Liberty's Lions

Dan LeRoy

Liberty's Lions

The Catholic Revolutionaries Who Established America

SOPHIA INSTITUTE PRESS
Manchester, New Hampshire

Sophia Institute Press
Box 5284, Manchester, NH 03108
1-800-888-9344

www.SophiaInstitute.com

Sophia Institute Press® is a registered trademark of Sophia Institute.

paperback ISBN 978-1-64413-116-9

ebook ISBN 978-1-64413-117-6

Library of Congress Control Number: 2021931348

For the priests and members
of St. Blaise and St. Monica Parishes,
and in memory of
Rev. Esber Tweel and Fr. James Krah

What tongue, human or angelic, may ever describe a power so immeasurable as that exercised by the simplest priest in Mass? Who could ever have imagined that the voice of man, which by nature hath not the power even to raise a straw from the ground, should obtain through grace a power so stupendous as to bring from Heaven to earth the Son of God?

—St. Leonard of Port Maurice

Contents

Liberty's Lions

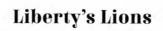

A Note about Footnotes and Endnotes

Most of the cited sources for this book are marked in the text with a footnote. Occasionally, if there is more to be said about a cited source, I have included the citation, along with the additional information, in the endnotes, rather than in the text of the book. If you see a source without a citation, it most likely means that the citation, and extra details about it, can be found in the endnotes.

Prologue

Song of the South

1

Drums rolled across the fields that September morning like a thunder-head. They promised a storm. In fact, a ferocious one had already struck. Another was on its way.

The air was already heavy here in the Low Country, at the tail end of summer. Well down the road, smoke from burning houses along the Stono River further thickened the atmosphere.

In a clearing at the side of the Pon Pon Road, a group of black men and women—at least sixty, perhaps as many as a hundred—were sing-ing and dancing.

The percussion of hand drums and gourds gave the music its pulse and punctuated the cries. One man waved a white banner, still crisp despite the humidity. Smiling, sweating people occasionally shouted "*Lukangu!*" It meant "Liberty," and that was what these joyful, excited revelers had gathered to celebrate.

The lieutenant governor of South Carolina, William Bull, had met them on the road earlier that morning. He was on his way to Charles Town[1] when he came upon the party, chanting and beating out tattoos on their instruments as they headed west, toward the Savannah River.

---

[1]   Today this city in South Carolina is known as Charleston.

Badly frightened, Bull and his four companions watched the procession for a moment or two. Then they ran.

That was cowardly, but wise. The marchers had already cut down twenty-one white South Carolinians. They would kill more before nightfall.

Soon, panicked militia members tumbled out of their pews in a nearby church and assembled at the edge of the field. They were joined by armed men from other towns. When they opened fire, it was returned: the group had stolen rifles from a local general store, as well as farming tools that could be used as weapons.

It's unclear how many of the marchers were killed by militiamen. Some members of the crowd were felled immediately; some would be executed later. Still others escaped into the woods, though most were eventually hunted down.

It seems at least a few marchers eluded capture and made it all the way to Spanish Florida, where freedom for runaway slaves beckoned. The presence of a Catholic-controlled colony to the south is one reason historians give for what happened that September morning. There were rumors of war between Britain and Spain. British officials believed the Spanish were openly encouraging slaves to escape as a border provocation.

The rebellion would ultimately be judged unsuccessful, though its effects would linger for decades—and not just in South Carolina. After all, the marchers had slashed and burned their way through the community, making real the worst nightmares of every plantation owner. One whispered account claimed the slaves had dismembered two local men they had encountered in the general store, and left their severed heads on the stairs.

"Whites' fears would quiet over time," historian Peter Charles Hoffer writes, "but none could ever fool himself or herself again that slaves were content in their chains."[2]

---

[2]   Peter Charles Hoffer, *Cry Liberty: The Great Stono River Slave Rebellion of 1739* (New York: Oxford University Press, 2012), 124.

Today, we remember the Stono River slave rebellion in 1739 as "the only large-scale slave rebellion in the British North American colonies," as Hoffer describes it.[3]

But was it also the first armed conflict in the New World between the British and Catholics demanding their freedom?

2

It makes for a compelling story, one that has been ably reconstructed by several scholars. In 1991, John K. Thornton analyzed the Stono Rebellion and pointed out several important details.

Many of the slaves who were part of the uprising were likely Kongolese, Thornton said. This was significant because the kingdom of Kongo[4] was both Christian and Catholic, and its educational system produced a high degree of literacy in Portuguese. This dovetails with reports that the rebellion was led by an educated slave, known alternately as "Jemmy" or "Cato."

In addition, Thornton noted, "significant numbers" of Kongolese slaves were likely ex-soldiers. They had probably been sold into slavery after being on the losing side of the civil wars that wracked central Africa during the early eighteenth century. That would account for the slaves' familiarity with the guns they stole from the general store.

And naturally, the prospect of escape to Spanish-controlled Florida would have been doubly attractive to Catholic slaves.

Writing a decade later, Mark M. Smith added further shading to this picture. In "Remembering Mary, Shaping Revolt: Reconsidering the Stono Rebellion," Smith pointed to the veneration of the Virgin Mary common among Kongolese Catholics.

The timing of the rebellion—Saturday and Sunday, September 8 and 9—has always been a source of intrigue. Some believed these dates were chosen because yellow fever had recently swept through the community,

---

[3] Hoffer, *Cry Liberty*, 1.

[4] The geography of the former kingdom of Kongo encompasses several modern countries, including the Democratic Republic of the Congo and the Republic of the Congo.

and whites were preoccupied. Others pointed to an announcement printed in local newspapers: white churchgoers would soon be required to come armed to worship. The rebellion might have been the slaves' last chance to catch their masters unawares on a Sunday, before this policy went into effect.

But Smith showed the rebellion could also have been timed to coincide with the feast of Mary's Nativity. And he gave several examples of how the slaves' "memories of Mary had helped shape the features, meaning, and precise timing of the revolt."[5] From the white banner the slaves waved to the fact that "the royal drum was also associated with Holy Saturdays in the Kongo, the day of the Madonna," Smith made the case that Mary was viewed as having a "protective and revolutionary power"—a power natural for the slaves to invoke.[6]

There were even examples in Kongolese history of Marian visitations—most prominently, when a "lady in white" appeared in the fifteenth century to the followers of Dom Afonso. A native king, Afonso was the founder of the faith in the Kongo, and was battling pagan forces. The "dazzling splendor" of this vision "blinded the enemy" and allowed Dom Afonso to emerge victorious.[7]

So, could a group of American Catholic slaves have planned an uprising that paid tribute to Mary and invoked her protection? Not everyone is convinced.

In his fascinating 2012 book on the rebellion, Peter Charles Hoffer argues against this interpretation. His retelling treats the insurrection as a spontaneous event. In this less dramatic tale, a work crew of slaves broke into the general store. Their goal was simply to get food and drink at the end of a miserable shift draining a nearby field. When they surprised two white men at the store, the slaves killed them both, and things rapidly spiraled out of control.

[5]   Mark M. Smith, "Remembering Mary, Shaping Revolt: Reconsidering the Stono Rebellion," *Journal of Southern History* 67, no. 3 (August 2001): 531, https://www.jstor.org/stable/3070016.

[6]   Smith, "Remembering Mary, Shaping Revolt," 530.

[7]   Smith, "Remembering Mary, Shaping Revolt," 530.

As Hoffer points out, with only one eyewitness account of the revolt—from Bull, who saw just a tiny part of it—we can merely guess at causes. And, as he noted, not all the slaves in the rebellion were necessarily Catholic. In addition, some of those in the field near Pon Pon Road were probably just onlookers, not participants.

Yet the story of Catholic slaves who rose up with the support and protection of the Virgin Mary might answer one of the persistent questions about the rebellion. Why did the slaves stop in the field, when they undoubtedly knew their pursuers could not be far behind?

Hoffer thought they were simply exhausted after their spree and could not have outrun mounted militia in any case. But it still seems strange to imagine the slaves simply giving up that September morning and waiting for their pursuers to attack.

Unless, perhaps, they believed they were not going to make their last stand alone, that Mary would defend them. Unless they believed they would be protected because their faith told them slavery was wrong and that those who had enslaved and pursued them were the ones who misunderstood God's law.

In that case, the "Account of the Negroe Insurrection in South Carolina" by Georgia's governor, James Oglethorpe—while also partial conjecture—has to be reconsidered. Describing the events of that fateful morning, this account from October 1739 stated: "They increased every minute by new Negroes coming to them, so that they were above Sixty, some say a hundred, on which they halted in a field, and set to dancing, Singing and beating Drums, to draw more Negroes to them, thinking they were now victorious over the whole Province, having marched ten miles & burnt all before them without Opposition."[8]

Could these rebels—some educated men and some Catholics—truly have believed "they were now victorious over the whole Province," unless they felt they had divine assistance?

---

[8] Mark M. Smith, *Stono: Documenting and Interpreting a Southern Slave Revolt* (Columbia: University of South Carolina Press, 2005), 13–15.

That interpretation raises all sorts of issues—not least because the rebels had just taken the lives of nearly two dozen people. The suggestion that violence was justified must also confront the terrible brutality of the event. As it was described shortly afterward:

> Next they plundered and burnt Mr. Godfrey's house, and killed him, his Daughter and Son.... They marched on towards Mr. Rose's resolving to kill him; but he was saved by a Negroe, who having hid him went out and pacified the others. Several Negroes joyned them, they calling out Liberty, marched on with Colors displayed, and two Drums beating, pursuing all the white people they met with, and killing Man Woman and Child when they could come up to them.[9]

But history is often problematic, and the possibility that the rebellious slaves saw their actions as divinely inspired and protected can't be discounted.

"It is hardly surprising," Smith wrote, quoting Thornton, that the Stono River slaves "'might have chosen to express their consternation at their enslavement in this strange land in religious terms.'"[10]

Although he believed the revolt was likely not religious but accidental in nature, the words of Peter Charles Hoffer seem appropriate here: "Some of what I found greatly disturbed me. But stories like Stono do not always reveal the heroes and villains we would like to find; rather, slavery demeaned and brutalized everyone it touched."[11]

Catholics in the United States have obviously not been demeaned and brutalized in the same ways, and to the same degree, as black Americans. But both groups share the knowledge of how discrimination can warp the promises of Scripture and liberty. In fact, their history is painfully intertwined, a braided umbilical cord that sometimes threatened to strangle the birth of a nation. Even today, that struggle can cause us to raise our hands to our own necks in discomfort.

---

[9] Smith, *Stono*, 13–15.
[10] Smith, "Remembering Mary, Shaping Revolt," 526.
[11] Hoffer, *Cry Liberty*, xiv.

3

This is not a book about the Catholic Church and slavery during the Revolutionary Era. If it were, it would be twice this length.

However, it's also impossible to write about one institution without referencing the other.

"Colonial Catholicism was clearly a southern institution in which the gentry were the most influential group and slaveholding was commonplace," Catholic historian Jay P. Dolan wrote in *The American Catholic Experience*. "The southern character of Catholicism goes a long way to explaining why in later years Catholics were reluctant to join the antislavery crusade."[12]

The reasons for Catholicism's southern tilt include the fact that Maryland, a southern colony with a southern agrarian economy, was home to most colonial Catholics. This was because it offered them — at least for a time — the religious freedom denied them elsewhere.

Another factor was the presence of Jesuit-owned farms, the major landholdings of American Catholics, which often employed slave labor.

But in truth, for all the historical detail available to us about the relationship between Church and slavery, the broad and important facts are already well known, and can be laid out in a paragraph.

The Catholic Church benefited from, and failed to condemn, the practice of slavery in America during this time. That characterization encompasses several of the figures mentioned in this book, as well as America's Founding Fathers of all faiths. Some tried to rationalize the practice; many admitted it was wrong. Because of the Church's teaching about the dignity of every human being, we see this as a particular, and particularly shameful, failing of Catholics. All that is difficult to contest, although it was in contradiction to what the Church's Magisterium officially taught.[13]

---

[12] Jay P. Dolan. *The American Catholic Experience: A History from Colonial Times to the Present* (Notre Dame, IN: University of Notre Dame Press, 1992), 123–124.

[13] See Steve Weidenkopf, "Did the Church Ever Support Slavery?," Catholic. com; https://www.catholic.com/magazine/online-edition/did-the

What this book does contest, however, is that this failure overshadows every other accomplishment of the founders and their historical peers. It does not mean that they were not great men. It *does* mean they were less great than they could have, and should have, been.

History can't be changed, but it can be examined. It ought to be studied in all its complexity. When we do so, it should be with the acknowledgment that the lens we look through, the lens that gives us the picture of this forgotten country, naturally distorts the image. We must make corrections, not just by remembering that we view a different time but also that we are looking at human beings—who are far too complicated to be studied with complete accuracy through our modern-day moral telescope, no matter how powerful it is.

That does not mean we should defend or ignore injustices that are apparent through any lens. The current moment in American history makes us rightfully uncomfortable about aspects of our past. We are uncomfortable, in part, because the more sensible among us recognize there are no easy remedies to undo what has been done, and left undone.

Yet we should also remember that Catholicism is not the only belief that can produce startling contradictions. To cite just one example, more than a few of the leading abolitionists who played a major role in ending slavery were also rabidly anti-Catholic. Some thought the two institutions—Catholicism and slavery—were equally evil. An American Party broadside published just prior to the Civil War stated:

> Roman Catholicism and slavery being alike founded and supported on the basis of ignorance and tyranny; and being therefore natural allies in every warfare against liberty and enlightenment; therefore, be it Resolved, That there can exist no real hostility to

---

-church-ever-support-slavery/. Given the better moral compass in Rome, for example, it's not surprising that Venerable Augustus Tolton received his training for the priesthood in Rome, not in post-slavery America, where it was considered unsafe for him to do so.

Roman Catholicism which does not embrace slavery, its natural
co-worker in opposition to freedom and republican institutions.[14]

To be on "the right side of history" is never quite as simple as we would
like it to be.

Trying to set the record straight is not, in itself, a remedy. To quote
George Washington, from a letter to Congress in 1776, it is, "comparatively speaking — no more than a drop in the Ocean."[15] (Back then, that
saying must have seemed much less a cliché.)

But there are fascinating and illuminating paradoxes here: stories of
great patriotism, and also of human frailty. Sometimes they exist side by
side; sometimes within the same person. There are men mentioned in this
book who owned slaves, and men who owned almost nothing. There are
those who made excuses for slavery, and others who fought passionately
against human bondage until the day they died.

They all have stories that need to be told, and understood. "The
greater our ignorance of any subject," Dr. Charles Hallan McCarthy
reminded members of the American Catholic Historical Association
almost a hundred years ago, "the more firmly are we attached to our
opinions about it."[16]

The revolutionary urge is generally to burn it all down and then rebuild
anew. The Carroll family of Maryland, about whom you will read a lot
in this book, knew something about that urge. As Catholics who were
the subject of persistent discrimination, it must have sometimes been a
tempting one, despite their wealth.

---

[14] James Hennesey, S.J., *American Catholics: A History of the Roman Catholic
Community in the United States* (New York: Oxford University Press,
1983), 145.

[15] "From George Washington to John Hancock, 25 September 1776," Founders Online, National Archives, https://founders.archives.gov/documents/
Washington/03-06-02-0305.

[16] Charles Hallan McCarthy, "The Importance of Stresses and Omissions
in the Writing of American History," *Catholic Historical Review* 10, no. 1
(April 1924): 38, www.jstor.org/stable/25012042.

Ultimately, however, they knew that there was much about their emerging America that was worth saving. The slower, much more difficult, but ultimately more rewarding, job was to improve the existing structure from within. That is what they, and the Catholics in this book, did.

The first step in that process is always accepting the burden that history places on each of us. It cannot be ignored, and it cannot be destroyed. We can only bear it by acknowledging and understanding it, in all its weight, depth, and nuance. May this book become some tiny part of that process.

Chapter 1

Bless Those That Curse You

1

Twenty-five years after the Stono Rebellion, and a thousand miles north, the drums once again murmured an ominous prophecy.

The military snares had been ricocheting through town since noon. The pounding increased as dusk gathered over the unlit cobblestone streets. Muttering swelled into shouts and then receded, like the waves lapping against the piers and wharves of Boston Harbor.

Earlier in the day, the sound of guns had echoed across the waters. The three cannons at Castle William, which protected the city from seaborne attack, erupted from the island fort. Now that evening had come at last, many of Boston's fifteen thousand inhabitants took to their homes and bolted the doors. On this night, the town's dozen constables were far outnumbered, and the mob ruled.

The wealthy peeked from behind linen curtains and hoped they wouldn't hear the sound of shattering window glass. Tavern keepers grumbled and resigned themselves to providing the free rum that was demanded on this day. And most mothers made certain their children were safe inside on the night of November 5.

It was Guy Fawkes Day in England, but here in the colonies, it was commonly known as Pope's Day. At the end of Pope's Day came Pope's Night, and the riotous celebrations that marked it drew thousands of people into the streets.

Guy Fawkes was a converted Catholic who plotted to blow up Britain's House of Lords with gunpowder. The Protestant king, James I, would also have been killed in the explosion, timed for the opening of Parliament on November 5, 1605.

The deadly plot was foiled at the eleventh hour, just a day before it was to take place, and Fawkes was executed. That didn't end hostilities between Protestants and Catholics in England, which had been ongoing since the Protestant Reformation. They led, almost a century later, to the Glorious Revolution of 1688 and the removal of James II, Britain's last Catholic monarch.

Fawkes's treason did, however, inspire a new tradition. British citizens began celebrating Guy Fawkes Day on the fifth of November by burning him in effigy. The custom traveled the ocean to the colonies.

But here, it would be the pope, rather than Guy Fawkes, who would be mocked and burned. Children allowed into the streets carried their very own dolls of the pontiff. The carved potato heads leered disturbingly at passersby.

As darkness descended on Boston and the late autumn winds whistled down the crooked lanes, you might have seen a huge carriage, nearly forty feet in length, come to a stop before one of the town's mansions. On the carriage's platform were several figures, lit by a huge oiled-paper lantern. The center of attention was a man seated in a throne-like chair. He wore velvet robes, a towering white wig, and an enormous gold-laced hat. The features etched into his mask were ugly and cruel. He was meant to represent the pope.

Behind him loomed a giant holding a pitchfork and clad in tar and feathers: Satan himself, the pope's ally. Both figures had false heads on poles that were controlled by boys hidden from sight.

There was also a woman on the platform, dancing a hornpipe to accompaniment from fiddles and drums. She was meant to represent the British performer Nancy Dawson, a symbol of corruption and immorality. Behind her, hanged in effigy, was the famous naval traitor Admiral Byng, who had been court-martialed in 1757 for refusing to fight. Around them capered boys as young as seven or eight, dressed in tarred and feathered costumes. They frequently kissed the figure of the devil, since they were meant to be his "imps."

The jeering throng that followed this carriage would have quieted long enough for a verse to be recited. It was the same verse that was "being recited in every village and hamlet in England on the same night," as the author Esther Forbes wrote centuries later:

> The Fifth of November
> As you well remember
> Was gunpowder, treason and plot,
>
> I know of no reason
> Why the gunpowder treason
> Should ever be forgot.[17]

With that, the mob roared its approval. Many people wore dunce caps; some blew conches — or "Pope's horns" — rang bells, or jangled strings of shells gathered from the nearby seashore. The inhabitants of the house, if they were wise, would provide at least a few coins for the procession. If they refused — or even if crowd members, many of whom had been drinking since the morning, simply got out of control — then the sound of rocks and bricks crashing through glass would probably follow.

Violence was common on November 5, and on this Pope's Day, in 1764, it had already occurred — with unusually tragic results. In Boston, there were two competing Pope's Day floats: one each from the city's North and South Ends. Both would parade through the streets civilly during the day, but when night fell the mobs would battle to see which could capture the other side's effigies of popes and devils.

This year, it appeared the battle would be postponed because of what had happened earlier in the day. As Boston resident John Boyle recalled in his memoirs, "a Child of Mr. Brown's at the North-End was run over

---

[17]   Esther Forbes, *Paul Revere and the World He Lived In* (Birmingham, AL: Palladium Press, 2005), 94.

by one of the Wheels of the North-End Pope and Killed on the Spot. Many others were wounded in the evening."[18]

Neither the age of the boy nor his full name is known, but the incident obviously unnerved the authorities. Merchant John Rowe added in his journal that "The Sheriff, Justices, Officers of the Militia were ordered to destroy both South & North-End Popes."

But the outmanned peacekeepers were no match for Ebenezer Mackintosh, the leader of the South- End gang. A shoemaker and wily organizer, Mackintosh managed to elude the police throughout the afternoon and protect the South End's effigy of the pope. And while the sheriff and his men were able to track down and destroy the North End pope, by nightfall it had been rebuilt under the direction of the group's "captain," shipwright Henry Swift.

The two carriages finally met at the bridge over Mill Creek, which marked the boundary of Boston's North End. Here an epic and bloody battle was fought. Boston resident Isaiah Thomas later recalled,

> With this the noise and tumult began, the blowing of conch shells, whistling through the fingers, beating with clubs the sides of the houses, cheering, huzzaing, swearing, and rising about all the din the cry "North end forever" or "South end forever." The devils on the stages were not the only or chiefest proof that the underworld was let loose. The procession that first reached the Mill creek gave three cheers and rushed on to meet their foes. As they approached the strife began; clubs, stones, and brickbats were freely used, and though persons were not often killed, bruised shins, broken heads and bones, were not infrequent.[19]

---

[18] Samuel Checkley, "Diary of the Rev. Samuel Checkley, 1735," in *Publications of the Colonial Society of Massachusetts*, vol. 12, *Transactions, 1908–1909* (Boston: Massachusetts Colonization Society, 2012), 290–291.

[19] Isaiah Thomas Jr., *The History of Printing in America: With a Biography of Printers, and an Account of Newspapers* (Worcester, MA: Isaiah Thomas Jr., 1810), 30.

Samuel Breck, a South-End participant, would look back years later and marvel, "In what a state of semi-barbarism did the rising generations of those days exist!"[20]

On this Pope's Night in 1764, the barbarism favored Captain Mackintosh and the South End, which emerged victorious. Mackintosh was named "First Captain General" of Boston's landmark "Liberty Tree," the famous elm that stood near Boston Common.

When the battle was over, Mackintosh led both gangs in procession past the common, through the gates of the town, and out onto Boston Neck, the narrow, marshy strip of land that connected Boston and Roxbury. There, in the shadow of the nearby gallows, both popes were set ablaze in a huge bonfire, and harmony reigned once again. Both North and South Enders stood together on the soggy ground, watching the smoke from the popes' bodies drift back across the causeway.

For their role in the violence of this day, both Mackintosh and Swift would face charges, though neither would ever be punished. But although no one knew it at the time, this Pope's Night would be the last of its kind in Boston.

The following year, in 1765, the event became a protest against the Stamp Act, which decreed that every legal document would require a stamp. The stamps were a form of taxation, although the law was never actually enforced. Mindful of the tragedy of the previous year, Boston residents made Pope's Night in 1765 a comparatively peaceful affair, directing their anger and energy at colonial officials — such as the colonial governor, Thomas Hutchinson.

But just as Guy Fawkes and his Gunpowder Plot would never be forgotten, neither would the reason for Pope's Day. A poem printed in *The Massachusetts Gazette* in 1766, "Extraordinary Verses on Pope Night," gives a sense of the prevailing sentiment toward the pope and Catholicism that still reigned in Boston:

---

[20] Samuel Breck, *Recollections of Samuel Breck, with Passages from His Notebooks (1771–1862)*, ed. Horace Elisha Scudder (London: Porter & Coates, 1877), 34.

"A Pagan, Jew, Mahometan, Turk, Strumpet, Wizzard,
    Witch;"
In short the Number of his Name's, Six Hundred Sixty six.
"How dreadful do his Features show?
"How fearful is his Grin?
"Made up of ev'ry Thing that's bad; He is the Man of Sin.
If that his deeden Self could see Himself so turn'd to Fun:
In Rage He'd tear out His Pope's Eyes, And scratch his
    Rev'rend Bum."[21]

2

Nearly a decade later, in 1774, the rage generated by the Stamp Act had reached a boiling point.

The past ten years had seen the colonies' struggle against their British masters intensify. The British expected the colonists to pay their fair share of the debt for the Seven Years' War, which had cost millions of pounds before concluding in 1763. The colonists insisted on representation in Parliament, and both sides were maintaining an increasingly tense stalemate.

More and more British soldiers crowded the streets of Boston, and their presence had brought misunderstandings and violence. Five people had died during the Boston Massacre in 1770, when panicky British officers fired into an unruly crowd that was pelting them with rocks and snowballs.

Now the British expected Bostonians to repay today's equivalent of a million dollars for the tea they had dumped into Boston Harbor in December 1773. This famous protest over British taxes on tea, and the colonists' lack of representation in Parliament, would soon lead to the British closing Boston Harbor. The city was essentially being held hostage.

---

[21] "South End Forever [cut] North End Forever. *Extraordinary Verses on Pope-Night. or, A Commemoration the Fifth of November, Giving a History of the Attempt, Made by the Papishes, to Blow Up King and Parliament, A.D.*" (Boston, 1768), in "Printed Ephemera Collection," Library of Congress, https://www.loc.gov/item/rbpe.03602800/.

Yet it was another act of the Crown that provoked the most outrage that autumn.

The Quebec Act was the last of a series of five measures dubbed the "Intolerable Acts" by colonists. What made it most intolerable was that it allowed French Canadians, many of whom were Catholic, full religious freedom, at home and in the colonies. The British hoped this would keep French Canadians from supporting the growing rebellion to the south. For the outraged colonists, it brought a British-approved "popery" directly into the Protestant heart of America.

As Robert Emmett Curran, the author of *Papist Devils: Catholics in British America, 1574–1783*, observes, "In the context of other imperial acts, the Quebec Act of 1774 looked particularly ominous." Curran points out that the previous decade had seen "passionate opposition to Anglican plans to appoint a bishop for the colonies, as the appointment of an Anglican prelate would be, so critics alleged, just the first step toward the establishment of popery in America." With its latest move in Quebec,

> the British government had confirmed the worst fears about its ultimate design to impose popery on the colonies. It had given Roman Catholicism a privileged position in the Canadian province by honoring the church's traditional status. It allowed Catholics to hold office without taking an oath impugning their religion. And it extended the southern border of Canada from the St. Lawrence River to the Ohio, seemingly bringing a vast area in the west under the control of the government in Quebec and making likely new alliances between Catholics and Indian tribes in the territory.[22]

American demagogues, Curran concludes, depicted the Quebec Act as a "harbinger ... of things to come in the rest of British America regarding traditional liberties and the place of Protestantism in society."

---

[22] Robert Emmett Curran, *Papist Devils: Catholics in British America, 1574–1783* (Washington, DC: Catholic University of America Press, 2014), 241.

The reaction from colonial leaders was swift. Future Broadway star —and immigrant—Alexander Hamilton warned that Canada would soon be flooded with Catholics from foreign shores:

> The preeminent advantages secured to the Roman catholic religion will discourage all protestant soldiers of whatsoever nation: And on these accounts the province will be settled and inhabited by none, but papists. If lenity and moderation are observed in administering the laws, the natural advantages of this fertile infant country, united to the indulgence given to their religion, will attract droves of emigrants, from all the Roman catholic states in Europe; and these colonies, in time, will find themselves encompassed with innumerous hosts of neighbours, disaffected to them, both because of difference in religion and government. How dangerous their situation would be, let every man of common sense judge.[23]

Three years earlier, John Adams had worried in his diary that he was living in a time "when the Barriers against Popery, erected by our Ancestors, are suffered to be destroyed, to the hazard even of the Protestant Religion."[24] He compared Great Britain to the governments of the Catholic nations France and Spain. The comparison was deliberately unflattering, and the Quebec Act did nothing to calm his fears. Adams felt it was "not only unjust to the People in that Province, but dangerous to the Interests of the Protestant Religion and of these Colonies."[25]

The dashing young doctor Joseph Warren, a leader of the anti-British Sons of Liberty in Boston, drafted a document called the Suffolk Resolves.

---

[23] Alexander Hamilton, "Remarks on the Quebec Bill: Part Two [June 22, 1775]," Founders Online, National Archives, https://founders.archives.gov/documents/Hamilton/01-01-02-0059.

[24] John Adams, "Adams' Diary Notes on the Right of Juries: 1771. Feby. 12," Founders Online, National Archives, https://founders.archives.gov/documents/Adams/05-01-02-0005-0005-0004.

[25] Robert J. Taylor, Mary-Jo Kline, and Gregg L. Lint, eds. *Papers of John Adams*, vol. 2, *September 1755–April 1775* (Cambridge, MA: Belknap Press of Harvard University Press, 1977), 152–156.

It harshly condemned the Quebec Act, calling it "dangerous in an extreme degree to the Protestant religion, and to the civil rights and liberties of all America."[26]

Warren, who would be dead within the year as one of the first colonial martyrs at Bunker Hill, gave the document to a loyal silversmith named Paul Revere. He ordered Revere to deliver it, express, to the First Continental Congress, which was meeting three hundred miles away in Philadelphia.

The year before his famous midnight ride, Revere journeyed day and night to get the Resolves into the hands of the congressmen. The members quickly approved the document and sparked a resurgence of the anti-Catholicism that had lain somewhat dormant over the past several years. That November 5, Curran notes, rival gangs in Boston even teamed up to burn a specially constructed "Union Pope."[27]

On behalf of the Congress, founding father John Jay wrote a letter to the British public about the Quebec Act. It stated that he and his fellow colonists were astonished "that a British Parliament should ever consent to establish in that country a religion that has deluged your island in blood, and dispersed impiety, bigotry, persecution, murder, and rebellion through every part of the world."[28]

The fears of the colonists were best summed up by John Adams, who wrote, in a letter to the reverend and doctor Jedidiah Morse, "The people said, if Parliament can do this in Canada, they can do the same in all the other Colonies."[29]

---

[26] Joseph Warren, "The Suffolk Resolves," September 9, 1774, no. 10, https://www.nps.gov/mima/learn/education/upload/The%20Suffolk%20Resolves.pdf.

[27] Curran, *Papist Devils*, 241.

[28] Continental Congress, "Continental Congress to the People of Great Britain, October 22, 1774," *Journals of the American Congress: From 1774–1788*, vol. 1, *September 5, 1774 to December 31, 1776* (Washington, DC: Way and Gideon, 1823), 30.

[29] "From John Adams to Jedidiah Morse, 2 December 1815," Founders Online, National Archives, https://founders.archives.gov/documents/Adams/99-02-02-6548.

Even as American and British troops began the Revolution in earnest, skirmishing in Boston at Bunker Hill and Prospect Hill, the colonists still hoped to persuade their British brothers of the error of their ways. Encampments in the city were so close to one another that American volunteers were able to distribute, behind enemy lines, a broadside addressed to the British military from "An Old Soldier." It read, in part:

> Gentlemen,
>
> You are about to embark for America, to compel your Fellow Subjects there to submit to Popery and Slavery. It is the Glory of the British Soldier, that he is the Defender, not the Destroyer, of the Civil and Religious Rights of the People....
>
> You will be called upon to imbrue your Hands in the Blood of your Fellow Subjects in America, because they will not admit to be Slaves, and are alarmed at the Establishment of Popery and Arbitrary Power in One Half of their Country. Whether you will draw those Swords which have defended them against their Enemies, to butcher them into a Resignation of their Rights, which they hold as the Sons of Englishmen, is in your Breasts.[30]

And among the many satirical verses written about the Quebec Act came one from John Turnbull, the acclaimed artist and future aide to George Washington. In it, he alleged England had:

> Struck bargains with the Romish Churches
> Infallibility to purchase;
> Set wide for Popery the door
> Made friends with Babel's scarlet whore.[31]

---

[30] Ephemera Collection, Library of Congress, https://www.loc.gov/resource/rbpe.0380300a/?st=text.

[31] Martin I. J. Griffin, "Revolutionary Catholic Notes," *American Catholic Historical Researches* 5, no. 4 (October 1909): 334, https://www.jstor.org/stable/44374787.

3

One of the most unpopular aspects of the Quebec Act was that it eliminated the loyalty oath for Canadians citizens who wanted to hold office. Elected officials now only had to pledge allegiance to King George III. They no longer had to deny their Catholic faith, if they practiced it, by denying transubstantiation, the invocation of saints, and the authority of the pope.

A sample of this sort of oath can be found at one of America's most-visited historic sites: Mount Vernon, the home of George Washington. It reads, "I ... do declare that there is no Transubstantiation in the sacrament of the Lords [sic] supper or in the Elements of Bread and wine at or after the consecration thereof by any person whatsoever."[32] This was the oath Washington had to pledge as a young soldier in the 1750s, to prove his loyalty to the Anglican Church and to the Crown.

A similar oath was demanded of officeholders in England, Scotland, and Ireland. This was why there were few, if any, Catholics in office there. And it became common throughout colonial America, as war with Britain loomed.

One of the Catholic priests in the colonies was the Jesuit Fr. Joseph Mosley, S.J. Writing to his sister from Talbot County, Maryland, during August 1775, he expressed his conflicted feelings about his support of independence and his duty to the Catholic Church.

"I am really between hawk and buzzard," he wrote. "I know not what step I best take."[33]

Fr. Mosley had been informed that the Maryland Legislature now required all priests to take a loyalty oath. He agonized over the decision.

---

[32] "Anti-Catholic Oath," George Washington's Mount Vernon, https://www.mountvernon.org/george-washington/religion/george-washington-and-catholicism/.

[33] Joseph Mosley "Letters of Father Joseph Mosley, S.J., and Some Extracts from His Diary (1757–1786) (continued)," comp. Edward I. McDevitt, S.J., *Records of the American Catholic Historical Society of Philadelphia* 17, no. 3 (September 1906): 301, https://www.jstor.org/stable/44207979.

One possible solution was to return to England, but he ruled that out as running away from his problem.

"Discontent or not, I see that I am a very necessary hand in my situation," Fr. Mosley advised his sister. "The gentlemen here won't hear of my departure."

In the end, the other Maryland Catholic priests agreed to take the oath, believing their loyalty to the American cause was that important. But because of a delay in getting this information to Fr. Mosley, whose parish was in a remote location, he fell under suspicion from the local authorities. Nevertheless, he agreed to refrain from public preaching until the matter could be resolved, which took the better part of three years.

When he presented himself to take the oath, he was told that the time to do so had expired. It took a special act of the legislature to allow him to preach again, and when he did, in 1780, he used the opportunity to explain himself to his congregation.

Fr. Mosley used the example of St. Paul, who "is much to be admired, for undertaking his own defence against the censures of the world, which judged him an evil-doer, because he was bound in chains, and in Caesar's custody."[34] And he assured his parishioners of his loyalty to America. He told them he only waited to take the loyalty oath to be sure that all members of the Maryland Catholic clergy acted in unison.

"I was resolved not to give any offense to Government," he said. "I acted according to all the reason and knowledge I had in the Canon Law."[35]

It was an extraordinary balancing act, made more remarkable by another point. All nine of the Jesuit fathers in Maryland, including Fr. Mosley, resisted the temptation to seek some easier assignment. Instead, they faced the challenge of dual loyalties head-on, remaining with their flocks as colonial — and soon American — citizens.

---

[34] Joseph Mosley "Mr. Mosley's Reasons for Not Taking the Oath of Fidelity to the State," *Woodstock Letters* 15, no. 2 (July 1, 1886): 137, https://jesuitonlinelibrary.bc.edu/?a=d&d=wlet18860701-01.2.2&e=-------en-20--1--txt-txIN-------.

[35] Mosley, "Mr. Mosley's Reasons for Not Taking the Oath of Fidelity to the State," 139.

4

These three sections remind us of something that many would like to forget: the history of America's founding is rich with examples of anti-Catholicism.

It wasn't just rowdy tradesmen and sailors, nor was it isolated to a particular geographic area like the Northeast. The ugly words and deeds were as common among those we rightly revere as the Founding Fathers of our nation. And they were present in even the most religiously tolerant of the colonies, such as Pennsylvania, Rhode Island, and Maryland.

What makes this vehement anti-Catholicism all the more stunning is that during the colonial era, Catholics represented a little more than 1 percent of the American population. Common estimates suggest between 1.2 and 1.6 percent of colonists were Catholic. In a nation of 2.5 million people, that amounted to between 30,000 and 40,000 Catholics. Outposts of the religion were few and far between. Before the Revolutionary War, Philadelphia was the only place in the British Empire where you could attend a public Mass.

Yet the memories of religious conflicts in England over the centuries, as the celebration of Pope's Night proves, were long and still bitter. At a time when the colonists were eyeing one another suspiciously, trying to decide who supported the cause of liberty and who was still loyal to the Crown, any other possible allegiance was grounds for suspicion. To be Catholic was, in most places, to declare yourself a part of a disreputable minority.

And that brings us to one of the most puzzling questions of the entire American Revolution. Why did so many Catholics apparently support it—even when, as in the case of Fr. Mosley, it required them to make choices that would be intolerable, even in a more tolerant place?

"It would be remarkable indeed if all Catholics could, of a sudden, have forgotten the animosity of the past, made friends of recent enemies, disavowed an allegiance of long standing, and substituted loyalty to an untried creation of doubtful legality," wrote Fr. Charles H. Metzger, in a 1949 study of Catholic Tories.

"Really the surprising fact is, not that there were Tories among the Catholics, but that in spite of the discrimination and persecution they had been subjected to in colonial days," he added, "so many Catholics did espouse the patriot cause."[36]

While we don't have verifiable numbers of loyalists among the colonies, historians guess that between 15 and 20 percent of the two million white colonists were loyal to Great Britain. If we use that figure for the thirty thousand to forty thousand Catholics in the colonies at that time, we come up with perhaps six thousand to eight thousand Tory Catholics.

What about the rest, the remaining twenty-four thousand to thirty-two thousand Catholic colonists?

Writing about Maryland Catholics, historian Fr. Gerald Fogarty, S.J., pointed to the similarities between the colonists' struggle and the battles Catholics had faced in England since the Reformation.

"When the patriots began arguing for no taxation without representation, no laws passed without the consent of the governed, and no parliamentary jurisdiction over the colonies, they found ready allies in the Maryland Catholics," he wrote. These Catholics, Fr. Fogarty added, "had been expressing the same theory since 1634."[37] We'll read more about this in the next chapter.

Robert Emmett Curran tries to solve this puzzle by citing the words of Fr. Charles Metzger, who "concluded that no other group in the colonies had a harder choice than Catholics did in deciding to be patriots, loyalists, or neutrals.

"In the end ... many, particularly those in Maryland, simply chose to forget the painful past and take the risk," writes Curran, "despite much

---

[36] Charles H. Metzger, "Some Catholic Tories in the American Revolution, Part I," *Catholic Historical Review* 35, no. 3 (October 1949): 277–278, www.jstor.org/stable/25015030.

[37] Gerald P. Fogarty, "Property and Religious Liberty in Colonial Maryland Catholic Thought," *Catholic Historical Review* 72, no. 4 (October 1986), 599, www.jstor.org/stable/25022406.

contrary evidence, that the future held an equality and freedom that Catholics had never known for most of their colonial history."[38]

5

Support of the American Revolution is remarkable among Catholics, given the abundant prejudices of the time. But Catholics did something more remarkable than just support the patriot cause: they helped *lead* it.

That is the primary goal of this book: to gather together, in one place and for the first time, the significant contributions of Catholics to the American Revolution.

For too long, the history of this era has been related strictly by the numbers. They say that Catholics were insignificant in the United States during the colonial period. And that history has been defined strictly by incidents like the ones that opened this chapter, which show the forces allied against these Catholics.

But history is not always the story of raw numbers, nor can it be understood solely through anecdotes. It is the story of people and their decisions. And the decisions of the relatively tiny group of Catholics who supported the revolutionary cause represent an amazing untold story from this era we think we know well.

That group of Catholics produced some of the greatest statesmen, thinkers, and military leaders of the day. They are the subject of this book, which also tries to answer the aforementioned question: *Why did they do it?*

There were so many Catholic heroes of the war that a single book can't do justice to all of them. Much more could be said, for example, about naval commodore Joshua Barney of Maryland, who served with honor in both the Revolution and the War of 1812, and was wounded defending the White House from British invaders. Certainly George Washington's loyal aide-de-camp, Lt. Col. John Fitzgerald—an Irishman who had a knack for trade and played an important role in Washington's Potomac Company—deserves more than just this brief mention.

[38] Curran, *Papist Devils*, 244.

Then there are the figures who remain elusive and who represent the unknown Catholic heroes and heroines of the war. Mary Waters was an army nurse from Dublin who was ready to give up medicine. She was talked out of it by Philadelphia priest Ferdinand Farmer, whom we'll read more about in chapter 10. He told her that "her skill in nursing was a commission sent her from heaven, which she was bound never to resign, and that she might merit heaven by it."[39] She listened, and the Continental Army benefited.

Famed physician Benjamin Rush thought Waters was fascinating enough to begin writing her biography in 1791. "Why not?" Rush asked. "Her occupation was a noble one—and her example may be interesting to thousands—Only a few men can be Kings—& yet Biography for a while had few other subjects." Rush told us that Waters sought out challenges: "Nothing but great danger rouses her into great activity and humanity."[40] Yet, besides these tantalizing details, we know little else about her life.

What is sure is this: despite all the obstacles arrayed against them, in spite of all the compelling reasons they had to stay loyal to Britain, or simply remain neutral, "American Catholics were overwhelmingly patriots," as journalist Donald R. McClarey notes. It's also certain that they "played a role in the American Revolution out of all proportion to the small fragment of the American people they represented."[41]

6

Contrary to some popular retellings of the story, the American Revolution was a close-run thing right up until Cornwallis's fateful engagement at Yorktown. As late as the spring of 1781, historian John Ferling pointed out,

[39] Hennesey, *American Catholics*, 60.

[40] Linda K. Kerber, *Women of the Republic: Intellect and Ideology in Revolutionary America* (Chapel Hill: Omohundro Institute of Early American History and Culture and the University of North Carolina Press, 1980), 74.

[41] Donald R. McClarey, "Catholics in the American Revolution," *American Catholic*, September 23, 2011, https://www.the-american-catholic.com/2011/09/23/catholics-in-the-american-revolution/.

Washington warned that his army was "exhausted" and the citizenry "discontented." John Adams believed that France, faced with mounting debts and having failed to win a single victory in the American theater, would not remain in the war beyond 1781. "We are in the Moment of Crisis," he wrote. Rochambeau feared that 1781 would see the "last struggle of an expiring patriotism." Both Washington and Adams assumed that unless the United States and France scored a decisive victory in 1781, the outcome of the war would be determined at a conference of Europe's great powers.[42]

In such a battle, are there any truly small moments? Could the contributions of anyone be truly negligible? And could the efforts of twenty-four thousand to thirty-two thousand Catholic colonists—especially those whose lives are detailed here—have truly made the difference?

Imagine them on the other side, and the question answers itself. And consider the estimate that 70 percent of the allied troops were Catholic—not an impossible number, when you remember how many of them were French and Spanish, as well as Irish and German Americans.

Throughout this book, such counterfactual arguments are necessary to make the larger point. What would the Revolution have been like without these Catholics?

The phrase "The stone the builders rejected has become the cornerstone" is one of the most familiar in the Bible. Appearing in the 118th Psalm (v. 22, NABRE), and referenced by the Old Testament prophet Isaiah (28:16), it is quoted by Jesus to the disciples and appears in three of the four Gospels (e.g., Matt. 21:42), as well as in the Acts of the Apostles (4:11) and 1 Peter (2:7).

It has also become secularized. It's familiar to non-Christians as a way of expressing an idea long associated with America. That is, sometimes the underdog comes out on top.

---

[42] John Ferling, "Myths of the American Revolution," *Smithsonian Magazine*, January 2010, https://www.smithsonianmag.com/history/myths-of-the-american-revolution-10941835/.

Liberty's Lions

The saying describes perfectly the condition in which colonial Catholics found themselves prior to the American Revolution, and their response to it. They could easily have allowed themselves to be rejected and discarded—something many of their fellow colonists wished for, vocally and publicly.

Instead, these underdogs sided with their underdog nation, and played a crucial role in forming it. These lions of liberty ignored prejudice, stood fast, and collectively became a "chief cornerstone" of the American Revolution—one without which it could never have been successful.

Chapter 2

First Citizen

1

Charles Carroll of Carrollton could see it all very clearly.

There were his fellow Americans, thousands of them. They were all poor, stark naked, and shivering. Winter would soon arrive.

The weather in Maryland had already turned frigid, with winds whipping in from the Atlantic. But the people had no clothes to wear because they could no longer afford to buy them from England.

Why didn't they simply make their own linens, woolens, stockings, and shoes? They couldn't: the law forbade it. The mills had been shut down, and even knitting in a private home had been declared a crime.

These Americans, defenseless against the hostile elements, were going to die, Charles Carroll knew. Disease and exposure would wipe out a great percentage of colonists.

And he thought the law that had sealed their doom "a very wise act." Because inevitably, their deaths would lessen tensions between Great Britain and America.

"If England forces her colonies to rebellion," Carroll observed, "she must take ye proper steps to make that rebellion ineffectual by reducing their strength, and ye most effectual way of doing this is by putting a stop to ye increase of our people."[43]

---

[43] Ellen Hart Smith, *Charles Carroll of Carrollton* (Cambridge, MA: Harvard University Press, 2014), 93.

Liberty's Lions

This grim scenario, which Charles Carroll sketched out in a 1767 letter to his friend William Graves in London, was, of course, a joke—a sarcastic response to the passage of the Townshend Acts that same year.

The acts, dreamed up by Britain's Chancellor of the Exchequer Charles Townshend, proposed to raise forty thousand pounds annually by taxing china, glass, lead, paint, paper, and tea.

These were all goods that Townshend calculated the colonists could not produce on their own. The money raised would pay the salaries of colonial governors and other officials. The British could even argue to Americans that their money was staying at home—although its purpose was to ensure that those officials remained loyal to Great Britain.

To call the acts a miscalculation would be kind. Protests and boycotts erupted in response. In fact, the acts were so unpopular that three years later, Parliament withdrew all the taxes except one. That tax was on tea, and the decision to keep it in place would be a fateful one.

Naturally, the farcical scenario Charles Carroll imagined in his 1767 letter never came to pass. But his satire masked a much deeper truth.

Carroll is rightly recognized by historians for several reasons. For many years, he was the most prominent and influential Catholic in America. He was certainly the richest—possibly the richest man in the colonies, period. He was the only Catholic to sign the Declaration of Independence, and the last of the signers to die, outliving John Adams and Thomas Jefferson by six years.

He was all of these things, and yet his letter to William Graves shows he was something else as well: a visionary.

A decade before the colonies declared their independence from Great Britain, a decade before Thomas Paine declared that Lexington and Concord had damaged the relationship with England beyond repair, Charles Carroll saw with certainty what was going to happen. He realized it would take a war to gain the colonies' freedom. And he could see what almost no one else at the time could imagine: that the colonies could actually win it.

It would take years for most of the other founders to reach the same conclusion. On the very eve of revolution, many of them still held out hope that the colonies could be reconciled with Great Britain. No "thinking man in all North America," Washington said in 1774, could possibly want "to set up for independency." Even four months after Lexington and Concord, Jefferson was still confessing he "would rather be in dependence on Great Britain, properly limited, than on any other nation on earth."[44]

Charles Carroll had given up that idea ages ago. Throughout America, people believed Great Britain would eventually back down from its unpopular policies, as it had before. Charles Carroll knew that was not going to happen. And he was ready for it.

Besides the fact that he was a naturally brilliant man, why did he come to these realizations so much earlier than his fellow founders? He might not have, if he hadn't been from Maryland. And if he had not been Catholic.

The experience of Maryland Catholics was markedly different than everyone else's in colonial America. But when that experience, and the truths it revealed, were applied to the colonies at large, independence was the inevitable result.

Charles Carroll of Carrollton was a lightning rod who helped direct that revolutionary energy. He was a good conductor: you could tell that just by looking at the coat of arms his grandfather reworked before he came to America. Over the image of a hawk in flight reads the new motto *Ubicumque cum liberate*—"Anywhere, so long as it be free."

Charles Carroll achieved numerous firsts in his long life. To give him his full due, perhaps the man who first contributed to the Revolutionary cause by writing letters he signed "First Citizen" should be considered the First Patriot as well.

2

The desire for freedom was a Carroll family trait. But if Charles Carroll was resolute—some might say stubborn instead—that was undoubtedly an inherited trait too.

---

[44] Thomas Jefferson, *The Writings of Thomas Jefferson*, vol. 1, *1760–1775*, ed. Paul Leicester Ford (New York: G. P. Putnam's Sons, 1892), 484.

His grandfather and his father—both also named Charles—were legendarily hard-headed, and not above spending a little time in jail to make a point. They were also proud Catholics who suffered for their faith, even though they lived in what was intended to be the most religiously tolerant of the colonies.

The Carrolls came from Irish gentry in County Offaly. However, the family lost much of its land and fortune when Oliver Cromwell confiscated Catholic property during the English Civil War. Charles Carroll the Settler was born in Ireland, educated at the French University of Douay, and got a job in London as a clerk to one of King James II's ministers. But greater opportunities in the colonies beckoned. The first Charles Carroll was a charming and persuasive young man, not yet thirty, who talked himself into the job of attorney general of Maryland.

He got out of England in the nick of time—just a month before the Glorious Revolution took place and King James II fled the country for France. The colonists in Maryland awaited directions from Lord Baltimore: would he instruct them to recognize William of Orange and Mary as the rightful rulers of England? But the messenger with Baltimore's instructions died en route to America, and some Protestants finally got tired of waiting. A mob led by former Catholic priest John Coode seized control of the government in St. Mary's City.

When King William was informed of the situation, he sent his own governor to run Maryland. Lord Baltimore was stripped of his powers as proprietor, and Charles Carroll the Settler was out of a job. The former attorney general wasn't shy about sharing his unhappiness. As a result, he was hauled to jail twice on charges that included "high misdemeanors," mutiny, and sedition against the government.

He found out making money was, if not the best revenge, then an acceptable substitute. Through his two marriages—the second to Mary Darnall, the daughter of the proprietor's chief agent—he added substantially to the land he'd been granted by Lord Baltimore. He used some of the sixty thousand acres he held to plant Maryland's signature crop, tobacco, and he also became one of Maryland's largest slave owners as a result. He ran a successful store in Annapolis, where he sold imported goods. He became a hard-nosed moneylender, sometimes to complaints from the community. And, of course, he was still an attorney — one who didn't mind taking unpopular cases, like when he defended two Catholic priests who dared say Mass.

He didn't care. He was brash and cocky, and in 1715, it even looked like he'd figured out a way to regain some of the power he'd been denied.

Charles Calvert, the third Lord Baltimore and a devout Catholic, was gravely ill and near death. Then his son, Benedict, publicly renounced Catholicism for the Church of England. It was a shameless attempt to convince the new British monarch, George I, to give the Calverts control of Maryland again. And it worked. Except that Benedict, only thirty-six years old, died just two months after his father.

Having some inkling that it might be beneficial, Charles Carroll the Settler had wisely planned a trip to England. He was in the country when both Calverts died, and even served as the attorney for Charles Calvert's grieving widow. After Benedict's unexpected death, the title of Lord Baltimore passed on to Benedict's son, Charles — then just a minor, aged fifteen.

Now the Calverts were back in control of Maryland, but the fifth Lord Baltimore had to be appointed a legal guardian, Lord Guilford. Charles Carroll the Settler used his charm and wit and went to work on them both. The signatures of Lords Baltimore and Guilford were on the commission Carroll proudly brought back to Maryland with him the next year.

It was a "remarkable" document, and one that made Carroll the chief agent of the proprietor in Maryland, as well as receiver general, escheator, and naval officer. In short, the commission effectively gave Carroll the powers of a colonial governor, including overseeing the collection of tax revenues.

The current governor, John Hart, exploded when he got a look at the commission. He immediately accused his "Papist" rival of bamboozling the innocent Lord Baltimore and his guardian. Hart and Carroll bickered constantly for the next two years, and Charles Carroll the Settler seemed to enjoy every opportunity to bedevil Hart.

The long-term consequences of the feud would be severe. A frustrated Hart took his case to the state assembly. He pointed out that Carroll had refused to take the oath of abjuration, which recognized the Protestant succession to the British throne. Carroll appealed to Lord Guilford in England, confident the man who had given him his commission would back up his claim. He'd never taken such an oath and didn't need to now.

This time, Carroll's faith in his own charm was terribly misplaced. It had also been compromised by one of his own relatives—his nephew, William Fitzredmond. Fitzredmond had reportedly committed the sin of offering a toast to James Stuart, the Catholic "Pretender" to the English throne.

Guilford revoked Carroll's commission in 1717 and affirmed that all officeholders needed to take the oath to King George. Guilford's decision wasn't just about officials in Maryland—it was also about defending the reputation of the proprietor he represented.

The new Lord Baltimore had followed in the footsteps of his father, who had renounced Rome for political gain. Lord Baltimore was no "Papist in masquerade," Guilford insisted, "but a true Protestant of the Church of England in which faith he is resolved to live and die."[45]

The state assembly wasn't through, either: the following year, it put an exclamation point on its decision by disenfranchising all Catholics in the colony. The message was clear. Catholics had enjoyed a period of tolerance, and perhaps even public influence, thanks in part to the irrepressible rogue Charles Carroll the Settler. But it was now officially, emphatically, over.

3

He died in 1720 without office and without the right to vote, but Charles Carroll the Settler's considerable holdings in Maryland were intact. Some of them were inherited by his second son, commonly called Charles Carroll of Annapolis. From his father he also got a legendary temper and his money-making acumen.

---

[45] Martin I. J. Griffin, "The Apostate Lord Baltimore and Acts of Hostility against the Catholics of Maryland," *American Catholic Historical Researches* 1, no. 2 (April 1905): 157.

The laws left Catholics "little else to do but make money and spend it," biographer Scott McDermott notes. Charles Carroll of Annapolis excelled in both pursuits.[46]

What he wanted most was to be a lawyer. He had been sent abroad to the Jesuit college at St. Omer in French Flanders for his education. But it was cut short by a pair of tragedies. First, his older brother, Henry, died at sea in 1719, on his way home from studying law in London. Then his father died the following year. Charles was called home to take over the family affairs while his younger brother, Daniel, remained in Europe to study.

If he didn't have a chip on his shoulder before, he did now. Years later, he would complain that he'd spent nearly forty years as the "constant servant of my family."[47] But the family he started himself was also his refuge from life's many disappointments. He doted on his beautiful cousin, Elizabeth, and the son they had together, Charles, who was born on September 19, 1737. This Charles would become the most famous Charles Carroll of all.

Charles Carroll of Carrollton grew up in relative ignorance of the situation Catholics faced in Maryland and of the ways it shaped his father's life. He would also not learn until later that he was illegitimate: Charles Carroll of Annapolis and Elizabeth Brooke were not married. This was shocking behavior for devout Catholics. It becomes more shocking when evidence suggests Charles Carroll of Annapolis refrained from marrying to test the heir to his fortune.

In his 2001 book, *Charles Carroll of Carrollton: Faithful Revolutionary*, Scott McDermott provides several letters as evidence that Charles Carroll of Annapolis "held the reward of legitimacy over his son's head until Carrollton proved himself worthy of a father's love."[48] That apparently

---

[46] Scott McDermott, *Charles Carroll of Carrollton: Faithful Revolutionary* (New York: Scepter, 2018), 34.

[47] Kate Mason Rowland, *The Life of Charles Carroll of Carrollton, 1737–1832* (1898; n.p.: Sagwan Press, 2018), 17.

[48] McDermott, *Charles Carroll of Carrollton*, 40.

did not occur until 1757, when Charles Carroll of Annapolis finally married Elizabeth.

"To survive and prosper as a Roman Catholic in a Protestant environment, Charley must accomplish the rigorous educational program laid out by his father—eleven years of study at Jesuit institutions in France and another five at London's Inns of Court,"[49] wrote Ronald Hoffman, who edited the definitive collection of the Carrolls' correspondence, in explaining this strategy.

Hoffman laid out the consequences: "And should the younger Carroll not become a man of strict self-discipline, sound faith, a master of mathematics, the humanities, commerce and business, and, most of all, of the law—what then? The legitimacy that would confirm his inheritance of the Carroll legacy would not be conferred upon him."

Yet the threat of disinheritance, McDermott suggests, helped create "a young man of impeccable character and excellent manners, without the gift of making friends."[50] Later, people would describe him as cold—even to his own wife. The one person to whom he was closest was always his imperious father. Even after he was happily married and had children of his own, Charles Carroll of Carrollton would say of his father, "He is the greatest comfort of my life."[51]

If the desire to win his father's love warped some aspect of his personality, though, it might also have driven him to pursue the cause of independence, as a way of proving his worthiness to his father—and, incidentally, to the rest of colonial America.

His early days, however, were blissfully innocent, spent as the third member of a close-knit trio with his "Mama" and "Papa." The three went back and forth between homes in Annapolis, on the banks of Spa Creek, and the family manor in Howard County called Doughoregan, a nod to the Carrolls' Irish heritage. Even as an older, wiser adult, the memory of

---

49 Ronald Hoffman, "The Carroll Family of Maryland," *Proceedings of the American Antiquarian Society* 117, no. 2 (October), 343, https://www.americanantiquarian.org/proceedings/44539656.pdf.

50 McDermott, *Charles Carroll of Carrollton*, 41.

51 McDermott, *Charles Carroll of Carrollton*, 82.

that time remained unblemished. "I shall never," he wrote wistfully to his father in 1761, "see such happy days again."[52]

Money was never an issue. Not only was Charles Carroll of Annapolis a good steward of the land and businesses he inherited, he managed to increase them, making himself one of the richest men in the colonies.

Moneylending was one of his primary revenue sources, and, like his father, he was known as a demanding creditor. That didn't stop customers, both Catholic and Protestant, from borrowing. (It didn't even stop members of his own family from paying the 5 percent commission he charged as executor of their legal transactions.)

There were two reasons he continued to relentlessly build his fortune, both rooted deeply in disappointment. The first was his thwarted dream of becoming a lawyer. The second was his religion.

The two causes were not unrelated. As he would tell his son years later, "had I been a lawyer, or deemed such, it's more than probably they would not have ventured to have imposed on me."[53] In this letter, *they* referred to "Characters" who were "ignorant, knavish or conceited." Undoubtedly, many of those "Characters" were the anti-Catholic citizens of Maryland under whom Charles Carroll of Annapolis suffered.

After losing the right to vote, and with loyalty oaths barring them from holding public office, Catholics in Maryland had reached an uneasy truce with the Protestants who now ran the colony. In the wake of the battle between John Hart and Charles Carroll the Settler, the latest proprietor, Charles Calvert, had written to Maryland citizens. He had now come of age, and his letter asked for peace between the two factions. The state assembly essentially offered Catholics a deal: it would keep its penal laws against them on the books. But if they were discreet in their worship, the laws would stay unenforced.

There were times during the eighteenth century when current events got Maryland Protestants riled up and that deal was threatened. Immigration was an issue that always promised controversy, because it often

[52] Smith, *Charles Carroll of Carrollton*, 27.
[53] Smith, *Charles Carroll of Carrollton*, 53.

meant adding Catholics to the colony. One example was when England sent Jacobite prisoners—partisans of the Stuarts who opposed the post-Glorious Revolution monarchs—to America to serve as convict labor. Another was when French Acadians, driven out of Canada by the British, migrated to Maryland.

Despite the best efforts of lawmakers, native "popery" also continued to grow in Maryland. Worship was driven underground, which meant Masses were often said privately at estates owned by wealthy Catholics. It was an American version of the gentry, manor Catholicism that had allowed the faith to survive in Britain—sometimes known as "Seigneurial Catholicism," after a seigneur, or feudal lord—and it was an increasingly popular one.

Between 1700 and 1760, the number of Catholic chapels in Maryland increased from fourteen to fifty. Charles Carroll of Annapolis had two: one at Doughoregan and one in Annapolis, with a full-time chaplain who served both.

Yet even if the authorities left the Carrolls and their neighbors to worship in peace, even if the penal laws were enforced arbitrarily, and sometimes not at all, they were still a constant reminder of just where Catholics stood in the colony that had once promised them freedom of conscience. There were the maddening Catch-22s, such as Catholics being barred from militia service but then being taxed because they did not serve. Or the hundred-pound fee Catholic parents had to pay if they sent their children overseas—to get the Catholic education forbidden at home. And of course, there was nothing a Catholic could do to change any of it, since he couldn't vote and was barred from holding office.

For all the polite social interaction between the two groups, Catholics knew they were second-class citizens, even if they had as much money as Charles Carroll of Annapolis. To a man who was oversensitive and already felt he'd been cheated of the career he truly wanted, the daily reminders of his place in society salted those wounds.

"He was as bitter as a man can be when he is intensely religious and really believes that this world does not matter," his son's biographer Ellen

Hart Smith wrote. "There were black moments when he hated Maryland and everyone in it."[54]

He hated it so much, in fact, that by 1757, he was ready to leave it all behind. And he felt he owed it to his son to explain why, in person.

4

When Charles Carroll of Annapolis made this momentous visit to France, he had not seen his only child for nearly a decade.

That was the sort of sacrifice parents had to make for the sake of a Catholic education. Charles Carroll of Carrollton was taught at home by his mother until he was ten. His parents then enrolled him at Bohemia Academy, a school on the border of Maryland and Pennsylvania. It was run covertly by Jesuits, who kept a low profile to avoid fines and persecution for violating the penal laws.

Charles attended Bohemia Academy with his older cousin, John "Jacky" Carroll. For both families, it was a means to an end: a way to prepare them for the rigorous schooling they would receive overseas at St. Omer. But this first-class learning came at great cost, and not just financial. The Atlantic journey was not just dangerous; it marked the beginning of a long separation that might well be permanent.

So, as the two boys bid their parents farewell that summer day on the wharf at Annapolis, the scene had to have been a wrenching one. Especially for Charles's parents, who were surrendering their only child—a small, frail boy, just ten years old.

The fears both families must have felt that day would unfortunately be well founded. John Carroll's father, Daniel, died unexpectedly in 1751, while John was still a student at St. Omer. Ten years later, Charles Carroll would still be abroad when he got news of his mother Elizabeth's death.

Both boys spent five years in French Flanders together. Charles graduated two years after that, when he was nearly seventeen. Charles Carroll's father made him promise to write home at least twice a year, and that's

---

[54] Smith, *Charles Carroll of Carrollton*, 26.

apparently exactly what he did. Meanwhile, none of John Carroll's correspondence from French Flanders seems to have survived.

But we do have some details of what life must have been like for the pupils. It was John Carroll, not his younger cousin, who truly seemed to excel at St. Omer. He seemed not to mind the regular diet of boiled milk and bread, nor the waking up at five each morning. And he quickly mastered the demanding curriculum of "little" and "great" figures, and upper grammar, with its emphasis on creating careful, polished writers and thinkers. "I believe Cousin Jack Carroll will make a good scholar," Charles Carroll predicted to his father in one of his required letters, "for he is often the first."[55]

Charles was certainly no slouch. He ranked consistently near the top of his class at St. Omer, even though most boys, like his cousin, were a year or two older. Although he disliked math, he enjoyed Latin and loved reading Cicero in his native tongue. What he felt for the ancient Roman philosopher would become a lifelong admiration.

As biographer Bradley Birzer explains in the book that took its title from that interest—*American Cicero: The Life of Charles Carroll*—his reading habits give us fascinating clues about this future statesman. He "devoured" the French theorist Montesquieu, who advanced the concept of a government where power is balanced between different branches. But Carroll apparently had little use for the philosophy of England's John Locke, who argued that man is born as a "blank slate."

In 1754, Charles Carroll headed for Rheims to continue his studies at the French Jesuit college. At some point, he transferred his studies to Paris, and it was there that Charles Carroll of Annapolis met his son in August 1757.

In a sense, he was meeting him for the very first time, since he'd only that year officially declared him as his son. We can imagine the discussion between them, whether it took place at some outdoor café or in Charles's rooms. Charles Carroll of Annapolis had reached the end of his tether. His face was red, his fists were clenched, his voice was choked. He had

---

[55] Smith, *Charles Carroll of Carrollton*, 31.

suffered for years — for most of his life — as a Catholic in Maryland, and his son was going to hear all of it.

How much his son actually knew about the situation back home is debatable. Years later, he wrote to his father asking for Maryland's provincial charter and confessed even then he was "perfectly ignorant"[56] of the situation in his native colony.

But he learned a lot on this August afternoon in Paris. As Ellen Hart Smith described it:

> Now at nineteen he was hearing family history he had never suspected before. All about the O'Carrolls in Ireland, who had been born so high and been brought so low. About his grandfather the Attorney-General, who had expected freedom in Maryland, but had never achieved it. About his own father, disenfranchised, mistrusted, fifty-five years old now, and still an onlooker in the affairs in the province where he had been born.[57]

His father had had enough, and now he was going to leave. He and a group of disgruntled Maryland Catholics were planning to ask King Louis XV for land somewhere in French-controlled territory — maybe Louisiana, along the Arkansas River — where they would not have to scrape and grovel. In fact, that was the main reason he was here in Paris.

The boy listened, rapt, to his father. But he was ready to dig in his heels. Not only was he uninterested in the career in law his father had been planning for him since birth, he also didn't want to see his family chased from their home. He would say later that he felt he had been banished overseas. In fact, he wanted to return to Maryland now.

If Charles Carroll of Annapolis was shocked or angered by his son's reaction, he must also have been proud. It was proof that Charles Carroll of Carrollton was a true, independent Carroll like his father and grandfather before him. Was this heart-to-heart talk the real beginning of the remarkable relationship between these two men? Or was it the

---

[56] Smith, *Charles Carroll of Carrollton*, 50.
[57] Smith, *Charles Carroll of Carrollton*, 36.

fact that the son was now officially the family heir? Perhaps it was a little of both.

Of course, this wasn't the end of their arguments. Charles Carroll of Annapolis continued to urge his son to study law. When the boy grew tired of laboring over the dry, dusty books, his father reminded him that even if he didn't plan to practice law, "would it not be of infinite advantage to England if every man who serves in Parliament were a sound Lawyer and well acquainted with the Constitution? ... Will it not enable you to state your own Cases?"[58]

In the short term, Charles Carroll of Annapolis would have his way. His son would stay overseas, first in Paris and then in London, to continue his studies. Even after the heartbreaking news of his mother's death in 1761 after a long illness, he remained abroad to finish his schooling, though he desperately wanted to return home.

Where home was located, however, was the second, and more important, argument that Charles Carroll of Carrollton would end up winning. He had quite a bit of help: it turned out that Louis XV was not really interested in granting the Maryland Catholics their own colony. We're told that the minister to whom Charles Carroll of Annapolis made the request was surprised by "the extent of the tract demanded,"[59] so the dream of escape from Maryland would remain only that.

The son now offered his father some consoling words. A French colony, he pointed out, might end up no better than an English one. "Religious persecution, I own, is bad," he wrote to his father in 1759, "but civil persecution is still more irksome." He added, "I know of no Catholick country where that greatest blessing, civil liberty, is enjoyed."[60]

In other words, trading one king for another was unlikely to get the Carrolls what they wanted: true religious freedom, and the payoff of that

---

[58] Smith, *Charles Carroll of Carrollton*, 52-3.

[59] B.U. Campbell, "Memoirs of the Life and Times of the Most Rev. John Carroll," *U.S. Catholic Magazine* 3 (1844): 40.

[60] Bradley Birzer, *American Cicero: The Life of Charles Carroll* (Wilmington, DE: ISI Books, 2010), 22.

motto Charles Carroll the Settler had inscribed on the family coat of arms: *Ubicumque cum liberate*.

All his life, Charles Carroll of Annapolis had dreamed of living any-where, as long it was free. In the end, he didn't have to uproot himself to make that saying come true. His son would help make it happen, right there in their home — in Maryland, in America.

5

When Charles Carroll finally returned to Maryland in February 1765, he had been gone for the better part of twenty years. Now an adult, he was slightly built and shorter than average. A famous portrait of the time shows a dark-haired young man with a long nose and a serious — maybe even imperious — expression. Yet his manners were impeccable, and he charmed his father's friends when he was reintroduced to Annapolis society.

In some ways, almost nothing had changed since he'd been gone. Catholics were tolerated, but only just. They could move easily enough in society — especially if they had as much money as the Carrolls — yet the laws that threatened them were still on the books, enforced or not, and the usual roadblocks to advancement were still firmly in place.

In other ways, there was nothing familiar at all. Annapolis had grown into "a London in miniature."[61] There were clubs, a thriving social scene, and every form of entertainment. The big house on Spa Creek was much emptier without Elizabeth Carroll, of course, and that was a change much for the worse.

Perhaps the greatest difference had to do with people's unhappiness with the Stamp Act, which had just been enacted. The measure, devised by British Prime Minister George Grenville, was a way of helping to pay for the Seven Years' War with France. It had concluded in 1763 with a British victory — and mountains of British debt. Parliament believed it was only right that the colonists should assume some of it, since it was their safety British forces had fought to protect.

[61] Smith, *Charles Carroll of Carrollton*, 65.

Some colonists didn't see it that way at all. To them, it was an in-fringement on the rights of colonial assemblies to tax their citizens. Mobs assembled up and down the American seaboard. They destroyed reams of the special stamped paper that was to be used for newspapers, legal documents, and even playing cards. And they threatened the lives of more than one stamp distributor.

It was coincidence, perhaps, that Charles Carroll chose this moment to change his name. Or, we should say, add to it. From this point, he signed himself "Charles Carroll of Carrollton." There was a practical reason for the switch: his father had just deeded him Carrollton Manor, in Frederick County. But Charles preferred to stay with his father in Annapolis. The name change seemed more symbolic: the true coming of age of the third Charles Carroll, who would both follow his family's footsteps and travel well beyond them.

He would do this at first through his opposition to the Stamp Act. Over the past few years, he had learned from his father's letters more and more of his family's history and persecution. Ever since the days of the O'Carrolls in Ireland—Catholics who lost property when Oliver Cromwell and his Roundheads seized it during the mid-seventeenth century—the family had been victimized by the British government. Charles might still say he would "chuse to live under an English govern-ment rather than under any other."[62] But that was a theoretical distinction only. He had lived for the past six years in London and knew firsthand the discrimination Catholics still faced there.

The crusade for a new, better, truly free land for his father, for himself, and for other Catholics, started here. "He saw the Stamp Act controversy," Ellen Hart Smith wrote, "clear-eyed, as an opening wedge."[63]

He summed it up in a letter to William Graves, a frequent correspon-dent. The issue was "allowing this unbounded power in a set of men at so great a distance, so little acquainted with our circumstances, and not immediately affected with ye taxes laid upon us, what security remains

---

[62] Birzer, *American Cicero*, 23.
[63] Smith, *Charles Carroll of Carrollton*, 78.

for our property? what fence against arbitrary enactions? are we to trust ye moderation of a British Parliament? have we reason to rely solely on that?"[64]

Charles Carroll of Carrollton knew, as few other Americans did in 1765, that they should not trust moderation, and had no reason to do so. He was certainly not the only patriot to question the British government that year. The fiery Virginian, Patrick Henry, compared King George III to both Caesar and Charles I, in a speech about tyranny that had his fellow legislators complaining of treason.

But as a Catholic, Charles Carroll also knew about things like "unbounded power," and having no "security for our property," and especially "arbitrary enactions," in a way no Protestant founding father could truly understand.

This was still a minority view. The Stamp Act might have inspired protests and even riots, but Americans were a long way from being ready for revolution. And if any colony was likely to stay loyal to the Crown, it was Maryland.

People there viewed the Stamp Act debate through a completely different lens. While other colonies objected to the Stamp Act on the grounds that it muscled in on the lawmaking turf of their *own* constitutions — especially their right to levy and collect taxes — Maryland had consistently argued that its constitution was the *same* as England's.

As author Maura Jane Farrelly points out, Maryland had long insisted on this similarity so as to curb the growth of Catholicism. After the Glorious Revolution, she said, Protestants thought that "to defend their liberty, they needed to preserve their English identity; to preserve their English identity, they needed to 'control the growth of popery in this province'; and to curb the growth of popery, they needed to solicit the help of Parliament."[65]

So Charles Carroll had, in effect, a double handicap to overcome. First, he was a Catholic, barred from voting or holding office, who was trying

---

[64] Smith, *Charles Carroll of Carrollton*, 74.
[65] Maura Jane Farrelly, *Papist Patriots: The Making of an American Catholic Identity* (New York: Oxford University Press, 2012), 227.

to insert himself into civic affairs where the law said he was unwelcome. Second, he had to contend with good Maryland Protestants, who would have had trouble agreeing with one of the major arguments against the Stamp Act, because Maryland officials had tied themselves so closely to English law and custom.

A Jesuit priest named Fr. Peter Atwood, S.J., had argued against this claim of Maryland officials all the way back in 1718. Lawmakers in the state assembly were trying to repeal the Act to Prevent the Growth of Popery in this Province. This wasn't because the Assembly suddenly felt friendly toward Catholics. It was just the opposite, in fact: the members claimed this 1704 statute had not prevented the "growth of popery" as much as they'd hoped.

That was technically true. Catholicism was on the upswing in Maryland, although some of that was due to immigration. So the Assembly proposed throwing out the law altogether, and instead deferring to English law, which was even *more* harsh toward Catholics. The rationale was that since Maryland and England shared the same constitution, English law could be applied where Maryland law had failed.

Atwood pointed out that this idea ignored not only Maryland's constitution, which was clearly a different document. It also failed to recognize the colony's unique history. "Liberty of Conscience" was the reason Maryland had been founded, he said, and it was a place where religious toleration was part of the collective identity.

Even though the Assembly was unable to repeal the anti-Catholic act and replace it with something more punitive, this didn't improve conditions much for Maryland Catholics in the short term. But an important truth had been revealed.

In short, in Farrelly's words, "Catholic colonists understood that to be English in Maryland meant something different from what it meant to be English in England."[66] This was the revelation that ultimately would ignite the Revolution. And Catholics understood it long before Protestants.

---

[66] Maura Jane Farrelly, *Anti-Catholicism in America, 1620–1860* (New York: Cambridge University Press, 2018), 93.

Wasn't the Revolution about taxation without representation? To some, it was. Annapolis lawyer and assemblyman Daniel Dulany, a Protestant, wrote perhaps the most widely read pamphlet against the Stamp Act. Titled *Considerations on the Propriety of Imposing Taxes in the British Colonies*, its argument boiled down to that oft-related phrase.

The pamphlet was well-received in the colonies: Charles Carroll, for one, approved. And it was influential abroad. William Pitt, who successfully argued for the Stamp Act's repeal in Parliament, agreed that while England could legislate for the colonies, that right stopped at taxation.

But within the "taxation without representation" argument is an implicit admission: *if* we receive representation, then taxation might be permissible. In his role as an American agent in London, Benjamin Franklin had sought colonial seats in Parliament for years, and there had been British statesmen willing to listen. If the proposal had been successful, history might well look different.

Catholics saw things differently. Their proposal was more radical: independence wasn't just a practical matter. It was a *necessity*, because the colonies were no longer what they had been.

Many years later, this idea would begin a famous introduction to a famous document: "When in the Course of human events, it becomes necessary for one people to dissolve the political bands which have connected them with another, and to assume among the powers of the earth, the separate and equal station to which the Laws of Nature and of Nature's God entitle them...."[67] What was that but the natural endpoint of Atwood's argument?

It would take Charles Carroll of Carrollton to make this idea crystal clear for his fellow Marylanders. He did it during a minor dispute with major implications.

---

[67] Thomas Jefferson, "Declaration of Independence: A Transcription," *America's Founding Documents*, National Archives, https://www.archives.gov/founding-docs/declaration-transcript.

6

By 1773, Charles Carroll had finally gotten married, to his younger cousin, Molly Darnall. A persistent theme among Carroll's biographers is the emotional distance Carroll seemed to maintain from his wife. But this union was always overshadowed by two failed engagements. In London, Carroll had unsuccessfully wooed the heiress Louisa Baker. Her father believed her too young for marriage, and her stepmother apparently disliked the American suitor.

Back home, he became engaged to another cousin, Rachel Cooke, who died the same month they were to be wed. For the rest of his life, Charles Carroll kept her picture and a lock of her hair in a secret drawer in his writing desk.

Molly had given him a daughter, Mary, who was now three, and two more children would follow. Four others died in childbirth, however, and Molly's health would always remain fragile. Frequently in pain, she became addicted to laudanum. This concerned Charles, and even more his father, who seemed to dote on Molly in a way her husband did not.

Meanwhile, three years before America declared its independence, unrest continued to simmer throughout the colonies. But Parliament had repealed most of the unpopular Townshend Acts, and there was hope the serious squabbles between Britain and America were past.

There was a recession in Maryland, however, thanks to falling tobacco prices. As money grew tight, the fees people paid to various government officials began to seem unnecessarily high. The Lower House of the General Assembly had agreed. In 1769, those lawmakers tried to get the fees lowered when they came up for renewal. But the Upper House — which contained some of these same officials earning higher fees — unsurprisingly disagreed.

Maryland's governor, Robert Eden, broke the deadlock and restored government services. But he did this by acting unilaterally, and restoring the old, higher fees. It was an unpopular move at the time, and as the recession deepened, it came under fresh scrutiny.

Then, on January 7, 1773, an anonymous letter appeared in *The Maryland Gazette*. It was a dialogue that set out to educate people who were complaining about the fees. Arguing against Governor Eden's decision was a character named First Citizen, who blustered ineffectively against the government's "Court-influence, and Corruption." But Second Citizen, the Gallant to First Citizen's Goofus, easily defended the governor and the increased fees.

"The blessings of Order," Second Citizen somewhat smugly informed First Citizen, "will still be preferred to the horrors of Anarchy."[68] And of course, there was no comeback to that.

That is, until a new dialogue appeared in the *Gazette* the next month. The characters were the same, but the content was much different. This time, First Citizen didn't just have answers for Second Citizen. He went on the attack himself. "Your attachment to government," he informed Second Citizen, "proceeds, I fear, more from personal considerations."[69]

This new First Citizen was devastatingly correct. As he knew, the author of the original letter was Daniel Dulany, who just happened to be a land commissioner and had personally benefited from the higher fees Governor Eden had reinstated. Meanwhile, the new, improved "First Citizen" of the follow-up letter was none other than Charles Carroll of Carrollton.

The argument that unfolded over the next few months in the *Gazette* was about much more than fees for government officials. It gave Charles Carroll a chance to revive and perfect Peter Atwood's ideas about Maryland's distinct character. The conduct of both letter writers would also have a substantial effect on the fortunes of Charles Carroll, as well as his fellow Catholics.

Fifteen years older than Carroll, Dulany was a formidable opponent. The son of an Irish indentured servant who had become a self-made man in Maryland, he'd inherited his father's fortune. There was more to him than just money, though. His pamphlet against the Stamp Act had been a game-changer. Charles Carroll himself admitted that Dulany was "indisputably ye best Lawyer on this Continent."

---

[68] Peter S. Onuf, ed., *Maryland and the Empire, 1773: The Antilon-First Citizen Letters* (Baltimore: Johns Hopkins University Press, 1974), 46.
[69] Onuf, *Maryland and the Empire*, 55.

Yet the perceptive Carroll also marked his adversary as "very Vain, Proud, & Designing & so much of a Politician as not to be ever scrupulous in ye Measures as he takes to answer his Ends."[70]

The fact that Dulany would use an anonymous letter to publicly defend a policy that enriched him speaks to those points. But the identities of both Dulany and Carroll became very quickly known — even after Dulany adopted the name "Antilon," which was a sticking plaster used to draw out infection.

The public ate it up. There was also family bad blood to spice up the feud. The fathers of both men had long disliked one another, and Charles Carroll of Carrollton had nearly dueled with Daniel Dulany's half brother, Lloyd, over some remarks he made about Carroll and his father.

On paper, the correspondence was a David and Goliath match. It seemed unfair: the older, established Protestant official against the young, unknown Catholic lawyer.

But people always enjoy rooting for the underdog. As he fitted rocks into his slingshot, Charles Carroll didn't disappoint. Dulany exposed his forehead by using the same argument he'd made against the Stamp Act.

Then, he had argued the issue was taxation without representation. But the fee debate was something different, he had Antilon lecture the public. *Fees* were not *taxes*. Furthermore, there was long precedent in England for having non-legislators set public fees — exactly what Governor Eden had done.

It was a consistent argument. And it was also wrong, according to Carroll's First Citizen.

What was true in England was not automatically true in Maryland. In fact, First Citizen showed that precedent in Maryland was markedly different. In 1692, the Lower House had rejected an attempt by the governor to do exactly what Governor Eden had done: set fees.

Therefore, Antilon's appeals to the English Constitution and English precedent were invalid. Maryland had its own constitution and its own history. They were two separate, and quite different, places. And at least

---

[70] Smith, *Charles Carroll of Carrollton*, 102.

some readers who devoured this series of letters couldn't have helped noticing that this argument might also apply to the controversy brewing between the colonies and Britain.

Dulany, a loyalist and Protestant, simply would never have thought of the dispute this way. But when it became obvious First Citizen was getting the better of him, things turned ugly. Antilon not only described the long-limbed Carroll as a "monkey" but also decided to out his opponent as a Catholic. Dulany was confident this nuclear option would finish off First Citizen.

"Who is he?" Antilon asked the public of his opponent, then proceeded to tell them. "He has no share in the legislature, as a member of any branch; he is incapable of being a member; he is disabled from giving a vote in the choice of representatives, by the laws and constitution of the country, *on account of* his principles, which are *distrusted* by those laws."[71]

As if anyone couldn't have guessed, Antilon spelled out exactly why: "He is not a Protestant."

The bomb went off, but Dulany was the victim. His mean-spirited attack was met with courtesy by First Citizen, who wrote that his opponent's abuse meant "we may fairly presume, that arguments are either wanting, or that ignorance and incapacity know not how to apply them."[72]

Carroll emerged the undeclared but widely acknowledged winner of the exchange. In this high-profile contest between Catholic and Protestant, the papist had won on both points and style. His opponent, meanwhile, had lost his cool and disgraced himself.

That May, candidates who supported the patriot cause and opposed Governor Eden swept into office. In July, the new Lower House of the Assembly voted unanimously to toss out the fees the governor had imposed. Remarkably, after the vote, they all marched through Annapolis to Spa Creek, the home of First Citizen. They made speeches to thank Carroll personally, because it was clear how important he had been to their cause.

[71] Onuf, *Maryland and the Empire*, 122.
[72] Onuf, *Maryland and the Empire*, 124.

Catholic or no, penal laws or no penal laws, Charles Carroll of Carrollton had become a public citizen, and a critically important one at that. He had successfully argued that Maryland tradition demanded religious tolerance. Now he was about to take that idea to places no one, not even his father, could have dreamed.

7

If there was one word that could not be applied to Charles Carroll of Carrollton, it would be "opportunist."

Over and over again, as we'll see, he had the chance to take advantage of his position. He consistently refused. That trend began in the summer of 1774, when—thanks to his triumph as First Citizen—he was chosen to be a delegate to the First Continental Congress. He refused, instead accompanying the state's delegation to Philadelphia as a mere observer.

What he observed was the Congress insulting all Catholics, in Canada and America, with its response to the Quebec Act, as we saw in chapter 1. His belief that Congress wasn't ready yet for an official Catholic member seemed accurate. But that certainly didn't change the view he had held for nearly the past decade about American independence. He repeated it that September in a letter to his father, back in Maryland: "I still think this controversy will at last be decided by arms."[73]

The easy thing for this rising political star to do would have been to simply convert. Why not abandon Catholicism for the Church of England, as many others had done for the sake of ambition? His friend William Graves urged him to consider it. The response he got was revealing. It shows that the idea of separating church and state was something Carroll was thinking about long before Thomas Jefferson, who often—mistakenly—gets credit for it.

Not only would he stay Catholic out of respect for his father, Charles Carroll wrote, but using a religious test to determine who was fit to serve was an idea he rejected. He was "a warm friend to toleration," because

[73] Smith, *Charles Carroll of Carrollton*, 123.

he'd seen how such tests had worked in Maryland. No Catholic should support the intermingling of church and state, given how often the state had worked against them.

"If my countrymen judge me incapable of serving them in a public station for believing ye moon to be made of green cheese," Carroll wrote, "in this respect their conduct, if not wicked, is not less absurd than my belief." He added, "And I will serve them in a private capacity notwithstanding."[74]

Yet in the spring of 1776, being a Catholic—for once—meant Carroll could serve them publicly. Congress had badly bungled relations with Canada following the Quebec Act. After complaining loudly to England about the way the act might empower Catholics, Congress then warmly invited the mostly Catholic nation to join it in arms against Britain.

The Canadians saw through the transparent ruse. So Congress needed an actual Catholic or two to send north, as proof of its sincerity. Here, Charles Carroll was the obvious choice. As John Adams put it, Carroll had money, he had a liberal education, and he spoke French. "And what is perhaps of more consequence than all the rest," Adams admitted, "he was educated in the Roman Catholic Religion and still continues to worship his maker according to the Rites of that Church."[75]

This time, Charles Carroll not only accepted; he also talked his cousin, Fr. John Carroll, S.J., into accompanying the delegation. He had some convincing to do. John Carroll, a priest who had returned to Maryland following the suppression of the Jesuits, was rightfully skeptical the mission could sway the Canadians. But he finally relented and joined Charles, Maryland lawyer and politician Samuel Chase, and elder statesman Benjamin Franklin on the journey to Montreal.

The story of that mission, its failure, and its long-term consequences, is better told in the next chapter, about Fr. John Carroll. But one thing worth noting is that the trip contributed mightily to the political—and military—education of Charles Carroll.

---

[74] Smith, *Charles Carroll of Carrollton*, 122–123.
[75] Smith, *Charles Carroll of Carrollton*, 137.

He observed the deplorable conditions of the forts where the party stayed along the way to Canada: Fort George, Fort Edward, Fort William Henry, Fort Ticonderoga, and others. He asked numerous questions, especially of their host and part-time traveling companion, colonial Gen. Philip Schuyler. Quickly, he gained a working knowledge of strategic locations, supplies, transportation, and the care and feeding of troops.

At the time, this might have seemed like polite curiosity. But the information Charles Carroll gained would become crucial to the country's survival soon enough.

While he and Chase were in Canada, however, the moderates ruled the Maryland Convention's vote on independence. The convention's initial recommendation to Congress was in favor of "a reunion with Great Britain on constitutional principles" to "increase the strength and promote the happiness of the whole empire."[76] That changed as soon as Charles Carroll returned to Annapolis. The man who had once been barred from holding office now swung Maryland's vote toward a break with Britain.

His reward was selection as a delegate to Philadelphia, where the formal Declaration of Independence was to be signed July 4. History shows us that "Charles Carroll of Carrollton" was the only Catholic to put his name to that document.

Far more significant for the actual realization of that independence, though, would be the appointment of Charles Carroll to a congressional committee no one remembers today. If he hadn't been part of that group, George Washington might never have become the father of his country.

8

Reevaluations of George Washington's military acumen have become a cottage industry in recent years. But facts are facts: after a string of surprising early successes, the first year of the Revolutionary War went badly on the American side. And Washington, the impressive-looking but inexperienced commander in chief, bore the brunt of the blame.

---

[76] Smith, *Charles Carroll of Carrollton*, 153.

The doubts were increased by a widely quoted complaint about Washington from one of his brigadier generals, an Irish soldier of fortune named Thomas Conway. That fall, Congress was abuzz about a letter Conway had written to Gen. Horatio Gates. It reportedly included the quote, "Heaven has been determined to save your Country; or a weak General and bad Counsellors would have ruined it."[77]

Historians have long debated whether there was an actual "Conway Cabal," as the alleged plot to dump Washington was called. Was Conway part of a group of conspirators actively trying to get Washington replaced? Or were the complaints about Washington unrelated, and simply the natural result of his uneven performance?

The question remains unresolved, but certain points seem clear. One is that Horatio Gates, who had taken credit for one of the few big colonial successes that fall at the Battle of Saratoga, seemed to be lobbying for Washington's job. So was Charles Lee, a British-born general who felt that he, not the less-experienced Washington, should have been named commander in chief in the first place.

Another point is that some powerful members of Congress had long held doubts about Washington. John Adams and his cousin Samuel were no great fans of the general. Neither were Richard Henry Lee of Virginia and his brother Francis. Nor was the Philadelphia representative Benjamin Rush.

So, whether there was a formal conspiracy against Washington is probably beside the point. As desertions from the army continued after the fall of Philadelphia, and after Washington and his troops retreated to Valley Forge to spend a legendarily miserable winter, he could certainly have been replaced.

In November 1777, the Congressional Board of War was reorganized. General Gates was its leader, and it was filled with enemies of Washington. It was enough to make a conspiracy theorist of anyone.

[77] "From George Washington to Major General Horatio Gates, 4 January 1778," Founders Online, National Archives, https://founders.archives .gov/documents/ Washington/03-13-02-0113.

Liberty's Lions

But Carroll managed to get himself appointed to a new committee that the Board of War convened. This group, the Committee at Camp, traveled to Valley Forge that winter to investigate conditions. It was hard to imagine a glowing report emerging from that trip. And it looked even less likely when Charles Carroll was called home to Maryland with news that his wife, Molly, was sick.

Biographer Ellen Hart Smith sarcastically imagined the reaction among Conway Cabal members: "His wife was extremely ill. Wonderful! ... The Lord giveth and the Lord taketh away; and, that being the case, He certainly seemed about to take Mrs. Carroll at a very opportune time."[78] That was because, as Smith saw it, "Washington's destiny, which Carroll thought was inextricably mixed with the destiny of America, certainly hung on the findings of that committee at Valley Forge."

The Lord, in this case, decided not to take Molly away. Not long after Carroll returned home, her condition improved. He was soon able to make the trip to Valley Forge. A grim scene awaited, familiar to any student of history.

If they were a city, the ragtag group of twelve thousand soldiers would have been the fourth-largest one in America at the time. But they lacked proper uniforms and shoes, tying bloody rags around their feet and huddling miserably around open fires for warmth. They also needed weapons: often, they drilled in the snow-covered fields with spontoons—makeshift bayonets constructed by lashing knives to poles. And proper food was in short supply. Most men were lucky to get meat once a week. Washington's own meager Christmas dinner had been burnt mutton with a side of hickory nuts.

Yet something miraculous was occurring. Under the tutelage of Gen. Friedrich Wilhelm August Heinrich Ferdinand von Steuben, a Prussian immigrant who called himself a baron, the army was somehow being whipped into shape.

Carroll, who had learned a lot during his trip to Canada two years earlier, noticed the improvement. But he was facing an uphill battle

---

[78] Smith, *Charles Carroll of Carrollton*, 177.

within the Committee at Camp. Gouverneur Morris of Pennsylvania, like Carroll, supported Washington. Two other committee members did not: Nathaniel Folsom of New Hampshire and Joseph Reed of Pennsylvania.

Reed's voice carried particular weight. Before his election to Congress, he had served as an adjutant general in the Continental Army, where he won Washington's trust. The feeling was not mutual. Reed confided his doubts in Washington's leadership to Charles Lee, in a letter that left Washington shaken when he learned of it.

That left Francis Dana of New York, the committee chairman. Carroll and Morris went to work on him at once.

Washington helped his own cause. Rather than publicly attack the men he described in private as a "malignant faction,"[79] he and his aide Alexander Hamilton prepared a thirty-eight-page letter in January 1778, detailing what needed to be done to improve the Continental Army.

Among the suggestions was the reorganization of the office of quartermaster general, which supplied the army. Washington knew that the current quartermaster, Thomas Mifflin, was a supporter of Horatio Gates. He suspected that his continual difficulties obtaining supplies weren't just an accident.

Then there was the evening when Francis Dana, out for a breath of air, was surprised to find Washington pacing furiously outside in the cold. "Congress, sir, does not trust me," he told Dana in a surprisingly emotional moment. "I cannot continue thus."[80]

But the lobbying effort of Charles Carroll must also have had its effect. The report Dana produced was a "negotiation" between Washington and his critics that became, in the view of Dana's biographer W. P. Cresson, "one of the most important documents of the Revolution."[81]

[79] "Washington to Gates, 4 January 1778."
[80] W. P. Cresson, *Francis Dana: A Puritan Diplomat at the Court of Catherine the Great* (New York: L. MacVeagh, Dial Press, 1930), 46.
[81] Cresson, *Francis Dana*, 44.

In the end, the Committee at Camp took many of Washington's suggestions. One of them had to do with the perpetually problematic post of quartermaster general.

In a report to Henry Laurens, the president of Congress, the committee assured him they would place "the Quarter Master's Department (as far as lies in their Power) upon such a Footing and in such Hands as will provide for the various Wants which now distress the Army and shakle [*sic*] the General."[82] The crisis had passed.

Spring at last came to Valley Forge, and with it arrived the news of an agreement with France. There was new hope at last for the patriots.

Yet what would have happened if Charles Carroll had not been at Valley Forge, determined to win his fellow committee members over on behalf of Washington? If the future military careers of Horatio Gates and Charles Lee are any indication, we can only shudder in relief.

Gates publicly apologized to Washington for whatever role he may have had in the Conway Cabal. He then ruined his reputation for good in 1780 with his disastrous performance in South Carolina at the Battle of Camden, which nearly got him court-martialed. Lee topped that by *actually* being court-martialed, following his retreat and refusal to follow Washington's orders at New Jersey's Battle of Monmouth in 1778. He might not be the only soldier to be cursed out by Washington in battle, but he is definitely the most famous.

These were the men who thought they were ready to lead the Continental Army. Charles Carroll knew better.

Meanwhile, Charles Carroll's biographers still puzzle over why he was not chosen to help America negotiate its alliance with France. It was, after all, one of the main reasons he had accepted a post in Congress. Even those who were personally no fans of his acknowledged he was the man for the job. When Arthur Lee, the brother of Richard Henry Lee, became

---

[82] "Committee at Camp to Henry Laurens," *Letters of Delegates to Congress*, vol. 9, *February 1, 1778–May 31, 1778*, February 24, 1778, American Memory, Library of Congress, http://www.memory.loc.gov/cgi-bin/query/r?ammem/ hlaw:@field(DOCID+@lit(dg009125)).

convinced Benjamin Franklin was mishandling diplomacy with the French, he proposed the name of "Mr. Carroll, the Catholic,"[83] as a replacement.

It may be that Carroll's wife was simply too ill for him to contemplate such a trip. It may be that he had made too many enemies in Congress already. It may be that he was involved in the negotiations in a way that records can't verify. In his 1918 biography of Carroll, Lewis Leonard quoted him as telling Washington and Franklin, "I am the one man who must be kept entirely in the background. It must not be known to a single soul that I am personally active in the matter."[84] But we don't know exactly what that quote means, nor where it came from.

It makes sense that Carroll would have been involved in negotiating with the French. But his letters are silent on this subject, and he is known to have destroyed some of them from this era. So we may never know whether Charles Carroll worked behind the scenes to convince the French to join the patriot cause. We can only guess, as well, at the influence he might have had as America's most prominent Catholic, in helping both sides accept the potentially problematic alliance.

Yet the role he played in keeping George Washington at the head of the Continental Army might have been Charles Carroll's most important wartime service to his country.

9

Charles Carroll went home to Maryland after his term ended in the summer of 1778. There had been talk of making him the president of Congress, a post that would once have been unthinkable for a Catholic to hold. The new French minister, Conrad Alexandre Gerard, confirmed that Carroll was the choice, "but it is feared he will not accept."[85]

The minister was right. Carroll told his friend Benjamin Franklin that Congress's "frivolous debates disgusted me."[86] Instead, Carroll served out

---

[83] Smith, *Charles Carroll of Carrollton*, 184.

[84] Lewis A. Leonard, *Life of Charles Carroll of Carrollton* (New York: Moffat, Yard and Company, 1918), 175.

[85] Smith, *Charles Carroll of Carrollton*, 186.

[86] Smith, *Charles Carroll of Carrollton*, 183.

the war years in the Maryland Assembly. He would play an important role in convincing his fellow assemblymen to ratify the Articles of Confederation. Like Washington and Alexander Hamilton, he could see the need for a unified central government.

He'd already played a major role in crafting Maryland's state constitution, which restored liberty of conscience and the right to vote to Catholics. This constitution also continued to restrict voting rights to property holders. In a letter he wrote to his father shortly after signing the Declaration of Independence, he had worried that putting power in the hands of all people without distinction might have a dangerous effect: "Anarchy will follow as a certain consequence; injustice, rapine & corruption in the seats of justice will prevail, and this Province in a short time will be involved in all the horrors of an ungovernable & revengeful Democracy, & will be died with the blood of its best citizens."[87]

The French Revolution would show this caution was prudent. But unlike his father, Charles Carroll was prepared to lose substantial amounts of money in the cause of liberty. What he feared more was the rule of the mob.

He also dependably voted against pay raises and pork barrel projects. When he helped pass a bill in 1779 that barred merchants from serving in Congress, there were good reasons for his support. He had only to look at his fellow Marylander Samuel Chase. Chase had been accused of what amounted to insider trading: he allegedly bought up flour and wheat when he learned in Congress that the army planned to purchase both.

Carroll could only shake his head at his former friend, whom he would call "the most prostituted scoundrel who ever existed."[88] He knew that the "preference of private to the public interest"[89] was a sure sign a politician was headed down the wrong path. If people asked why a wealthy businessman like Charles Carroll should be allowed to serve in Congress

---

[87] Hoffman, "The Carroll Family of Maryland," 340.
[88] McDermott, *Charles Carroll of Carrollton*, 171.
[89] McDermott, *Charles Carroll of Carrollton*, 170.

while merchants should not, the answer was probably that merchants did not always share Charles Carroll's ethics.

As had been the case when First Citizen got the best of Antilon, Carroll's example was the most powerful tool he had to change people's minds about Catholics. It was little wonder, then, that when the Articles of Confederation needed replacing, he was asked to participate in a convention to draft a new constitution. There were no longer family issues to keep him in Maryland: his beloved father had died in 1780 after a fall, and Molly, who witnessed the accident and was traumatized by it, followed him in death two weeks later. Only one of his three children—his youngest daughter, Kitty—remained at home.

But there were other obligations besides family. Samuel Chase had thrown his influence behind a scheme to flood Maryland with newly printed paper money. The proposal would help people who were indebted—not coincidentally, people like Chase. Charles Carroll, however, knew the inflation that would be created could wreck the state economy. He missed the Constitutional Convention so he could help defeat Chase's plan in the Maryland Assembly. His cousin Daniel Carroll traveled to Philadelphia instead.

Charles outlined for Daniel a proposal to rework the Articles of Confederation. This plan was more noteworthy, as Philip A. Crowl wrote in the *American Historical Review*, "for its limitations than its scope."[90] Rather than merely invest power in a strong central government, it proposed limiting the influence of democracy on state governments. Only property owners could vote, and their elected delegates could remain in office as long as they "give satisfaction."

The goal was to protect property rights against the mob. Carroll had always believed in a government that combined "the energy of monarchy" and "the wisdom of aristocracy" with the "integrity, common interest, & spirit of a democracy."[91]

---

[90] Philip A. Crowl, "Charles Carroll's Plan of Government," *American Historical Review* 46, no. 3 (April 1941): 588.

[91] McDermott, *Charles Carroll of Carrollton*, 199.

What emerged from Philadelphia was in some ways distant from his plan, but Charles Carroll still supported it. He and Daniel Carroll defended the new Constitution against vicious attacks by Samuel Chase and the antifederalists, and ensured Maryland would vote to ratify.

When his old friend George Washington was elected America's first president, Charles Carroll allowed himself to be chosen one of Maryland's first two senators. But he wasn't in Congress long before he remembered all the reasons he had left a decade ago: the endless speeches, the focus on trivialities such as titles for officials. "I am already tired of my situation and wish to be at home," he wrote to his daughter Mary in April 1790, "where I could employ my time more to my satisfaction than in this place."[92]

When Congress voted that members could not also serve in their state legislatures, Carroll got his wish. He resigned in 1792, and even Washington couldn't talk him into another federal job: negotiating with hostile Native American tribes on the Western frontier.

It was always unlikely that he'd accept—just as it was unlikely he would have accepted a much bigger and more historic opportunity.

10

Most people know that John F. Kennedy officially became America's first Catholic president in January 1961. Far fewer people know about the man who could have beaten him to the punch by nearly 170 years.

In the spring of 1792, George Washington was ready to call it quits. He had a sense of obligation every bit as strong as Charles Carroll's, but he didn't have his old friend's ability to say no. After resigning his commission as commander in chief, he'd returned to his beloved Mount Vernon. There, he intended to sit "under his vine and under his fig tree" in peace, one of his favorite quotes from the Bible (Mic. 4:4).

He'd been talked into reentering public life as America's first president, but his first term had worn him down. Worse trouble was ahead:

---

[92] Smith, *Charles Carroll of Carrollton*, 247.

there was open warfare in his cabinet between Treasury Secretary Alexander Hamilton and Secretary of State Thomas Jefferson. Both men wanted his ear, but Jefferson was also beginning to work behind the scenes against him.

The newly formed Federalist Party began to panic. What if Washington decided to step down? Jefferson was waiting in the wings as a challenger, and Vice President John Adams was no sure thing as Washington's successor.

James McHenry, a surgeon from Maryland who later became Washington's secretary of war, had a plan. As he wrote to Alexander Hamilton in August of 1792, "I mentioned Mr. Carroll as proper to be brought forward to oppose a man"—he meant Jefferson—"whom I suspect the antifederalist interest will unite in supporting." McHenry did not think Carroll would succeed, but he thought the effort was worthwhile regardless.

Hamilton told McHenry that Washington was probably going to run again. But he added, "If it turns out otherwise, I say unequivocally—I will cooperate in running the gentleman you mention, as one of the two who are to fill the two great offices."[93]

Under the rules of the time, the runner-up in the presidential election became vice president. It does not seem impossible, though, that with the backing of Hamilton—and perhaps Washington as well—Charles Carroll could have won the highest office in the land. As Ellen Hart Smith pointed out, in 1792, Jefferson had yet to reach his peak of popularity, "and even four years later was defeated by John Adams, a much less likely Federalist than Carroll."[94]

Would there have been anti-Catholic efforts to defeat Carroll? Undoubtedly. Yet he had won the respect of Protestants, time and again, because of his brilliance, his hard work, his modesty, and his ethics. Betting against him had been a bad wager for nearly thirty years.

---

93 Smith, *Charles Carroll of Carrollton*, 246.
94 Smith, *Charles Carroll of Carrollton*, 246.

"But no use to speculate," Smith sensibly added. "Carroll probably would have refused this too, as he had most of the political opportunities that had come to him."[95]

Had political firsts been his goal, Charles Carroll could certainly have had more of them. Had he wanted more power or more riches, he could have had those, too. Had he been truly ambitious, we might be singing the songs from a hit Broadway musical about his life.

All Charles Carroll really desired, though, was the free country that his family, and his father especially, had dreamed of for years. He didn't get to witness its full expression. But he lived long enough, at least, to glimpse its contours on the horizon.

11

Charles Carroll of Carrollton was ninety-five when he died. That's close to triple the average life span during this time. He was lucky to keep his health until the very end: in his last year, he could still be found riding the horses he had always loved.

But the third act of his life was one of both reflection and disappointment. It's probably true that most people lucky enough to have such a third act find a similar experience. In a life like Charles Carroll's, so closely connected with the republic he helped create, the things on his mind in his waning years loom a little larger.

In our tumultuous modern times, we may find remarkable overlap between his concerns and our own. That would be appropriate: Charles Carroll always was a visionary.

One of his disappointments was political. The man who had always put Maryland first and who had won it over in spite of his Catholicism, was turned out of the state senate in 1800. It was an ugly campaign. The Republican Party of Thomas Jefferson was ready to end the reign of Federalists. Anyone who stood in the way of this new American revolution was going to be bulldozed.

[95] Smith, *Charles Carroll of Carrollton*, 247.

The sentiment of those standing against him should be familiar to contemporary Americans. "Shall the people be dictated to by this lordly nabob because he has more pelf [money] than some others?" one editorial in the *Republican Advocate* demanded. "Has he more virtue, more honor, more honesty than a good industrious farmer?... Set Charles Carroll at defiance!"[96] That he had proven, time and again, that his honesty and virtue were above reproach meant nothing now. Neither did the surprisingly peaceful revolution he helped lead. The populist mob had spoken.

Just as those in the political minority wonder today what their fate will be in an increasingly intolerant society, Charles Carroll was also forced to confront such thoughts. One night during that unhappy October of 1800, on the way to his daughter's house, he and his son-in-law Richard Caton were caught in a violent thunderstorm. They took shelter in a humble cottage, where a kindly mother fed boiled potatoes and milk to her children. Sitting comfortably by the fireside as the elements raged around them, Charles Carroll pondered the fate of an outcast.

"It occurred to me that in the course of a few years I might be driven into exile by the prevalence of a miserable faction, and forced to shelter in as poor a house the remnant of a life, a considerable part of which had been faithfully devoted to my country's service," he wrote later to his son. But he resolved to take such "frowns and snubs of Fortune with resignation and fortitude."[97]

These were two qualities he needed in abundance in dealing with his adult children. His political career often meant he'd been an absent father. Now he made sure they were all well situated. But the time he'd spent away had long-lasting effects.

Carroll's children, Scott McDermott notes, had been raised "by their opium-addicted mother, their doting grandfather, and a corps of slaves.

[96] Edward S. Delaplaine, "Chief Justice Roger B. Taney—His Career at the Frederick Bar," *Maryland Historical Magazine* 13, no. 2 (June 1918), 109–142.
[97] McDermott, *Charles Carroll of Carrollton*, 216.

It should come as no surprise that the next generation of Carrolls lacked discipline and emotional balance."[98]

Despite his wealth, Carroll also couldn't ensure that his beliefs would transfer as readily to his children as his money would. A letter he wrote in 1821 to his son, Charles Carroll of Homewood, captures the sorrow of any parent whose child fails to follow them in their faith.

> In writing to you I deem it my duty to call your attention to the shortness of this life, the certainty of death, and of that dread judgment, which we must all undergo, and on the decision of which a happy or miserable eternity depends. The impious said in his heart, there is no God. He would willingly believe there is no God; his passions and the corruption of his heart would feign persuade him that there is not; the stings of conscience betray the emptiness of the delusion: the heavens proclaim the existence of God, and unperverted reason teaches that he must love virtue, and hate vice, and reward the one and punish the other....
>
> The approaching festival of Easter, and the merits and mercies of our Redeemer ... have led me into this chain of meditation and reasoning, and have inspired me with the hope of finding mercy before my judge and of being happy in the life to come, a happiness I wish you to participate with me by infusing into your heart a similar hope. Should this letter produce such a change it will comfort me, and impart to you that peace of mind, which the world cannot give, and which I am sure you have long ceased to enjoy.[99]

The words were sadly prophetic. An alcoholic, Charles Carroll Jr. would precede his father in death. Four years later, Charles Carroll of Carrollton could only write, to his son's widow, "I presume that he expressed anguish and repentance for the life he led; the course of which both of us have more cause to lament than his end. He has appeared

---

[98] McDermott, *Charles Carroll of Carrollton*, 118.
[99] Smith, *Charles Carroll of Carrollton*, 277.

before a judge, the searcher of hearts and most merciful. Let us pray that he has found mercy at that dread tribunal."[100]

That dread tribunal occupied much of Charles Carroll's thought during those last years. The question of slavery must have been a significant part of those ruminations.

Much could be, and has been, written about the Carroll family's history as slaveholders. The history of American Catholicism, which is rooted in places such as Maryland and Louisiana, is inextricably tied to slavery. From the Jesuit plantations to the estates of the landed gentry, slaves played a major role in advancing the fortunes of Catholics in the South.

As a Maryland legislator, Carroll made multiple, unsuccessful attempts to gradually emancipate all slaves in the state. One of those bills, in 1797, would have required all female slave children to be educated. At age twenty-eight, they would have been freed—and then expected to educate the rest of their families. Without education, he believed, immediate manumission would simply be cruel.

Carroll usually owned between three hundred and four hundred slaves, who worked on his plantations and in the family ironworks in Baltimore. His record as a slave owner is relatively humane and consistent with his ideals. He tried not to break up families. He made sure there was weekly religious instruction.

But Carroll, like many of his fellow founders, still knew slavery was wrong. He apparently told Charles Beaumont, the traveling companion of French historian Alexis de Tocqueville, that slaves were unnecessary for sugar, rice, and tobacco farming. Whites would suffer at first if slavery were abolished, Carroll said, but they would soon get used to the change, and even "accomplish twice as much as the slaves."[101]

Frustrated by his legislative failures to abolish slavery, Carroll wrote in 1820 that "it is admitted by all to be a great evil; let an effectual mode of getting rid of it be pointed out, or let the question sleep forever."

[100] McDermott, *Charles Carroll of Carrollton*, 247.
[101] Birzer, *American Cicero*, 183.

There *was* an effectual mode, of course—at least for Charles Carroll. The richest man in America could simply have manumitted all his slaves. He talked about it. He seems to seriously have considered it. Three times, Ellen Hart Smith claimed, "he nearly lost his temper to the extent of doing so."[102]

But, with only a few exceptions, he did not. Instead, he supported the American Colonization Society, a group that aimed to start a colony of free American blacks in Africa. In his nineties, Carroll served as the president of the Maryland branch. After his death, the society would be responsible for helping found the nation of Liberia.

It wasn't the same thing as freeing his own slaves, though. Ellen Hart Smith defends this decision as Carroll not wanting to show up his less well-off neighbors, who could not afford to free their slaves.[103] It's one of the few unconvincing arguments in her biography. By 1810, after individual manumission was permitted, Maryland had freed a fifth of its slaves and contained more free blacks than any other state. So many Marylanders did free their slaves, and there should have been no insurmountable obstacle to prevent Carroll from doing the same.

In the end, Carroll—again, like many of his fellow founders—simply failed to tackle the issue, politically or personally. These men would all be gone before the festering wound they left unlanced finally exploded in 1861.

Perhaps Carroll compared the Christian treatment of slaves to their fate in other cultures. In his eighties, still true to his student days, he embarked on an ambitious three-year study of religion. He asked his cousin John Carroll—by this point America's first archbishop—to make him a list of books. Then he added to it volumes from every tradition. There were Roman Catholic books, and Judaic books; pre-Christian books from Greece and Rome; Islamic books, deistic books, and even atheistic ones. It was a one-man comparative religion class.

Why did he do it? It wasn't simply boredom: there was always plenty to keep him occupied. The reason had something to do with his character.

---

[102] Smith, *Charles Carroll of Carrollton*, 269.
[103] Smith, *Charles Carroll of Carrollton*, 269.

He had been a faithful Catholic all his life, if not as openly devout as his father or his cousin John. Now he needed to be sure that the doctrines he had been taught added up. He didn't want to be one of those people who "must rest their religious faith on their instructors."[104]

He concluded that the beliefs that had driven him were valid ones. He also told his daughter-in-law, Hattie, that he bore "no ill will or illiberal prejudices against the sectarians which have abandon[ed] that faith; if their lives be conformable to the duties & morals prescribed by the gospel, I have the charity to hope & believe they will be rewarded with eternal happiness, tho they may entertain erroneous doctrines."[105]

But in his beloved library, he'd finally had the freedom to test an idea he'd outlined years earlier, when his friend William Graves tried to convince him that converting to the Church of England would be a good career move.

"Upon conviction only a change of religion is desirable," he told Hattie, "on a concern so seriously interesting to all of us no worldly motives should sway our conduct."[106]

He was past worldly motives now, even though the older he got the more people sought him out as a link to America's revolutionary past. That link finally broke on the frigid evening of November 14, 1832, at his daughter Mary's home in Baltimore. After receiving the Host one final time, the old man died peacefully in his sleep. The old cliché about the "end of an era" was, for once, appropriate.

After a funeral Mass at the Basilica of the Assumption in Baltimore, mourners spent the afternoon processing back to Doughoregan Manor through a cold and steady rain. As the autumn light dimmed, Carroll was buried "in a vault he himself had prepared under the spot where he used to pray in his chapel, on the Gospel side, near the altar."[107]

---

[104] Smith, *Charles Carroll of Carrollton*, 272.

[105] Smith, *Charles Carroll of Carrollton*, 275–276.

[106] Smith, *Charles Carroll of Carrollton*, 275.

[107] Archbishop William Lori, "Offered for the Eternal Salvation of Charles Carroll of Carrollton, of the Deceased Members of the Carroll Family, and of All the Faithful Departed," November 22, 2013, Archdiocese of

A special service was held there in 2013, at the old family chapel, for Charles Carroll's eternal salvation. The archbishop of Baltimore, William Lori, set the scene.

He imagined Charles Carroll, kneeling alone in prayer as he stared up at the Blessed Sacrament in the brass tabernacle. We can see him too, especially in his old age. He is still slight and even more frail. His clothing is still modest, with old fashioned lace at his cuffs and buckles on his shoes. His hair is now long and white, and his face is a map of wrinkles in the candlelight. In that map is traced much of the history of the country he played such an important role in founding.

"Here, in the presence of the Eucharistic Lord," Archbishop Lori said, "the only Catholic signer of the Declaration of Independence must have prayed for himself, for his family, and for his fledgling nation."

The sorrows of his family, and his country, show that undoubtedly not all his requests came to pass. But the history of America, and its unprecedented religious freedoms, suggest that many of them did.

Baltimore, https://www.archbalt.org/offered-for-the-eternal- salvation-of-charles-carroll-of-carrollton-of-the-deceased-members-of-the-carroll-family- and-of-all-the-faithful-departed/.

Chapter 2 Supplement

Of Dangerous Consequence

Catholicism's Parallel History in England and Maryland

To understand Charles Carroll of Carrollton, it's necessary to understand Catholicism in Maryland and how it developed.

And to understand Maryland Catholicism, it's necessary to understand Catholicism in England during the same period. As a British colony, America generally followed the trends set across the Atlantic — including the prejudices.

Maryland was, in theory, unique, thanks to the number of Catholics that lived there and the religious tolerance that marked its founding. Yet that also meant that anti-Catholic laws which applied to very few actual citizens in other colonies were more practical, and practiced, in Maryland.

If we could pick one word to describe the Catholic experience in England and America in the nearly 250 years between King Henry VIII's break with Rome and the Revolutionary War, it would probably be "disappointment." At least, disappointment at the way officials in both places viewed Catholics.

There were periods of tolerance, and even times of optimism and hope. But tolerance was often withdrawn, and hopes were usually dashed. And in America, those hopes were dashed most notably, and often, in Maryland.

As Maryland's 1649 Act Concerning Religion put it, "inforceing of the conscience in matters of Religion hath frequently fallen out to be of dangerous Consequence in those commonwealthes where it hath been practised." That was as true in Maryland as it was in England.

Because the conjoined history of the two places is so complex, we might be able to better follow it in the form of a chart:

The Event	Henry VIII breaks with Rome so he can legally divorce Catherine of Aragon and marry his lady-in-waiting, Anne Boleyn.
The Response	Parliament passes a series of acts, including the 1534 Act of Supremacy, establishing Henry VIII as the head of the Church of England.
The Result for Catholics in England	Between 1536 and 1540, monasteries are dissolved and their property seized. Some Catholics who oppose the act, such as Sir Thomas More, are executed.
The Event	King Henry's son, the boy king Edward VI, takes the throne and rules from 1547 to 1553.
The Response	Protestant reformers take a more active hand in changing worship in the Church of England.
The Result for Catholics in England	The Latin Mass is replaced by the Book of Common Prayer. Catholic statues are destroyed and several common practices of worship are forbidden.
The Event	Mary (Tudor) I, a Catholic, becomes queen in 1553.
The Response	Mary and her supporters attempt to reconcile the Church of England with Rome.
The Result for Catholics in England	Catholic worship is legal. But Mary's persecution of Protestants, many of whom are burned at the stake, earns her the nickname "Bloody" Mary.

The Event	In 1558, Elizabeth I, the daughter of Henry VIII and Anne Boleyn, becomes queen.
The Response	Elizabeth begins her reign with the Act of Supremacy and the Oath of Supremacy, both aimed at abolishing the pope's authority.
The Result for Catholics in England	Anyone who wants to hold public or church office must take the oath, which affirms the monarch as the head of the Church of England.
The Event	Pope Pius V issues *Regnans in Excelcius* in 1570. This papal bull states that Elizabeth is not the rightful ruler of England and should be deposed.
The Response	Elizabeth I can now plausibly claim that Catholics are treasonous. Beginning in 1581, she responds with a series of harsh measures against Catholics.
The Result for Catholics in England	Celebrating Mass becomes an act of high treason; fines are imposed for not attending Church of England services; and many priests are executed as martyrs. Not surprisingly, the number of professed Catholics in England declines.
The Event	James I, the son of Mary, Queen of Scots—executed by Elizabeth I, who feared she would try to claim the English throne—becomes king of England in 1603.
The Response	The Gunpowder Plot of 1605 is foiled when a group of conspirators, including Guy Fawkes, are caught just before they can blow up Parliament and the king in an attempt to establish a Catholic monarchy.

Liberty's Lions

The Result for Catholics in England	Despite the plot, James vacillates between prosecuting and tolerating Catholics during his rule, which lasts until 1625. He walks a fine line, because recusancy fines—which are paid by those who do not attend the mandatory Church of England services—are essentially a tax on which the government has become dependent.
The Situation for Catholics in Maryland	One of James I's acts of toleration is to give one of his courtiers, the Catholic George Calvert, the title of Lord Baltimore.
The Event	The Anglican Charles I becomes king in 1625. Two years later, he marries the Catholic Henrietta Maria of France.
The Response	Charles's court, which includes several "Papists" (actually, most are High Anglicans like Charles himself), clashes with a Parliament increasingly dominated by Puritans—members of the Church of England who want to purge it of its "popish" influences.
The Result for Catholics in England	The clash between courtiers (Cavaliers) and Parliamentarians (Roundheads) culminates in the English Civil War, a series of conflicts that last nearly a decade (1642–1651) and ends in victory by the Roundheads. In 1649, Charles I becomes the first English king to be executed; the monarchy is abolished; and Oliver Cromwell becomes the Lord Protector of England, Scotland, and Ireland. Catholics throughout these three countries are persecuted, and their landholdings are seized.

The Situation for Catholics in Maryland	In 1632, Charles I approves Lord Baltimore's charter for a proprietary colony in America. When George Calvert, the first Lord Baltimore, dies, his son Cecilius takes over the title and the charter. Two hundred settlers, most of them Protestant, land in Maryland in 1634. The next fifteen years are filled with disputes between Protestants and Catholics. The colony is briefly under Protestant rule from 1645–1646, and Jesuits are expelled. But the same year Charles I is executed, the Maryland Assembly passes the Act Concerning Religion. It becomes the first legal protection for all Christians in England or America.
The Event	The Restoration of the English monarchy occurs when Charles II takes the throne in 1660.
The Response	Well aware of the fate of his father, Charles II pursues the same mixed path of tolerance and repression. He takes a Catholic wife, and signs the Treaty of Dover with France's King Louis XIV, who promises him money if he becomes publicly Catholic. But Charles II is careful not to overplay his hand in Protestant England. He becomes a deathbed convert instead.
The Result for Catholics in England	Charles II is able to suspend the penal laws for "Nonconformists." Parliament pushes back, and Catholics are subjected to a Test Act that forces all officeholders to swear allegiance to the king and Church of England. It also demands they deny the doctrine of transubstantiation, which states that during the Consecration, bread and wine are transformed into the Body and Blood of Christ.

Liberty's Lions

The Situation for Catholics in Maryland	After the death of Cecilius Calvert, his son Charles becomes the third Lord Baltimore in 1675. During his rule as governor and proprietor, Maryland's major crop, tobacco, begins a long decline in value. Harsh new laws binding slaves to servitude for life are passed. Unlike Charles II in England, Calvert alienates many citizens by policies that openly favor Catholics. Voting privileges are reserved for large landowners, who are predominantly Catholic.
The Event	The Duke of York, James II, becomes the last Catholic ruler of England in 1685.
The Response	James's ascendancy to the throne has been feared by non-Catholics for years. In 1678, false allegations of a "Popish Plot" to assassinate King Charles II and crown James II creates anti-Catholic hysteria. James II ignores the sentiment against him and promises to bring back toleration for both Catholics and Protestants.
The Result for Catholics in England	During James II's brief reign (1685–1688), he makes moves friendly to Catholics (and dissident Protestants). One is the Declaration of Indulgence, which effectively repeals the Test Act. When Parliament disagrees, James disbands it, and gives Catholics prominent military, political, and academic jobs. However, he continues to make powerful enemies.
The Situation for Catholics in Maryland	Charles Calvert travels to England in 1684 to defend himself against charges of favoring Catholics. He will never return to Maryland. In his absence, his nephew George Talbot and fellow Catholic William Joseph mismanage affairs and raise tensions among Protestants. The Calverts are about to lose control of the colony they have held for more than five decades.

The Event	James II's son, James Francis Edward, is born in 1688.
The Response	English Protestants' longtime fears of a Catholic dynasty now seem real. Protestant noblemen beg William of Orange—the husband of James's older daughter, Mary (who is also a Protestant)—to take the throne. William II arrives in Devon in November 1688 with an army. James II flees to exile in France, and is declared to have abdicated the throne.
The Result for Catholics in England	The Glorious Revolution heralds a decidedly inglorious eighteenth century for English Catholicism. Catholics become publicly invisible, as a series of laws restrict their right to own property, inherit land, vote, or hold office. They are forced to pay special taxes, and while Masses still occur, priests are subject to fines and imprisonment. Violent persecution of Catholics never returns to Elizabethan levels, although anti-Catholic violence does follow the Papists Act of 1778, designed to reduce discrimination (and help recruit Catholic soldiers). Catholicism declines throughout England, reaching an estimated low of about 1 percent of the population by 1800.
The Situation for Catholics in Maryland	As is the case in England, Maryland Catholics ultimately lose many rights. They cannot serve in the military or hold office. Meanwhile, the Calverts lose control of the colony to the Crown. Although William III surprisingly extends liberty of conscience to Catholics in 1693, when he dies persecution in the colony begins again. In 1704, An Act to Prevent the Growth of Popery forbids priests from offering Mass or baptizing anyone who is not Catholic—i.e., conversions are forbidden. "Papists" are barred from teaching—even their own children. In 1718, Catholics also lose the right to vote. Yet, unlike the situation in England, in Maryland Catholicism continues to grow—both by immigration and by the underground practice of the faith on private property. Jesuit priests continue to serve the colony and even quietly run a school during the 1740s and 1750s.

Maryland was founded by George Calvert, also known as Lord Baltimore. He was a Catholic nobleman who died before he could act on the charter he had been granted by King Charles II for a proprietary colony north of Virginia called "Terra Mariae."

To be more precise, Maryland was a palatinate: a territory under the jurisdiction of a governor who had nearly the power of a king. It became an important distinction. This power was allowed under the "Bishop of Durham Clause," which had been granted in the eleventh century to the bishopric of Durham, near the Scottish border. Because of its remote location, Durham functioned a lot like a sovereign nation.

George Calvert's son Cecilius received his father's title and the Maryland charter. Meanwhile, Cecilius's brother Leonard served as colonial governor for the group of about two hundred colonists who sailed from England in 1633.

Although neither George nor Cecilius would ever set foot on American soil, both men had a profound influence on American history. The colony they founded was an experiment in religious tolerance. Even before the *Ark* and the *Dove* set sail for Maryland, Cecilius warned their "Gentleman Adventurers" — especially the Catholics — to be respectful of their fellow religionists. "Treat the Protestants with as much mildness and favor as Justice will permit," he advised.

That was practical advice for a company — and soon a colony — that included more Protestants than Catholics and was chartered by an Anglican monarch besides. But, despite a stormy religious history almost from the beginning, Maryland's assembly did produce the Act Concerning Religion — commonly known as the Toleration Act — in 1649. It guaranteed freedom of conscience to all Christians, the first legal promise of tolerance in American or British history.

It was also the payoff of Maryland's status as a palatinate. This law guaranteed Catholics freedoms they had never legally enjoyed in Britain. It forever put Maryland on a separate path from the Crown, no matter how much Protestants loyal to England protested. One day, that path would lead to revolution — not just in Maryland, but throughout the colonies.

The short-term consequences were more modest. The Toleration Act was repealed in 1654, then reinstated three years later. It remained in place until fallout from the Glorious Revolution in England reached the colonies.

When that happened, the tenuous balance between Catholics and Protestants was upset. The Calverts lost control of the colony they had run for nearly three-quarters of a century. Catholics in Maryland eventually were stripped of the right to vote and hold office, and were subjected to numerous other restrictions and special taxes.

From the beginning of the eighteenth century to the start of the Revolutionary War, the best Maryland Catholics could hope for was that the many penal laws on the books would not be strictly enforced. The price for this deal was silence: Catholics in the colony had to keep their worship secret and their beliefs quiet in public. The faith went underground, nourished behind closed doors on the Jesuit plantations and the manors of the wealthy, and served largely by circuit-riding priests.

Yet Catholicism also grew in Maryland under these challenging conditions. It was waiting, perhaps, for the advocate who could bring it back into the light—someone like Charles Carroll of Carrollton.

Chapter 3

The Pope Who Helped the Patriots
The Suppression of the Jesuits and
the Liberation of Fr. John Carroll

1

In his room at the House of the Seven Towers, as night fell at last, Father John Carroll fingered his rosary beads.

Then he breathed a silent prayer — for his death.

Today, September 20, 1773, had been the lowest point of his thirty-seven years. Much of that time had been filled with self-imposed hardship. But he was now trapped in Bruges, near Belgium's northwest coast. Any hope he'd maintained for the future was gone.

Maybe you've seen the city of Bruges. It's one of the best-preserved medieval towns in Belgium, and it even gave its name and location to the 2008 black comedy, *In Bruges*.

For Carroll, however, the events of this day could only be described as a tragedy. He was a prisoner in the House of the Seven Towers, a huge stone building also known locally as *Domus Anglorum*. With him were fifteen other priests and more than a hundred students at the Great College of the English Jesuits.

Once, more than a century earlier, King Charles II had been exiled in this same building, while Oliver Cromwell's Commonwealth ruled England. But this fourteenth-century structure in the heart of Bruges now housed a different group of outcasts.

Liberty's Lions

Along the nearby canal, the first autumn breezes from the North Sea stirred. From his room, Carroll heard the scuffling of footsteps on the cobblestone Hoogstraadt outside and the murmur of voices. Occasionally, he saw the flicker of a match and sniffed the scent of pipe smoke. There had been armed guards posted outside the Great College since early this Monday morning. They kept their watch tonight to ensure no priests or students tried to escape.

Carroll pulled his black cassock more tightly around him, against the evening chill. Wearily, he thought back on the events of this day, which now seemed as if they'd taken place a lifetime ago.

At 7:00 a.m., the college had been surrounded, then invaded. It was a carefully planned operation that had been weeks in the making. The news of Pope Clement XIV's suppression of the Society of Jesus had traveled quickly across Europe that summer. Local officials across the continent were now charged with delivering that news officially—and, for the Jesuits, unpleasantly.

Jacque Hyacinthe Van Volden, a civic official from the Council of Flanders, led a procession of assistants into the school. Van Volden was businesslike, though mild-mannered. His second-in-command, however—a twenty-five-year-old commissary named Louis Maroucx d'Opbracle—stared haughtily at the priests as the orders were read.

There were a lot of them. There was a lengthy explanation of Van Volden's commission, then a copy of a papal bull officially suppressing the Jesuit order. Then, from Brussels, letters patent that outlined the conditions of this suppression in the Austrian Netherlands. There were a lot of conditions, too. The priests could not leave the college building. Corresponding verbally or by letter with anyone outside the college was forbidden. The priests were told they no longer had authority over their students, who ranged in age from ten to twenty-two.

The Jesuit fathers had each been forced to sign the Act of Submission. This document formally released them from their vows to the Society of Jesus. They could join another order "or place themselves as secular priests under the jurisdiction of the Bishop where they might reside."[108] But their work as Jesuits was finished.

To add insult to injury, the local officials believed the Jesuits were hiding treasure in the *Domus Anglorum*, and were determined to find it. Fr. Charles Plowden, S.J., who would later pen a first-person account of the raid, recalled the sneering Maroucx bursting in,

> attended by a rout of smiths, joiners, and carpenters; he confined all the prisoners under guard in a separate room, while the work-men armed with poles and iron tools proceeded to beat up the quarters, in order to draw imaginary treasures into light from supposed lurking-holes and dark recesses, which, it was imagined, their acquaintance with the material part of architecture would best enable them to discover.

They searched, they probed, during a whole morning, every wall, floor, ceiling, beam, desk, and table; they even pulled up the board on which the tailors worked, and at length retired in the vexation of disappointment, leaving the prisoners to contemplate the odious scene in silent amazement and despair.[109]

A similar routine had been enacted at the Little College nearby, where about eighty boys, aged five to nine, were students. All the Jesuits in Bruges were left to process the news that their whole lives' work was now, officially, over.

Fr. Carroll had known this day was coming, as had his fellow priests. When he'd accepted his current job as prefect of the sodality at Bruges earlier that summer, he was well aware of just how suspicious the locals were of the Jesuits. The suppression of the order had spread like a virus throughout Europe over the past decade and a half. And Carroll had seen this terrible outcome clearly a year ago, when he had been traveling as a

---

[108] Sydney Fenn Smith, *The Suppression of the Society of Jesus*, ed. Joseph A. Munitiz (1902; Leominster, UK: Gracewing, 2004), 256–257.

[109] Maurice Whitehead, *English Jesuit Education: Expulsion, Suppression, Survival and Restoration, 1762–1803* (Burlington, VT: Ashgate, 2013), 88.

tutor. He was chaperoning Charles-Phillippe, the eighteen-year-old son of the English Catholic nobleman Lord Stourton.

In October 1772, the pair's European travels took them to Rome. There, Carroll was shocked by the open hostility to Jesuits. He knew the Society of Jesus had already been dissolved in Portugal, France, and Spain. Elsewhere on the continent, sentiments against the Jesuits still ran high.

Yet even here in the Eternal City, opinion had turned against the order. The danger seemed certain enough that Carroll told his friends not to give away his affiliation when addressing letters to him. He was also forced to avoid Jesuit houses during his visit, and felt angry skulking around Rome like a "sneak-thief."[110]

He had no choice. Rumors had been flying for years that Pope Clement XIV would give in to pressure from the royal courts of France, Portugal, and Spain, and officially suppress the Jesuit order. In fact, people had long believed that Giovanni Vincenzo Antonio Ganganelli, the only Franciscan in the College of Cardinals, had been chosen as pope precisely *because* he was willing to disband the Jesuits.

When Ganganelli's predecessor, Clement XIII, died in 1769, John Carroll was filled with foreboding. "Nothing could have happened more unfortunate to us," he wrote to his older brother, Daniel.[111]

Four years later, John Carroll's prediction had come terribly true. Now he was unable even to send another letter to his brother to let him know how right he had been.

He had last written to Daniel a little more than two weeks earlier, on September 5, when the Jesuits at Bruges had gotten the news of Pope Clement's suppression order. In that letter, the years of dread descended with their full, crushing weight.

"I am not, and perhaps never shall be, recovered from the shock of this dreadful intelligence," John Carroll wrote on September 11, 1773.

---

[110] Annabelle McConnell Melville, *John Carroll of Baltimore: Founder of the American Catholic Hierarchy* (New York: Charles Scribner's Sons, 1955), 33.

[111] Melville, *John Carroll of Baltimore*, 33.

"The greatest blessing which in my estimation I could receive from God would be immediate death."

"But if he deny me this," John Carroll continued, trying desperately to snatch a silver lining from the cloud of gloom that enveloped him, "may his holy and adorable designs on me be wholly fulfilled."

Then he wrote something even more prescient than the predictions he'd been making for months about the fate of his order.

"You see now that I am my own master," Carroll told his brother, "and left to my own discretion."[112]

It's not likely he knew it that night in late September, as guards prowled the perimeter of the Great College and the stunned priests and students huddled inside. But those holy and adorable designs John Carroll wrote about would, indeed, be wholly fulfilled. And they would depend on him becoming his own master—free of the ties to his order and to Europe.

There might not have been a successful American Revolution—or a Catholic Church as we know it in America—if both those things had not come to pass.

2

Why were the Jesuits suppressed? It's a question that has puzzled historians almost since it occurred.

As Maurice Whitehead, the author of the study *English Jesuit Education: Expulsion, Suppression, Survival and Restoration, 1762–1803*, put it, "any attempt to provide a single, all-embracing explanation of the destruction and ultimate suppression of the Society is fruitless."

But Whitehead does list several contributing factors. Outside the Church, the Jesuits had made enemies of Protestants, who believed the Society of Jesus was involved in behind-the-scenes intrigue designed to topple their kings. Inside the Church, there were quarrels with other religious orders. The Jansenists in France thought the Jesuits were morally

---

[112] Msgr. Peter Guilday, *The Life and Times of John Carroll*, vol. 1 (New York: Encyclopedia Press: 1922), 23.

lax. The French Gallicans believed they were working with the pope to undermine the French bishops' leadership. The Franciscans were engaged in a long-standing dispute with the Jesuits over missionary outreach in China. And there was jealousy from all quarters over the success and prominence the Jesuits had achieved since their founding in 1540.

All of this found its way into the papal bull read to the Jesuit priests that traumatic September morning in Bruges. The brief, *Dominus ac Redemptor*, issued on August 16, 1773, was described by John Carroll's biographer Msgr. Peter Guilday as "one of the unfairest pontifical acts in the history of the papacy."[113]

In it, Pope Clement XIV admitted he was yielding to the wishes of "our beloved sons in Jesus Christ, the Kings of France, Spain, Portugal, and the Two Sicilies"[114] and suppressing the Jesuits in order to keep peace throughout Europe, and throughout Christendom. The pope, the brief explained, has to be willing to destroy institutions that are dear to him, to maintain that peace.

The Jesuits in Bruges were there, in fact, because they had been turfed out of St. Omer in 1762, when the Society of Jesus was expelled from France. St. Omer was where John Carroll and his younger cousin Charles had gone to school. Now what was left of the order would be on the move again.

Before that happened, John Carroll and some of his fellow Jesuits found out just how far the authorities would go to maintain the peace Pope Clement XIV prized. On the night of October 14, Austrian officials again stormed the college and arrested Fr. Carroll and two other priests. Thanks to the intervention of a Catholic nobleman from Britain, Baron Arundell of Wardour, the priests were soon released, but they could no longer stay in Belgium.

Baron Arundell offered Carroll the job of family chaplain at the castle in Wiltshire. But after a brief stay there, Fr. Carroll decided to end nearly a quarter-century of life in Europe and return home to Maryland.

[113] Guilday, *The Life and Times of John Carroll*, 47.
[114] Guilday, *The Life and Times of John Carroll*, 47.

As he made plans to sail for America in the spring of 1774, there were definite consolations. He hadn't seen the family home at Rock Creek since he was a boy. He would be reunited with his aging mother, as well as his siblings.

But the man who gave this happy news to his brother, Daniel, was also chastened by the events of the past year or two. As he whiled away his exile at Wardour Castle, John Carroll's future was anything but certain.

"I shall have the comfort of not only being with you," he wrote gloomily to Daniel that winter, "but of being farther removed from the scenes of distress of many of my dearest friends, whom God knows, I shall not be able to relieve."[115]

3

The painting glows with hues of yellow and orange, just as the waters of Annapolis Harbor must have done that October night.

If you examine *The Burning of the Peggy Stewart*, a mural by Jack Manley Rosé, you might imagine you're seeing a depiction of the Boston Tea Party. It isn't, although the two events are related. The painting shows instead a lesser-known moment in Revolutionary War–era history — but one that illustrates perfectly the strange new Maryland to which Fr. John Carroll had returned.

When the *Peggy Stewart* dropped anchor on October 15, its owner, an Annapolis merchant named Anthony Stewart, paid the customs taxes on the British goods in its hold. That included two thousand pounds of tea, wrapped in blankets.

That violated the boycott colonial leaders had imposed against paying taxes on British tea. The past December, the Sons of Liberty had protested these taxes by dumping, in today's terms, a million dollars' worth of tea into Boston Harbor.

Stewart was well-known as a loyalist, and he and his father-in-law had gotten into trouble for violating colonial boycotts before. This was the last straw. Outraged citizens chased him into his house, where he barricaded

---

[115] Guilday, *The Life and Times of John Carroll*, 33.

himself with his pregnant wife and daughter, Peggy, for whom the ship was named. The mob quickly built a gallows outside and presented the frightened Stewart an ultimatum: either the tea and the ship burned, or he would be hanged.

It wasn't much of a choice. As the crowd cheered and jeered, Stewart set the ship on fire, gathered up his family, and left town for good.

Fr. John Carroll did not witness the burning of the *Peggy Stewart*, but the news would soon have reached him at Rock Creek. Undoubtedly, it caused him to reflect on how much the Maryland of his youth had changed.

When he was born on January 19, 1736, John Carroll entered one of Maryland's most wealthy and distinguished family lines. It was also one of the most confusing: the number of Charleses and Daniels alone makes sorting out the genealogy tricky.

John's father, Daniel, a merchant from Prince George's County, was of Irish descent. His mother, Eleanor Darnall, was of the manor born. When they joined their fortunes, they were able to provide a secure and happy upbringing for their six children, on the plantation Eleanor inherited from her parents.

Meanwhile, Daniel's importing business and general store thrived during John's childhood. One tragedy darkened the family history: the couple's oldest son, Henry, drowned at the age of nine, when his brother John was just four years old.

The Carrolls persevered, despite the severe restrictions on Catholics during this period in Maryland's history. "Popish priests" could not offer Mass, nor could children be baptized. Catholics could not vote, and some had their land taxed twice—to help support the local militia that Catholics were not allowed to join. Even parents who wanted to send their children overseas to receive the Catholic education forbidden at home were to be charged one hundred pounds for the privilege.

John Carroll's mother had been educated abroad herself—a rarity for women at the time—at a convent school in Flanders. So she tutored John and his siblings at home, until the boys were old enough for more formal schooling. When he turned twelve, John, nicknamed "Jacky," was sent to Bohemia Manor, a new school on the northeastern border of Maryland and Pennsylvania.

Housed in a brick building not far from the Jesuit rectory at St. Francis Xavier Church, Bohemia Manor also educated John's cousin, Charles. Another notable student was their friend Robert Brent, who became the first mayor of Washington, DC.

Little is known about Bohemia Manor, partly because the Jesuits were forced to run it in near-secrecy. "The Jesuit fathers were too wise to set down records which, if found, would circumstantially sentence them to life imprisonment," Charles Carroll's biographer Ellen Hart Smith would later note. "Its activity was regulated much like that of another Maryland institution of a bygone day, the speakeasy."[116] That is, as long as the Jesuits went about their business quietly, the authorities were willing to turn a blind eye.

The school apparently started in the mid-1740s, but it soon attracted the notice of Protestants in the area, including an outspoken Episcopal priest named Hugh Jones. The trouble he helped stir up in the local press evidently played a role in the Bohemia academy closing down. Yet, at least into the 1750s, the school served about twenty students in two courses of study. Enough records survive to tell us the names of some of the students who attended and a few of the details about what they studied. The school offered a classical course that cost forty pounds a year and an "English" course that went for thirty pounds annually, both with bed and board included.

The goal of sending boys like John and Charles Carroll to Bohemia was a limited one, anyway: to prepare them for a more formal and rigorous Catholic education abroad. For Catholic families at the time, that generally meant enrolling their sons at St. Omer, the Jesuit academy in French Flanders. So, within a year, the Carroll cousins would be on a ship to France. John would be taking the place of his older brother, Daniel, who was returning to Maryland to help run the family businesses.

[116] Smith, *Charles Carroll of Carrollton*, 29.

The practical-minded Charles Carroll would say, years later, that the education he and his cousin received at St. Omer was "only fit for priests."[117] There was no doubt, then, that John Carroll was headed to the Jesuit novitiate after his time at St. Omer was over.

In September 1753 he traveled to the novitiate in Watten, Belgium, where he spent two years before taking his vows. After that, it was on to study philosophy and theology at the English College at Liège, where he was ordained on February 14, 1761, and where he would teach philosophy afterwards. The details of his whereabouts on the Continent are unclear during this time, though it seems sure that he was at Liège well into the 1760s.

Now entering his thirties, Fr. Carroll must have presented a reassuring figure to the boys who came to Liège. The depictions of him that survive all show him as an older man. But from them, we can guess that he was on the portly side and no more than average height. Like most of the Carrolls, his most prominent feature was his nose. His hair, swept back behind his ears, was probably beginning to recede. It might, even then, have started its transition from brown to gray. In his traditional black cassock, Fr. Carroll would have seemed serious. And it seems likely that the boy who was "often the first" at St. Omer showed a formidable intellect to students. But his expression was probably kind, and his voice was soft.

He wrote regularly to family members in Maryland, including his older brother, Daniel, from both Liège and Bruges. At least once, in 1764, he complained about the lack of return letters from the colonies, telling his brother that, if not for contact with their uncle, "I should be at a loss to know whether my friends there were dead or alive."[118] But throughout the 1760s, there had been no guarantee he would ever return to America.

Even as the net was closing around the Jesuits in 1773, John Carroll seemed focused on a future in Europe. He relocated to Bruges early that summer, where he was surrounded by good friends like Fr. Charles

---

[117] Smith, *Charles Carroll of Carrollton*, 33.
[118] Melville, *John Carroll of Baltimore*, 20.

Plowden. Then the shock waves hit, one after another. The official suppression of the Jesuits. The ugly breakup of the colleges at Bruges. His arrest and exile to England. Suddenly, events had brought him back home.

He was heartened to see his mother again, and on her estate at Rock Creek, he enjoyed material comforts he had forgone as a Jesuit. Yet the comfort of Mass was denied him, and other Catholics, by law. So he began offering daily Mass in his mother's home. It all continued the old Maryland tradition of "manor Catholics" that had traveled across the ocean from Britain. The faith was maintained on private estates where the authorities couldn't — or at least, usually didn't — intrude.

When the crowds quickly got too large, he constructed on the property a tiny frame chapel, which he called St. John's. There he held Sunday Masses in what became the first parish in Montgomery County. Fr. Carroll also began visiting nearby communities on horseback, so that rural Catholics could also worship and have their confessions heard. When he wasn't serving as a priest, he continued his studies: not just ancient literature, but current events as well — like the burning of the *Peggy Stewart*.

The desire for independence was beginning to catch flame across the colonies, and Fr. John Carroll was not immune. After all, he was suddenly a "free" man — a man without an order. He had been cast adrift, but was beginning to sense that freedom brought with it new possibilities.

"Catholics contributed nothing to the support of religion in its ministers; the whole maintenance fell on the priests themselves," he wrote of the situation at the time. "The produce of their lands was sufficient to answer their demands."[119]

He was speaking about the Jesuit properties in the colonies, and the fact that the priests who ran them now had almost no guidance and support for their mission. But he was about to get a mission of his own — one that would have fateful and unexpected consequences for him, for his native colonies, and for Catholicism in America.

[119] Guilday, *The Life and Times of John Carroll*, 59.

4

On the eve of the most important trip of his life, Fr. John Carroll had the sick, certain feeling it was destined for failure.

His reasons were sound, and in the short term, he was right. But nevertheless, Carroll was talked into traveling to Canada in the spring of 1776. His companions were his cousin Charles Carroll, Maryland lawyer and assemblyman Samuel Chase, and the venerable Dr. Benjamin Franklin.

Their mission seemed impossible from the very start. They were sent to Montreal, where they were tasked by colonial authorities to win over skeptical Canadians—Catholics especially—to the rebel cause. It got worse when the quartet reached its destination, to encounter a hostile bishop and a group of hosts who were expecting money and got only assurances of friendship and religious tolerance.

Those assurances fell flat in light of recent events. Two years earlier, Great Britain had issued the Quebec Act. Besides expanding the boundaries of Quebec as far south as the Ohio River, it essentially restored the French culture of the province, which had been lost to Britain after the Seven Years' War ended in 1763. Most important, it allowed Catholics to practice their faith freely.

If it seemed like a calculated move, it assuredly was. After all, just two decades earlier, Great Britain had forcibly evicted nearly seven thousand native Acadians from Nova Scotia. It was one of the more shameful recent examples of English treatment of Canadian Catholics, and the memory of it was certainly fresh.

But the Quebec Act was prudent policy, as well. Sir Guy Carleton and Lord North, who devised it, realized the British Empire could benefit from allowing native cultures in its colonies to remain intact. Carleton made the point persuasively, in person, to Parliament: the claims of fifty thousand Canadians, almost all of whom were French and Roman Catholic, "must be superior to those of the 600 British immigrants."[120]

So while the Quebec Act was certainly strategic—making sure that the colonies' northern neighbor would become a British ally, or at least

[120] Melville, *John Carroll of Baltimore*, 42.

stay neutral in the coming conflict—it would also become "the master-plan for British government in 'the second empire' which flourished after the American colonies were lost," in places like India, according to author Annabelle Melville.[121]

That was bad enough for the prospects of the American delegation. But the colonial response to the Quebec Act made a difficult job all but impossible.

Colonial leaders classified the Quebec Act as the fifth of five "Intolerable Acts." The other four, including the Boston Port Act that closed Boston Harbor, and the Quartering Act that forced colonists to house British soldiers, were punishment for the Boston Tea Party of December 1773. This new act, however, might have been the most intolerable of all.

Some founders were certain the act would do far more than just protect the religious freedom of Canadian Catholics. Alexander Hamilton was one of many who viewed it as a plot: to establish the Catholic religion throughout the colonies via immigration.

As an immigrant himself, Hamilton might have been charged with hypocrisy—but that was just a teaser for the colonists' upcoming about-face.

Just days after responding with outrage to Parliament, the Congress issued the Canadians an offer to join them in rebellion. Recognizing that Canadians already possessed religious freedom, Congress made a more sophisticated case: that this freedom was actually an insult, because it was not something the British king could bestow. Instead, it came from God. If it did not, the British could—and by implication, probably would—take it away someday. Therefore, the tie that bound these two British provinces—"the mutual devotion to liberty"[122]—would overcome all their differences, and made them natural allies for independence.

It was a surprisingly cogent argument, but there was no way it could overcome its clumsy presentation. Copies of the Congress's letter to Parliament and the Canadians circulated widely, and colonial leaders

---

[121] Melville, *John Carroll of Baltimore*, 42.
[122] Farrelly, *Anti-Catholicism in America*, 71.

were mocked at home and abroad for what everyone plainly saw as double-dealing.

Yet even though the appeal to Canada failed, the colony was too important to simply ignore.

In early 1776, Thomas Paine's *Common Sense* was electrifying the colonies. The author insisted that the "shot heard 'round the world" at Lexington and Concord the previous year was the breaking point in relations with Great Britain. But the colonists, Paine warned, had only a limited window in which to pursue independence. The pamphlet was a best seller and helped persuade even Washington, Franklin, and Jefferson — all of whom had believed a peaceful settlement was possible — that it was time to act.

Once that course was decided, the strategic significance of Canada came to the forefront — even if asking the Canadians to forget about the recent colonial insults to Catholics was a tall order. The colonists' French agents recommended sending a delegation to Montreal, then under American control, to make their case in person. The two-faced policy was "ridiculous,"[123] as Annabelle Melville acknowledged, but a party was selected regardless.

Wealthy, distinguished, and Catholic, Charles Carroll of Carrollton was an easy choice. The hot-tempered Maryland attorney Samuel Chase was a more unusual one: nicknamed "Old Bacon Face" by his colleagues on the bar, he would sign the Declaration of Independence and serve on the U.S. Supreme Court, but his career was pockmarked by controversies and disputes.

The star of the delegation, of course, was Dr. Franklin, who had just turned seventy. He'd returned the previous year from Great Britain, where he'd spent two tours of duty trying to persuade British officials to honor American interests. He had ultimately been unsuccessful; in fact, when he left England in 1775, many there were convinced he was a troublemaker and intriguer. But his standing in the colonies had only risen, especially among people who favored independence.

---

[123] Melville, *John Carroll of Baltimore*, 44.

The colonists had enough sense to try hedging their bets further. Charles Lee, who would become a general in the Continental Army, had a suggestion for the ideal fourth member of the Canadian delegation.

"I should think that if some Jesuit or Religieuse of any other order (but he must be a man of liberal sentiments, enlarged mind, and a manifest friend to Civil Liberty) could be found out and sent to Canada, he would be worth battalions to us," Lee wrote to John Hancock in February 1776. "Mr. Carroll has a relative who exactly answers the description."[124]

He did indeed. But when Fr. John Carroll received the letter from his cousin Charles, one morning early that March, he had good reasons for turning down the invitation.

There's no doubt it must have left him terribly conflicted. For one thing, John Carroll had been home at Rock Creek plantation for less than two years. He was still busily engaged in building a post-Jesuit career for himself as a circuit priest to the surrounding area. He knew well, of course, about the attitudes of colonial leaders toward Catholics. And he was far from sure that a priest was the best person to get mixed up in politics. As he wrote at the time: "The nature and function of the profession in which I have engaged from a very early period in life, render me, as I humbly conceive, a very unfit person to be engaged in a negotiation of so new a kind to me. I have observed when ministers of religion leave the duties of their profession to take a busy part in political matters, they generally fall into contempt, and sometimes even bring discredit to the cause in whose service they are engaged."

In short, Fr. Carroll thought Congress should know "how little service they can hope to derive from my assistance."[125]

Yet, against his better judgment, he relented. He traveled north later that month, stopping in Philadelphia to get advice from another former Jesuit. Fr. Ferdinand Farmer, S.J., the "priest on horseback," is the subject of chapter 10. We don't know the substance of their discussion at Old St. Joseph's Church, but it's certain Farmer gave him a letter of introduction

---

[124] Melville, *John Carroll of Baltimore*, 44.
[125] Melville, *John Carroll of Baltimore*, 45.

to Fr. Pierre-René Floquet, S.J.—a letter that would cause both Carroll and Floquet future grief.

Fr. Carroll might still have changed his mind about the trip if he'd known how unrealistically congressional leaders viewed his role. No less than John Adams, who called Fr. Carroll "a gentleman of learning and Abilities," believed that having him available to offer the sacraments to Catholics "such as have been refused (them) by the Toryfied priests in Canada"[126] would be a difference-maker.

But it was never going to be that simple. However they'd gotten it, the Quebec Act had brought religious freedom to most Canadian Catholics, and their own leaders warned the flock to beware of the Americans. In particular, Jean-Olivier Briand, the bellicose bishop of Quebec, drew a line in the sand.

Briand had held his job since 1766, when King George III allowed him to be appointed. This concession to Rome was an early hint of the geopolitical pragmatism that led to the passage of the Quebec Act. Bishop Briand became immediately popular with his new flock and loyal to his British colleagues—in particular, Sir Guy Carleton, the governor of the province.

Once he was appointed, Briand became the closest Catholic bishop to the American colonies. Based on an April 1773 letter to the Canadian priest Fr. Bernard Well from Fr. Ferdinand Farmer, there was even talk of having Briand visit the colonies to administer Confirmation—which Farmer counseled against, warning him of colonial hostility to bishops.

The feeling was mutual. Whatever he may have thought about confirming American Catholics, the bishop had no sympathy at all for American independence.

In 1775, Bishop Briand released a pastoral letter that backed Carleton, and Britain, to the hilt.

"Your oaths and your religion impose on you the essential obligation to defend your country and your king with all your power," he commanded Canadian Catholics. "Close your ears, therefore, dear Canadiens, and

[126] Melville, *John Carroll of Baltimore*, 44.

do not listen to these seditious men who seek to make you unhappy, to extinguish the feelings of submission to your legitimate superiors that your upbringing and religion have engraved on your hearts. Carry out with joy everything you are told to do by a beneficent governor whose only care is for your interests and your happiness."[127]

Now, on the eve of revolution, some of those "seditious men" were showing up on Bishop Briand's doorstep. He would be sure to greet them unkindly—Fr. Carroll most of all.

5

The four Canadian commissioners crossed the Delaware River into New Jersey in early April. They rode a ferry run by Irish immigrant Patrick Colvin, a little-known but crucial Catholic hero of the Revolution.

Their coach made its way into New York for a brief stopover. An uneasy peace held in the almost-empty city, where soldiers were working frantically to fortify General Washington's new headquarters. But the British Army loomed just off Long Island, and an invasion seemed imminent.

The commissioners disembarked for a small boat, which carried them up the Hudson River to Albany. There their host was Gen. Philip Schuyler. At the family mansion on the outskirts of town, the party rested—and Charles Carroll, in particular, found himself captivated by the charms of the general's two daughters: "lively, agreeable, black-eyed"[128] Eliza and Peggy. The former, of course, would become Mrs. Alexander Hamilton and, a couple of centuries later, a Broadway star.

The Schuylers accompanied the party as far as Saratoga. After thirty miles of terrible roads, they were greeted by six inches of April snow. The roads got worse, and when the party crossed Lake Champlain,

---

[127] Gilles Chaussé, "Bishop Briand and the Civil Authorities," in *A Concise History of Christianity in Canada*, ed. Terrence Murphy (Toronto: Oxford University Press, 1996), Quebec History Encyclopedia, http://faculty.marianopolis.edu/ c.belanger/quebechistory/encyclopedia/Bishop BriandandtheCivilAuthorities.html.

[128] Smith, *Charles Carroll of Carrollton*, 140–141.

John Carroll chose to sleep under the awning onboard their boat, wrapped in blankets, rather than go into the woods like his fellow passengers, who made "a covering of the boughs of trees, and large fires at their feet."[129]

On finally reaching Montreal on April 29, the commissioners were greeted by a welcoming committee that included Brig. Gen. Benedict Arnold. At his home an "elegant supper" and glasses of wine were served to the weary and grateful travelers. After the meal they were entertained by "a large assembly of ladies, most of them French," who sang for their guests. John Carroll found it all "very agreeable."[130] It seemed a promising beginning.

The hospitality was a mirage, and the problems with the mission became immediately apparent. The first had to do with money. If the Canadians were expecting anything at all from the commissioners, it was that they had come to settle the bills colonial soldiers had run up over the past several months—as well as the worthless notes of credit they'd sometimes offered as payment.

"It is impossible to give you a just idea of the lowness of the Continental credit here," Benjamin Franklin informed Congress. "Therefore, till the arrival of money, it seems improper to propose the federal union of this province with the others."[131]

But the appeal to the religious sympathies of Canadian Catholics got an equally chilly reception, thanks in large part to Bishop Briand.

On March 20, Congress had drawn up a set of instructions for the commissioners. The most noteworthy of all was the one aimed at Catholic Canadians. It read: "You are further to declare that we hold sacred the Rights of Conscience, and may promise to the whole People solemnly, in our Name, the free and undisturbed Exercise of their Relegion, and to the Clergy the full, perfect, and peaceable Possession and Enjoyment of all their Estates, that the Government of

---

[129] Guilday, *The Life and Times of John Carroll*, 150.
[130] Melville, *John Carroll of Baltimore*, 55.
[131] Melville, *John Carroll of Baltimore*, 51.

every Thing relating to their Relegion and Clergy shall be left entirely in the Hands of the good People of that Province, and such Legislature as they shall constitute."

There was one caveat: "provided however that all other Denominations of Christians be equally entituled to hold Offices and enjoy civil Privileges and the free Exercise of their Relegion and be totally exempt from the Payment of any Tythes or Taxes for the Support of any Relegion."

It hardly mattered, because these were freedoms the Canadians already enjoyed under British rule. And Fr. Carroll found it difficult to answer pointed questions about the colonists' well-known anti-Catholic views. Later that summer, in fact, a loyalist Irish priest, John McKenna, escaped to Bishop Briand's protection in Montreal after being run out of New York—a living example of why Canadians weren't ready to listen to the commissioners' claims.

The letter of introduction John Carroll presented to Fr. Pierre-René Floquet not only didn't improve matters, it helped put Floquet on the outs with his bishop.

Fr. Floquet was the last of the Jesuits in Canada, following the disbanding of the Society of Jesus. He was living in the Jesuits' old residence in Montreal, where Fr. Carroll visited him that May. Carroll had dinner there and he offered Mass once in Floquet's church.

That was enough to compromise his loyalty to the Crown in the opinion of Briand, who threatened to place Fr. Floquet under an interdict and banish him from Montreal. If Briand had been expecting an apology from his wayward priest, that isn't quite what he received.

In a letter dated June 15, 1776, Floquet accepted his fate—and then went on to make a frank accounting of some other ways he had disobeyed Briand's orders.

"Here is my public confession. I do not like the Quebec Bill, and I have said so too openly," he wrote. "This has made enemies for me of all those who are responsible for it. I treated the Bostonnais [the name given the Americans] considerately from human respect. Had I appeared as violent against them as did many others, the fury of the storm would have fallen on my head—I being the only Jesuit in Montreal—should have served as an example to others, and I should perhaps have caused the persecution of our missionaries in Pennsylvania and in Maryland."[132]

Fr. Floquet further confessed that he'd offered Communion secretly to American militiamen, and went easy on them in the confessional to boot.

Not surprisingly, the interdict was imposed. Floquet was exiled to Quebec, and although he was recalled later that year and the interdict lifted, he never won back the bishop's good graces. "Fr. Floquet has behaved very badly," his exasperated bishop would say later. "He does not believe that he was wrong and says so when he is not afraid of his listeners."

By that point the American delegation had retreated in defeat and despair to the colonies. Once they'd taken stock of the smallpox-ridden troops, and heard the news that a fleet of British warships had landed a thousand men to repel the American siege of Quebec, leaving Canada seemed not just like a practical matter but also one of personal safety.

"We are afraid it will not be in our power to render our country any further services in this colony," the commissioners informed Congress on May 10.[133] It was something of an understatement.

Benjamin Franklin threw in the towel first. Even before reaching Canada, he admitted his health probably made the trip unwise. "I begin to apprehend that I have undertaken a fatigue that at my time of life may prove too much for me," he'd lamented to his friend Josiah Quincy in April, while waiting for the ice to melt at Saratoga. "So I sit down to write to a few friends by way of farewell."[134]

That eulogy might have been tongue in cheek. It certainly turned out to be premature. At first Franklin overcame the hardships the party faced, such as sleeping on hard wooden floors and the challenge of keeping clean. He even entertained his younger companions by composing

[132] Martin I. J. Griffin, *Catholics and the American Revolution*, vol. 1 (Ridley Park, PA: published by the author, 1907), 106–110.

[133] Melville, *John Carroll of Baltimore*, 52.

[134] H. W. Brands, *The First American: The Life and Times of Benjamin Franklin* (Norwalk, CT: Easton Press, 2002), 507.

songs for them, and he had an endless supply of amusing stories. "Nothing is serious enough to suppress the humor that bubbles up in Franklin," Charles Carroll wrote admiringly.[135]

But after six weeks on the road, Franklin was now suffering from the rashes, boils, and lesions that affected many travelers of this time, as well as the gout that bedeviled him so often that he would later write an imaginary "dialogue" with it.

He'd also realized quickly that, without money, there was no more good to be done in Canada. So he departed abruptly on May 11. The American forces would not be far behind, abandoning Canada the very next month.

Fr. Carroll, who had grown fond of Franklin and could see the pain he was enduring, decided to follow his fellow commissioner and help him get home as comfortably as possible. "Believe me, my Dear Sir, that no one can wish your welfare more ardently, or bear a greater regard for you," Carroll wrote to Franklin that day from Montreal, begging him to wait at St. John's until he could catch up.[136]

When he did, it took two days for Fr. Carroll to secure them a carriage for their long and arduous trip back to the colonies. The trip was made more difficult than necessary by a last-minute request from Mrs. Thomas Walker, the wife of the merchant who had hosted them in Montreal. She requested a ride to Saratoga, and as the carriage — now filled with her luggage — bumped and jostled its way south, Franklin's aching legs turned his temper sharp.

He would not, however, forget the kindness of Fr. Carroll. "As to my self, I find I grow daily more feeble," he wrote to his fellow commissioners, Charles Carroll and Samuel Chase later that month, "and think I could hardly have got along so far, but for Mr. Carroll's friendly Assistance and tender Care of me."[137]

---

[135] McDermott, *Charles Carroll of Carrollton*, 130.
[136] "To Benjamin Franklin from John Carroll, 11 May 1776," Founders Online, National Archives, https://founders.archives.gov/documents/Franklin/01-22-02-0257.
[137] Guilday, *The Life and Times of John Carroll*, 103.

In time, that care would be repaid in a way that benefited Catholics all across America. And though neither Franklin nor Fr. Carroll could have known it then, the Canadian mission would ultimately prove not to be the utter failure it first seemed. Bishop Briand and unhappy local business owners might have given the commissioners the cold shoulder but others were listening to their message.

After the commissioners left, significant numbers of the bishop's flock rebelled. Even after the American forces withdrew, there were many Catholics whose opinion turned against the Crown. The bishop blasted the unfaithful in a scathing pastoral letter in June 1776 — "What an abyss of sin you have plunged into.... How many sins you have committed before God!" — but even he admitted it had little effect. "My authority is not respected any more than yours," he wrote to a loyalist priest. "Like you, I am called an Englishman.... I should put all the churches, even most of the diocese, under interdict."[138]

If the commissioners had not secured Canada's assistance as an ally, they had at least preserved the "benevolent neutrality" of Canadians.

"After this episode Bishop Briand could no longer be considered the undisputed leader of the nation. The gulf between the clergy and the people had widened, even if the latter had not intended to call into question their adherence to Catholicism. A breath of freedom had touched them," reads an entry in *The Quebec History Encyclopedia*, which continues, "The letter of 26 October 1774 from the American Congress, and the appeal for liberty issued on 28 October 1778 by the Comte d'Estaing, vice-admiral of the squadron sent by France in support of the rebel colonies, had given Canadiens their first taste of democracy and freedom. From then on they would always be reluctant to come to the defence of the king or British interests, or to follow the instructions of their religious leaders in this regard."[139]

Undoubtedly, the patience and kindness of Fr. John Carroll helped win some Canadian hearts and minds to the patriot cause, just as those same qualities won over the suffering Benjamin Franklin. But inside the

[138] Chaussé, "Bishop Briand and the Civil Authorities."
[139] Chaussé, "Bishop Briand and the Civil Authorities."

stuffy, cramped carriage in that May of 1776, Carroll's thoughts may have been dark ones indeed.

He had never wanted to go to Canada and thought it was a fool's errand from the start. Now, some observers allege, he was thinking of a situation even more desperate. Had he survived the dissolution of the Jesuits only to lose his life in the Catholic Church instead?

6

John Carroll has been the subject of at least two major biographies. The first, *The Life and Times of John Carroll*, was published in 1922. Written by Catholic priest and scholar Msgr. Peter Guilday, it runs close to a thousand pages and truly deserves the term "magisterial." The second, shorter work appeared in 1955. Author Annabelle Melville's *John Carroll of Baltimore* condenses his life into a more imaginative, accessible volume.

Yet neither book claims that Fr. Carroll was excommunicated by Bishop Briand. Neither does the subject come up in Carroll's correspondence. So it's hard to trace where the idea entered the public consciousness.

It certainly became news when it was mentioned in August 2008 at the annual Knights of Columbus convention in Quebec. The person who brought it up was the late Cardinal John Foley, who spoke at the convention's traditional "States Dinner."

At the gathering, Cardinal Foley asked a public favor of Quebec's Cardinal Marc Ouellet. The request dated back to the Canadian mission of 1776.

"Bishop Briand saw no reason for Canadians to join the American colonies against the British, and he was very annoyed that a Catholic priest should be among those seeking to encourage Canadians to risk their religious liberty in what he considered to be a dubious cause," Cardinal Foley told the Knights. "So he excommunicated Fr. Carroll—and there is no record of which I know that such an excommunication has ever been lifted."[140]

---

[140] "Cardinal Foley Entertains Knights' Dinner, Asks for Lifting of Excommunication," Catholic News Agency, August 5, 2008, https://www.catholicnewsagency.com/newss/cardinal_foley_entertains_knights_dinner_asks_for_lifting_of_excommunication.

The exchange, reported by the Catholic News Service, was light-hearted, and Cardinal Ouellet, it is suggested, agreed to "lift" the excommunication. But the casual nature of the encounter belies a number of serious issues.

The most obvious is that Carroll didn't outwardly behave like a man who had just been denied the sacraments and expelled from the Church. He returned to Rock Creek in early June, where his mother and two youngest sisters, Mary and Elizabeth, awaited. And he wasted little time in beginning to offer Mass again at the family chapel.

Now in his forties, he also continued his demanding work as a circuit rider to spread the faith. "I have care of a very large congregation," he wrote in February 1779 to his old friend from Bruges, Fr. Charles Plowden. "I often have to ride twenty-five or thirty miles to the sick; besides which I go once a month between fifty and sixty miles to another congregation in Virginia."[141]

If Carroll didn't act as though he'd been excommunicated, then the simplest explanation is that he wasn't. A search of the archives of the Archdiocese of Quebec turns up no record of such an event. "I did not find paper relating specifically to John Carroll," reports archivist Pierre Lafontaine, "much less an excommunication."

This wasn't the first time such a question had been posed to the archdiocese. In 2011, a similar request for information was made. But the archivist at the time, Lafontaine notes, also "found no document as accurate."

A bigger problem with the alleged excommunication is that Fr. John Carroll would eventually become the first American bishop. "It would be surprising," Lafontaine notes, "that the Pope appointed Bishop a priest who had been excommunicated several years earlier."

How could such a mistake happen? The simplest explanation, Lafontaine offers, is that people have simply gotten Fr. Carroll mixed up with Fr. Pierre-René Floquet. Both men were in Montreal at the same time, and it's undoubtedly true that both got on the bad side of Bishop

---

[141] Melville, *John Carroll of Baltimore*, 55.

Briand. In fact, as we've seen, Carroll's presence undoubtedly led to the interdict against Floquet—which some might have gotten confused with the more serious punishment of excommunication.

Maybe a more interesting question than how such an error occurred is why people apparently believed it. The answer might lie in the way circumstances realigned the loyalties of American Catholics—especially former Jesuits.

With the dissolution of the Society of Jesus, American Jesuits were also freed from the authority of the English provincial who had supervised them. Three years later, the Declaration of Independence put an exclamation mark on the former Jesuits' own independence.

The English prelate cut ties with the American clergy. As a 1905 account in the Jesuit publication the *Messenger* put it, Fr. Carroll and his fellow priests "were placed in a novel and anomalous situation: ecclesiastically, they were nullius jurisdictionis."[142]

The only Jesuit supervisor in America at the time was Fr. John Lewis, who had been appointed vicar general before the war. But Lewis was older and hardly up for the challenges that freedom presented the former members of his order.

John Carroll, however, was thinking about these opportunities as the Revolution raged around him, and then came to its surprising conclusion at Yorktown. He was also considering how Rome might respond to the new landscape. By the fall of 1783, as the Treaty of Paris officially ended the war, he was hearing rumors from his friend Fr. Charles Plowden that Jesuit holdings in America might now be an attractive target for a takeover.

His response is noteworthy for a few reasons. One is that these rumors clearly made him angry. Normally gentle and deferential, his reply to Fr. Plowden shows a surprising fieriness. Another is that his words reveal a man who has gone all-in on the American experiment—even if it meant going against the wishes of Rome.

---

[142] Fr. Edward I. Devitt, S.J., "Centenary of the Restoration of the Jesuits in the United States," *Messenger* 44, no. 2 (August 1905): 117.

"They may be assured that they will never get possession of a sixpence of our property here," Carroll wrote—and by "they" he meant the Vatican's Sacred Congregation for the Propagation of the Faith, otherwise known as Propaganda—"and if any of our friends could be weak enough to deliver any real estate into their hands or attempt to subject it to their authority, our civil government would be called upon to wrest it out of their dominion."

"A foreign temporal jurisdiction will never be tolerated here," Carroll added defiantly. "They may send their agents when they please; they will certainly return empty-handed."[143]

Much has been written about the way Fr. Carroll, and other Catholics of the time, challenged the church's temporal—that is, worldly—authority. As historian Stephen Klugewicz noted, "There was a tradition in English Catholic thought, echoed in the apologetic writings of American Catholics, that denied the Pope's temporal authority. But this theory generally defined the Pope's temporal power as his power to interfere in the civil concerns of countries—to depose kings, for example."

Carroll's interpretation of the idea went further. "The suggestion was that the Church hierarchy wielded no power over Americans in non-ecclesiastical matters, especially in the area of property rights."[144] In short, the man who went skeptically to advance the colonial cause in Montreal had become a patriot. And he had also come up with a plan to protect the considerable Jesuit holdings in America, and turn them into the basis for an authentic Catholic Church in America—one as free from foreign influence as possible.

Author Maura Jane Farrelly points out that the common colonial slur "popery" can be seen as not just anti-Catholic. It also, she argues, reflected colonists' distrust of authoritarianism—a word that signified "both a *cause* and *effect* of tyranny."[145]

---

[143] Melville, *John Carroll of Baltimore*, 59.

[144] Stephen M. Klugewicz, "An Extraordinary Revolution: The Creation of the Catholic Church in America," The Imaginative Conservative, May 17, 2011, https:// theimaginativeconservative.org/2011/05/john-carroll-and-creation-catholic.html.

[145] Farrelly, *Anti-Catholicism in America*, 83.

John Carroll, too, had cause for concern about this sort of "popery." Years after the Revolution, his recollections of Pope Clement XIV were still fresh — and bitter. His arguments against the Curia, according to Jesuit historian Fr. James Hennessey, S.J., were theological, political — and, he admits, emotional: "colored by memories of 1773."

So, in 1790, Carroll warned his old friend Fr. Plowden about jumping unthinkingly to the defense of the Holy See.

"Remember the iniquities and oppressions of popes such as Ganganelli, and you will be careful to obey and respect their orders, within the line of their rightful jurisdiction," Fr. Carroll wrote. What Plowden should never do, he cautioned, was to allow that jurisdiction to stretch further, into worldly matters — "which sooner or later always does harm."[146]

It's worth considering the situation John Carroll found himself in during the Revolutionary War, and the harm he probably felt had been done to him. His religious order had been messily disbanded by the pope. His ties to England had been cut, and with London as the intermediate link between the colonies and Rome, that connection had been affected as well. Meanwhile, the freedom he had unexpectedly gained had given him the opportunity to imagine the Catholic Church in a distinctively American milieu, one he would undoubtedly have a significant part in building from the ground up.

Even though Fr. John Carroll was apparently never excommunicated, he had good reasons to declare his own *qualified* American independence — an independence in political matters, at least — from Rome

7

What did Benjamin Franklin think about religion? Unlike many of his fellow founders, we have a reasonably accurate picture. Not long before he died in 1790, Franklin was asked by Ezra Stiles, the president of Yale College, to commit his beliefs to paper.

---

[146] James Hennesey, S.J., "'An Eighteenth Century Bishop: John Carroll of Baltimore,'" *Archivum Historiae Pontificiae* no. 16 (1978): 173–174, www .jstor.org/stable/23563998.

Franklin, then eighty-four, obliged, giving a short statement of his "Creed." He believed in one God, who created the universe and governs it. This God should be worshipped, and the best way to do so "is doing Good to his other Children. He thought Jesus was the greatest moral teacher of all. Was He divine? Franklin wasn't sure. He also wasn't inclined to investigate the question. With typical wit, he said it was "needless to busy myself with it now, where I expect soon an Opportunity of knowing the Truth with less Trouble."[147]

What did Franklin think of Catholics, specifically? He did approve of the typical anti-Catholic prejudices of the time, such as loyalty oaths. Yet Franklin might have been second only to George Washington — the subject of chapter 12 — in the careful way he avoided publicly criticizing Catholics. That tolerance would lead John Adams to note, with both sarcasm and a touch of jealousy, "that Catholics thought him almost a Catholic. The Church of England claimed him as one of them. The Presbyterians thought him half a Presbyterian, and the Friends believed him a wet Quaker."[148]

But what Franklin thought of one Catholic, in particular — Fr. John Carroll — would have dramatic consequences for the Church in America.

The intrigue that surrounded the end of the Revolutionary War, and the negotiated peace that followed, is labyrinthine in its complexities. That was especially true at the Vatican, which was now under new leadership. Pope Pius VI, who had become head of the Church in 1775 after Clement XIV's death, recognized that the new world order would necessarily mean changes in American Catholicism.

Although the pope had dissolved the bonds between the Church in America and London during the war, it was time for a rethink of how that Church would be overseen. And given the nature of the struggle for

---

[147] John Fea, "Religion and Early Politics: Benjamin Franklin and His Religious Beliefs," *Pennsylvania Heritage* 37, no. 4 (Fall 2011), http://www.phmc.state.pa.us/portal/communities/pa-heritage/religion-early-politics-benjamin-franklin.html.

[148] Alf J. Mapp Jr., *The Faiths of Our Fathers: What America's Founders Really Believed* (Lanham, MD: Rowman and Littlefield, 2005), 35.

American independence against the rule of a foreign monarch, it became increasingly clear the new Church would need a native-born leader.

Franklin, who had been in Paris during the war, was the go-between in a series of delicate negotiations between the French government, the Vatican, and the newly independent colonies. He helped convey two simple wishes from the Continental Congress. One was that Congress wanted to steer clear of religious matters. In return, foreign powers — such as the Vatican — should also avoid getting mixed up in American temporal issues.

Fr. John Carroll himself had made similar points over the past few years. In 1782 he began devising a plan to protect Jesuit estates from seizure. A year later, his call for a meeting of clergy led to a roundtable at a former Jesuit residence in Whitemarsh, Maryland. A half-dozen priests attended, including Carroll's theoretical boss, Fr. John Lewis, S.J. From this meeting came a petition to Rome, asking that Lewis be named their superior. The Church in America, the petition read, "can no longer have recourse" to leaders "in different and foreign states."[149]

The Vatican finally agreed with the sentiment, but not with the group's choice of leader. Lewis was in his sixties and had maintained a low profile during the Revolutionary years — something Carroll himself had complained about. Fr. Carroll, on the other hand, was not yet fifty and had the energy and respect to make him an obvious candidate.

His old friend Benjamin Franklin thought so. He had always remembered the kindnesses that Carroll had shown him on that uncomfortable trip home from Canada. The exact nature of what he said on Fr. Carroll's behalf is not known, but others believed Franklin was the deciding factor.

Carroll's friend Fr. John Thorpe, an English ex-Jesuit who lived in Rome, handled negotiations between American Catholics and the Vatican. In July 1784, he wrote to Carroll, telling him how much his letters had impressed Vatican officials and convinced them "that you are eminently qualified for the dignity which Dr. Franklin has commended on

---

[149] Guilday, *The Life and Times of John Carroll*, 170.

you." The notification from the Vatican that followed also suggested that Fr. Carroll's appointment as superior would "especially" please Franklin.

It would be another five years before Carroll would officially be elected the first Catholic bishop of the United States of America. His comments prior to his election read a lot like his misgivings shortly before the Canadian mission of 1776. He thought himself "entirely unfit for a station in which I can have no hopes of rendering service," and openly hoped that his fellow priests would choose another candidate.

Again, he had good reasons to be wary. The subject of bishops in America had been a hot-button issue for decades—and not only for Catholics. Back in 1765, when the English Catholic bishop Richard Challoner had suggested from London that it might make sense to create an American version of his job, he drew a rebuke from Charles Carroll of Carrollton.

"For many years past attempts have been made to establish a Protestant Bishop on this continent," Carroll pointed out, "and yet such attempts have been as constantly opp'd thro the fixed avertion ye people of America in general have to a person of such a character."[150]

The problem, again, was a "popery" that wasn't really about the pope, nor even Catholicism. Instead, it was the fear that having a foreign power appoint a bishop to oversee its American flock meant giving in to authoritarianism. This was why Fr. John Carroll worked so hard on a plan for a truly American expression of the Catholic Church, and why he declared flatly that "a foreign temporal jurisdiction will never be tolerated here."

The gains made by Catholics during the Revolution and afterward had been real and substantial. Even when Rome acquiesced and allowed the Americans to choose their own bishop, the term still carried baggage. Fr. Carroll undoubtedly feared the word and its implications more than he did the job, for which just about everyone could see he was the natural choice.

What he feared more than the word, however, was the idea that Rome would appoint its own bishop if he turned down the job—a prerogative

[150] Guilday, *The Life and Times of John Carroll*, 155–156.

the Vatican was careful to preserve. So, when Carroll finally accepted the vote of his fellow priests in May 1789, he led not just the Catholic Church but American Christianity into new and largely uncharted waters.

The sailing would never be smooth. In the short term, the new bishop of Baltimore would contend with shortages of priests, and the challenges of westward expansion. He would be called upon to adjudicate disputes that threatened to tear apart parishes. He would face attacks from priests who left the faith, and would struggle with the thorny issue of balancing power between priests and laity. Meanwhile, history would look critically on the relationship between the Church and slavery, something encoded deeply in the southern origins of American Catholicism.

But the successes were undeniable. He oversaw construction of the nation's first cathedral, today called the Basilica of the National Shrine of the Assumption of the Blessed Virgin Mary. His lifelong interest in education and his realization that America needed more priests led to the foundation of Georgetown University in 1791. He convened the first diocesan synod in America that same year, and became the country's first archbishop in 1808.

Most important, Archbishop John Carroll steered the young Church through the crucial first years of its existence. When he died in 1815, he left behind an American Catholicism that enjoyed numbers and freedoms that would have been unthinkable just a half century earlier.

And through it all, as his biographer Annabelle Melville summarized so well, he never deviated from a core conviction: "that while in affairs spiritual he was always a true son of Rome, in concerns temporal and political he was first and last an American."[151]

8

Did Pope Clement XIV inadvertently help win the American Revolution, through his suppression of the Jesuits? Even a shameless author would have to admit the idea is at least partly hyperbole.

---

[151] Melville, *John Carroll of Baltimore*, 61.

Yet the unexpected freedom Clement granted the American Jesuits at least allowed them to make a choice. It was a difficult and sometimes painful one. For some, like Maryland priest Fr. Joseph Mosely, S.J., who agonized in 1776 about whether to return to England, it was "truly between Hawk and Buzzard."[152]

It stands in contrast, however, to the example of Fr. Floquet in Montreal, who served under the authority of Bishop Briand and was punished for it. Had the society and its ties to London existed, how many Jesuits would have felt comfortable taking the patriot side?

The suppression didn't just free John Carroll. In chapters 10 and 11, we will meet two other Jesuit priests who also played significant roles during the Revolution. Those were roles they most likely could not have assumed if the Society of Jesus had stayed intact.

While we don't have precise records of their influence, we can certainly speculate. For example, Fr. Mosely reported that all 250 of his male parishioners had declared their allegiance to the patriot cause—at his direction.[153]

Meanwhile, there is an even stronger case to be made that the suppression made American Catholicism as we know it possible.

"Although it may not have seemed so at the time, the Suppression of the Society of Jesus was one of the best things to happen to the American Catholic Church," contended Jesuit priest Raymond A. Schroth, S.J. "If the church had a founder, it was John Carroll; but if the Society had not been pulled out from under him when he was a young Jesuit traveling, studying, and teaching in Europe, he most likely would have gone on to become a professor—never the first American bishop."[154]

Which takes us back to that room in Bruges where we started. In some alternate reality, it is 1776 and autumn has come to Belgium again. A

---

[152] "Letters of Father Joseph Mosley, S.J.," 301.

[153] Curran, *Papist Devils*, 262.

[154] Raymond A. Schroth, S.J., "American Jesuits, Buried and Brought Back, Part II: The Maryland Plantation Jesuits," *America*, November 18, 2014, https://www.americamagazine.org/issue/american-jesuits-buried-and -brought-back-part-ii.

North Sea breeze whistles down the Hoogstraadt, but Fr. John Carroll is snug inside the House of the Seven Towers.

Tonight he fingers his rosary beads, but his prayer in this alternate dimension is a simple one: of gratitude for his vocation and of guidance for the young Jesuit scholars he teaches.

A New World away, there is news of revolution. Fr. Carroll worries about his family in Maryland, but it's hard to say when — or if — he will see them again. His calling is here, with the Jesuits, who have survived the efforts of their enemies to disband them. In this reality, the pope elected to do the job, Clement XIV, died before the suppression could be finished.

So the crisis has passed, and Fr. John Carroll, S.J. is secure in a familiar place. With satisfaction, he blows out his candle. As he sinks into sleep, he wonders what will happen in his home country. We might wonder, too, without him there to help guide it.

Luckily, American Catholics — and all other Americans — will never have to find out.

Chapter 3 Supplement

A Man of Few Words

There is a third Carroll among the founders. He is the mystery man of the famous Carroll trio that includes his brother John and their cousin Charles Carroll of Carrollton.

Although he's the least known of the three Carrolls, the few words for which Daniel Carroll is best known have made his impact on America just as significant as that of his more famous relatives.

His contributions to our Constitution loom large every four years when we elect a new president. They loom even larger every day, for anyone who enjoys the freedom to worship as they choose.

Perhaps instead of describing Daniel Carroll as mysterious, we should simply call him "overlooked." It's not that the facts of his life are particularly ambiguous. We know he was born in 1730, that he was a student at St. Omer, and that his brother John took his place there in 1748 when he returned to Maryland.

"Young Daniel, fortified by Latin, some Greek, a ready knowledge of French, and a familiarity with philosophy, undertook to learn the practical management of a Southern plantation," wrote historian Richard J. Purcell.[155] Daniel Carroll was forced into learning this skill when his father died unexpectedly in February 1751.

---

[155] Richard J. Purcell, "Daniel Carroll, Framer of the Constitution," *Records of the American Catholic Historical Society of Philadelphia* 52, no. 2 (June 1941): 69, https://www.jstor.org/stable/ 44209385.

We know Daniel Carroll inherited his father's business and prospered, becoming a successful importer, planter, and landowner. We know he married Eleanor Carroll, the first cousin of Charles Carroll of Carrollton: this connected the two family lines, and increased Daniel Carroll's already significant holdings. We know Eleanor died in 1763, and that, by the time of her death, she had given Carroll a son (Daniel III, who was eleven at the time) and a daughter (Mary, then nine).

We know, because Daniel Carroll mentioned it in a letter to an Irish relative in 1762, that if Charles Carroll of Carrollton had died, then Daniel's son, Daniel Carroll III, would have inherited the substantial fortune of Charles Carroll of Annapolis, one of the richest men in America. We know that, tragically, both of Daniel Carroll's children preceded him in death. We also know that after a period of mourning for his wife, he visited his brother in Europe the next year.

We know that when the Maryland state constitution allowed Catholics to hold office, he served in the Maryland Assembly, and as a member of the Confederation Congress during the Revolutionary War. We know he became a delegate to the Constitutional Convention in 1787, and that he served in the first U.S. Congress two years later.

We know his friendship with George Washington led to several opportunities. After the Revolution, "the trading and manorial families of Maryland and Virginia grew interested again in the improvement of the Chesapeake and Potomac waterways," Richard Purcell wrote, "and their union with the western country was no longer underestimated."[156] The imagined link between those waterways and the west was never discovered, but Carroll joined Washington and several other heavy hitters to invest in their development. In addition, Washington named Daniel Carroll one of three commissioners who surveyed the land that became the District of Columbia.

We also know two key points that have become Daniel Carroll's bullet-pointed biography. He was one of only five men to sign both the Articles of Confederation and the Constitution he helped draft to replace

[156] Purcell, "Daniel Carroll, Framer of the Constitution," 76.

them. He was the only Catholic to sign the Articles, and he and Thomas Fitzsimons were the only Catholics to sign the Constitution.

All that is well established, and yet personal details about his life are scant. In 1943, Sr. Mary Virginia Geiger wrote a full-length biography that is a model of careful scholarship. It includes meticulous research about Daniel Carroll's landholdings, about the inventory of the store he inherited from his father, and about his attendance and voting record as a public servant. But about the man responsible for these acquisitions and accomplishments surprisingly little survives.

Perhaps if he'd lived as long as his cousin Charles, there would have been more stories. Instead, he seems to have been frequently ill. His health caused him to turn down a request from Congress to help negotiate peace terms with southern Native American tribes, and his illnesses are frequently cited as reasons for his absences and lateness.

He arrived late to the Constitutional Convention as well. However, a 1787 letter written before the gathering offers the rare personal reflection that his "nervous complaints" were under control, thanks to "moderate (but dayly) exercise, temperance, and attention." He added that his "health, Thank God, is much better than it has been for several years past."

Yet he died in May 1796, just three months after his mother. Archbishop John Carroll's biographer Annabelle Melville said Daniel "never recovered from the blow of her departure."[157]

The previous four years had also been stressful and unpleasant. Carroll was the most active of the three commissioners George Washington chose to oversee the construction of the nation's new capital. That meant Carroll clashed frequently with Pierre L'Enfant, the imperious architect of Washington, DC.

"The commissioner's patience was sorely tried on more than one occasion," wrote Annabelle Melville.[158] The Frenchman had an ambitious blueprint for the area, and some of it involved land owned by Carroll's family and friends.

[157] Melville, *John Carroll of Baltimore*, 161.
[158] Melville, *John Carroll of Baltimore*, 156.

In one case that raised the blood pressure of both Carroll and Washington, L'Enfant ordered a house under construction to be demolished because it was in the way of his plans. The home belonged to Carroll's father-in-law, who was out of town at the time. He had to be told the bad news: that his house had been bulldozed because L'Enfant had decided to put five decorative fountains on the site.

Perhaps Daniel Carroll was simply a more private person than his more famous brother and cousin. He was apparently neither as devout a Catholic as Archbishop John Carroll nor as great a statesman as Charles—despite the fact that he called George Washington and James Madison friends. Much of his work was done behind the scenes. During the Revolution, he used his business connections to supply patriot troops with essentials like salt, flour, linen, and blankets.

He had a reputation for generosity, and his fellow delegate to the Constitutional Convention, William Pierce of Georgia—not known for flattery—called him "possessed of plain good sense."[159] His best-known portrait shows a dark-haired man with the prominent Carroll nose and a cleft chin. But the look he gives the artist is as inscrutable as the details of his personal life.

That leaves his work. We could best describe his legacy as a few small phrases that have had an outsized impact. At the Constitutional Convention, it was Daniel Carroll who moved that the U.S. president be selected "by the people" instead of "by the legislature" as originally written.

He teamed up with Pennsylvania delegate James Wilson, a future Supreme Court justice, "in the cause of popular sovereignty. The Scotch Presbyterian and the Irish Catholic found they had much in common.... They shared with each other a firm belief in the sovereignty of the people and an unshaken confidence in the republican institutions of government," wrote Catholic historian J. Moss Ives in his book *The Ark and the Dove: The Beginning of Civil and Religious Liberties in America.* "Wilson and Carroll were among the few who were at all times and for all purposes in favor of the people exercising their choice of rulers.

[159] Purcell, "Daniel Carroll, Framer of the Constitution," 80.

"It was not until the closing days of the convention that the majority swung to the support of the doctrine that Wilson and Carroll had advocated from the beginning," Ives continued. "The president never would have been the choice of the people had it not been for the combined work and influence of Wilson and Carroll."[160]

In the first Congress, Carroll proposed a similar change to the Tenth Amendment. He requested that "or to the people" be added to the phrase, "The powers not delegated to the United States by the Constitution, nor prohibited by it to the States, are reserved to the States respectively."[161]

He might be best remembered, though, for his defense of the First Amendment's establishment-of-religion clause, although his brother John sometimes mistakenly gets credit for it. Some of his fellow congressmen argued there was no need to include such language, believing it was silly to imagine they would ever try to establish a state religion. But as a Catholic, Daniel Carroll knew all too well not to take that belief for granted.

He also voiced a strong belief that presidential electors should be chosen by popular vote in each state—something not specified by the Constitution but which he believed was evident regardless.

In short, he supported a strong federal government, like his fellow Federalists, but he put more faith in the voters than his cousin Charles had.

As a congressman, Daniel Carroll also joined his two better-known relatives—as well as Pennsylvania congressman Thomas Fitzsimons and New York merchant Dominick Lynch—in drafting a congratulatory letter to George Washington after he was elected president. Written on behalf of all United States Catholics, the letter read in part:

From these happy events, in which none can feel a warmer interest than ourselves, we derive additional pleasure by recollecting,

[160] J. Moss Ives, *The Ark and the Dove; the Beginning of Civil and Religious Liberties in America* (1936; New York: Cooper Square Publishers, 1969), 372.

[161] "The Constitution of the United States: A Transcription," America's Founding Documents, National Archives, September 24, 2018, https://www.archives.gov/founding-docs/ constitution-transcript.

that you, Sir, have been the principal instrument to effect so rapid a change in our political situation. This prospect of national prosperity is peculiarly pleasing to us on another account; because whilst our country preserves her freedom and independence, we shall have a well founded title to claim from her justice equal rights of citizenship, as the price of our blood spilt under your eyes, and of our common exertions for her defence, under your auspicious conduct, rights rendered more dear to us by the remembrance of former hardships.

As the letter to Washington noted, Catholics had seen a rapid change indeed in their political situation. In those few eloquent words of thanks, the influence of Daniel Carroll—a man of few words, yet well-chosen ones—is certainly present.

Chapter 4

The Philadelphia Story

1

The traffic is only a murmur in Philadelphia's historic Old Town. It's a picture-perfect summer morning, and part of the perfection is the remarkable quiet. Take a seat on a wooden bench outside Independence Hall, let your mind wander, and you can almost convince yourself one of the founders might come hurrying across the square, late for a meeting that will determine the future of the republic.

Part of the silence, though, is uneasy. Echoes of the turbulent first half of 2020 still linger. There are whispers from COVID-19 lockdowns, and the screams of violent civil rights protests. Walk past the restored brick row houses, churches, and historic buildings, and you'll see Black Lives Matter signs and black metal gates, now locked. The two phenomena aren't unrelated: after the spring of turmoil, vandalism is a constant fear. Khaki-shirted National Park Service employees mill around outside the landmarks, keeping a watchful eye on the nearly empty streets.

There are signs of life in the Old Town. A florist throws open her door to the public and a stream of cooled air escapes. A used bookshop employee unloads a delivery from a battered brown van. Restaurants try to lure back customers with cheerful signboards on the sidewalks. Yet everything seems somehow furtive—as if the powers that be will frown on this reopening if it gets too public, too loud.

That's sort of how it feels when you visit Old St. Joseph's, the oldest Catholic church in Philadelphia.

It's one of the most historically significant sites in the city. As a shrine to religious freedom alone, Old St. Joseph's would be worth your attention. When it was opened in 1733, it was the only place in the British Empire where you could attend a public Mass.

In addition, the church's redbrick bulk takes up a substantial chunk of real estate in downtown Philadelphia. But you could easily walk right past and never realize it's there.

Located on the corner of Fourth and Walnut, the front of the church is set back from the street and obscured by a stand of walnut trees. It's affectionately known as "the church in the alley." That's because you have to enter from the back, through a narrow side street named Willings Alley. Even after you make your way through the wrought-iron gates, the church doesn't present itself immediately. It's as if it's still wearing camouflage.

A local Catholic author, Agnes Repplier, once described it well: a "church as carefully hidden away as a martyr's tomb in the catacombs."

The subterfuge was by design. It reflected the uncertain legacy of religious freedom here in the most tolerant of the thirteen original colonies. The guarantee of conscience Pennsylvania promised its Catholic citizens was real, yet often tested.

Even the author of Pennsylvania's groundbreaking "Charter of Liberties and Privileges" wasn't a fan of Catholics. Pennsylvania's founder, the Quaker William Penn, is rightfully noted for his promise of religious freedom, in the 1701 charter, to all residents of the colony "who shall Confesse and Acknowledge one Almighty God the Creator upholder and Ruler of the world."

Penn's charter also allowed anyone who professed belief in "Jesus Christ, the Savior of the World," to hold public office—an equally rare concession in colonial America. This was at a time, after all, when Catholics were losing their rights to worship, to vote, and to hold office in Maryland, formerly the most tolerant colony toward Catholics. And Penn had tried to recruit settlers from Germany, in particular—surely importing many of the Catholics who would help plant the seeds of the faith in Pennsylvania.

Yet when he heard reports of Mass being said in Philadelphia—and it apparently happened as early as 1707—Penn wrote to the colony's governor demanding an explanation.

"There is a complaint against your government, that you suffer publick Mass in a scandalous manner," Penn said. "Pray send the matter of fact for ill use is made of it against us here."[162]

"Here" was, of course, England, where Penn was undoubtedly under pressure to keep Catholicism out of his colony.

"Penn did not love Catholics, but he was Christian enough not to hate them to death," explained the Jesuit historian Fr. Francis X. Talbot, S.J. "He might write a 'Seasonable Caveat against Popery,' he might condemn 'The Scandal of the Mass,' but he would also defend the right of the Catholic to liberty of worship in vigorous pamphlets and broadsides."[163]

Yet Penn's son Thomas, who became the next proprietor of Pennsylvania along with his two brothers, could hardly be called an ally. In February 1742, he told Thomas Cookson, a surveyor in Lancaster County, that he was "well pleased" Cookson had given Lutherans and Calvinists lots for churches. He was even happier Cookson had not granted lots to any Catholics, sniffing that "these people should be discouraged as much as possible."

So Old St. Joseph's founder, Fr. Joseph Greaton, S.J., probably realized early on that Pennsylvania's religious tolerance was far from assured. He was undaunted by the challenge; he might even have relished it. It turned him into a master of disguise.

2

Joseph Greaton was a Londoner and a Jesuit priest, who also went by the name "Josiah Crayton." He appears to have settled in Philadelphia in 1729, after nearly a decade spent in Maryland. But it's likely Fr. Greaton

---

[162] Eugene B. Gallagher, "Two Hundred and Fifty Years Ago: The Beginnings of St. Joseph's Church," *Records of the American Catholic Historical Society of Philadelphia* 93, no. 1/4 (March–December 1982): 5–6, https://www.jstor.org/stable/44216420.

[163] Gallagher, "Two Hundred and Fifty Years Ago," 5–6.

had been visiting Philadelphia for years to celebrate Mass in private homes. He got away with it because he dressed as a Quaker.

Certainly, "when he was appointed to secure ground and to establish a permanent chapel in Philadelphia he was quite familiar with the city and the temper and spirit of the colonists. He so identified himself with the town that he always claimed to be a citizen of Philadelphia," Eugene B. Gallagher wrote.[164] In particular, Fr. Greaton got along well with Quakers. Maybe it was the disguise.

According to author Eleanor Donnelly, Fr. Greaton was wearing his Quaker getup when he approached a wealthy matron not long after he arrived in Philadelphia. He had been told she was Catholic, and took the chance of revealing himself to her as a Jesuit. She was reportedly so excited to see a real live priest that "she went through the neighborhood, and invited her Catholic acquaintances to come and see a Catholic priest in her house. This was soon filled with Catholics, for the most part Germans."[165]

Fr. Greaton quickly got down to business. He began a subscription on the spot to raise funds for a permanent church. The money he collected helped purchase a rectangular property east of Fourth Street and bordered on the north and south by Walnut Street and Willings Alley.

On that site, in 1731, Fr. Greaton constructed a two-story "Jesuit mansion."[166] He lived there, and began celebrating Mass in his house. He was allowed to offer Mass in his residence, but the home he erected was simply camouflage. He had more building to do.

Fr. Greaton immediately began work on a chapel, which was attached to his home "like an out-kitchen."

"It was only a room eighteen feet by twenty-two," wrote Donnelly, "whose modest proportions might have recalled the living-room of the Holy Family at Nazareth, or the Cenacle of the Apostles at Jerusalem."[167]

---

[164] Gallagher, "Two Hundred and Fifty Years Ago," 1.
[165] Eleanor C. Donnelly, *A Memoir of Father Felix Joseph Barbelin, S.J.* (New York: Christian Press Association, 1886), 91.
[166] Gallagher, "Two Hundred and Fifty Years Ago," 4.
[167] Donnelly, *A Memoir of Father Barbelin*, 93.

Another writer described it as "a little church with a chimney instead of a cross."[168]

According to Donnelly's book, the first Mass was said in this tiny chapel in February 1732. There were probably fewer than a dozen worshippers present.

The "modest proportions" and "out-kitchen" disguise of the chapel were no accident. There were immediate complaints to the government about the rumored "popish chapel." By 1734, Lt. Gov. Patrick Gordon was reporting the church to the Provincial Council.

"He had no small concern to hear that a house lately built in Walnut Street was set apart for the exercise of the Catholic religion; it is commonly called the Romish chapel, where several persons, he understands, report on Sundays to hear Mass openly celebrated by a Popish priest," the report read in part.

The council did its homework and discovered that since Queen Anne had approved William Penn's "Charter of Liberties and Privileges," this trumped previous anti-Catholic laws in England. A victorious Fr. Greaton responded in language that sounds a lot like the defiant colonists four decades later. (Richard Henry Lee would copy the wording, in fact, in his June 1776 resolution urging Congress to officially break free from Great Britain.)

"We are, and of right ought to be, free and independent of all civil authority, retarding, restricting or debarring religion," Fr. Greaton declared. "It is not toleration we claim. It is freedom we demand and will maintain."[169]

That didn't keep Old St. Joseph's free from harassment. Legend has it Benjamin Franklin himself advised Fr. Greaton to keep the entrance of the chapel inconspicuous and to install an iron gate in front.

It was good counsel. At least twice, the chapel was attacked by Protestant mobs, and Quakers apparently came to the rescue. During Britain's

---

[168] Sr. Blanche Marie, "The Catholic Church in Colonial Pennsylvania," *Pennsylvania History: A Journal of Mid-Atlantic Studies* 3, no. 4 (October 1936): 248, https:// www.jstor.org/stable/27766216.

[169] Gallagher, "Two Hundred and Fifty Years Ago," 6–7.

war with Catholic Spain in 1740, "a mob of fanatical Presbyterians, with axes in their hands," planned "to destroy a Catholic chapel. Ten or twelve Quakers stopped them, exhorted them and they dispersed without effecting their design."[170]

Then, in July 1755, "when the French and Indians inflicted such a terrible defeat upon General Braddock at Fort Duquesne and the remnants of his army, crushed and bleeding, staggered into Philadelphia, an angry mob gathered to destroy the church, and only by the heroic, persistent efforts of the Quakers, was it finally persuaded to desist."[171]

The little church, though, continued to grow. By 1757, Greaton's successor, the Jesuit Fr. Robert Harding, S.J., built a larger chapel. It measured a spacious forty by sixty feet, but still wasn't large enough to keep up with the increase in parishioners. By that point, there were 378 members of the congregation. That number probably included some of the Acadian refugees from Canada who had made their way south after being forcibly relocated by the British.

The new chapel of Old St. Joseph's was not only too small, its aesthetics apparently left something to be desired.

"The Church was badly lighted and worse ventilated," wrote a parishioner of the time. "The few windows in the north and south walls merely afforded what is termed 'a dim religious light.' Transgressors who sought religious grace, found in that little Chapel naught to distract their minds or their eyes, in the way of ornamental art or gaudy show."[172]

In its third iteration, Old St. Joseph's became a little less spartan. The church was rebuilt yet again in 1838, and refurbished in 1886. If you find the entrance in Willings Alley and make your way inside, you'll see Old St. Joseph's as it must have looked around the time of those renovations.

---

[170] Martin I. J. Griffin, "Rev. Joseph Greaton, S.J.: Planter of the Faith in Philadelphia and Founder of Old St. Joseph's Chapel," *American Catholic Historical Researches* 16, no. 2 (April 1899): 94–95.

[171] "Two Milestones in Jesuit History," *Woodstock Letters* 62, no. 2 (June 1933), 295–296, Jesuit Online Library, https://jesuitonlinelibrary.bc.edu/?a=d&d =wlet19330601-01.2.9.

[172] Donnelly, *A Memoir of Father Barbelin*, 90.

The style is described as "Greek Revival merging into Victorian." The pale yellow walls and the yellow-and-gold mosaic windows—a simple, yet modest, alternative to more intricate stained glass—project warmth. Look above and you'll see an eighteen-foot-round painting titled *The Apotheosis of St. Joseph*, by the Italian artist Filippo Costaggini, who is also responsible for the frescoes in the U.S. Capitol Rotunda. Look behind you, on the rear wall, and you'll find the letter George Washington wrote to American Catholics in 1790, after his election as the nation's first president.

Jesuit fathers still offer Mass, just as they did close to three centuries ago. Perhaps all twelve of the people who gathered there for the daily Mass one summer afternoon not long ago, knew they were doing so in the place "that upheld the right of Catholics to free and open worship at a time where nowhere else under the British flag was it permitted—not even in London itself."[173]

Or maybe they didn't. Maybe they had no idea that not far away from this chapel, a Jesuit priest in disguise had once asked a wealthy old woman, "Have the Catholics a Church?"[174]

When the lady answered, "No, they have none," the priest began taking steps—careful, circumspect, yet also bold and brave—to fix that problem. And the rest is history: not just of the Catholic Church, but of America as well.

3

When St. Joseph's expanded in 1757, it needed more room for the dead, as well as the living. Colonial Catholics were permitted to own land for a cemetery, and it was this loophole that allowed Fr. Robert Harding to buy a plot of land that would eventually house a larger church.

Harding bought a piece of property near Old. St. Joseph's, between Fourth and Fifth streets. In a neat little piece of historical irony, he

---

[173] Martin I. J. Griffin, "Old St. Joseph's Philadelphia, Birthplace of Religious Freedom," *American Catholic Historical Researches* 4, no. 3 (July 1908): 284–288, https://www.jstor.org/ stable/44374760.

[174] Donnelly, *A Memoir of Father Barbelin*, 90.

purchased it from Joseph Shippen, the father of Peggy Shippen — who would later marry the Catholic-despising Benedict Arnold.

The cemetery was apparently founded in 1759. And after taking two subscriptions to raise money, a new church was opened next to the graveyard in 1763. Old St. Mary's then became the "Sunday church" in Philadelphia, thanks to its expanded seating. Old St. Joseph's, where the priests lived, served as the site for smaller daily Masses.

The new church would also be visited by even more colonial luminaries than St. Joseph's. It was Old St. Mary's that future president John Adams referred to in a famous 1774 letter to his wife, Abigail. That was where Adams marveled, condescendingly, "Here is everything that can lay hold of eye, ear, and imagination, everything which can charm and bewitch the simple and ignorant, I wonder how Luther ever broke the spell."

Adams was one of many members of the Continental Congress who visited Old St. Mary's. George Washington also came to Mass twice — once in 1774 with Adams at the same vespers service mentioned above, and once again during the Constitutional Convention. We have no record of what he thought of the Mass, however, beyond his notation that he visited a "Romish Church."

On the other hand, we know exactly what the traitorous Benedict Arnold felt about the Mass he attended at Old St. Mary's, a requiem in May 1780 for Don Juan De Miralles, "'a Spanish gentleman of distinction' known as the Spanish agent."

In the recruiting letter Arnold addressed to members of the Continental Army after his treachery was revealed, he tried to win patriots back to the Crown by playing on anti-Catholicism.

"Do you know that the eye which guides this pen lately saw your mean and profligate Congress at mass for the soul of a Roman Catholic in Purgatory," Arnold demanded in his October 1780 letter, "and participating in the rites of a Church, against whose antichristian corruptions your pious ancestors would have witnessed with their blood."[175]

---

[175] Griffin, *Catholics and the American Revolution*, vol. 1, 257.

Nevertheless, Old St. Mary's was the site of two memorable celebrations during the war. One was on July 4, 1779, and marked the third anniversary of the Declaration of Independence.

"It is the first ceremony of the kind in the thirteen States," wrote Conrad Alexandre Gérard de Rayneval, France's American representative, "and it is thought that the éclat of it will have a beneficial effect on the Catholics, many of whom are suspected of not being very much attached to the American cause. My Chaplain delivered a short address which has obtained general approbation, and which Congress has demanded for publication."[176]

That chaplain was Abbé Seraphin Bandol, one of a hundred French priests who served with the military. A number of congressmen and state officials were present and joined in singing the "Te Deum."

An even larger gathering occurred two years later after the patriot forces — with the assistance of the French — trapped Cornwallis at Yorktown and essentially ended the Revolution.

On Sunday, November 4, 1781, just two weeks after that military triumph, Old St. Mary's was packed with French and American glitterati. The world had turned upside down, and it was time to thank the God who had made it possible. As author Eleanor Donnelly wrote, "The Church, which was filled to its utmost capacity, was brilliantly illuminated, the altar especially was ablaze with lights, and was decked with its richest ornaments. The French Ambassador invited Congress to be present, and his invitation was gladly accepted; and besides Congress, which attended in a body, headed by their President, Hon. Thomas McKean, the most distinguished inhabitants, military and civil, were likewise present."[177]

When trying to find a place friendly to the many French Catholics in attendance, there wasn't a lot of choice. The only other chapel in the colonies where a public Mass could be celebrated was Old St. Joseph's, located right up the street, and it wasn't big enough to hold such a crowd.

---

[176] Martin I. J. Griffin, "The Te Deum at St. Mary's, Philadelphia, July 4th, 1779," *American Catholic Historical Researches* 3, no. 4 (October 1907): 318, https://www.jstor.org/stable/ 44374700.

[177] Donnelly, *A Memoir of Father Barbelin*, 115.

Liberty's Lions

The theme was "God's Strange Providence." And what, asked Abbé Bandol, who once again gave the homily, could have been more strangely provident than the new friendships between America and France, and between Protestants and Catholics?

"Who, but he, in whose hands are the hearts of men, could inspire the allied troops with the friendships, the confidence, the tenderness of brothers?" he inquired. "How is it that two nations once divided, jealous, inimical, and nursed in reciprocal prejudices, are now become so closely united, as to form but one?" It wasn't the politicians and it wasn't the generals who did it, the abbé continued: it was the divine will.[178]

As the enormity of the American victory set in, the people in the pews had to acknowledge, as author Robert Emmett Curran, puts it, that "there was no longer an inherent conflict between being a good Catholic and a good citizen."[179]

On the feast of St. Bonaventure recently, a half-dozen worshippers gathered in the St. Mary's chapel for the early Mass. In the early morning, the interior of the church was dim and cool. The previous night's shadows still lurked amidst the dark-wood pews, beneath a deep-blue ceiling flecked with tiny gilt stars.

The priest entered, said a few words, then exited abruptly. His headset microphone wasn't working. In the lull, it was hard not to think about the men who offered Mass here for the founders—men such as Abbé Bandol—trying to lift their voices above the mumbling and creaking from the pews.

Somehow, the abbé and his fellow priests made themselves heard—not just in this church, but throughout an emerging nation.

4

It's when you step outside Old St. Mary's, however, that you really have a chance to appreciate the Catholic contribution to the Revolution. To

[178] Griffin, "The Te Deum," 311.
[179] Curran, *Papist Devils*, 264.

the right of the church is the cemetery that was part of the reason Old St. Mary's was constructed.

"One can go to St. Mary's graveyard, and, compiling the history of those whose ashes make the very ground you tread upon, write the history of our country," the Philadelphia Catholic historian Martin Griffin wrote. "The very sun, in its beyond a century's shining upon the old church, has never beamed more brilliantly [than] in the lives of many who are buried within the consecrated earth of the old churchyard."[180]

On this brilliant summer morning, Griffin's words seem exactly right. Three of the lives he mentions, in particular, are worth examining. All three were military heroes of the American Revolution. And all three were native Irishmen.

That last point is noteworthy, since Philadelphia's Catholic population was still predominantly German at the time. Yet Irish Catholics, who began emigrating to Philadelphia in 1719, would have had special reasons to join the patriot cause.

Most of them were born less than a hundred years after Oliver Cromwell's brutal invasion of Ireland, which stripped Catholics of their land and forced thousands—including children—into exile. Yet by the time these Irishmen appeared on the scene, repression of Catholics had been the norm for so long in Ireland that hardly anyone could remember any different. Catholics couldn't vote, have a profession, hold office, or own land. Priests were barred from the country on penalty of death. Catholic farmers could keep only a third of their annual harvests, and even speaking Gaelic was banned.

"If it had been possible to pass a law barring the sun from shining on Irish Catholics," author Tim McGrath jokes, "the Protestant Parliament would gladly have done so."[181]

---

[180] Martin I. J. Griffin, "The Story of St. Mary's," *American Catholic Historical Researches* 10, no. 1 (January 1893): 2.

[181] Tim McGrath, *John Barry: An American Hero in the Age of Sail* (Yardley, PA: Westholme, 2011), 5.

Many of those Catholics found their way to America. In Pennsylvania, "the vast majority of Catholic patriots were of Irish origin," writes Robert Emmett Curran. Partly, he contended, this was because the Irish Catholics were more urban. German Catholics were more isolated geographically, and therefore politically. Located in Pennsylvania's farm country, far from military targets like Philadelphia, they were less likely to encounter marauding British troops.

Martin Griffin's research suggested that about 300 Irish Catholics from Pennsylvania served in Pennsylvania's military during the Revolution. Considering the total number of Catholics in the colony could not have been much more than 1,500 at the time, it's an impressive percentage.

Some of them attended Mass here at Old St. Mary's. Some — including the three men we'll meet next — rest here still.

5

When, exactly, the churchyard at Old St. Mary's was officially opened is a matter of some debate. The first burial appears to have been an infant named Ann White. She was the daughter of a local merchant, James White, who was also one of the trustees in the land purchase. Ann White died in 1759 — the year that signs outside the cemetery claim the graveyard was founded.

That isn't the only bit of uncertainty among these monuments. If you stroll midway through the burial ground, you'll encounter a rectangular marble slab with lots of writing chiseled into it. The names are mostly members of the Maitland family of Philadelphia. You have to scan down the stone about two-thirds of the way before you find the name Thomas Fitzsimons.

The only clue that this grave marks the resting place of an historic figure is the small brass-edged plaque to the right. There, in 1937, the Pennsylvania Constitution Commemoration Committee commemorated, on the 150th anniversary of the Constitution, the burial site of one of its two Catholic signers.

Thomas Fitzsimons is listed with his wife, Catherine, and his sister Ann, who married into the Maitland family. There's still much we don't know about his beginnings. Most people believe he was born in Ireland in 1741, but where is less clear: Clare, Belfast, Wicklow, and Limerick are among the possibilities.

Neither is it sure when he and other family members came to America. There are records of a Philadelphia merchant named Thomas Fitzsimons Sr., who died in 1760. Along with Thomas Fitzsimons Jr., he contributed to the fund to buy the St. Mary's churchyard. Apparently, both father and son helped buy this land.

The obscurity surrounding Fitzsimons extends to his last name, commonly spelled a half-dozen different ways, including "Fitz Simons," "FitzSimons," "FitzSimmons," and "Fitzsimmons." It sometimes appears in multiple versions in the same document. And the questions about him are even present in one of the most famous artworks in America.

If you've ever visited the U.S. Capitol, you've probably seen Howard Chandler Christy's large oil painting, *Scene at the Signing of the Constitution of the United States*. It was unveiled in 1940, and in it you can view the faces of almost all the thirty-nine delegates to the Constitutional Convention.

But you can't see Thomas Fitzsimons — because in his research, Christy was unable to locate a picture of him. So his face is obscured by the arm of Pierce Butler of South Carolina, whose face is, in turn, blocked by the arm of his fellow South Carolinian, Charles Pinckney.

It wasn't until 1965 that a portrait of Fitzsimons was discovered. The artist is believed to have been Gilbert Stuart, who painted so many of the founders. The picture dates from the early nineteenth century, when Fitzsimons would have been about sixty years old. It shows a distinguished-looking man in a quiet, dark coat, his gray hair swept back.

There's a bronze statue of Fitzsimons a few streets over, in the National Constitution Center, that strikes a similar attitude. There, Fitzsimons cradles his chin with his right hand, looking down, apparently deep in thought.

He might have been thinking about money. Fitzsimons was a merchant — perhaps like his father before him — and it was his financial expertise more than his military contribution that made him indispensable to the new republic. Alexander Hamilton gets most of the credit for the founding of a national bank and for having the national government assume public debts, but it seems certain he got not just support, but also advice, from Fitzsimons.

It was business that got him involved in the patriot cause. Some records suggest he first worked as a clerk in a countinghouse. He married Catherine Meade in 1763, and that year he joined the business of his two brothers-in-law, Garrett and George Meade.

The Meades were also Catholics of Irish descent. Their father, Robert, was a merchant who emigrated to Philadelphia and also spent time in the Caribbean. Robert Meade's children were educated in Barbados, and it was hardly a surprise that the Meade brothers' new business included imports from the West Indies: rum, sugar, and slaves.

The Meades and Fitzsimons were probably part of the protests against the Stamp Act that took place in Philadelphia during October 1765. In fact, the boycott of British goods by Philadelphia merchants might be overlooked historically: it could be called "the first pledge of honor in the record of American Independence."[182]

It was Philadelphia merchants, and their threat in the fall of 1773 to tar and feather captains who unloaded East India tea in their port, who inspired the Boston Tea Party that December. After the British closed the port of Boston in response, local businessmen went on high alert. If it could happen in Boston, then why not in Philadelphia?

When Paul Revere rode into the city to spread that urgent news in May 1774, he delivered it at the newly constructed City Tavern, on Philadelphia's east side. The tavern still stands today, and despite its name, it was far more than a local ale joint. It had five levels, three dining rooms, and "the second-largest ballroom in the New World."

A group of as many as three hundred prominent Philadelphians hurriedly gathered there the next day, to draft an indignant response to send back with Revere. Thomas Fitzsimons was one of the most important of those men. Despite his Catholicism, he was part of the

---

[182] Griffin, "Rev. Joseph Greaton, S.J.,"103.

inner circle of fifty or sixty merchants who were decision-makers in America's largest city.

He had developed a reputation not just as a fair and levelheaded businessman but also as one who gave back to his community. In 1771, he'd been named vice president of a new group, the Friendly Sons of St. Patrick. Formed, appropriately enough, on St. Patrick's Day, it became a powerful fraternal organization, and was certainly a political stepping-stone. But it had a noble goal: to help migrants from Ireland, who often arrived in America with little more than the clothes on their backs.

Fitzsimons's election to Pennsylvania's Committee of Correspondence in 1774 was more significant. He became the first Catholic elected to public office in the colony. That was despite the "test oath" denying transubstantiation that officeholders in Pennsylvania were required to take. It was an oath "no Catholic could take,"[183] and apparently Fitzsimons did not.

Along with Charles Carroll of Carrollton's selection to the Maryland Committee of Correspondence, Fitzimons's election showed colonial patriots officially putting the cause of liberty ahead of anti-Catholicism. And it was an important post: the committees were a sort of "shadow government" among patriots, offering them the chance to communicate between colonies.

The result of that communication was the decision to convene the First Continental Congress. It met that September in Philadelphia's Carpenter Hall—just a block or two down South Fourth Street from Old St. Mary's.

Fitzsimons was not one of the Pennsylvania delegates, so he missed some of the unpleasantness when the Congress unleashed its attack on Catholicism following the Quebec Act. But he might have escorted George Washington to a Mass at Old St. Mary's that fall.

[183] Martin I. J. Griffin, *Thomas FitzSimons: Pennsylvania's Catholic Signer of the Constitution of the United States* (Philadelphia: Press of the American Catholic Historical Researches, 1887), 52.

Washington's diary entry of October 9, 1774, notes that "led by cutiosity [sic] and good company he attended the Romish Church." Martin Griffin asked, "Whom more likely to have been the 'good company' to 'lead' to our church than Thomas FitzSimons, the only Catholic then in official prominence, and one of the conveners of the Congress Washington was attending."[184]

Six months after that Mass, a colonial militiaman fired the shot heard round the world at Concord's North Bridge, and America was at war. Much has been written about the inexperience of the colonial army, and Thomas Fitzsimons was certainly a perfect example of a patriot soldier who had to learn on the job. He is also, however, an example of something less noticed: a successful local businessman who was willing to use his connections—and risk his livelihood—for freedom.

Because Pennsylvania was founded by Quakers, who were pacifists, there was no state militia. So "the local Patriots had to organize a military force from the ground up by forming volunteer units, called "Associators." Thanks to his wealth and wide-ranging connections in the community, Fitzsimons contributed significantly to this speedy mobilization," wrote Robert K. Wright Jr. and Morris J. MacGregor Jr. in *Soldier-Statesmen of the Constitution.*

"When Philadelphia's contingent of infantry (today's 111th Infantry, Pennsylvania Army National Guard) was organized, Fitzsimons, as a captain, raised and commanded a company in Colonel John Cadwalader's 3d Battalion."[185]

While the British were attacking New York City in the summer of 1776, Fitzsimons's troops were helping guard the New Jersey shoreline. That winter, when the British staged a surprise invasion of New Jersey, Fitzsimons and his company covered George Washington's retreat to the Pennsylvania side of the Delaware River.

[184] Griffin, *Thomas FitzSimons*, 52.

[185] Robert K. Wright and Morris J. MacGregor, *Soldier-Statesmen of the Constitution* (Washington, DC: Center of Military History, U.S. Army: 2007), 88–89.

The conditions were hostile, and the poorly trained, poorly equipped troops suffered as autumn turned into winter. Yet Fitzsimons did his best to mitigate the hardships. Just before Christmas, he traveled to Bristol, Pennsylvania, to seek a discharge for the son of Sergeant William Young, who was "exceedingly unwell," and another sick soldier. The boy's grateful father wrote in his diary, "Our Captain very kind to our men."[186]

On Christmas night, Washington surprised drunken Hessian troops at the Battle of Trenton, winning a legendary victory. Fitzsimons's company did not take part in the famed crossing of the Delaware. Yet his kindness was once again recorded: there is a diary entry from a local woman who recalled that his well-behaved soldiers "stopped to bless and thank me for the food I had sent them."[187]

Fitzsimons left active duty in the army at the end of January 1777. His next job was on a board that oversaw the piecemeal Pennsylvania navy. It was an important task: the little fleet of privateers was charged with safeguarding the critical port of Philadelphia, as well as Delaware Bay. The makeshift defenses he helped create held for months, until the British captured Philadelphia that fall. But the experience taught him a larger lesson.

According to *Soldier-Statesmen of the Constitution*, "With Philadelphia, along with his home and business, in enemy hands, Fitzsimons came to understand that no matter how well organized and defended one state might be, its safety depended ultimately on the united strength of all the states."[188]

That led Fitzsimons, who became a Federalist, to insist on a strong national government. Even before the war ended, he joined forces with wealthy Pennsylvania merchant and investor Robert Morris. Together, they found ways to fund the army and navy, even when that meant both men had to use their own money to do it. Their frustrations in dealing with the individual colonies convinced them of the need for the national banking system proposed by Alexander Hamilton.

---

[186] Griffin, *Thomas FitzSimons*, 56.

[187] Griffin, *Thomas FitzSimons*, 58.

[188] Wright and MacGregor, *Soldier-Statesmen of the Constitution*, 90.

Naturally, Fitzsimons also became a proponent of dumping the ineffective Articles of Confederation for a new national constitution. He was elected to represent Pennsylvania at the Constitutional Convention in 1787, and became one of two Catholics to sign the document. But his most important—and surprising—role might have been in getting his state to ratify the constitution, something we'll read about later in this chapter. (During the convention, he also, most likely, escorted George Washington to Mass again at Old St. Mary's.)

Most of Fitzsimons's contributions to the convention, and later in Congress, dealt with financial policy. Fisher Ames, a Massachusetts congressman who disliked the Irish, described Fitzsimons in a revealing little sketch: "He is supposed to understand trade, and he assumes weight in such matters. He is plausible though not overly civil; is artful, has a glaring eye, a down look, speaks low and with an apparent candor and coolness."[189]

Something worth noting about Fitzsimons's financial views is that he was a supporter of protective tariffs. While tariffs are often a dirty word in today's free-trading world, Fitzsimons advocated them to secure American jobs and promote fairness. He wanted to give "our working-men a competitive chance in supplying the needs of our people." And he insisted that the first principle of taxation "is that the weight of the taxes fall not too heavily in the first instance upon any particular part of the community."[190]

Populist sentiments like these helped keep Fitzsimons well-liked. That was not, however, his principal concern. When he planned to endorse Gen. Arthur St. Clair for governor of Pennsylvania in 1790, he was advised St. Clair was almost certain to be defeated by his popular fellow general, Thomas Mifflin.

"I conceive it to be a duty to contend for what is right," Fitzsimons replied, "be the issue as it may."[191]

---

[189] Richard J. Purcell, "Thomas Fitzsimons: Framer of the American Constitution," *Studies* 27, no. 106 (June 1938): 285, http://www.jstor.org/stable/30097546.

[190] Griffin, *Thomas FitzSimons*, 68.

[191] Griffin, *Thomas FitzSimons*, 95.

He soon got a chance to apply those noble sentiments to his own political career. In 1794, Fitzsimons was narrowly defeated in the congressional election by John Swanwick. Swanwick was not a Catholic but did hold a pew at Old St. Mary's and was a friend of the "priest on horseback," Fr. Ferdinand Farmer. He was also a foe of Hamilton's national bank.

Fitzsimons was turned out of office by just fifty-eight votes. Yet the loss, his former friend James Madison exulted in a letter to Thomas Jefferson, was a "stunning change for the aristocracy."[192] By "aristocracy," Madison meant the Federalist Party, which was beginning to implode during George Washington's second term. Fitzsimons was a high-profile Federalist scalp; more would follow as Jefferson began his march to the presidency.

There were plenty of other things to keep Fitzsimons busy. Since 1781, he had been a director of the Bank of America, which he helped found. He served as president of Philadelphia's chamber of commerce and as a trustee of the University of Pennsylvania and helped found the Insurance Company of North America.

But as proof of the old saying that "no good deed goes unpunished," Fitzsimons would be undone trying to help his old friend Robert Morris. The "financier of the Revolution" had invested heavily in land—too heavily, as it turned out. Fitzsimons loaned Morris more than $150,000 to cover his debts, but Morris could not repay him. Fitzsimons consequently went bankrupt, and his only consolation was that it could have been worse: Morris, once the richest man in Philadelphia, spent three years in debtors' prison.

In an 1806 letter to Bishop John Carroll, Fitzsimons confessed, "The period which has elapsed since we last parted has not been a pleasant one. Many unpleasant things have occurred, but they are now passed, and I know your kindness will be gratified to know that we are comfortably situated." He and his wife, Catherine, had downsized to a modest home on Arch Street, a mile or two from Old St. Mary's. But he took care to

---

[192] Griffin, *Thomas FitzSimons*, 100.

mention the church to the bishop: "Your friends at St. Mary's acquit themselves most highly."[193]

Catherine died of consumption in 1810 after a long illness. During her decline, Fitzsimons wrote to Carroll, "You may therefore judge what my situation is, with this connection of forty-five years. Whenever that separation shall take place I am left without a reed to lean on." He looked forward to "the more consoling hope of a meeting hereafter that is even denied us here."[194]

In the end, he lived little more than a year after her passing. Bishop Michael Egan of Philadelphia was a frequent guest at the little house on Arch Street during Fitzsimons's final illness. After one of those visits, he wrote to Archbishop Carroll: "Mr. FitzSimons is seriously indisposed. I often visit him and have spoken to him on the subject that ought to interest him the most. He thanks me and promises he will when he gets better."[195]

As the bishop predicted, however, he did not improve, and died at age seventy on August 26, 1811. What was it he promised Bishop Egan he would do when he got better? We don't know. His last years were filled with reversals, many of them public. Perhaps it was related to one of those situations; perhaps it was personal.

Everyone knew of Fitzsimons's disappointments. His obituary read in part, "He possessed an uncommon firmness of mind upon all occasions except one, and that was when his friends solicited favors from him."[196] The favors he granted the new republic, however, are even now being repaid.

6

Who first came up with the term "The United States of America"? For a long time, the answer baffled historians.

[193] Griffin, *Thomas FitzSimons*, 106.
[194] Griffin, *Thomas FitzSimons*, 107.
[195] Griffin, *Thomas FitzSimons*, 110.
[196] Griffin, *Thomas FitzSimons*, 110.

Was it George Washington? Thomas Jefferson? Benjamin Franklin? Thomas Paine?

Legendary *New York Times* columnist William Safire dug into the mystery in 1998 but didn't produce a definitive conclusion. It wasn't until 2013 that Byron DeLear, writing in the *Christian Science Monitor*, named the creator—who had been mentioned in a 1951 book by historian Curtis P. Nettels, but apparently forgotten.

The answer to the question is "none of the above." But you can find it on a small marble stone in St. Mary's churchyard, placed there by a Knights of Columbus chapter.

Brig. Gen. Stephen Moylan, who is honored with this marker, may be best remembered as George Washington's assistant during the American Revolution. Yet, in a letter written on January 2, 1776, he put the immortal phrase "The United States of America" in print for the very first time.

The modest context of the words probably has something to do with the letter's obscurity. Moylan wrote to Gen. Joseph Reed, Washington's aide-de-camp, that "I should like vastly to go with full and ample powers from the United States of America to Spain."[197]

It's not exactly the Declaration of Independence, is it? Instead, it's a very practical request: Moylan apparently had business contacts in Spain that could have helped the colonists. And, as DeLear also pointed out, it seems unlikely Moylan would have used the phrase if he hadn't heard it somewhere else first: namely, from his boss, George Washington.

But let's give Moylan the glory here. It's a deserved contrast to the obscurity in which he still lingers. Without a single surviving portrait of him, we have to use our imaginations to fill in around his distinguished record of service.

Moylan was born in Cork in 1737, the son of a merchant and the Countess of Limerick. It was a well-off, and devoutly Catholic, family.

---

[197] Byron DeLear, "Who Coined 'United States of America'? Mystery Might Have Intriguing Answer," *Christian Science Monitor*, July 4, 2013, https://www.csmonitor.com/USA/Politics/2013/0704/Who-coined-United-States-of-America-Mystery-might-have-intriguing-answer.

Moylan's two sisters took vows as Ursuline nuns, and his brother, Francis, became the bishop of Cork.

However, the penal laws in Ireland at the time made it necessary to educate the boys abroad. So Stephen and Francis were sent out of Ireland to school—possibly in Lisbon, Portugal, which is where Stephen entered the family shipping business.

It's not clear exactly when Stephen came to the colonies. Years later, a visiting French nobleman described him as a "gallant and intelligent man who had lived long in Europe and has traveled through the greatest part of America."[198] But in 1768, at age thirty, Moylan had certainly settled in Philadelphia. Over the next few years, he became the owner or part-owner of several ships, and was evidently a success in the import and export trade.

Like his fellow Catholic Thomas Fitzsimons, Moylan used his business connections to overcome prejudice against his faith. The two men crossed paths frequently in Philadelphia. In fact, Moylan became the president of the Friendly Sons of St. Patrick, the same fraternal group in which Fitzsimons served. It was primarily made up of "prosperous merchants,"[199] many of whom were involved in trade with Europe and the West Indies. But besides Moylan and Fitzsimons, merchant George Meade was the only other Catholic.

Groups like the Friendly Sons were a unifying force, then, among Philadelphia Protestants and Catholics. So were the increasingly restrictive British acts that threatened local businessmen. There was anger over the closure of Boston Harbor after the city's famous Tea Party. The fear that the port of Philadelphia might be shut down next turned merchants of both faiths into patriots.

[198] Frank Monaghan, "Stephen Moylan in the American Revolution." *Studies* 19, no. 75 (September): 486, https://www.jstor.org/stable/30094651.
[199] "Colonel Stephen Moylan: 2nd Quartermaster School Commandant, June 1776–September 1776," U.S. Army Quartermaster Corps, https://quartermaster.army.mil/bios/previous-qm-generals/quartermaster_general_bio-moylan.html.

We aren't sure when Moylan made up his mind about the colonial cause, but by early 1776, he was chomping at the bit for a full-fledged revolution.

"Shall we never leave off debating and boldly declare Independence?" he wrote, exasperated, to Joseph Reed. "That and that only will make us act with spirit and vigour. The bulk of the people will not be against it—but the few and timid always will,—but what can be expected of a contrary conduct? Can it be supposed possible that a reconciliation will take place after the loss of blood, cities and treasure already suffered, but the war must come to every man's home before he will think of his neighbour's losses."[200]

By this time, Moylan had already joined the Continental Army. He had impressed John Dickinson, a Philadelphia solicitor and future Founding Father, who recommended him to General Washington. Washington obliged, and named Moylan the army's muster-master general.

Moylan's title might sound strange to those outside the military. He wasn't actually a general—that term simply meant that his job applied to the entire army. Keeping muster required him to report "how many men were really available, and what was the condition of their equipment and training."[201] That task was anything but simple—especially for an army so disorganized.

Surveying the ragtag collection of recruits in August 1775, just days before Moylan joined, Gen. Joseph Reed wrote, "We heard, and we find it true, that the Army was a disorder and confusion, that the Officers were not only ignorant and litigious but scandalously disobedient, and in the last action of them proved such notorious cowards that the very existence of the army, and consequently the salvation of America, depended upon an immediate reform."[202]

---

[200] Monaghan, "Stephen Moylan in the American Revolution," 482–483.
[201] Joseph F. X. McCarthy, "Stephen Moylan: An American Military Career," Peter & Lynne's Place, http://www.pmoylan.org/pages/family/KenMoylan/Stephen_Moylan.html.
[202] Martin I. J. Griffin, "Stephen Moylan: Muster-Master General ...," *American Catholic Historical Researches*, 5, no. 2 (April 1909): 105, https://www.jstor.org/stable/44374763.

Moylan himself observed that "the deficiency of public spirit in this country is much more than I could possibly have an idea of."[203] Yet he slowly helped bring some of that needed reform to the army.

His expertise was also needed to help outfit the ships in America's independent navy of privateers and prepare them for war. In this case, "war" didn't usually mean attacking British warships. Instead, the privateers more often made pirate raids on unarmed shipping vessels, helping the colonists capture necessary food, arms, and ammunition.

However, when the crew of one ship was captured, and the captain threw his papers overboard, Moylan counseled mercy. "In any other war he would suffer death for such an action, but we must show him and all such who fall into our hands that Americans are humane as well as brave," he wrote to the captain of the American vessel in December 1775. "You will, therefore, treat the prisoners with all possible tenderness."[204] Once the war began, he pleaded for similar mercy for a Quaker physician who had treated both American and British soldiers.[205]

Moylan had been filling in as Washington's secretary and right-hand man when Reed was absent. He was officially promoted to aide-de-camp in March 1776. The general needed "a good many writers" to handle his correspondence, and Moylan was one of the most trusted.

Just three months later, Moylan's rise continued. He was given the rank of colonel and appointed by the Continental Congress to the post of quartermaster general. His job was to keep the entire Continental Army supplied.

That was an almost impossible duty, made more difficult by the doubts that were already beginning to surface about Washington's leadership. Following complaints about the condition of the army in the fall of 1776, Moylan was pressured to resign as quartermaster. He was replaced by Gen. Thomas Mifflin, who had done the job before — and was also no friend of Washington.

[203] Griffin, "Stephen Moylan," 119.
[204] Griffin, "Stephen Moylan," 121.
[205] Griffin, "Stephen Moylan," 149.

Although the army's problems were largely due to lack of money, Moylan fell on the sword in a long, humble letter of explanation to Congress. He declined the offer to lead his own battalion and instead pledged to serve as a volunteer. "I can assure the Congress, that I am very willing to Sacrifice my Life, when Calld upon," he wrote, "in the glorious Cause which from the principle, I have voluntarily engaged in."[206]

He did keep volunteering with Washington, but Moylan soon found his place on horseback. In January 1777 he was given command of a light horse regiment. It was nicknamed "Moylan's Horse," and it immediately helped the Continental Army win the Battle of Princeton. Moylan's dragoons followed up Washington's surprise attack, chasing and harassing the retreating British troops.

In a letter to financier Robert Morris, Moylan was still gushing about the feeling "we all enjoyed when pursuing the flying enemy. It is unutterable—inexpressible. I know I never felt so much like one of Homer's Deities before. We trod on air—it was a glorious day."[207] To sow more confusion and fear among the enemy, members of the Horse took to wearing red coats from British soldiers captured at Saratoga, until Washington insisted this was alarming too many civilians.

Moylan would soon have a rival: the Polish horseman Casimir Pulaski, whom we'll read about in chapter 6. The two were both strong-willed and frequently feuded at Valley Forge before Pulaski departed to start his own legion. That left Moylan to command the army's cavalry.

In the middle of the war, Moylan himself was conquered—by love. In a postscript of a 1778 letter to Washington, he wrote that he was engaged to Mary Ricketts Van Horne, the daughter of a New Jersey militia commander.

The description of Moylan at the time might be as good a picture of him as we're likely to get, and he sounds a bit like a dandy. His new bride, we're told, was fascinated by his "merry appearance, the latter enhanced by his red breeches, bright green coat and bear skin hat." That

---

[206] Griffin, "Stephen Moylan," 137.
[207] Griffin, "Stephen Moylan," 144.

charming ensemble was apparently "too great for the Middlebrook beauty to withstand,"[208] and they were married at Trenton that October. They had two daughters; Thomas Fitzsimons was one of the godparents when the oldest, Maria, was baptized at Old St. Mary's years later.

Despite the perpetual difficulties of finding good men and good horses, Moylan and his dragoons saw action in some of the Revolution's most memorable battles — from the near disaster at Monmouth in 1778 to the climactic Battle of Yorktown in 1781. In the long lull that followed Cornwallis's surrender, the cavalry was reabsorbed into the army, but Moylan was promoted to brigadier general.

He returned to Philadelphia after the war. There he lived quietly until his death in April 1811, serving as Pennsylvania's commissioner of loans and spending time on his farm in Chester County. However, his four-story brick home on Fourth and Walnut streets was evidently the site of frequent gatherings. "General Moylan was emphatically a gentleman of the old school; he was remarkable for his hospitality," a magazine writer recalled in 1861. "Having two daughters, one of whom was very fascinating, his house attracted many young persons."[209]

Unlike many of his fellow patriots, Stephen Moylan has apparently given his name to few towns, schools, bridges, and other landmarks. Instead, he gave our country *its* name — something none of the more famous founders can claim.

7

It's easy to identify the most prominent of the three Irish Catholics on our churchyard tour. There's an ornate monument in his honor in front of Old St. Mary's. You can also see his statue a few blocks away, on Independence Mall. He's motioning toward the horizon, in the direction of the ocean, and holding a spyglass — reminders that he made his reputation at sea.

People will argue forever about whether he or the more flamboyant John Paul Jones deserves to be called the Father of the American Navy.

---

[208] Griffin, "Stephen Moylan," 175.
[209] Griffin, "Stephen Moylan," 234.

But there's no doubt John Barry, the nation's first commodore, has an impressive claim on the title. As his biographer Tim McGrath describes it, invoking baseball legends, he's the steady "Lou Gehrig" to Jones's flashier "Babe Ruth."

There's also no doubt that the six-foot four-inch Barry was every bit as formidable on land as onboard a ship. For proof, consider how Pennsylvania came to ratify the Constitution.

Delegates from all thirteen states had spent the sweltering summer of 1787 in Philadelphia, drafting the new constitution to replace the weak and ineffective Articles of Confederation. Barry and his naval colleagues supported the Constitution: they felt it was their "last, best chance to get paid" for their service during the Revolution. But the Constitution had to be ratified by every state, and it had its enemies.

In Pennsylvania, most of those foes were from the rural districts. They distrusted the idea of a strong federal government, and they were led by James McCalmont, a state militiaman and legendary Indian fighter from Franklin County. The towering McCalmont was considered by many the toughest man in the Pennsylvania Assembly.

He was also wily. When it became clear that September that the Federalists easily had enough votes for ratification, McCalmont sent his supporters home. Now the Assembly lacked a quorum and it was set to adjourn for the year. Instead of being the first state to ratify the Constitution, as its supporters hoped, it now seemed Pennsylvania's vote would be postponed. That would give McCalmont's side time to lobby for the Constitution's defeat.

His strategy might have worked if he'd left town like most of his supporters. But confident they'd won, he and Jacob Miley, from Dauphin County, lingered at Maj. Alexander Boyd's inn on Sixth Street. That was where Barry and a gang of sailors found them.

Only two more assemblymen were needed to reach a quorum, and Barry and his men got both of them. They dragged McCalmont and Miley kicking, screaming, and thrashing through the streets of Philadelphia, past crowds of wondering onlookers, and into Independence Hall. Up three flights of stairs they all went, until, bloodied and bruised, the two snarling antifederalists were dumped into the Assembly's chamber. There, they were recorded as "no" votes—and the Constitution was ratified.

If that sounds rough, Barry learned early on that life is rarely a picnic—especially not for the son of a Catholic tenant farmer, who served at the whims of Protestant landowners. Born in the village of Rosslare on Good Friday 1745 in a thatched-roof, one-room cottage, John Barry was the oldest of five children. From an early age, he helped out on the farms where his father James worked. Yet there still wasn't enough money or food to support so many children.

Young John always found the nearby ocean alluring. And he idolized his Uncle Nicholas, a ship's captain who offered his nephew an escape. At age nine, John Barry became a cabin boy on his uncle's ship. It was a life as demanding as the tenant farming he left behind, and more dangerous besides. The quarters were dark and cramped, the food was sometimes rotten, and disease might lurk in any port. But the ship also meant freedom from the drudgery and prejudice of Ireland.

Barry spent the next half-dozen years as a sailor, getting a nautical education that would one day prepare him to live his dream as captain of his own ship. The place it happened was Philadelphia, where he came to live in 1760. He had a relative there, Jane Barry Wilcox, and was quickly employed as a crew member on numerous voyages to the West Indies, a major trading port for Philadelphia merchants.

By 1766, he had met his first wife, Mary, whom he wed at Old St. Joseph's the next Halloween. He also became a ship's captain, taking over a schooner named the *Barbadoes*. As the cliché goes, Barry was truly married to the sea. Author Tim McGrath notes that when Mary Barry died in 1774 of an unrecorded illness, she and her husband had been together "for less than six months in a marriage of just over six years."[210] Barry's frequent, and successful, trade missions to the Caribbean were the reason.

Yet when war beckoned, and the need for defense on the ocean became apparent, the future Father of the Navy was treated more like a stepchild instead.

[210] McGrath, *John Barry*, 37.

8

The Continental Navy was first proposed by John Adams, and the idea was promptly laughed out of Congress. But by the autumn of 1775, the thought was worth taking more seriously. Congress bought two armed ships, and began adding more as war became likely. Yet while John Barry had twenty years of nautical experience, he was passed over time and again for the command of those vessels. Instead, he had to swallow his pride and refit them for combat—a job he performed so quickly and efficiently that it seemed he might be landlocked forever.

When his turn finally came, though, he made the most of it. As captain of the brigantine *Lexington*, he recorded the American navy's first combat victory against a British warship in April 1776. He and his crew chased down the *Edward* just off the Virginia Capes, blowing a hole in her stern and forcing her surrender.

That triumph established Barry as a British nemesis. "I have chaced him several times but can never draw him into the sea," a frustrated captain, Andrew Snapes Hamond, wrote to Lord Dunmore later that month.[211] While one of the many legends about Washington's 1776 crossing of the Delaware on Christmas night is that Barry crossed with him—he did not; the ice was too thick, and by the time he arrived, the Battle of Trenton was over—he continued to vex English captains as the war progressed.

In fact, Barry was so highly regarded, that in the fall of 1777 he was approached by a messenger—whose identity has never been revealed—with an offer from Lord Richard Howe. In a secret meeting in his captain's cabin, the mystery man offered Barry twenty thousand pounds and a commission in the British Navy to switch sides. He could even keep command of his ship.

One can only imagine the emissary quaking as a furious Barry drew himself up to his full height and rejected the offer out of hand. He still sounded angry when he wrote about it later. "I spurned the eydee [idea] of being a Traitor," he said indignantly.

[211] McGrath, *John Barry*, 79.

He did not, however, spurn the idea of remarriage. His new wife, Sarah Keen "Sally" Austin, was the popular daughter of a local merchant of Swedish descent. She was also a member of a local sewing circle that kept busy by making American flags. The most famous member was Betsy Ross, whose home is a familiar tourist attraction on nearby Arch Street in Philadelphia's Old Town. Ross's creation of the first American flag might be legend, but the attraction between the young seamstress Sarah and the imposing Irish captain was real.

The couple were married in July 1777 at Philadelphia's Christ Church by an Anglican minister. Just two years later, however, Sarah converted to Catholicism. She was baptized—along with a slave named Judith—at Old St. Mary's.

In the bleak midwinter of 1777, as Washington's hungry troops huddled around their open fires at Valley Forge, Barry offered one of the few bright spots for the patriots. Commanding a makeshift flotilla, he conducted a series of daring maneuvers on the Delaware River. He and his men set fire to British haystacks along the coastline, captured goods from enemy vessels, and gave cover to soldiers bringing the army at Valley Forge desperately needed food and supplies.

An even riskier mission on the Delaware followed in March of 1778. Barry used another patchwork collection of boats to capture two British transports and an armed schooner called the *Alert*. The next day, in a raging nor'easter, he successfully escaped from a British attempt to recapture the ships. The *Alert* was deliberately run aground on Reedy Island, but Barry didn't lose a single soldier.

General Washington wrote to Barry a few days later, "to congratulate you on the Success which has crowned your Gallantry."[212] He also thanked Barry for his gift of a huge cheese and some pickled oysters that Barry had liberated from the *Alert*. The real prize, though, was a collection of letters that provided vital information for the patriots.

As is so often the case, it's one of Barry's failures that might best illustrate his character. That September, commanding the frigate *Raleigh*,

[212] McGrath, *John Barry*, 166.

Barry was pursued by the British into unfamiliar waters off the coast of Maine. He lost the ship, and thanks to a midshipman who might have been a traitor, he was unable to sink it before the British captured it.

But he protected his crew, most of which evacuated in rowboats. "Saved 85 in number," Barry wrote tersely afterward.[213] He was never one to boast, but the Eastern Navy Board did it for him. "Perhaps no ship was ever better defended," the official report read. "Captn Barry's conduct is highly approved here, and his men are greatly pleased with him."[214]

They were pleased because despite his rugged appearance, he was known as a fair captain—and a devout one. At sea he was known for beginning each day with Bible readings for the crew. Today you can see Barry's well-thumbed family Bible, in fact, resting on the altar of the chapel at the Naval Academy in Annapolis.

Yet, while he occasionally displayed a sense of self-deprecating humor, he was a captain no one sensible dared cross. Barry put down three mutinies in his career. One of them was in March of 1781, aboard the *Alliance*, the thirty-two-gun frigate he next commanded.

When he rooted out the conspirators, the punishment was brutal: they were hung by their thumbs, so that their feet could not quite reach the deck. As the tendons in their hands tore from the pressure, their bare backs were flayed with a cat-o'-nine-tails. The leather strips were tipped with beads or bits of metal, and were wiped clean of blood and gore after every "stripe."

"Savage as they were," Tim McGrath writes, "Barry's methods were his only recourse; they saved the lives of his officers and loyal sailors as well as his own."

His most famous battle took place that May, off the coast of Newfoundland. The *Alliance* was sandwiched between two British warships, the *Atlanta* and the *Tresspassy*, and Barry was riddled with shrapnel from a canister shot. His shoulder was shredded and his left arm hung useless, but he stayed in command until blood loss caused him to drop.

---

[213] McGrath, *John Barry*, 195.
[214] McGrath, *John Barry*, 196.

When he was visited belowdecks by his second-in-command, Lt. Hoysted Hacker, the news was all bad. The *Alliance* was in "frightful condition." Casualties were high. Even the wind was against them. But when Hacker asked for permission to strike the ship's colors—in other words, surrender—Barry roared his dissent.

"No Sir, the thunder!" he bellowed. "If this ship cannot be fought without me, I will be brought on deck; to your duty, Sir."[215] It seemed the elements heard Barry's cry as well. A sudden wind filled the *Alliance*'s sails, and the battle resumed. After four bloody hours, the two British crews admitted defeat. Barry's reward for his heroism was a long recovery from his injuries—and the welcome news that the *Alliance*'s hull would be sheathed in copper.

9

For all his revolutionary service, though, it was only after the war that people began to truly recognize John Barry's greatness. One of them was President George Washington, who in 1797 presented Barry with Commission Number One in the U.S. Navy.

That May, his flagship, the U.S.S. *United States*, was launched from Humphrey's Shipyard in Philadelphia. It was a forty-four-gun frigate that Barry personally outfitted, and it was needed immediately. The "Quasi-War" with France, fought at sea, demanded the services of Barry, now a commodore.

After that, he hoped for one more mission. Barry dreamed of finishing his career in the Mediterranean battling the Barbary pirates, raiders from North Africa who were plundering American ships and holding their crews hostage. Yet when the order finally came, Barry sadly declined it: the old sailor knew his asthma had made him far too weak for another voyage. He died at his home in Strawberry Hill, a neighborhood in northeast Philadelphia, on September 12, 1803.

[215] John Barry Kelly, "Named in Honor of Commodore John Barry," USS Barry, 1995, https://www.public.navy.mil/surfor/ddg52/Pages/Namesake .aspx.

John Barry's memorial is one of the grandest in this small cemetery at Old St. Mary's, its three-tiered construction honoring the great man and both his wives. Always a plainspoken man, the commodore would undoubtedly have disliked the tributes offered during his military funeral here, on a sunny, brisk Wednesday morning.

He might have been far more comfortable, though, with what was said upon the launch of the U.S.S. *United States*. He was a proud man, but these words are a reminder of the cause he served, which was always more important: "A political state must be formed by the Union of many talents which by their very diversity make one excellent whole. Federal people, this frigate is an emblem of our United States. Taken asunder an hundred bateaux might be made from her, but a sloop of pirates could sink them all; so would you by discord, become a prey to foreign or domestic tyranny! Respect then your National Union as the pledge of general security and happiness!"[216]

10

There's still a hush in the old churchyard, in the heart of a thoroughly modern, deeply divided, and increasingly anxious metropolis. We are far from the madding crowd the novelist Thomas Hardy once described; only an occasional runner or dog walker passes on the street outside this summer morning.

In the unusual stillness, we might recall a quote from the British author and apologist G. K. Chesterton. He said Christianity has continually been reborn, "for it had a God who knew the way out of the grave."

The liberty these Catholic lions fought for, in the name of that God, also knows its way out of the grave. Thanks to their efforts, and the efforts of others resting peacefully here, that liberty is all around us. It's here in Philadelphia's Old Town. It's in the rest of the city. It's in the rest of the nation these men helped create—whether anyone realizes it or not.

---

[216] Martin I. J. Griffin, *The History of Commodore John Barry*, reprinted from the *Records of the American Catholic Historical Society*, ed. F. T. Furey (Philadelphia: American Catholic Historical Society, 1897), 136.

Chapter 5

The Most Important Receipt in American History

1

The complaint could have been made yesterday.

"In discussing America's lack of vision and the failure of its colleges and universities to teach adequately to the American youth their own history, I had occasion to say that if the ten most brilliant students of the senior classes of the ten leading universities were asked the simple question, 'How did aid first come to America from France?' that not 5 percent could answer the question correctly."[217]

But the sentiment is actually more than a hundred years old. It comes from lawyer and congressman James Beck, in his introduction to Catholic scholar Elizabeth Kite's 1918 biography of Pierre-Augustin Caron de Beaumarchais.

Who was Beaumarchais? Exactly.

To theater lovers, he was the creator of two comedies — *The Barber of Seville* and its sequel, *The Marriage of Figaro* — that became world-famous in their musical adaptations, the latter created by Mozart. Beaumarchais was also a watchmaker, an inventor, a publisher, a musician and composer, and a diplomat, among his many professions.

---

[217] Elizabeth Sarah Kite, *Beaumarchais and the War of American Independence* (1918; Whitefish, MT: Kessinger Publishing, 2010), 12.

He also, in all likelihood, saved the American Revolution.

"During the spring of 1777, ammunition, guns, and the complete military equipment for twenty-five thousand men, amounting in value to no less than five million French livres, were landed on the American coast," Kite wrote.[218]

In today's funds, that's nearly three billion dollars in military aid. It was a godsend to the cash-strapped colonies, whose currency was worthless, whose credit was nonexistent, and whose Congress lacked the power to officially raise a single cent. The Continental Army was so poor that it lost the Battle of Bunker Hill in 1776 because its soldiers ran out of gunpowder and had to retreat.

All this aid arrived a year before France officially entered the war on the side of the patriots. The supplies came through a dummy corporation called Roderigue Hortalez and Company. It was invented by Beaumarchais to covertly funnel assistance to the rebels, and was funded by France and Spain, as well as his own fundraising for the fake business.

In the early days of the Revolution, it "functioned like one of Beaumarchais' own well-oiled watches."[219] Keeping a close eye on the secret enterprise was the new French foreign minister, the Comte de Vergennes, who shrewdly used the revolutionary passion of Beaumarchais to further a more calculating end.

Vergennes wanted revenge for France's humiliating defeat to Britain in the Seven Years' War. But he realized the French weren't ready yet for a military confrontation. Secretly funding the rebels weakened England while buying France more time to rebuild its armed forces. And it allowed the French to dump outdated muskets and cannons, which they planned to replace anyway.

As early as 1774, France—along with Spain and the Netherlands—were probably funneling supplies to the colonies. Some of these goods were received by Col. Jeremiah Lee, a wealthy Massachusetts merchant

[218] Kite, *Beaumarchais and the War of American Independence*, 31.

[219] Streeter Bass, "Beaumarchais and the American Revolution," Studies Archive Index 14, no. 1, September 22, 1993, Central Intelligence Agency.

who died on the eve of the Revolution. But the scheme involving Beaumarchais was on a much larger scale.

On Vergennes's orders, the phony company began with a million livres
of seed money from the French treasury. In his biography of Beaumarchais,
Harlow Giles Unger calls the receipt the playwright received — from Vergennes's fifteen-year-old son, Duvergier, to further muddy the trail — "the
most important receipt in American history."[220] That is no exaggeration.

Beaumarchais had first schemed with American gadfly Arthur Lee.
The pair developed a plan to trade French gunpowder for American
tobacco. Now, money in hand, Beaumarchais teamed with Connecticut
merchant Silas Deane.

Deane had been sent to France to get supplies and volunteers for the
war effort. As 1777 was perhaps the bleakest year for the Continental
Army, we can only imagine how much worse it might have been without
the under-the-table funding Beaumarchais provided.

One of the few bright spots for the patriots that summer and fall was
the surrender of the British at Saratoga. It gave the Northern Army
control of the strategically critical Hudson Valley. Even more important,
this victory is often marked as the war's early turning point: the win that
convinced the French to officially become America's ally the next year.

But the army that helped win this decisive victory had *already* been
outfitted and supplied by the French — thanks to Beaumarchais and his
fictitious company.

2

The watchmaker father of Beaumarchais, André-Charles Caron, was a
Calvinist who converted to Catholicism. This was a good business decision in early eighteenth-century France. In 1685, King Louis XIV had
revoked the Edict of Nantes, which had protected Calvinists and other
Protestants from persecution.

---

[220] Harlow G. Unger, *Improbable Patriot: The Secret History of Monsieur de
Beaumarchais, the French Playwright Who Saved the American Revolution*
(Hanover NH: University Press of New England, 2011), 212.

Elizabeth Kite noted, however, that André-Charles "retained his Calvinistic character."[221] A case in point is a long letter he wrote to his son after throwing him out of the house for the usual teenage hijinks: drinking, carousing, and womanizing around town. The letter spells out precisely, and severely, the conditions by which Pierre-Augustin would be readmitted to the family home.

The boy meekly complied, vowing to work harder and make his father proud. He did. Not long afterward, he created an escapement mechanism that allowed watches to become smaller, thinner, and lighter. This ultimately led him to pursue a successful lawsuit when an older watchmaker tried to steal his idea. And it got the attention of King Louis XV, allowing the young inventor of humble beginnings entry into the fabulous world of the royal court.

Beaumarchais kept channeling his urge for excitement into bigger and broader pursuits. He was handsome, filled with reckless energy, and boundlessly creative. He took the name "Beaumarchais" from the property left to him by his first wife, whose husband was a royal courtier that he cuckolded. He killed one man in a duel and was challenged to others. He worked as a spy in London, delighting in the games of cloak and dagger.

The word that surfaces in every biography is "rogue." Few men seem to have been better suited for the title.

"What a man," gushed the French writer Voltaire. "He has everything—pleasantry, seriousness, vigor, pathos, eloquence of every kind, and yet he strives after none of them." Beaumarchais would return the favor after Voltaire's death by publishing his complete works as a tribute.

Appropriately enough, given his background of intrigue, there is a CIA dossier of sorts on Beaumarchais. The agency uses it for historical background, and it includes this posthumous assessment: "Psychologically, Beaumarchais was an incurable adolescent to whom life was a continuous drama in which he played a succession of leading roles. What made him extraordinarily successful was his ability to absorb with his whole

[221] Kite, *Beaumarchais and the War of American Independence*, 45.

being whatever role he was playing at the moment, to the exclusion of any other."

3

The role of Beaumarchais as a Catholic, however, is a different story. We know with certainty that he *was* one. What is less clear is the kind of Catholic he was.

Like most of the men in the following chapters, Beaumarchais was a European child of the Enlightenment. The gospel that excited him most was written by Jean-Jacques Rousseau. The Genevan philosopher had electrified France in 1762 with his famous assertion that "man is born free, but he is everywhere in chains."[222] Society—especially its focus on, and defense of, property ownership—is what warps man, Rousseau believed.

Rousseau did spend some time as a Catholic convert, but his beliefs were certainly not Christian in any orthodox way. He saw traditional Christianity, in fact, as an obstacle to his goal: finding a "civil religion" everyone in society could agree upon. His views had far more to do with the French Revolution than the American one.

But Beaumarchais admired him enough to make him a character—the lovesick young page, Cherubino—in *The Marriage of Figaro*. And Beaumarchais was undoubtedly not the only Frenchman who linked Rousseau's belief in the equality of all men to the patriot cause.

Perhaps Beaumarchais's contrary nature made him unlikely to ever be more than a lukewarm Catholic. Referencing his father's Huguenot background, one biographer wrote, "his recollection of the religion of his ancestors probably added its influence to his natural instinct for opposition."[223]

---

[222] *The Major Political Writings of Jean-Jacques Rousseau: The Two Discourses and Social Contract*, trans. and ed. John T. Scott (Chicago: University of Chicago Press), 163.

[223] Louis Léonard, *Beaumarchais and His Times: Sketches of French Society in the Eighteenth Century from Unpublished Documents*, trans. Henry S. Edwards (New York: Harper, 1857), 41.

That "natural instinct for opposition" showed itself in his plays, which lampooned the aristocracy—including the Church—and drew the ire of monarchs. Louis XVI prevented *The Marriage of Figaro* from being shown in France for years. When the show finally made it to the stage in 1784, Louis probably wished he'd stuck to his guns.

The play quickly became must-see theater. Beaumarchais had moved the setting from France to Spain, but crowds still roared in response to speeches like Figaro's takedown of the count: "Because you are a nobleman, you think yourself a great genius—Nobility, fortune, rank, position! How proud they make a man feel! What have you done to deserve such advantages? Put yourself to the trouble of being born—nothing more! For the rest—a very ordinary man. Whereas I, lost among the obscure crowd, have had to deploy more knowledge, more calculation and skill merely to survive than has sufficed to rule all the provinces of Spain for a century!"[224]

Beaumarchais's "natural instinct" also may have played some role in the way he advocated for the rights of minority Protestants in France. "During his long and brilliant career," a history of the Huguenots in France stated, "Beaumarchais never forgot his 'new Catholic' background"—in other words, his family's Huguenot roots.[225]

In fact, Beaumarchais believed passionately in the plight of the oppressed, wherever they were. He also wasn't shy about using his influence on their behalf.

He demanded of King Louis XVI, "How can you allow your vessels to take by force and bind suffering black men whom nature made free and who are only miserable because you are powerful?"

Turning his attention from African slavery to affairs in Poland, where Russia, Prussia, and Austria had conspired to grab Polish land, Beaumarchais

---

[224] Pierre Augustin Beaumarchais, *The Barber of Seville* and *The Marriage of Figaro*, trans. John Wood (1964; Harmondsworth, UK: Penguin Books, 2004), 138.

[225] Geoffrey Adams, *The Huguenots and French Opinion, 1685–1787: The Enlightenment Debate on Toleration*, (Waterloo, ON: Wilfrid Laurier University Press, 1992), 257.

also asked, "How can you suffer three rival powers to seize iniquitously upon and divide Poland under your very eyes?" This was a particular sore spot, since the sufferers in Poland were mostly fellow Roman Catholics, and since the French had been appealed to for help.

Like many of the patriots who came from Europe, though, Beaumarchais would find the true outlet for his frustrated revolutionary aspirations across the Atlantic.

"We must aid the Americans," Beaumarchais insisted to Louis XVI. For "you cannot have the peace you desire unless you prevent at all costs peace between England and America ... and the only way to accomplish this is to supply aid to the Americans to make them equal to England."

It was a winning argument — in both France and America.

4

The patriots' cause benefited from more than just the money Beaumarchais raised and the supplies he smuggled. He was also critical in exporting some of the Revolution's military difference-makers from Europe to the colonies.

This was no small task, as the CIA report on Beaumarchais notes. "In Europe no military events of significance had taken place since the end of the Seven Years' War and unemployed soldiers were everywhere in evidence. Many offered their services to the Commission in Paris and Beaumarchais was of invaluable assistance in sorting out the riff-raff from the competent soldiers."

There was quite a bit of riffraff, in fact. "After nearly a decade and a half of boring peace," H. W. Brands writes, "the warrior class of the continent wanted work." So did fresh-faced boys seeking adventure in the colonies, and even surgeons who desired practical battlefield experience.

Benjamin Franklin, who had by this time come to Paris, was asked for recommendations so often that he put together an all-purpose letter. It concluded, "As to this gentleman, I must refer you to himself for his character and merits, with which he is certainly better acquainted than I can possibly be."

That was a joke; the fact that everyone and his brother wanted a commission was not. This frustrated George Washington, who asked

Franklin to stop flooding the ranks of the Continental Army with no-hope officer candidates. "Every new arrival is only a source of embarrassment," Washington wrote, "to Congress and myself."

But, as Brands points out, "there were a few diamonds amid the dross." We'll meet some of those diamonds in the next couple of chapters.

What most of them have in common is the Catholic Faith they shared with Beaumarchais, and the fact that his efforts were what brought them to America. The money he requested, and invested, went to fund not just the weapons and supplies that were so desperately needed by the colonists. It also paid for the passage of many soldiers who turned the tide for America.

Those soldiers took great personal risks in coming to America, of course. Some of them paid with their lives for the Revolutionary cause. Yet it should be remembered that many had little to lose in joining the patriots. Brian Morton and Donald Spinelli make this point in their book about Beaumarchais, comparing him to the most famous Revolutionary import, Lafayette.

"In 1777, when he arrived in America, he was aged twenty, thirsting for fame," they wrote of Lafayette. "He risked his life, but at his age this was little compared to the rewards of glory. He possessed, as Jefferson would put it later, 'a canine appetite for popularity and fame.'"[226]

In fact, that "canine appetite" very nearly ended the schemes of Vergennes and Beaumarchais when they'd barely gotten off the ground. Today we rightfully think of Lafayette as one of the architects of American liberty. But his youthful recklessness and arrogance could also have helped doom the American Revolution before he ever set foot on colonial soil, as we'll read in chapter 8.

Beaumarchais knew a little something about recklessness and arrogance. But, unlike Lafayette, he didn't have a noble family and a personal fortune to fall back on if his impetuous nature got the best of him. He was forty-three when he proposed his funding scheme, and stood to lose everything if it failed.

---

[226] Brian N. Morton and Donald C. Spinelli, *Beaumarchais and the American Revolution* (Lanham, MD: Lexington Books, 2003), 334.

"He was aware that the failure of war or a change in French policy could easily lead to his own bankruptcy," Morton and Spinelli wrote. "He knew that appeals to the French court after the fact would go unheeded."[227]

Beaumarchais would find, unfortunately, that appeals to Congress after the fact had a similar effect.

5

Like several other people in this book, Beaumarchais found it extraordinarily difficult to get America to reimburse him for the financial sacrifices he made on its behalf.

The web of intrigue in which he operated may have been partly to blame. Lost in the secretive founding of Roderigue Hortalez and Company was the fact that it still operated like a normal business. There were expenses, and Beaumarchais certainly hoped to turn a profit, in addition to doing a good deed.

His relationship with Deane didn't help Congress's understanding of this fact. Deane was recalled to America in 1778 under a cloud and denounced as a traitor. According to Prof. Thomas Schaeper, who spent years researching Deane and wrote a fascinating book about his findings, Deane was the victim of a whispering campaign by Beaumarchais's old ally, Arthur Lee.

Lee, the younger brother of Virginia Congressman Richard Henry Lee, was well-known for his jealousies and hotheaded temperament, as well as his anti-Catholic sentiments. Cut out of his father's will by two of his older siblings, he lived the rest of his life nursing this grudge. He wanted to be the colonists' sole representative in France, and among those he tried to undermine was Benjamin Franklin himself.

He was also stung because he'd been replaced by Silas Deane in Beaumarchais's scheme. So Lee claimed the French government's investment in Roderigue Hortalez and Company was a gift. Therefore, the thinking went, invoices submitted by Beaumarchais and Deane seeking reimbursement were fraudulent.

---

[227] Morton and Spinelli, *Beaumarchais and the American Revolution*, 334.

Part of the problem was something Deane had written to the Continental Congress back in 1776, claiming everything Beaumarchais "says, writes, or does, is in reality the action of the [French] Ministry." This careless remark was interpreted as proof that French aid was, indeed, a present. And, as author Larrie D. Ferrario notes, it "would unintentionally lose Beaumarchais a fortune."[228]

Despite the fact that both Beaumarchais and Deane had invested their own money in the operation, their claims were denied. Deane wound up in London, broke and sick, before dying mysteriously onboard a ship that was returning him to America. Congress's dispute with Beaumarchais, meanwhile, would stretch on for years.

When Alexander Hamilton investigated his claims in 1793, he discovered Beaumarchais was owed more than two million francs. But Congress managed to bargain that amount down to zero. It did so partly by claiming that the money Beaumarchais had spent belonged to America all along—the "gift from France" defense—and partly by claiming interest.

Beaumarchais made his final appeal in 1795 directly to the people. "Americans, I have served you with indefatigable zeal and I have received, throughout my life, only bitterness as a reward for my services," he wrote. "I die your creditor. Allow me therefore, now that I am dying, to bequeath you my daughter, that you may endow her with a portion of what you owe me."[229]

They eventually did—but not until 1835, decades after his death, for just pennies on the dollar. It was a sad and ignoble way to close the ledger on the Revolution's most significant individual financier.

So it's a good thing, at least, that Beaumarchais could look back with pride on the career of the man whose support he considered his best expenditure.

"Never did I make an investment that gave me so much pleasure," Beaumarchais wrote in 1778, "for I put a man of honor in the right

[228] Larrie D. Ferreiro, *Brothers at Arms: American Independence and the Men of France & Spain Who Saved It* (New York: Alfred A. Knopf, 2016), 57.
[229] Bass, "Beaumarchais and the American Revolution."

place.... His glory is the interest on his money and ... I do not doubt that, on these terms, he will repay me with usury."[230]

This man was neither a Frenchman nor a Pole. Beaumarchais was speaking instead about the German credited with turning around the fortunes of the Continental Army: Baron Friedrich Wilhelm von Steuben, who drilled Washington's troops at Valley Forge. Beaumarchais had loaned him the money for his voyage to America.

Von Steuben had been a soldier of fortune in several countries. His price was right: he'd offered to volunteer, with his pay contingent on the outcome of the war. Some historians claim von Steuben was also available because he had been drummed out of the Prussian army for homosexuality.[231]

Regardless, his effect on the patriot army was undisputed. One soldier would claim that he seemed to be the personification of Mars, the Roman god of war. His drills were precise and relentless, and even included an aide who could swear at the troops in English—which von Steuben could not speak. The satisfaction with which Beaumarchais viewed his small loan for von Steuben was warranted—even though he was apparently never repaid.

Beaumarchais was probably never repaid for similar loans that he made on behalf of the more than one hundred foreign volunteers who sailed to the colonies in ships that he owned. Throughout 1777, these volunteers would reach the shores of America to bolster the patriot cause. Some added particular military and technical expertise. Some brought little more than enthusiasm and a willingness to die for a cause.

Some, however, came because their faith had taught them the value of freedom—a freedom that had proven frustratingly elusive in their own nations. Two of those men, both natives of Poland, are the subject of two chapters that follow.

---

[230] Bass, "Beaumarchais and the American Revolution."
[231] Erin Blakemore, "The Revolutionary War Hero Who Was Openly Gay," *History*, February 6, 2020, https://www.history.com/news/openly-gay -revolutionary-war-hero-friedrich-von-steuben.

In the ledger of Beaumarchais, there is an unpaid receipt for one of them, in the sum of 480 livres. Like von Steuben, this officer also spent time at Valley Forge. Like von Steuben, he also played a major role in the reformation of the American army. His story is even more fascinating, though, and his effect on the Revolution was every bit as dramatic — as we'll see next.

Chapter 6

Polish Patriots . . .

1

All afternoon, he had knelt in prayer before the Black Madonna.

Now evening was blushing at the edge of the western horizon. In the hushed little chapel, with its intricately carved dark wood and the lingering scent of incense, Casimir Pulaski had made his decision.

He rose, knees aching, and smoothed his small mustache. Though he stood not quite five feet, four inches, his stature was far greater on the battlefield. It broke his heart to realize he must abandon it.

For the past five years, he and his family had tried their best to defend Poland from Russian incursions. The Pulaskis were part of a group called the Bar Confederation, but, at times, it had seemed as though their family was acting alone. Casimir's nobleman father had warned for years that Poland needed to defend itself against the Bear to its east, as the country degenerated into a Russian protectorate. He had started planning the armed resistance when Russia interfered with the selection of Poland's new king. He and his sons had won over many of the people, as well as some foreign allies.

The French soldiers who came to Poland, though, were more hindrance than help. And Poland's monarch, Stanislaus August Poniatowski, was the former lover of Russian empress Catherine the Great. He fiddled while Russia, as well as Prussia and Austria, plotted to carve up his country.

In October 1771, a group of Polish revolutionaries tried and failed to kidnap the king. Casimir Pulaski was not one of the abductors, but the dashing young horseman, who rode as if he'd been born in the saddle, was blamed anyway. He had proven himself the fiercest enemy of foreign interference in Poland—especially interference designed to weaken the Roman Catholic Church, which was part of Catherine's design.

That made him "Public Enemy Number One of Russia," and his Knights of the Holy Cross—named for the small red cross each man wore on his cap—became the bane of the Russian army. Catherine ordered imprisonment for anyone who helped him. A Russian commander offered a more visceral warning. His soldiers chopped off the hands of a dozen peasants accused of assisting Pulaski and sent the severed appendages to Warsaw.

Now Pulaski was accused of not just kidnapping but regicide—in a country that had never killed a king. It was a serious, even shocking, charge. King Stanislaus took full advantage, using it to win public support for crushing the resistance.

Casimir Pulaski had fought valiantly, but now he was trapped. He and his soldiers were sheltered in Jasna Góra Monastery at Częstochowa, one of the holiest sites in Poland. Since the seventeenth century, it had also been a fortress. Built on a hill, the monastery was ringed by strongly fortified walls and a moat. But the monastery was now surrounded by Russian troops, with Prussian and Austrian reinforcements nearby.

The greatest treasure at Jasna Góra was the icon of the Black Madonna. Four feet high, it depicted the Virgin Mary and the Infant Jesus. Legend held that St. Luke the Evangelist had painted it on a tabletop from the Holy Family's home. The images of Mother and Child had turned dark, thanks to age and constant exposure to incense smoke.

There were also two deep scars on the Virgin's right cheek, where the icon had been slashed by raiders in 1430. As he gazed on those wounds, Casimir Pulaski was reminded of the prayers he'd said as a boy, at the shrine to the Virgin Mary that his family kept in their manor at Winiary.

Many believed that the Blessed Mother had once interceded to protect the Polish people. In 1655, the monks and a band of local volunteers made a miraculous defense of Jasna Góra against German troops working for Sweden. It was the key event of a war known simply as "The Deluge." In gratitude, the Polish king consecrated the country to the protection of the Virgin Mary.

Was another such miracle possible, more than a hundred years later? Casimir Pulaski had prayed it might be. After all, just a year earlier, he had found himself in a similarly grim situation at Jasna Góra, and he and his men had repelled the Russian forces.

This time felt different. The fighting had already claimed Pulaski's father and older brother, Francis. Russian troops had burned down his family home in Winiary, near Warsaw, and Pulaski believed—mistakenly —that his mother and sisters had been killed.

As he looked around the monastery, he thought about the kindness of its monks and the bravery of his soldiers. He gazed again on the solemn expression of the Black Madonna, gesturing toward the Christ child as He reached up for her face.

Was he ready to be responsible for the destruction of all he saw around him—this precious relic, and all these precious lives? Taking a deep breath of the sweet spring air and then exhaling slowly, he knew he was not.

There was only one gun in the fort with any powder left. Gently, he laid it down. He would surrender in hopes of sparing the monastery. But he was confident he'd have another opportunity to avenge his beloved country.

Casimir Pulaski could not have known that evening, in June 1772, that this chance would never come. As he left the sanctuary of Jasna Góra for a Russian concentration camp, he was also saying his final farewell to Poland.

2

He spent the next five years as a virtual exile. It isn't clear why or how such a wanted man was somehow paroled by the Russians, but he escaped the country before they could change their minds—which they soon enough did. There was still a price on his head: he had been sentenced to death for the plot against the Polish king. That he was innocent made no difference. His reputation was ruined across Europe. He tried to join the French army and was rebuffed.

When he and a few countrymen drifted into Turkey to fight against the Russians, his identity was discovered. The Russians refused to sign a peace treaty with Turkey unless Pulaski surrendered. Disguised in the baggy trousers and turban of a Tartar, he and his fellow Poles barely escaped in a fishing boat, landing in Smyrna on the Aegean coast.

Penniless, he later reached Marseilles, where in 1775 he was thrown into a debtors' prison. Friends eventually bailed him out, but no one was interested in a thirty-year-old ex-revolutionary. He'd had some heroic exploits in Poland. But what use were they now?

Certainly none in Poland, which had been partitioned eagerly by Russia, Prussia, and Austria not long after he left the county. The warnings Joseph Pulaski had given all those years ago had come true. Now Polish independence looked further away than ever.

The odds looked even longer in America. But in the autumn of 1776, Casimir Pulaski loitered on the docks and watched the ships in Marseilles loading supplies for the colonists. Those supplies were being shipped under the Spanish flag, in crates stamped with the name of the phony company Roderigue Hortalez and Company. The covert aid was a badly kept secret. Pulaski suspected the Americans might just be desperate enough to take a chance on him.

When he was finally able to reach Paris to meet with Benjamin Franklin, it turned out he was right. Pulaski had the help of Chevalier de Rulhiere, a writer and diplomat who was a member of the French Academy. Ruhliere had known Joseph Pulaski, and now he vouched for his son to Franklin: he was a freedom fighter, not a foreign intriguer.

Franklin sometimes embellished the recommendations he sent to Washington; this one needed no gilding. "Count Pulaski of Poland, an officer famous throughout Europe for his bravery and conduct in defense of the liberties of his country against the three great invading powers of Russia, Austria and Prussia will have the honor of delivering this into your Excellency's hands."

Soon enough, it would be Casimir Pulaski who delivered Washington—and along with him, the Revolutionary cause.

3

September 11 is a date, of course, that will forever live in infamy in American history. Had the events of September 11, 1777, gone slightly differently, there might be little American history at all.

If you stand on the banks of Brandywine Creek today, you can look upstream and imagine the scene as it must have been on that late-summer day, nearly 250 years ago. The east and west branches of the river, a tributary of the Christina, unite not far from the battlefield. They meander peacefully together through Chester County, Pennsylvania, on their way to Wilmington, Delaware, where they flow into the Delaware River. At what seems like every riverbend, huge sycamores cross their ancient limbs over the waters, draping leaf fronds like garlands just above the placid surface.

Many have thought these scenes along the Brandywine are among the most beautiful in America, including the painter Andrew Wyeth. You can see some of his canvases in the restored gristmill nearby that serves as a museum. Wyeth, who grew up close to the battlefield, was haunted by the river—and by the battle fought near it. One of those trees, his artist son Jamie would say, a buttonwood estimated to be more than five hundred years old, "heard the battle"[232]—a fact that fascinated his father.

Philadelphia sits about twenty-five miles to the east. The colonial capital was what General Washington and his troops were trying to save this September morning. The battle fought would be the largest, in terms of troop numbers, in the entire Revolution. The thirty thousand soldiers were divided almost evenly among the two sides.

But Washington made an error that nearly proved fatal. He believed his forces had blocked off all possible ways across the Brandywine for Sir William Howe's forces. They had not. And the fog that had saved

[232] W. Barksdale Maynard, *The Brandywine: An Intimate Portrait* (Philadelphia: University of Pennsylvania Press, 2015), 197.

Washington the previous year, covering his desperate exit from Brooklyn Heights in New York, this time worked against him. It rose thickly from the creek beds, obscuring Gen. Charles Cornwallis's British infantry as they forded the river upstream.

While Hessian Gen. Wilhelm von Kynphausen diverted the Continental Army at Chadds Ford, the British stealthily outflanked Washington on the right. It was too late to do anything but retreat, and even that possibility looked bleak. Maj. Gen. Nathaniel Greene's men bravely tried to assist the escape, but once again, Washington seemed to be just moments from capture.

Then, just as the British were ready to break the American line and perhaps crush the rebellion for good, they were surprised by a small band of horsemen. Their leader seemed to be an acrobat in the saddle and was a striking sight. He wore a navy-blue dolman—an eastern European military jacket decorated with interlaced white trim across the front. On horseback, he looked taller than his actual height. Some of that was his bearskin hat, called a busby, which was decorated with a hanging tassel. And some of it was his sheer gutsiness.

The British couldn't have known that Casimir Pulaski had been practicing stunts on horseback since he was a small boy in Poland. They also couldn't have known that his "cavalry" consisted of about thirty troops a desperate Washington had allowed him to press into action just moments earlier. But they *did* know, as the mystery rider wove his horse nimbly through the smoke of artillery fire, that he'd interrupted their plans.

The British army might have tried to pursue the retreating patriots to Chester. But with Pulaski and his horsemen swarming like a cloud of hornets, they changed their minds. With nothing to stop his victorious march into Philadelphia, General Howe decided not to chase Washington.

It was a turning point, though at the moment, it seemed no more than a reprieve. Exhausted American troops straggled into Chester well into the wee hours of the morning. Their losses had been high: more than twelve hundred killed or wounded. The numbers would have been much higher without the daring of Casimir Pulaski.

"Pulaski, with his usual intrepidity and judgment led them to the charge and succeeded in retarding the advance of the enemy—a delay that was of the highest importance to our retreating army," wrote Paul Bentalou, a French captain in the Continental Army.[233]

The Battle of Brandywine Creek was Pulaski's first military duty in America. He had been so impatient for action that when he fought, he hadn't even received his commission. Just four days later, Congress presented it, naming him a brigadier general in charge of cavalry—the "Commander of the Horse." If the American cavalry has a father, it is undoubtedly the Polish general who saved the Father of America at Brandywine.

4

Cavalry, of course, simply refers to soldiers on horseback. That has been a military tradition since there have been men, horses, and war. Even before Casimir Pulaski set foot on American soil, Congress had granted George Washington the authority to develop a cavalry force of three thousand men. So why does Pulaski deserve such credit?

A major reason is that the horsemen the Continental Army had were poorly equipped and even more poorly trained. Just as Baron von Steuben revolutionized American troops with his demanding discipline, Pulaski brought exacting new standards to the cavalry. And just as von Steuben turned his regime into a volume called *Regulations for the Order and Discipline of the Troops of the United States*—known as the "Blue Book," for short, because of the paper used for its cover—Pulaski set down regulations for the cavalry, rules that long outlived him.

Those rules codified the innovative way Pulaski envisioned the cavalry. During his five years of warfare in Poland, he had been perpetually outnumbered and outgunned. In the time-honored tradition of military underdogs, he'd successfully adopted guerrilla tactics to combat his

---

[233] Martin I. J. Griffin, "General Count Casimir Pulaski," *American Catholic Historical Researches* 6, no. 1 (January 1910): 11–12, https://www.jstor.org/stable/44374799.

enemies. That included his use of cavalry as an offensive weapon. Instead of just scouting and protecting the army's flanks, Pulaski saw its role as far more daring.

Good horsemen could disrupt a much larger force, as his stinging attacks had proven at Brandywine. And his arsenal of stunts was breathtaking: he could drop his hat on the ground and circle back to snatch it while hanging off the side of his horse. Or he could flip his pistol in the air and catch it in the middle of a complex riding maneuver. His father and older brother, Francis, had taught him tricks like these years ago.

Pulaski's concept of a guerrilla cavalry should have been an easy sell for the Continental Army, which had used a similar strategy on the ground against the superior British forces. There was resistance, however, and that failure of imagination—a failure General Washington shared—frustrated Pulaski.

It's easy to forget that when he joined the Continental Army, he had been a soldier for roughly half his life, and a leader of soldiers for most of that time. As author Alex Storozynski points out, "Pulaski had more combat experience than anyone in the Continental Army."[234] Undoubtedly, it was galling to see his plans foiled by men who had spent little or no time on the battlefield.

Then again, Pulaski was never one to suffer indignities quietly. "Vain" and "arrogant" are two words historians often use to describe him, and "impetuous" was frequently applied to his actions, on and off the battlefield. A humorous example of his reputation was a report in the *Rivington's Royal Gazette*, a loyalist newspaper, from the fall of 1778. It claimed Pulaski was summoned by George Washington after a congressman proposed repealing the Declaration of Independence:

> He had scarcely uttered the words before the President sent a message to fetch the Polish count, Pulaski, who happened to be

---

[234] Alex Storozynski, *The Peasant Prince: Thaddeus Kosciuszko and the Age of Revolution* (New York: Thomas Dunn Books, 2010), 47.

exercising part of his legion in the courtyard below. The Count flew to the chamber where the Congress sat, and with his saber, in an instant severed from his body the head of this honest delegate. The head was ordered by the Congress to be fixed on top of the liberty pole of Philadelphia, as a perpetual monument of the freedom of debate in the Continental congress of the United States of America.[235]

It was true, though, that Pulaski rarely had an opinion he was unwilling to share. And he began sharing them almost immediately upon joining the patriot forces — in spite of the fact that he spoke almost no English.

He argued against the Continental Army decamping to Valley Forge in the winter of 1777, remembering his successes fighting in the snow in his homeland. He clashed repeatedly with Washington's chief of staff, Stephen Moylan, who became Pulaski's successor as the army's commander of cavalry.

Ultimately, he ran afoul of Washington himself. Pulaski had taken over a unit that was the army's stepchild, and his standards were high — perhaps too high for the raw material he'd been given. At one point early in 1778, Washington wrote to Trenton, where Pulaski and cavalry were headquartered, to remind him, "Your officers complain that the Cavalry undergo severer duty now, than they did while they were in Camp. As rest and refreshment are two of the principal objects of your removal from Camp, I hope you will, by proper arrangements give your men and Horses, an opportunity of reaping these benefits from their winter Quarters."[236]

At that point, Pulaski resigned his commission and succeeded in getting authorization from Congress to form his own elite unit instead. Washington backed the measure, and Pulaski was assigned a group of about three hundred cavalry and infantry troops.

---

[235] Francis Casimir Kajencki, *Casimir Pulaski: Cavalry Commander of the American Revolution* (El Paso: Southwest Polonia Press, 2002), 130.
[236] Griffin, "General Count Casimir Pulaski," 39.

Pulaski's Legion included several immigrants and fellow Catholics, including a few former members of his Knights of the Holy Cross. One of them was a cousin from Poland named John Zelinski. The most significant addition was the Hungarian nobleman Michael Kováts, an expert horseman who became the colonel commandant of the Legion.

Pulaski chose a site near Baltimore for his headquarters, which might have allowed some of his men to participate in Mass at private chapels. Yet equipping his troops to his standards created problems. He was often forced to dip into his own funds for supplies. At one point, his sister Ana, who had survived the Russian attack on the Pulaski home years earlier and had become a nun, sold some family property at his request and sent him the money.

But Washington also wrote to complain about Pulaski's habit of appropriating property from locals he suspected of being Loyalists. Pulaski's impatient nature reveals itself again: he was neither a receipt-keeper nor a pencil pusher.

The Legion's combat record was checkered. In October 1778, at Little Egg Harbor in New Jersey, they were ambushed. Pulaski was willing to accept deserters into his ranks, and the Legion was double-crossed by a former British soldier who gave away their position.

Pulaski then begged to be sent south, and Washington obliged early the next year. The Legion traveled seven hundred grueling miles to South Carolina, one of the longest marches of the war.

When they reached Charleston in May 1779, the city was surrounded by the British and considering surrender. Pulaski wasted no time in putting his pet strategy to the test. Barely giving his troops time to rest, he used a group of cavalrymen to try luring Gen. Augustine Prevost into an ambush.

Historians are divided on the outcome. American losses were high: two of those killed were Kováts and Zelinski. Prevost's decision to fall back to Beaufort Island, meanwhile, may have been made because he knew a larger American force was on its way. Still, a British major called Pulaski's troops "the best cavalry the rebels ever had," and Charleston was spared until the following year. Pulaski, however, would not be so lucky.

5

"His attitude was to cost him dearly on more than one occasion," Pulaski's biographer Clarence Manning wrote, "but he maintained it to the end."[237]

Casimir Pulaski's finale was representative of much of his military career. It was paradoxical: an impulsive move that produced little short-term gain. Yet it was undeniably heroic, and it ensured his legend would long outlive him.

He'd been suffering from malaria since he arrived in Charleston, where mosquitoes clustered in the humid summer. The city welcomed the flamboyant Polish cavalier, and during his better moments, he thought about returning there to settle. But he was still sick when he traveled to the Georgia coast that September. He was meeting a long-awaited French fleet, led by Adm. Jean Baptiste Charles Henri Hector, the Comte d'Estaing.

Pulaski's Legion and Admiral d'Estaing's four thousand troops were to link up in an attempt to recapture British-held Savannah. They would be joined by another two thousand American soldiers led by Gen. Benjamin Lincoln. It would be a rematch with British Gen. Austin Prevost, and this time, luck seemed to be on the patriots' side.

A series of errors and mishaps changed those odds. Overly confident of success, d'Estaing offered Prevost the chance to surrender. The British general asked for twenty-four hours to consider the offer. The request was naively granted, allowing reinforcements time to reach Prevost. He admitted later to Parliament that he couldn't have held the city for ten minutes if d'Estaing had attacked. Meanwhile, the British burned and sank several of their own ships, blocking French vessels from reaching the troops or even shelling the city.

Using slave labor working around the clock, the British heavily fortified Savannah, a town of about four hundred homes. They dug a ditch around the city and destroyed all causeways across it. To reach the British, the patriot troops would have to make long, careful detours, or cross

---

[237] Clarence Augustus Manning, *Casimir Pulaski: A Soldier of Liberty* (New York: Philosophical Library, 1944), 204.

swampland that, with one wrong step, could suck soldiers and horses under.

Regardless, an all-out frontal assault on Savannah was planned for the early morning of October 9. Perhaps it might still have succeeded, but at the eleventh hour, the patriots were betrayed by a defector, who gave the plans for the attack to Prevost. When the French and American troops feinted, the British knew to ignore the bait.

The soldiers had no choice but to pick their way through the swamp to reach the Spring Hill redoubt that d'Estaing had chosen to assault. They were mowed down by the redcoats. Admiral d'Estaing was one of those who fell.

Casimir Pulaski saw the admiral wounded and acted without a second thought. Under heavy fire, he rushed to "the murderous spot."[238] As Pulaski did this, he was struck by a piece of grapeshot. Grapeshot was essentially a cloth bag filled with iron balls; it got its name because it looked like a bunch of grapes. One of those "grapes," the size of a twenty-five-cent piece, ripped a hole in Pulaski's groin.

Nearly nine hundred French and Americans were wounded or killed in the failed siege. The injured Pulaski was removed, delirious and fever-ridden, to the American merchant ship *Wasp*.

There he suffered for the next four days as French and American doctors tried and failed to stop the deadly spread of gangrene. "Jesus, Mary, Joseph," were his last reported words. If he wore on his tunic, as some reports claim, a medal honoring Our Lady of Czestochowa, he may have clutched it as he breathed his last. He was just thirty-four years old.

Gangrene is accompanied by a foul-smelling discharge when it's caused by infection. So the story told afterward made an unpleasant sort of sense: Pulaski's body was given a burial at sea, and the *Wasp* lowered its flags and fired a salute in tribute to honor him.

Congress followed suit later that month. While his last communication with them had been an indignant demand to be repaid for expenses,

---

[238] William W. Gordon, "Count Casimir Pulaski," *Georgia Historical Quarterly*, 13, no. 3 (September 1929): 221, http://www.jstor.org/stable/40576081.

they wasted no time in commissioning a memorial. They didn't realize they were also beginning a mystery that would take nearly 250 years to solve.

6

Savannah has grown substantially since that fateful autumn day in 1779, but the grid of its original layout remains. Shaded by massive live oak trees and drooping Spanish moss, the city's twenty-two squares offer tourists a place to rest from the Georgia heat as they plan which historic home to visit next.

One of the most famous is Monterey Square. Located at Bull and Wayne streets, the southeast corner offers a close look at the redbrick facade of the Mercer-Williams House. Flanked by palm trees on each side, the site of John Berendt's famous true-crime tale, *Midnight in the Garden of Good and Evil*, retains its eerie charm.

The dominant piece of architecture in Monterey Square, though, is the monument to Casimir Pulaski. Designed of Italian marble by New York sculptor Robert Eberhard Launitz, it soars into the foliage. A depiction of the lady of liberty peers into the trees at its top, while a relief of Pulaski on horseback decorates the base. When Lafayette visited America in 1825 as an old man on his farewell tour, he laid the cornerstone for the monument himself.

What's inside the monument, however, has been the source of controversy since the 1850s. Historians and scientists have spent decades trying to settle the question definitively.

The accounts of Pulaski's burial at sea were contradicted by the *Wasp*'s captain, Samuel Bullfinch. In 1971, Polish-American scholar Edward Pinkowski uncovered a letter from Bullfinch. Although it did not mention Pulaski by name, it seemed to confirm that his body was not thrown overboard but was instead taken from the ship to nearby Greenwich Plantation.

"I likewise took on board the Americans that were sent down, one of which died this day," Bullfinch wrote to Gen. Benjamin Lincoln, "and I have brought him ashore and buried him."

Liberty's Lions

At Greenwich Plantation, Pulaski was apparently buried by torchlight, to deter grave robbers. In 1853, Gen. William Bowen—the grandson of the plantation's owners—located a skeleton at the burial site. He buried it in the vault inside the Pulaski monument.

Edward Pinkowski insisted for years that his research proved the skeleton was there. In 1996, he was finally proven correct during repairs to the crumbling monument. But the skeleton in the corroded metal box baffled researchers. The pelvis and jaw angle appeared female.

It would take DNA testing years to reach the point where the bones could be compared to a sample from Pulaski's grandniece. A mitochondrial DNA test reportedly proved to be a match, and a 2019 documentary on the Smithsonian Channel reignited questions about Pulaski's background.

Was he actually a woman living as a man? Was Pulaski, perhaps, intersex—having both male and female characteristics? Did he have a condition known as congenital adrenal hyperplasia, in which a genetic female is exposed to high levels of testosterone in the womb? Could that explain the combination of his mustache and receding hairline with feminine skeletal features?

An excited press corps and activists treated the revelations as proof the general was hiding a shocking secret. But what the investigation determined beyond the identification of the bones was less clear. Researchers pointed out there was no evidence Pulaski's friends or contemporaries ever thought of him as anything but a man. There was also no evidence Pulaski ever believed himself to be different from other people.

Except for what he could do on the battlefield. Which, after all, is the reason people remain interested in his career almost 250 years later.

Anthropologist Virginia Hutton Estabrook of Georgia Southern University, who examined the bones, did the best job of putting the discovery in perspective.

"Pulaski is Pulaski is Pulaski," Estabrook said. "What he did, his accomplishments don't change."[239]

---

[239] Brigit Katz, "Was the Revolutionary War Hero Casimir Pulaski Intersex?" *Smithsonian Magazine*, April 29, 2019, https://www.smithsonianmag

Yet an even better epitaph is the one given by Pulaski's old foe, King Stanislaus. It sums up Pulaski's heroism on two continents, and why it matters even today.

"Pulaski died as he lived," the Polish monarch remarked, on learning of his adversary's death. "A hero, but an enemy of kings."[240]

.com/smart-news/was-revolutionary-war-hero-casimir-pulaski-intersex
-180971907/.

[240] Griffin, "General Count Casimir Pulaski," 117.

Chapter 7

... and Postponed Promises

1

It's spring, and the cherry blossoms are in bloom once again by the Potomac River. Walk up the steps here on the south bank of the Tidal Basin, in the gathering twilight, past the colonnade. Under a shallow dome, you'll find Thomas Jefferson. Nineteen feet high and cast in bronze, he stares past the ionic columns, out to the east, toward the White House he once inhabited.

You've probably seen the statue, in person or at least as a photograph. You probably know at least a few of the quotations etched into the marble walls. What you might not have noticed is the fur coat Jefferson is wearing, as he stands there, frozen in time, in the center of his memorial.

The coat was a gift from the Polish general Tadeusz "Thaddeus" Kościuszko, a man for whom the saying, "He'd give you the shirt off his back" could have been coined.

Kościuszko was well-known for awarding soldiers his rings and jewelry instead of medals. He was once visited in America by the Miami Indian Chief Little Turtle, who brought him a combination peace pipe and tomahawk. Kościuszko was so moved that he sent the chief away laden with gifts, including his own eyeglasses and his favorite set of pistols.

Kościuszko gave Jefferson the fur, which he had been presented by Czar Paul I when he was freed from captivity. It was just about the only gift from the double-talking Russian leader Kościuszko was willing to accept. During his lifetime, he refused to touch the thousands of rubles the czar deposited for him in a London bank, considering it blood money.

Czar Paul was only one of the many leaders who let Kościuszko down during the last two decades of his life. There was King Stanislaus, whose weakness had lost Kościuszko's beloved Poland. There was Napoleon, who pledged to help the country regain its freedom but instead used the trusting Polish people to further his own ends.

There was his own Catholic Church, too: the priests in Poland who refused to help the Polish serfs win their freedom but profited from their labor, and who tried to save their own necks by bargaining with Russia and other foreign powers. Kościuszko had grown tired of listening to everyone's promises.

But he would have been disappointed most of all, perhaps, by Jefferson, who still wears Kościuszko's fur coat during his lonely vigil. The two men loved each other like brothers. Yet Kościuszko wanted just one thing from Jefferson: to live up to the words he'd written in the Declaration of Independence. And it was the one thing Jefferson was unwilling, or unable, to do.

Where were the leaders who would do as Kościuszko had done, who would not only pledge to help the peasants but live like them as well, immune from bribes and flattery?

The only one who was close was George Washington, under whom Kościuszko had served with honor in the Continental Army. In December 1783, when Washington made his emotional farewell to his troops at New York's Fraunces Tavern, he gave the Polish engineer a special gift: his cameo ring from the Society of the Cincinnati. This elite society was named after the Roman general Cincinnatus, famed for leaving his farm to lead the republic to victory—and then spurning power by returning home afterward.

That was also an accurate description of Washington, of course. But as Kościuszko's biographer Alex Storozynski notes, no one in attendance could have realized that "Washington was passing the baton to the next farmer-general who would lead his nation against foreign invaders in the name of liberty."

To call Thaddeus Kościuszko the Polish George Washington sounds like a stretch of the truth — until you hear his life story. He was not only a beloved leader but a principled one as well. That combination is rare enough. But then, so are men who have played a crucial role in not just one revolution, but two.

2

Like his countryman Casimir Pulaski, who was born just one year earlier, Thaddeus Kościuszko grew up comfortably. His father, Ludwig, oversaw a midsize estate on Poland's eastern border, near present-day Belarus. Although the farm was modest, it was worked by a group of thirty-one peasant families.

Polish landowners had the right to demand a period of unpaid labor — called a corvée — from their tenants. Since some landowners set the corvée at six or even seven days a week, many serfs were little better than slaves. Ludwig Kościuszko, however, treated his serfs kindly, and taught his four children to do the same.

Thaddeus, the youngest, took this admonition to heart. The desire to see freedom and equality for all became the animating principle of his life. "Serfdom is a word," he would later write, "that must be cursed by all enlightened nations." Kościuszko would also curse discrimination of all kinds, including prejudice that harmed blacks and Jews.

Yet he was no attention-seeking daredevil, like Pulaski. His hero was, instead, the ancient Greek general and statesman Timoleon.

A member of the oligarchy, Timoleon led Corinth and Sicily to victory against the tyrant state Carthage, brought peace to his people — and then retired, rather than prolong his career. "He overthrew tyrants, set up republics and never demanded any power for himself," the admiring boy said.

Kościuszko was exposed to these lessons as a student at the Catholic Piarist Fathers College at Lubieszow. The school's curriculum had been designed by the reformist priest Fr. Stanislaw Konarski. He was dedicated to educational reform in Poland, and introduced his pupils to a wide-ranging set of lessons.

He was also closely associated with the man who became Thaddeus Kościuszko's patron: King Stanislaus August Poniatowski. Thaddeus had long dreamed of being a soldier, and he got his chance at age eighteen, when the newly formed Royal Knight School was looking for recruits.

Kościuszko went to Warsaw to study a variety of military subjects, from topography and mapmaking to swordsmanship and fort construction. He was such an eager student that he tied a string to one hand each night. In the hallway, he left the string's other end, asking the night watchman to pull it at 3:00 a.m. so he could rise extra-early to study.

The king was impressed by the dedicated young recruit, who soon faced a test of loyalty. Some Polish nobles, including the family of Casimir Pulaski, wanted to overthrow King Stanislaus. The monarch had taken the throne in 1763 after a rigged election funded by his former lover, Empress Catherine the Great. Members of the Bar Confederation understandably feared Stanislaus would be no more than a Russian-controlled puppet.

Now twenty-three, Thaddeus Kościuszko was conflicted. He believed deeply in independence for Poland, but he decided against throwing his lot in with the rebels. Instead, in the fall of 1769, he went to Paris to further his studies: at the Royal Academy of Painting and Sculpture by day, and with private military tutors at night. The quietly intense young man had a natural gift for engineering, and he studied carefully the French infrastructure around him.

Paris was abuzz at the time with the thoughts of writers such as Voltaire and Rousseau, whose ideas were still two decades from sparking a revolution in France. Kościuszko also became fascinated by a philosophy called physiocracy, which argued for free markets and against the feudalist system of countries like Poland.

When he returned home in 1774, however, he got a forceful reminder that the old ways were still very much in effect. He fell in love with Louise Sosnowska, the daughter of a wealthy nobleman, after he began tutoring her and her sister.

The dashing young captain with the turned-up nose was handsome, his thick brown hair tied back in a ponytail. He charmed Louise with his gentle flirting, but it became clear she was out of his league financially. Her father had already arranged a more suitable marriage, so Kościuszko appealed to the king for help.

King Stanislaus knew a little something about the problems of getting involved with a more powerful woman, and he advised Kościuszko to lay off. Instead, Kościuszko planned an elaborate scheme to abduct Louise and elope. Their carriage was stopped, however, before the couple could reach a priest. Lord Sosnowski's guards knocked the young captain unconscious, and Kościuszko was haunted by the older man's haughty dismissal of the affair: "Pigeons are not meant for sparrows."

But pigeons *could* be prosecuted by vengeful noblemen, and Lord Sosnowski also wanted revenge. In October 1775, the lovelorn Kościuszko fled Poland to save his life. He first sought a position in the Saxon court at Dresden, then traveled to Paris to try joining the French army. When those two possibilities fizzled, he was introduced to the French playwright, watchmaker, and spy, Pierre Augustin Caron de Beaumarchais.

Beaumarchais, as we saw in chapter 5, was beginning to recruit soldiers for the American rebels. His scheme—creating a dummy company to funnel weapons and supplies to the colonists—was about to be funded by the French and Spanish governments.

The colonists also needed soldiers, and Beaumarchais sent them plenty. But what they *really* needed, to plan their forts and design their defenses, were engineers. They were about to get one of the best.

3

Benjamin Franklin was known for being able to find the humor in humorless situations. As the serious young man leaned earnestly toward him, he realized this was one of those moments.

It was August 1776, and in a few months, Franklin would be on his way to Paris. There he would be inundated with applications from foreign mercenaries who wanted to join the Continental Army. But the young man before him was hoping for the same sort of commission. He had survived a shipwreck in Martinique, then found his own way to Philadelphia on a fishing trawler.

Now he was in Franklin's shop on a sweltering summer afternoon, demanding to be given a placement test in engineering or military architecture. Franklin pushed up his spectacles with a finger and chuckled. "Who would proctor such an exam," he gently asked his visitor, "when there is no one here who is even familiar with those subjects?"

Instead, Thaddeus Kościuszko was given an assessment in geometry, which he passed. He would also pass most of the other tests he was given in the Continental Army—even though it took his superiors some time to realize his expertise.

His first job was to help design a series of defenses for Philadelphia, which the British were expected to attack. This brought him into the orbit of Gen. Horatio Gates, who was assigned command of forces around the city early in 1777. Kościuszko became close with Gates, which gave him a powerful ally for a while.

The older man was mightily impressed with his new Polish engineer, "the only pure republican I ever knew. He is without dross." This friendship, however, drew the quiet and modest Kościuszko unwillingly into the Revolution's plentiful personal intrigue.

One of the most remarkable things about America's success in the Revolution is not just the long odds against the patriots, but the way petty jealousies threatened to derail the cause at every turn. Later that year, as just one example, Gates was named as part of the "Conway Cabal" that sought to replace George Washington as commander in chief. The leading contenders for the job were Charles Lee and Gates himself.

But that was only one of the many simmering personal conflicts threatening to explode at any time. Gen. Philip Schuyler was another rival of Gates, who was unhappy when Gates took over the Northern Army in the spring of 1777. Feeling unappreciated and underpaid despite his bravery and military successes, Maj. Gen. Benedict Arnold also sulked on the periphery after Gates's appointment.

These squabbles trickled down when Kościuszko received his next assignment: to survey the defenses at Fort Ticonderoga, a star-shaped stone fort nestled between Lakes George and Champlain in upstate New York. He recommended placing cannons on the bluffs of Mount Defiance, but the fort's own engineer, feeling threatened by the highly touted new import, disagreed.

Some people *did* agree with Kościuszko. Unfortunately, they were British Gen. John Burgoyne and his chief of artillery, Gen. William Phillips. On July 4, 1777, they had soldiers drag cannons up the undefended hill and fire directly into the fort. The only reason some patriot troops were able to evacuate Ticonderoga was because Kościuszko had supervised the construction of a floating log bridge across Lake Champlain.

The next time the Continental Army faced Burgoyne, at Saratoga in September, the results would be far different. After the embarrassment at Ticonderoga, people were ready to listen to Kościuszko. He was sent out to find a place where the army could make a stand. And when he found "an elevated pasture above the road to Albany along the Hudson, Kościuszko's eyes lit up," as author Alex Storozynski recounts, "and he galloped his horse around in circles on the hill and exclaimed, 'This is the spot!'"[241]

It was a densely wooded plateau called Bemis Heights, just south of Saratoga. Kościuszko built up the colonial positions on the elevation, knowing the British would be faced with an impossible choice: be picked off on the narrow path below or scatter into the thick forests on either side.

Gen. Daniel Morgan's crack team of Virginia sharpshooters took care of the first part, and when the redcoats retreated into the woods, Benedict Arnold rallied his troops to chase them. Burgoyne was expecting reinforcements, but Gen. William Howe's troops had headed for Philadelphia to capture the bigger prize. So, by mid-October, Burgoyne was forced to surrender. It was effectively the end of his military career.

Among all the terrible news the patriots received that fall and winter of 1777, Saratoga was the bright spot. It was the decisive victory the French had been waiting for, which allowed them to make their secret support of the rebels public.

Of course, the bickering for credit began almost immediately. Arnold and Gates both vied to get the lion's share of the glory for this important

[241] Storozynski, *The Peasant Prince*, 33.

victory. It made Gates, in particular, seem like a viable candidate to replace George Washington.

But a year later, when the Conway Cabal had faded into memory and Gates had apologized to General Washington for his role in the intrigue, he was sober-minded enough to mention the real architect of Saratoga.

"The great tacticians of the campaign were the hills and forests," he admitted to Dr. Benjamin Rush, "which a young Polish Engineer was skillful enough to select for my encampment."[242]

4

Now came the big assignment. In March 1778, Kościuszko was sent to West Point, the project dearest to Washington's heart. The general had wanted a fort there for years, ever since he sailed up the Hudson and "marked with his eye the positions best adapted to command the passage."[243]

The three existing forts in the area had been hastily constructed and were poorly situated. They were the opposite of the "Gibraltar on the Hudson" Washington envisioned. And the two engineers assigned to work on this project were also a study in contrasts.

Colonel Kościuszko kept his mouth shut, did his work, and got along with just about everyone. It wasn't just West Point's commander, Gen. Samuel Parson, who believed the Polish soldier was "disposed to do everything he can in a most agreeable manner."[244]

The same could not be said of Lt. Col. Louis de la Radiere, the French engineer originally assigned to the project. Disagreeing with everyone else—including Washington—about the best site for the fort, he sketched out a massive stone structure downriver.

Radiere was dismissive and rude to everyone he worked with—Capt. Edward Boynton described him as an "impatient, petulant officer"—and

---

[242] Storozynski, *The Peasant Prince*, 39.

[243] George Bancroft, *History of the United States of America, from the Discovery of the Continent*, vol. 5 (1885; Boston: Little, Brown, and Company, 2017), 432.

[244] Jonathan Kruk, *Legends and Lore of the Hudson Highlands* (Charleston, SC: History Press, 2018), 76–77.

Maj. Gen. Israel Putnam dismissed his scheme for the fort as the work of a "paper engineer."[245]

The commander of the Hudson Highland, Gen. Alexander McDougall, put things somewhat more delicately: Kościuszko, he offered, was "esteemed by those who have attended the works at West Point, to have more practice than Col. DeLaradiere, and his manner of treating people more acceptable."[246] Washington himself, who quickly got fed up with Radiere's delays and complaints, admitted Kościuszko "is better adapted to the genius and temper of the people."[247]

Kościuszko, in turn, would have to adapt his design to the hilly terrain. He managed this, military historian Nicholas Sambaluk explained, by developing "a sophisticated solution that used the numerous hills to turn the dilemma back onto an attacker since the new layered defenses formed a succession of obstacles to overcome."[248]

Those obstacles included thirty-seven different forts, redoubts, and ramparts. And protecting the river itself was "Washington's Watch Chain," developed by Capt. Thomas Machin, a 1,700-foot-long set of iron links floating on sharpened logs.

During the more than two years he worked on the project, Kościuszko also had time to plant a garden of wildflowers on a rocky cliff that looks down on the Hudson River. He used the spot as a quiet retreat to meditate; it remains there today, and cadets at West Point sometimes use it for the same purpose.

Washington had well-known difficulties in remembering the correct name of his remarkable young Polish engineer. But, however he spelled

---

[245] "To George Washington from Major General Israel Putnam, 13 January 1778," Founders Online, National Archives, https://founders.archives .gov/documents/Washington/03-13-02-0190.

[246] "To George Washington from Major General Alexander McDougall, 13 April 1778," Founders Online, National Archives, https://founders .archives.gov/documents/Washington/03-14-02-0461.

[247] "Washington to Gates, 4 January 1778."

[248] Nicholas Michael Sambaluk, "Making the Point—West Point's Defenses and Digital Age Implications, 1778–1781," *Cyber Defense Review* 2, no. 2 (Summer 2017): 150, https://www.jstor.org/stable/26267348.

it, he knew Kościuszko had helped give him the impregnable defense at West Point that he'd been seeking.

It was so formidable, in fact, that the only way anyone could hope to breach the defenses was from the inside, with the help of a turncoat.

Enter Benedict Arnold.

5

Even in this history-starved age, just about everyone recognizes the name Benedict Arnold—and its most common synonym: "traitor."

Fewer people, however, realize what Arnold was offering the British during the summer of 1780, as he schemed to sell out the colonies for a reward of twenty thousand pounds. That would be Thaddeus Kościuszko's plans for West Point—in Washington's view, the "key to America." This was the prize Arnold promised to turn over to his new allies.

Even today, no one knows exactly what motivated Arnold. Libraries have been written to settle the point, but the truth died with him in London in 1801, where he finished out his life in exile. Was it simple greed? Was it professional jealousy? Was it the constant pain from his war wounds? Was it the fear his pretty young loyalist wife, Peggy Shippen, would cuckold him? Was it all of the above, or was it some other factor that will remain forever unknown? Possibly even Arnold himself couldn't have answered the question.

Regardless, had Thaddeus Kościuszko not gotten his way and left West Point for the Revolution's southern theater, Arnold's plot would never have gotten as far as it did. Kościuszko would have immediately recognized something was wrong when Arnold took over the command of the fort that August and began rescinding the plans the engineer had so carefully developed.

Arnold never did find Kościuszko's blueprints, which were hidden in a chest at his boardinghouse, so he copied them as best he could based on his own observations. If he'd had Kościuszko's plans, the timetable of his deception might have been moved up.

Perhaps then, Arnold's British contact, Maj. John André, would have been riding through the autumn woods near Tarrytown, New York, on a different day that September 1780. Perhaps he would never have been stopped by three curious sentries, who therefore never would have discovered, stuffed inside one of his boots, Arnold's own scrawled plans of the fort.

But that's exactly what happened, and the plot quickly unraveled. André was executed as a spy, and Arnold narrowly escaped from West Point into a waiting British warship.

The Hudson was the dividing line of colonial America. Had the British seized control of West Point and strategic control of the river it overlooked, they could then have focused on crushing the rebellious North.

Now Britain had to turn its attention to the loyalist South. Once again, Kościuszko helped frustrate their efforts.

He arrived too late to see his mentor and friend, Horatio Gates, suffer one of the worst losses of the Revolution. The man his troops affectionately—or mockingly—called "Granny Gates" wilted in the August heat at Camden, South Carolina. His inexperienced troops were routed, and Gates beat a hasty retreat without them. He made it all the way to North Carolina before he stopped, and made himself a laughingstock in the process.

Kościuszko served instead under Gates's replacement, Nathaniel Greene. Greene racked up exactly the same number of wins in the South as Gates: zero. But his strategy was the embodiment of the old saying, "Lose the battle; win the war."

Greene's job was to keep the Southern Army a step ahead of the British forces in a war of attrition. Kościuszko helped by engineering portable flatboats that allowed the patriot troops to continually elude the redcoats' clutches. The most memorable example came in February 1781, during what came to be called the "Race to the Dan."

On Valentine's Day, General Cornwallis was tantalizingly close to catching Greene's troops, who were exhausted after a march of nearly two hundred miles. Defeat seemed imminent, and for the Continental Army it would have been a devastating loss. But at Irwin's Ferry on the Dan River, Kościuszko's boats allowed the narrowest of escapes—so close that the patriots were able to jeer at the British troops from the opposite side of the Dan.

It was an especially bitter sight for Cornwallis. For three weeks and 250 miles, he had chased the patriots through the mud, rain, and sleet. But he'd failed, by the width of the Dan River. And it foreshadowed his much bigger loss that summer at Yorktown.

That battle would be the last major conflict of the Revolution, although the fighting continued sporadically throughout the next year. Kościuszko's unit fought what is sometimes recognized as the final battle, at James Island in South Carolina, near the end of 1782.

It would be some time before he got there, but Kościuszko was thinking of home. It had been ten years since Poland was partitioned, losing almost a third of its territory. Russia, Prussia, and Austria had claimed chunks of Poland following the end of the Bar Confederation rebellion led by Casimir Pulaski.

Kościuszko hoped to secure a commission to lead a Polish cavalry regiment. But he knew the landscape had changed.

"Drawing the tickets in the lottery of chance for so many years," he wrote to Nathaniel Greene, the day before he departed America in July 1784, "I am too well acquainted to depend on probabilities where even certainties are so often doubtful."[249]

Kościuszcio's caution was well-founded. Yet for a gloriously short while, it looked like the lottery ticket he and Poland had drawn was a winner.

6

Voices soar above the clangor of bells from St. John's Cathedral. They are singing "Te Deum Laudamus," a Latin hymn that means "God, We Praise You." A joyous crowd has gathered on the cobblestone street outside the church, welcoming a triumphant King Stanislaus.

The deputy of the Sejm, the Polish assembly, happily waves a copy of the new Polish Constitution. Stanislaw Małachowski says this document will create a government "finer than both" England's and America's. Just behind him, head bandaged from a war wound, Thaddeus Kościuszko proudly holds aloft the flag.

[249] Storozynski, *The Peasant Prince*, 118.

You can see it all in a famous oil by Jan Matejko, who painted the scene a hundred years after the adoption of Poland's new constitution. The Constitution of 3 May 1791, as it's commonly called, isn't historically accurate: Matejko intentionally depicted several people who weren't actually there in Warsaw that day.

One of them was Kościuszko. He had become a general in the Polish army and was defending the Russian border at the time. But his importance to the event certainly merits his inclusion.

Since he'd arrived back in Poland at the end of 1784, Europe had struggled to orient itself to the American Revolution. There was optimism on the part of reformers, and fear in the ruling classes. In Poland, people were speaking up for the rights of burghers—businesspeople who wanted to be able to own land and have representatives in the Sejm—and even serfs.

An important voice belonged to the Catholic priest Fr. Hugo Kollontay, a leader in the movement to reform Poland. He became an ally of Kościuszko, already a symbol of independence thanks to his heroism in America.

The unlikeliest ally of reform was King Stanislaus, long derided as a Russian stooge. Yet he was now under pressure from more than just Catherine the Great. The French Revolution, which began in 1789, had put the entire European aristocracy under a microscope.

Stanislaus really may have believed the new constitution would create opportunities for Poland, by liberating the burghers, affirming religious freedom, and making the country an attractive destination for business. Or endorsing the constitution might simply have been a result of his well-honed instinct for self-preservation. Better to give up some power than to have it all taken away.

Either way, Stanislaus became a national and international hero when he took the oath affirming Poland's new direction. The document was modeled on the U.S. Constitution, giving Poland separation of powers, a bicameral legislature, and a judicial branch. From Edmund Burke in England to George Washington and Thomas Jefferson in America, the praise poured in for Europe's first constitution.

And though Kościuszko felt it didn't go far enough—protections for Jews and serfs were still lacking, he thought—he still signed it and encouraged his men to give it their support.

When he took the oath that momentous May afternoon before the Sejm, King Stanislaus declared, "I swear before God that I won't regret it."[250]

But he did. And it only took a single year.

7

The new constitution had powerful enemies. One of them, of course, was Catherine the Great, who stood to lose her influence over Polish affairs. Others were the Polish nobles—the Targowica Confederation—who resented the loss of power and profits the constitution represented. It was perhaps inevitable that the two sides would join forces to bring down Poland's new republic.

In May 1792, Russia invaded Poland. What followed was a three-month war that ended when King Stanislaus pursued a diplomatic solution—in other words, a second partition of Poland, which reduced its population to just a third of what it had been in 1771.

It was a crushing disappointment, not just because of the loss of territory and pride but also because Kościuszko had proven he could hold his own against the numerically superior Russian forces. In one battle, at the small farming village of Dubienka, he managed a stalemate despite being outnumbered five to one. His genius for battle planning and fortification helped the Poles continually repel the Russian army, in onslaught after bloody onslaught. Even the opposing general, Mikhail Kachowski, praised Kościuszko's "passionate plan,"[251] which led to so many losses on the Russian side.

Kościuszko wanted to keep fighting, but King Stanislaus insisted he surrender to Kachowski. That ceremony was exceptionally bitter for Kościuszko. "After shaking hands, I thought, how easy it would be to

[250] Storozynski, *The Peasant Prince*, 149.
[251] Storozynski, *The Peasant Prince*, 163.

beat them, if our country had the energy and sense of its own freedom and the real enthusiasm of its citizenry," he wrote later. "I left disgusted, with tears in my eyes."[252]

Two years later, he returned as the commander in chief of a new rebellion. Dressed in a peasant's robe made of sheep's wool, he led a coalition that included peasants, Jews, ex-army members, and dissident priests.

The uprising began in a Krakow monastery on March 24, 1794. Kościuszko "assisted at a low Mass in the Capuchin church, where the officiating priest blessed the leader's sword" next to a statue of the Virgin Mary, as biographer Monica Mary Gardner wrote. "'God grant me to conquer or die,' were Kościuszko's words, as he received the weapon from the monk's hand."[253] He then dedicated himself to the new movement by invoking "God and the innocent passion of His Son."[254]

With the Proclamation of Polaniec that May, Kościuszko offered freedom to the serfs—and criticism of the noblemen who had sold out Poland for their own gain.

Although it was inspired by the French Revolution, this movement would be different. The insurgents in Paris lived by Denis Diderot's famous maxim that no one would truly be free until the last king was strangled with the entrails of the last priest. But Kościuszko had neither their hostility toward religion nor their appetite for bloodshed.

He proved the difference after a group of rebels in Warsaw took justice into their own hands that June. They hanged a local bishop and several other prisoners, and Kościuszko punished them severely. This didn't endear him to the French revolutionaries, but he insisted even traitors deserved lawful treatment.

That summer might have been Kościuszko's finest moment on the battlefield. His peasant army defended Warsaw for nearly two months against a brutal siege by Russian and Prussian troops. Once again, Kościuszko's

[252] Storozynski, *The Peasant Prince*, 165.
[253] Monica Mary Gardner, *Kościuszko: A Biography* (1919; Charleston, SC: Nabu Press, 2010), 97–98.
[254] Storozynski, *The Peasant Prince*, 182.

talent for planning frustrated a superior force. Meanwhile, "his modesty and good nature did wonders to keep morale high in a city that was constantly under cannon fire."[255] He spent his nights in a tent outside a palace, sleeping in his robe to be ready for action.

The invading armies withdrew early in September, but the Russians soon returned. Along the muddy banks of the Wisla River near Maciejowice, Kościuszko made his last stand. In the driving autumn rain, the Polish peasants were massacred by the Russian army, whose soldiers bayoneted even those who begged to surrender. Catherine the Great, furious at being defied, was determined to finally crush the rebellion.

To motivate the troops, she'd placed a substantial bounty on Kościuszko's head. Yet, after he was thrown from his horse into the muck, the Russians didn't even recognize him at first. He was still dressed in his peasant's robe, and they casually stabbed him in the back and leg with their bayonets. The Russians laughed, too, when Kościuszko stuck his pistol into his mouth to spare himself this final indignity.

But he was out of bullets, thank God, and out of luck in his battle with the Russians. The revolution, and Poland, were both finished.

8

After being hauled across the frozen wastes of Russia to St. Petersburg, Kościuszko spent the next two years as the prisoner of Catherine the Great. He won his freedom only with her unexpected death from a stroke in November 1796.

Catherine's son Paul visited Kościuszko's room in the Marble Palace shortly after the empress's death. The new czar called himself a friend. He certainly owed no allegiance to the memory of his mother, who'd had his father killed, then took the throne, when he was only eight.

But Czar Paul proposed a devil's bargain. To win his own release, and the freedom of twelve thousand Polish prisoners of war, all Kościuszko had to do was say the word. The word, however, was an oath to the czar. No more rebellions—and therefore, no more Poland.

[255] Storozynski, *The Peasant Prince*, 199.

Kościuszko gritted his teeth and took the oath. He lived for more than twenty years afterward, and there probably wasn't a day he didn't regret what he'd done.

In those final two decades of his life, he never gave up the hope of returning to Poland and helping liberate his country. As a sign of his intent, he publicly returned the funds Czar Paul had deposited for him in a London bank, although the angry czar refused to accept the money, vowing he would "accept nothing from traitors."

Yet while both Napoleon and the new czar of Russia, Alexander, promised Kościuszko they would help him work for Polish independence, he soon found neither man was serious about it.

Though his dream of an independent Poland remained elusive, Kościuszko had another goal he was sure he could achieve. To do so, he would use most of the back pay Congress had awarded him for his wartime service — nearly twenty thousand dollars, with interest.

As early as 1780, Kościuszko had been puzzled about the contrast between Thomas Jefferson's famous declaration that all men are created equal and his ownership of slaves. For his part, Jefferson realized Kościuszko was not just a theoretical abolitionist. "He is as pure a son of liberty as I have ever known," he wrote to Kościuszko's former commander, Horatio Gates, "and of the liberty which is to go to all, and not to the few or rich alone."[256]

The two men corresponded regularly and grew increasingly close as the years passed. Jefferson tried to persuade Kościuszko to settle down in America. When it became clear this was a futile dream, he proposed they should be buried there instead, side by side.

The aging Kościuszko — battle-scarred and living as simply as possible in Switzerland — wanted something different.

Most of his dreams, he had to admit, had fallen well short of expectations. He had been unable to free the serfs in Poland. He'd also never

---

[256] "From Thomas Jefferson to Horatio Gates, 21 February 1798," Founders Online, National Archives, https://founders.archives.gov/documents/Jefferson/01-30-02-0083.

found anyone to replace his first, and only true love, Louise Sosnowska. While the "peasant prince" remained attractive to women, even in his old age, he never married. That unfulfilled first romance loomed large over the rest of his life.

But for twenty years he'd nursed a final wish: he wanted to use his back pay to buy the freedom of as many of Jefferson's slaves as possible. He wrote it in a will in May 1798, before he left America, and he repeated this wish to Jefferson multiple times. "The fixed designation" of his assets, he wrote to Jefferson in September 1817, "after my death is known to you."[257]

When Kościuszko died the very next month, after being thrown from a horse near Lake Geneva, Jefferson had his chance to address the dichotomy between his words and actions. But friends and relatives of Kościuszko inevitably appeared to stake their own claims to the will. Even before these competing claims surfaced, Jefferson pleaded that the will was too complicated and he was too old to deal with it. In federal district court, he relinquished the executorship.

Almost all Jefferson's slaves would be sold following his death in 1826. Some were families, separated by the auctioneer's gavel. Slavery's "fire bell in the night," which Jefferson famously confessed had awakened him in terror, didn't ring loudly enough to make him follow his friend's wishes.

It's perhaps fortunate that Kościuszko didn't live to witness that betrayal. He was never able to understand how otherwise upright and moral men, both secular and religious, could fail to recognize the human dignity of all God's creatures. And it often caused him to rebel against the priests and bishops of his own Catholic Church, who he believed should have been first to affirm that dignity. "There is no faith," he told his countrymen in 1794, before he made his last stand, "that would forbid a man to be free."[258]

His struggles did not, however, cause him to lose his own faith. Near the end of his life, Kościuszko wrote a personal prayer for the human race.

---

[257] Storozynski, *The Peasant Prince*, 277.
[258] Gardner, *Kościuszko*, 116.

Despite his Enlightenment leanings and his belief in man's responsibility to the state, it is not the prayer of a deist. It explicitly mentions Jesus as man's Savior, and it reads like the cry of a man desperate to see Christ's justice done—and a man who is also old enough to recognize how unlikely that is in this world.

Almighty God, who enlivens the world's millions with your spirit,

Who has ordered me to live in this valley of tears for designs hidden from me,

Grant that I may wend my way through it over roads pleasing to You;

Let me do good; keep me from evil; restrain the unruly impulses of my impetuosity;

Let me come to know your genuine truth unmarred by any human error.

Bless, O God, my country, my relatives, my friends, my benefactors, my countrymen—the whole human race.

And when my last hour comes, when my soul takes leave of my body, grant that I may stand before Your countenance in the dwelling of the blessed and comprehend the mystery of the world which today is beyond my comprehension.

Do not send me to eternal perdition; but permit me to stand before Your countenance in the abode of the blessed.

I ask this through Jesus Christ our Savior. Amen.[259]

9

While they didn't live parallel lives, Casimir Pulaski and Thaddeus Kościuszko certainly had much in common. They helped win a revolution in America they could not accomplish in their homeland, despite their valiant, underdog efforts. They both survived with a price on their heads, put there by a foreign czarina hostile to the Roman Catholic Church and an independent Poland. That price reflected Catherine the

---

[259] Storozynski, *The Peasant Prince*, 274–275.

Great's acknowledgment of their charisma and leadership and the honor with which they served on the battlefields of two nations.

Both men were military innovators, and both lived up to the ideals of the new country they helped found. It's appropriate that their names can be found all across America, then: on bridges, towns, counties, schools, and highways.

In the long, strange, summer of 2020, their lives would intertwine again.

Protesters around the country damaged and toppled monuments following the death of Minneapolis resident George Floyd, who was killed by a policeman during an arrest. Not far from the White House, on the National Mall, statues of both Polish patriots were defaced.

It's impossible to know whether the people who proudly scrawled "BLM" across the base of Kościuszko's monument realized his feelings about slavery and the way he tried to act on them. The irony that he believed only education could lift the oppressed out of poverty would almost certainly have been lost on the vandals.

A year earlier, a statue of Pulaski in Baltimore's Patterson Park had also been spray-painted with graffiti. If they could have heard it, the response of one Baltimore resident would probably have sounded familiar to both Pulaski and Kościuszko. "There's certain historical figures that I don't think should be idolized, but I don't know anything about him, so I guess I can't really comment," a local man told a Baltimore TV station. "But in general, graffiti's bad."[260]

It was the sort of verbal shrug both men heard often, more than two hundred years ago, that allowed them to lose their beloved country. If their statues could speak, they might well have had a warning for the people in their adopted homeland, who seemed convinced a republic can sustain itself without any sacrifices.

---

[260] "Pulaski Monument Vandalized with Spray Paint in Baltimore's Patterson Park," WJZ 13–CBS Baltimore, May 23, 2019, https://baltimore.cbslocal.com/2019/05/23/pulaski-monument-vandalized-patterson-park/.

"I came here, where freedom is being defended," Casimir Pulaski once told Benjamin Franklin, "to serve it, and to live or die for it." Meanwhile, in Poland, Thaddeus Kościuszko lamented that his country lacked "the energy and sense of its own freedom and the real enthusiasm of its citizenry" to truly remain independent.

For now, at least, their statues still stand—a reminder that between freedom and bondage, indifference is a third option that never lasts for long.

Chapter 8

She Stooped to Conquer:
The Other Lafayette

1

When Lafayette predicted that the United States would never entertain an aristocracy or a king, Frederick the Great responded, "Monsieur, I knew a young man who, after visiting countries where liberty and equality reigned, got it into his head to establish all that in his own country. Do you know what happened to him?"

"No, Sire," Lafayette replied.

"Monsieur," the king grinned, "he was hanged."[261]

2

The stench of raw sewage never abated. At any moment, the suffocating silence might be lacerated by the "horrible music"[262] of a prisoner's moans from the courtyard below, as a metal rod tore flesh from back and neck. When food arrived, it had to be picked with greasy fingers out of filth-encrusted pots.

After more than three years in this Moravian prison, little more than a skeleton was left of the man. His hair had fallen out, and weeping sores

[261] Harlow G. Unger, *Lafayette* (New York: Wiley, 2003), 213.
[262] Jason Lane, *General and Madame de Lafayette: Partners in Liberty's Cause in the American and French Revolutions* (Lanham, MD: Taylor Trade, 2003), 228.

were visible through his rags. The woman had not been here as long but was in even worse shape. She'd become bloated: her arms and legs were so swollen she could barely move them. When she did, the blisters that covered them erupted into open wounds.

But every night, before the lights were extinguished, they embraced on the same wooden pallet. Then their two girls helped her rise painfully to her feet, and the three crossed the dim and dirty hallway to their own cell.

They were together again, a family again, at last.

No horrors could be worse than what they'd already survived. For more than a year, the woman had been locked in a cell in Paris, wondering when her neck would be roughly jammed into the grooves of the guillotine. Her mother, sister, and grandmother took their turns during the height of the Terror. She barely escaped hers.

The man was only saved because he was no longer in France. Instead, he'd been imprisoned in a series of airless dungeon cells in Austrian and Prussian jails. There he was kept under lock and key out of spite: he was blamed for the French Revolution that had thrown Europe into chaos and had all monarchs looking nervously over their shoulders. The prisoner had tried desperately to stop the madmen who raped and robbed, tortured and murdered, in the name of revolution. That meant nothing to King Frederick William II, the nephew of Frederick the Great.

"As it is you who put your king in irons," the Duke of Saxe-Teschen had written disdainfully to him when he was first jailed, "as it is you who were the principal instrument of all the disgraces that overwhelmed that unfortunate monarch, it is only too just that those who are working to reestablish his dignity should hold you until the moment when your master, having recovered his liberty and his sovereignty, can, according to his sense of justice or clemency, dictate your fate."[263]

The king of France, Louis XVI, that "unfortunate monarch," would not be able to dictate anyone's fate now: he'd been beheaded by the baying mob in Paris, early in 1793. But King Frederick still meant to teach

---

[263] James R. Gaines, *For Liberty and Glory: Washington, Lafayette, and Their Revolutions* (New York: W. W. Norton, 2009), 374.

his captive a lesson. So Frederick transferred the man to an even fouler prison, in Olmütz, Moravia, in present-day Czechoslovakia.

There, his wife and their two daughters came to visit. More than that: at his wife's insistence, they came to stay. They would all share the man's fate.

"My cherished thought is that when one is condemned to ostracism," she had written to him beforehand, "one can endure it with his wife and his children."[264] They would find this letter in his billfold after he died.

When she made this stunning demand, the Austrian emperor, Francis II, shrugged. She would find her husband well-nourished and well-treated, Francis said, after granting her a brief audience. Both claims were lies.

"Your presence will be an added pleasure," he told her.[265] Even though it seemed he was mocking her, that claim turned out to be true.

When she and the girls had spied the towers of the prison from the window of their carriage on the October morning they'd arrived at Olmütz, she fought back tears. To think she was this close to her husband again! Then she led their girls in a prayer—one of her mother's favorites, Tobit's "Song of Praise":

> Blessed is God who lives for ever,
> and blessed is his kingdom.
> For he afflicts, and he shows mercy;
> he leads down to Hades, and brings up again,
> and there is no one who can escape his hand.
> Acknowledge him before the nations, O sons of Israel;
> for he has scattered us among them.
> Make his greatness known there,
> and exalt him in the presence of all the living.
> (Tob. 13:1–4)

---

[264] Lane, *General and Madame de Lafayette*, 224.

[265] André Maurois, *Adrienne: The Life of the Marquise de La Fayette*, trans. Gerard Hopkins (London: Jonathan Cape, 1961), 296.

She gazed up at the forbidden towers in the leaden autumn sky. "How the ordeal before us is to be endured," she whispered, "I do not know."[266]

But they found a way. She managed to write an entire biography of her mother in the margins of a book, using a toothpick dipped in ink. She and the girls used fabric from their skirts to patch her husband's clothes, and they made him a pair of shoes from her corset. And they were together again—that was the most important thing of all.

Even when fever kept her from sleep and her swollen limbs itched and ached, she refused to leave the prison. The king told her that if she sought treatment elsewhere, he would not let her return to her husband's cell. "I will not expose myself," she replied in a voice edged with steel, "to the horror of a new separation."[267]

Her daughters watched in wonder. "Despite her suffering, she seemed happier than she had ever been," one of them marveled. "It is hard for me to describe how happy she was. To understand, you have to recognize the fear she had lived with for so long—during the frequent separations and endless adventures that took my father away from home into great danger. She had spent the previous three horrible years alone without hope of ever finding him again. Now her lifelong dream was fulfilled."[268]

Eventually, Gilbert du Motier—better known as the Marquis de Lafayette—would be released from prison, along with his wife and daughters.

He was the adopted hero of one revolution, and helped unleash another in his home country, an uprising he could not contain. He is an icon to all revolutionaries, and a cautionary tale to all of them as well. He was more revered than any king, and he also paid a terrible price for the glory he deservedly won.

His wife, Adrienne de Lafayette, paid an even greater and more painful cost. Yet she shared all his sufferings with every bit as much courage and grace.

---

[266] Maurois, *Adrienne*, 298–299.
[267] Lane, *General and Madame de Lafayette*, 230.
[268] Unger, *Lafayette*, 312–313.

You probably know his story, or at least the most glorious parts of it. But there would have been no story at all without her, and her remarkable, resilient faith.

3

If there is a future saint lurking anywhere in this book, she is here in this chapter.

She didn't fight a single redcoat during the American Revolution. In fact, she never set foot on colonial soil. Her contributions to the freedom of the United States are not recorded in any history book, because the contributions of families—especially those of faithful wives—are usually relegated to a paragraph or two, or maybe just the footnotes, if they are acknowledged at all.

The American Revolution boasted its share of remarkable women, and remarkable spouses. Martha Washington, Abigail Adams, and Eliza Hamilton are three of the best-known among the many who faced the agonies of long separation and the trials of what amounted to single parenthood. They stoically endured their spouses' public humiliations; in Eliza Hamilton's case, those humiliations included the revelation of her husband's unfaithfulness. All three richly deserved the salutation Alexander Hamilton used in his final letter to Eliza: "Best of wives, best of women."[269]

But none of them had to face down a slavering mob at bayonet point. None of them had to play hardball with dimwitted and shifty government officials to recover her family's stolen property. None of them had children whose parents lived for years in the shadow of a revolution turned monstrously evil, children who would later recall of their parents, "Not once in those days did she see him leave the house without the feeling that she might be saying her adieux to him for the last time."[270]

---

[269] "From Alexander Hamilton to Elizabeth Hamilton [4 July 1804]," Founders Online, National Archives. https://founders.archives.gov/documents/Hamilton/01-26-02-0001-0248.

[270] Unger, *Lafayette*, 239.

And as far as we know, none of them prayed daily, with the devotion of St. Augustine's mother, St. Monica, that her unbelieving beloved would return to the faith.

Adrienne de Lafayette did all these things, and more. Her husband, the Marquis, is the hero of the American Revolution. Yet he might not even be the greatest Lafayette in his own family.

4

The little red-haired boy had a serene, angelic face. But he grew up haunted.

In 1759, when he was two, his father was killed by a British cannonball at the Battle of Minden, during the Seven Years' War. That loss draped itself over Lafayette's thoughts like a funeral shroud. He felt compelled to live up to his family's proud military history, which stretched back to the Crusades and included a relative who fought alongside Joan of Arc.

In the old stone chateau on the hillside at Chavaniac, where he spent most of his time as a lonely only child, Lafayette dreamed of revenge for his father. The schemes he would one day propose against the British during the Revolutionary War were hatched here as he stalked the drafty halls, studying portraits of his heroic ancestors.

He desperately wanted a father. But three of the four most important people in his life were powerful women instead.

The first was his grandmother, Marie-Catherine de Suat, dame de Chavaniac. She was as imposing as the mansion that shared her name. The old woman was also fair, and her advice was sought by people from miles around. She taught the boy that sharing the harvest with the local peasants was the right thing to do, and that everyone deserved respect. His love of equality was developed at his grandmother's knee.

The second significant woman in his life was not his mother, who died when he was just thirteen. Instead, it was his mother-in-law.

The orphaned Lafayette had joined the King's Musketeers, with some help from his great-grandfather. There the new musketeer caught the eye of the duc de d'Ayen. He was a nobleman and chemist and was seeking a husband for his second daughter, Marie-Adrienne.

The duke's wife, Henriette Anne Louise d'Aguesseau, however, did not approve. Marie-Adrienne was only a baby of twelve, after all. The pair were too young to marry, and besides, the duchess mistook Lafayette's shy and awkward nature for coldness.

After months of arguments, she and the duke worked out a deal. Lafayette would live with the family in their mansion at Versailles. He would be told of the arrangement; his new bride would stay ignorant. Henriette d'Ayen would watch the prospective bridegroom closely for two years before consenting to the match and then informing her daughter.

If she sounds imperious and meddlesome, she wasn't. The duchess was a beautiful and remarkable woman. Educated in a convent, she also kept up with the latest writers and ideas. She kissed her daughters each morning before she left for Mass, and taught them using texts both old (the Bible, of course, and classic poetry) and new (the scandalous works of Voltaire).

Her bedchamber, with its intricate crimson tapestries, was their classroom. Lively discussions with her children took place while she did her sewing, sitting in her favorite high-backed wing chair by the fireplace. They read, they wrote letters, and they talked about the issues of the day. "They were taught to think for themselves," notes author Jason Lane.[271]

While she considered her future son-in-law aloof at first, she soon warmed to him and became his greatest ally. The duchess didn't just see future greatness in Lafayette. She saw that his revolutionary dreams were more than just the glory-hungry fantasies of a callow young man. And she understood, to her sorrow, that a great many people might be hurt by those dreams. One day, she herself would pay the ultimate price for them.

What about the third, and most important, woman in Lafayette's life? That was his young bride Adrienne, "a rather plain girl with a pale, oval face, large sad eyes, and a composed expression."[272]

---

[271] Lane, *General and Madame de Lafayette*, 9.
[272] Lane, *General and Madame de Lafayette*, 10.

She was serious, devout, and deeply unsure of herself. Her mother allowed her the unusual step of delaying her First Communion, because she didn't feel ready to receive the Eucharist.

She felt the same way about her prospective husband. Did she love him at first sight? The reports conflict; Adrienne later denied it. But she certainly adored him by the time her mother revealed Adrienne's impending marriage to the handsome young soldier who had been living under their roof. She was fourteen, and she stayed head over heels for the rest of her life. "What joy it was for me to learn, after more than a year, that my mother already looked at him as her son," she recalled.[273]

Yet still she felt unworthy. It can't have helped her confidence to know that Lafayette was also pursuing a beautiful noblewoman, Aglaé d'Hunolstein. Aglaé rejected him at first, but after he returned from the American Revolution, they carried on a passionate affair. After it broke off, Lafayette would begin an even more serious relationship with another courtier, Comtesse Diane-Adélaïde de Simiane.

The countess was reportedly the most beautiful woman in France. She and Lafayette continued their affair for thirty years—even after her husband killed himself, reportedly because he was jealous of Lafayette.

It helps here to remember the personal and historical context, as Jason Lane points out. The French have traditionally been tolerant of extramarital relationships, and in Lafayette's day, they were common. He was little more than a boy, in an arranged marriage, to boot. Even Adrienne was aware of her father's affairs and saw that her parents' marriage had survived them.

"Lafayette did love his wife," Lane writes. "However, his love would not fully develop until he matured, until she matured as well."[274]

Undoubtedly, that is true. But even though Adrienne went to great lengths to spare her husband the "inconvenience" of her jealousy, the pain Lafayette caused must have been real, and considerable. Lane points out that in 1787, following the suicide of the Comte de Simiane, Adrienne drafted her first will. "Why would a healthy young woman," he asks,

[273] Unger, *Lafayette*, 10–11.
[274] Lane, *General and Madame de Lafayette*, 15.

"confident in her faith, wealthy and highly placed in society, a woman with beautiful children, supportive mother and sisters, married to the most idolized man in France, draw up a will?"[275] It's a good question.

Wracked with insecurity and doubt, Adrienne fell back on the one thing that gave her comfort, when her husband did not.

"Most important," Lane writes, "she was a fundamentally strong person with absolute faith in God's will."[276] That faith would be tried almost immediately after they married, and frequently throughout their union together.

5

Most people know that George Washington became the father Lafayette had never known, and that Lafayette became the natural son he never had. At their very first meeting, at Philadelphia's City Tavern, Washington clapped a big hand on the shoulder of the gawky young officer and told Lafayette to think of him as a "father and a friend."[277] Nineteen, nervous, and awed by the six-foot two-inch commander in chief, Lafayette later gushed in his diary, "Although he was surrounded by officers and citizens, it was impossible to mistake for a moment his majestic figure and deportment; nor was he less distinguished by the noble affability of his manner."[278]

The friendship deepened throughout the years. Lafayette named his only son after the general. Meanwhile, in December 1784, Washington was so heartbroken when he parted from Lafayette—for what he correctly predicted would be the last time—that immediately afterward he wrote the French general a melancholy letter.

---

[275] Lane, *General and Madame de Lafayette*, 76.

[276] Lane, *General and Madame de Lafayette*, 16.

[277] Lane, *General and Madame de Lafayette*, 33.

[278] Marc Leepson, "George Washington and the Marquis de Lafayette," in *The Digital Encyclopedia of George Washington*, ed. James P. Ambuske, George Washington's Mount Vernon, https://www.mountvernon.org/library/digitalhistory/digital-encyclopedia/article/george-washington-and-the-marquis-de-lafayette/.

"I often asked myself, as our carriages separated, whether that was the last sight I ever should have of you," Washington confessed, back at Mount Vernon. "And though I wished to say no, my fears answered yes."[279]

So it's ironic that Lafayette was used as a pawn, not once, but twice, in plots to replace his mentor as commander in chief. In the first case, at least, the planners were foiled for the same reason they were nearly successful: Lafayette's youthful naivete.

As we read in chapter 5, French playwright and spy Pierre Augustin Caron de Beaumarchais and American agent Silas Deane secretly funneled French supplies and foreign soldiers to the colonial cause. The French foreign minister, Vergennes, was happy to covertly help arm and outfit the colonists, but that wasn't all he wanted. Eventually, he intended the French to be in charge of the colonial forces—with a military dictator.

"All means to reduce the power and greatness of England," Vergennes craftily counseled the twenty-year-old King Louis XVI, "are just, legitimate, and even necessary, provided they are efficient."[280]

Vergennes had the perfect, efficient, candidate to lead the colonial forces: Victor-François, the duc de Broglie. De Broglie had years of military experience, including serving as a general in the Seven Years' War. But under his command, the French had lost the crucial Battle of Villinghausen in 1761, and his reputation needed rehabilitating. Here was his chance. Even Silas Deane signed off on the scheme.

De Broglie invited Lafayette, whom he had commanded at Metz, to a dinner with some of his fellow freemasons and England's Duke of Gloucester. The duke was the brother of England's King George III, and he had harsh words for Britain's policies in America. Fired up by the freemasons' talk of liberty, tolerance, and republicanism—but knowing nothing of the plan to replace Washington—Lafayette decided to enlist.

---

[279] "From George Washington to Lafayette, 8 December 1784," Founders Online, National Archives, https://founders.archives.gov/documents/Washington/04-02-02-0140.

[280] Unger, *Lafayette*, 19.

That was hardly welcome news to de Broglie, who correctly saw that the eager young soldier could muddle his scheme. He appealed to Lafayette's dead father: de Broglie had seen him killed in battle, and he couldn't risk seeing the boy meet a similar fate. His words, however, had precisely the opposite effect on Lafayette. The chance to avenge his father was the most appealing thing about the whole adventure.

While Lafayette lacked experience, he had plenty of money. Deane reluctantly commissioned him a major general in December 1776, and noted "his high birth, his alliances, the great dignities which his family hold at court"[281] as assets. Deane was more right than he knew.

But what happened next was an international comedy of errors. Vergennes was furious when he heard of Lafayette's rash decision. Sending the son-in-law of a well-known French nobleman to fight against the Crown—while the two nations were ostensibly at peace—might alert Britain to the covert aid France was providing to the colonies.

Lafayette's father-in-law was equally incensed: the boy was deserting the French military. And he had left his pregnant wife at home while he rushed off to seek glory. The duc d'Ayen ordered Lafayette back home in the strongest possible terms. Reading their letters, Lafayette agonized, going back and forth about leaving.

Meanwhile, Baron Johann von Robais de Kalb—a German-born soldier of fortune who had invented his own royal title—was growing antsy. He was a conspirator in the plot to replace Washington. De Broglie had decided to make use of Lafayette's enthusiasm and funding, and Kalb was now to escort Lafayette to America. When they got there, Kalb's job was to lay the groundwork for de Broglie to take over the Continental Army. But Lafayette's dithering was making that task more difficult.

The young soldier had been so anxious to get started that he bought his own transportation, the *Victoire*, to sail to the colonies. Yet as he waited for the ship to be outfitted, he made things worse by traveling to London. There he met King George III and loudly defended the Americans to

[281] Unger, *Lafayette*, 22.

the royal court. It was not only embarrassing; it also made the British far more watchful of France, just as Vergennes had feared.

Chastened, Lafayette left abruptly for Paris, where he stayed in hiding, afraid to face his father-in-law and his pregnant wife. Then he rode secretly to Bordeaux, disguised as a postillion. He stayed one step ahead of the king's soldiers, who had orders to bring Lafayette back to Paris.

Even at the last possible moment, as the *Victoire* finally departed for Spanish waters, Lafayette confessed to an exasperated Kalb that he was guilt-ridden and thinking about returning home after all. "If he had not been on board the ship and under way, I think he would have gone home," Kalb wrote to his wife. Kalb added that in his opinion, this would have been a good idea.[282] And no wonder.

By this point, nearly everyone in France was following the exploits of the young marquis, which were anything but secret. Some rooted him on, and some just shook their heads.

But his wife, who had not even been given a goodbye—and who had given birth to their second daughter in his absence—refused to blame him. Not even when he wrote to her with typical enthusiasm and insensitivity, "I have been much put about, dear heart, at having received no news of you for two posts. Fortunately, I know you are not sick but only lazy."[283]

His young wife "quickly came to his defense in the only way that was possible—by saying nothing," wrote her biographer Constance Wright. "Adrienne hid her grief and preferred to be thought childish or unfeeling rather than to swell the chorus of disapproval."[284]

That was because her mother patiently counseled her through this crisis. The duchess had already cooled down her husband, which was significant. If Lafayette had been caught, the duke could have had his son-in-law clapped in irons for deserting or sent to some far military frontier.

---

[282] Unger, *Lafayette*, 26.
[283] Maurois, *Adrienne*, 61.
[284] Wright, *Madame de Lafayette*, 24.

Undoubtedly, when the duke received a letter from his son-in-law that implored his "dear papa" to "not lose your affection for me" as "I am very desirous of deserving it,"[285] his wife helped convince him Lafayette's motives were sincere.

"She had less taste for ambition, thirst for human glory, and attraction for enterprises than any one in the world," Adrienne later wrote of her mother. "However, she judged what Monsieur de Lafayette did as it was judged two years later by the rest of the world.

"Her feelings for him made it possible to soften my own heartbreak," she added. "She herself informed me of the cruel departure and took care of consoling me."[286]

There would be no consolation for de Broglie. By the time the *Victorie*'s crew reached Philadelphia on July 27, 1777, the only soldier accepted by the Congress was Lafayette — and that was only because he offered to fight without pay.

Baron de Kalb was eventually able to threaten Congress into accepting him into the army. He grew to admire Lafayette, and later died heroically at the Battle of Camden, in South Carolina.

But de Broglie's dreams of becoming military dictator of America were roundly rejected by Congress. And thanks in part to Lafayette's public shenanigans, the French were in no position to force the issue. Vergennes gritted his teeth and kept planning. Score one big point for inexperience.

6

Lafayette's brief involvement in the second plot against Washington was the result of something everyone quickly learned about the young major general: he had just as much bravery and ambition as he did money.

A list of Lafayette's unrealized goals during the American Revolution is telling. He proposed an invasion of the British-held West Indies. He suggested teaming up with Spain for a joint invasion of Florida, then wanted to retake British-held New York City. And he enthusiastically

---

[285] Lane, *General and Madame de Lafayette*, 23–24.
[286] Lane, *General and Madame de Lafayette*, 27.

backed the most audacious scheme of all: an assault on England itself. Working with Benjamin Franklin, he helped develop a plan to attack Britain's largely undefended coastlines. Only the onset of winter forced this idea to be scrapped at the eleventh hour.

In each of those instances, Lafayette hoped to lead his troops to victory. His desire for glory was certainly part of it. But the need to avenge his father might have been even stronger.

So, when a group of anti-Washington plotters in Congress hoped to replace the commander in chief in the fall of 1777, they tried to get supporters of the general out of the way, as we saw in chapter 2. That's why Lafayette was proposed to lead an expedition to British-held Canada. It seemed like the perfect temptation: one that would satisfy Lafayette's desire for prestige and preoccupy an important Washington ally.

The Board of War's offer to Lafayette was, in fact, alluring, as he admitted in a letter to Washington that December.

Speaking of Thomas Conway, the Irish-born general who gave his name to the Conway Cabal trying to oust Washington, Lafayette wrote, "That gentleman had engaged me by entertaining my head with ideas of glory and shining projects, and I must Confess for my shame that it is a too certain way of deceiving me."[287]

But this time Lafayette was too self-aware and suspicious to be taken in by the conspirators. The Canadian invasion—and the schemes of the Conway Cabal—ultimately came to nothing.

The larger truth behind the targeting of Lafayette was that it affirmed his importance. Even though the young Frenchman had no combat experience when he entered the Revolution, from his very first battle he proved he was a natural soldier. Courage, tactical savvy, coolness under fire, the ability to rally discouraged and outnumbered troops—Lafayette had it all.

It's true that his money and connections were equally important to the Americans. He frequently used his own fortune to outfit the "poor nacked"[288] soldiers under his command. When he returned to France

---

[287] Lane, *General and Madame de Lafayette*, 38.
[288] Lane, *General and Madame de Lafayette*, 38.

for a year in 1779, he helped convince the prime minister, the Count of Maurepas, to send an expedition to America. It would be led not by Lafayette—who of course wanted the job badly—but by the Comte de Rochambeau, the subject of the next chapter, who helped end the Revolution at Yorktown.

And when the war reached its final stages, it was Lafayette's requests to the French ambassador in Philadelphia, the Chevalier de la Luzerne, that helped secure the foreign funding to put the patriot cause over the top.

Yet a survey of Lafayette's military career in America reveals a remarkable general, though one involved in less significant battles than his reputation might suggest. In his very first engagement, at the Battle of Brandywine in September 1777, he was wounded in the leg, yet managed to rally the patriot troops and help cover Washington's retreat. Like his fellow Catholic Casimir Pulaski, his actions during the retreat impressed the general; Washington cited Lafayette for his "bravery and military ardour."[289] And as was the case with Pulaski, the Battle of Brandywine was the beginning of bigger things for Lafayette.

That November, his leg not fully healed, he led a reconnaissance mission that routed a company of Hessians at the Battle of Gloucester in New Jersey. In his first solo command, and outnumbered eight to one, he calmly eluded a British trap at the Battle of Barren Hill in May 1778. Somehow, he lost almost no soldiers.

After he returned from France in the spring of 1780, Lafayette spent a frustrating year. The American cause was floundering, and Britain's "southern strategy" seemed to be paying off. The fleet the French had promised finally arrived but was smaller than expected. Inflation was devastating the American economy, and Lafayette, greeted on his return from France as a hero, was reduced to patrolling New York and New Jersey. Then, that fall, the news of Benedict Arnold's betrayal rocked the patriots.

---

[289] "Marquis de Lafayette," American Battlefield Trust, February 2, 2017, https://www.battlefields.org/learn/articles/marquis-de-lafayette.

The next spring, Washington sent Lafayette south in pursuit of Arnold, who was terrorizing Virginia. Lafayette found Arnold "repugnant"[290] and at one point refused his request for a prisoner exchange. But Lafayette also turned down a chance to have sharpshooters assassinate the traitor.

Just how deeply this speaks to Lafayette's character is illustrated by another fact. The attempt on Arnold would have been made while he was walking, vulnerable, on a nearby beach with another British general: William Phillips, who had been in charge of the attack in which Lafayette's father was killed. Badly as he must have wanted to kill both men—especially the soldier he blamed for his father's death—Lafayette refused to do so when he thought the circumstances were less than honorable.

Lafayette never caught Arnold, and he convinced himself that Phillips's death that spring—from typhoid fever, not from a cannonball fired by one of Lafayette's soldiers—was divine retribution for his father. But his harassment of General Cornwallis's troops that spring and summer definitely set the stage for the Battle of Yorktown, in which he participated.

Though the war would officially last another eighteen months, Lafayette knew well what Yorktown meant.

"The play is over," he wrote after the battle, "the fifth act has ended."[291] His own drama, however, had barely begun.

7

When he finally arrived home for good in 1782, following the American Revolution, Adrienne fainted into her husband's arms.

Years later, she confessed to Lafayette that the moment played into one of her worst fears: "of seeming importunate, of being an embarrassment to your delicacy." But she added, "You ought not be dissatisfied with what did show."[292] She was right: her fainting spell was only a teaser for a far deeper and more profound devotion.

[290] Lane, *General and Madame de Lafayette*, 62.
[291] Gaines, *For Liberty and Glory*, 160.
[292] Lane, *General and Madame de Lafayette*, 73.

To this point, Adrienne had been a dutiful wife. She had not only sacrificed Lafayette to fight a revolution, one she too supported. She had also spared him her jealousy, her fears, her embarrassment, and perhaps even her anger. Adrienne had given him three children during the course of the Revolutionary War, including Anastasie and George Washington Lafayette. She had also suffered the loss of the oldest, two-year-old Henriette, while he was gone. She would bear him a fourth, Marie Antionette — named for the queen, but usually called Virginie — the year he returned.

But as Lafayette began to agitate for the same sort of sweeping change in France that he'd helped bring about in America, Adrienne showed there was far more to her than the stoicism of the stay-at-home wife.

She supported Lafayette's campaign for the rights of Protestants, acknowledging the errors French Catholics had made in persecuting them. When he brought home a fourteen-year-old Protestant orphan, John Caldwell, following a 1784 trip to America, she welcomed the boy into her home. When Lafayette angrily protested at the boy being forced to attend Mass at his boarding school, she backed up her husband. As her daughter Virginie put it, "Her enlightened zeal for religion made her wish that there should be no further injustices committed in its name.... She regarded as a great crime any attempt to hinder the liberty that God wished to give men and likewise to push, for reasons of self interest, a decision that conscience alone is able to dictate. She wished to attract to Catholicism, but for spiritual reasons."[293]

More practically, she displayed an economic sense Lafayette himself lacked. He had been deeply moved by the plight of the slaves he saw in America and bought a plantation in Cayenne, French Guiana, with the goal of freeing its slaves. Not only did Adrienne encourage him to buy a second plantation, she took over the project, working with Jesuit priests from the *Seminaire du Saint Esprit*. "He left this enterprise to a great extent in the hands of Adrienne," wrote her biographer André Maurois, "who was more methodical and persevering than he."[294]

[293] Lane, *General and Madame de Lafayette*, 87.
[294] Maurois, *Adrienne*, 145.

There were, however, limits to both her tolerance and her duty to her husband. When the French Revolution led to the state's takeover of the Catholic Church, Adrienne refused to participate in Masses conducted by "juring" priests—priests who had taken the oath of loyalty to the French government. And she invited nonjuring priests into her home, even though doing so was increasingly risky for her husband and family as the revolution became more and more radical.

"Adrienne fully understood the difficulty of [Lafayette's] ambiguous position," Maurois wrote, "but thought it her duty for that very reason to stress her personal devotion to orthodox Catholicism."

"It is always dangerous to lay hands on religion," he added, "because it inspires heroic opposition by setting the transitory at odds with the eternal."[295] Adrienne would soon prove the truth of this sentiment.

8

Lafayette had not envisaged the revolution he now saw evolving before him, and it disgusted him as nothing in the American Revolution had ever done.[296]

At the moment described above, in July 1789, the French Revolution was not even a week old. The belief that the "Terror" of the revolution was something that occurred near the end, when things slid out of control, that the beheadings and bloodshed were some frustrated expression of failed politics, is simply untrue.

The movement began with butchery. When mobs stormed the Bastille, they also beheaded the prison warden and Paris's provost of merchants. Then the assailants giddily smeared their faces with blood from the corpses' ruined necks.

A week later, another mob hanged and decapitated seventy-four-year-old Joseph Foulon. He was a wealthy speculator accused of driving up the price of grain; the unverified rumor was that he'd said people could eat grass if they couldn't afford wheat. The crowd filled his mouth with grass

[295] Maurois, *Adrienne*, 145.
[296] Unger, *Lafayette*, 243.

and manure, then shoved his bloody head into the face of his shocked son-in-law, who was passing by. "Kiss papa!" they laughed.[297]

What the French Revolution became at the end, it was at the beginning as well. And what it was not—anything like the American Revolution—it never could have been. This was the bitter truth Lafayette did not grasp.

The revolution was sparked by multiple flashpoints, and money was the first. France was buried in debt, thanks to its involvement in the Seven Years' War and the American Revolution. There was no easy way to get more funds. The nobility and clergy paid no taxes on property, and the lower classes were already overburdened. The king, Louis XVI, had a good heart but a weak will.

Financial crisis was exacerbated by the weather: a historic, torrential hailstorm in the summer of 1788, followed by a drought, a brutal winter, and massive spring floods. Bread became hard to find and impossible to buy. Yet the revolutionary ideas of writers like Rousseau and Voltaire had been fermenting like yeast for years. Now they rose, along with the public's anger.

The people had Lafayette on their side, and for a while that seemed like enough. For the first year of the revolution, he almost single-handedly held the country together. Later, he saved the royal family more than once. But no one will ever know precisely how many priests and bakers and common people he also spared from hangings or torture or dismemberment. And, irony of ironies, it was common people who ended up being the most common victims of the revolution.

At various points, Lafayette could have been a dictator with powers even Napoleon never commanded. Once the frightened nobles and priests of the Assembly realized what was about to happen, some got down on their knees and wept, begging Lafayette to take command of the city and country—to save them, as he'd helped save the American patriots.

He tried his best. But over and over again, Lafayette refused to accept the unlimited power he was offered. He would emulate his mentor George

---

[297] Lane, *General and Madame de Lafayette*, 129.

Washington: he would show the French people he was as incorruptible as his American idol.

"Think what he could have done if he had not had an honest soul, and say if you know how many men in history to compare with him," wrote Deputy Adrien Duquesnoy of the National Assembly. "Absolute master of an immense army that obeys him blindly and disciplines itself every day, strong in the enthusiasm of the people and the esteem of the public; what could he have not done if he had been wicked."

It was one of the most noble gestures in history. But France was not the United States. Lafayette's principled refusal to take power created a vacuum eagerly filled by the revolutionary Left—the "Jacobins" who were already plotting how to get him out of the way.

To get a sense of what they were like, Harlow Giles Unger's biography of Lafayette is an excellent source. The descriptions of the repulsive revolutionaries are not just ad hominem attacks. There was the "foul, ill-kempt Swiss dwarf"[298] with skin disease, the journalist Jean-Paul Marat; the "ugly but nonetheless glib lawyer"[299] Georges-Jacques Danton; and the "hideously pockmarked, leonine face"[300] of the ex-convict and sadist Comte de Mirabeau. Their unpleasant physical characteristics, however, were just outward signs of the inner corruption that soon soaked the streets of Paris in blood.

Eventually, of course, Lafayette lost control, and the mobs turned on him too. Once King Louis XVI made a failed run for the Belgian border despite Lafayette's insistence that the king would stay in Paris, he was a marked man. Yet even before then, it was the mob that was dictating terms to Lafayette.

It was inevitable they would come for his family, as well.

When they first did, in the summer of 1791, Lafayette was gone. He was at the Champ de Mars, the field where just a year earlier the revolution had been celebrated. Now he was trying to put down a riot. Part

[298] Unger, *Lafayette*, 249.
[299] Unger, *Lafayette*, 235.
[300] Unger, *Lafayette*, 227.

of the crowd broke away and went looking for his family instead. The terrified children heard the voices outside, screaming "Kill his wife and take him her head!"

"She took us in her arms with tears of joy, and saw to all the necessary precautions against the impending danger with impressive calm and a tremendous sense of relief," Adrienne's daughter Virginie later wrote.[301]

It was a close call. A year later, the national mood was even uglier. Lafayette had gone on the run. He was wanted for treason, and his enemies in government—led by the tiny madman Maximilien Robespierre, a radical lawyer and the ugliest character of them all—would have been all too happy to have his head.

But Lafayette instead was arrested and imprisoned by Austrian authorities. To them, Lafayette was the architect of the revolution and a threat to monarchs everywhere. Not radical enough for the radicals, and far too radical for the aristocrats, Lafayette was virtually friendless in Europe.

"I make no excuse, neither to my children, nor to you, for having ruined my family," he wrote Adrienne, with typical candor and tactlessness. "There is not one of you who would wish to owe his fortune," he claimed, to "conduct contrary to my conscience."[302]

Perhaps not, but it would be Adrienne to whom they would ultimately owe much of their fortune. It was the beginning of her finest hour—an hour that lasted until the end of her life.

9

First, she would protect the children.

Painful as the separation was, she sent them all away. George Washington and his tutor, Felix Frestel, were hidden in a mountain village; they would later be shipped to America, where the boy's namesake himself supervised their care. The girls were also packed off to a governess, but Adrienne relented when they begged to be reunited with her.

[301] Maurois, *Adrienne*, 207.
[302] Unger, *Lafayette*, 286.

So Adrienne, her daughters, and Lafayette's elderly Aunt Charlotte relocated to the family château at Chavaniac, where the marquis had grown up. It was three hundred miles south of Paris, but it certainly wasn't safe, either, as three thousand prisoners would be butchered there during the 1792 September Massacres.

Looters and brigands roamed the countryside, and revolutionary fervor gripped the country. The home of a man now considered a traitor to the nation could be attacked at any time. While the girls nervously watched the roads, Adrienne calmly made an inventory of the house in case it was sacked, and wróte letters on her husband's behalf to French officials, as well as to her son's namesake, George Washington.

Soldiers finally forced their way into the chateau on September 10. With them was the local commissioner, Alphonse Aulagnier, "a sinister-looking man in a rust-coloured riding coat."[303] His orders were to arrest Adrienne and her children, and he seized several letters from Lafayette as evidence. Loyal Anastasie, who was hiding with her governess, escaped and was taken to Le Puy, along with her mother and great-aunt.

Yet the patient Adrienne managed to talk her way out of jail. The local counselors were moved by her request to read her husband's letters, which turned out to reveal nothing but the love of husband and wife. They agreed to place her under house arrest at Chavaniac, where she could watch over the girls and Aunt Charlotte.

The reprieve was blessed but brief. In November 1793, Adrienne was arrested again. This time, she was separated from the children and Aunt Charlotte and imprisoned in Brioude, about fifteen miles to the north-west. Then, in May, the news got much worse: she was transferred to Le Pressis, the Paris prison for those about to be tried by the Revolutionary Tribunal. The next stop was almost always the guillotine.

While even George Washington felt he could offer little more than prayers for the Lafayettes, another Founding Father served as Adrienne's guardian angel. Gouverneur Morris, the American minister in Paris, was one of the more colorful characters of his era. A vain and unrepentant

---

[303] Maurois, *Adrienne*, 232.

aristocrat with a wooden leg (he had lost his limb in a carriage accident), Morris was horrified by the revolution of the rabble he'd just witnessed.

Morris had loaned Adrienne money before her imprisonment. When she languished on the revolution's death row, he firmly reminded French officials that putting to death Lafayette's wife would put America at odds with the newly republican France. His ultimatum probably saved her life.

Her mother, grandmother, and sister Louise would not be so fortunate. In July 1794, when the blood ran thickest during the Terror, the three women ascended the platform at the Place du Trône.[304] Located on the eastern edge of Paris, the site of the guillotine was now so busy that the condemned were crammed into wagons each day and transported to the public executions.

A nonjuring priest, Fr. M. Carrichon, had arranged to attend in disguise so that he could offer the three women absolution. They could not find him in the crowd at first, and he was moved to see their distress as they sought him out. Then a sudden thunderstorm broke, and violent winds and rain lashed across the execution site. Things looked hopeless — until Adrienne's mother, the Duchess d'Ayen, caught sight of the priest in his red waistcoat. He remembered:

> Immediately they bent their heads with an air of repentance, contrition, tenderness, hope, and piety. I raised my hand, and, though with covered head, pronounced the entire formula of absolution, and the words which follow it, very distinctly, and with the deepest earnestness. They joined in this more perfectly than ever. I can never forget the holy picture, worthy of the pencil of Raphael, of that moment when, for them, all was balm and consolation.
>
> Immediately the storm relaxed and the rain diminished. It was as if they had come only to insure the success of what my friends and I had so ardently desired. I blessed God for it, and they did the same. Their appearance showed contentment, security, and cheerfulness.[305]

[304] Today known as Place de la Nation.
[305] Duchesse de Duras, *Prison Journals during the French Revolution*, trans. Mrs. M. Carey (New York: Dodd, Mead, 1891), 219–220.

Though she had lost nearly everything, Adrienne felt the same way when she was finally released from house arrest in 1795. Her freedom was thanks in part to James Monroe, who had replaced Gouverneur Morris as the American minister to France.

But her thoughts, as always, were with her husband. Adrienne had been through a terrible ordeal. It had weakened her body but strengthened her mind and her faith. She knew now what she had to do and felt blessed to have the chance. At once, she wrote to Lafayette at Olmütz: "If to the joy of being with you I may be allowed also the added happiness of serving you, then nothing remains but for me to join with you in blessing Him who governs all things, and in whose eyes this miserable life is of so little importance that He has permitted those for whom we mourn to have been so cruelly deprived of it, yet can at the same time make what remains of it for us so truly precious."[306]

10

When Adrienne offered herself and her daughters up for imprisonment at Olmütz, the Austrian war minister, Count de Ferraris, tried to talk her out of it. His motive was almost certainly not altruistic.

"He was probably thinking more about the consequences for the empire than for Adrienne and her daughters," writes Jason Lane. Ferraris likely suspected "that the incarceration of the females would lead to an international clamor for the release of the family."[307]

If so, he was absolutely correct. All across Europe, people rallied to the cause of the Lafayettes. In songs, in artwork, even in a one-act play called *The Prisoner of Olmütz, or the Conjugal Devotion*, the family's plight in the dank Austrian dungeon inspired melodrama and the support of millions. This time, Adrienne was not just the wife of the tale — she was also the heroine.

It would take two years, however, for the Lafayettes to win release, as Adrienne grew sicker and sicker. The revolution in France was spent, but

---

[306] Maurois, *Adrienne*, 290.
[307] Lane, *General and Madame de Lafayette*, 226.

diplomacy crawled. President George Washington had to tread carefully: tensions with France were rising, and he was trying to keep the country as an ally. Meanwhile, in Great Britain, Tory leader William Pitt the Younger crowed in Parliament that he delighted in seeing revolutionaries "drink to the dregs the cup of bitterness they have prepared for the lips of others."[308] Everyone knew he was talking about his nation's old adversary, Lafayette.

In the end, a new leader helped negotiate the Lafayette family's freedom. But Napoleon Bonaparte was wary. He knew a martyred Lafayette could be a powerful opponent, so he resolved to keep him out of the country.

Napoleon knew he was up against a formidable general. What he didn't realize was that he was also up against the general's equally formidable wife.

Following the family's release from prison, Adrienne met with Napoleon. The diminuitive consul was polite but clearly wanted Lafayette elsewhere. So Adrienne forced the issue. Obtaining a fake passport for her husband, she advised him to immediately come to France from Holland, where he was staying.

When he did, Napoleon was predictably angry. Yet Adrienne stayed calm, knowing she had the upper hand. Napoleon had not yet consolidated his power and still wanted to be thought of as a "friend of liberty."[309]

In a second meeting, Adrienne pointed out that bringing home France's greatest-ever friend of liberty would be a public relations coup. Napoleon grudgingly agreed. Now that Lafayette was already in the country, it was better for the time being to merely insist that he keep a low profile. Napoleon might have been a genius on the battlefield, but as a negotiator, Adrienne easily bested him.

The Lafayettes returned to La Grange, the chateau Adrienne had inherited from her mother and lost during the revolution. She'd recovered

[308] Lane, *General and Madame de Lafayette*, 231.
[309] Lane, *General and Madame de Lafayette*, 247.

it before joining her husband in prison. Located in Seine-et-Marne, in the north of France, the gray stone castle and its grounds became a headquarters for the extended family: the three children, various grandchildren, and a constant parade of guests.

The money to support it came largely from Adrienne's labors. Wracked by constant pain from swollen limbs and skin lesions, she spent years slowly tramping from one government office to another in Paris, trying to recover family property lost in the French Revolution.

Accompanied by her daughter Virginie, she had other duties as well. One was getting the government to remove the proscriptions it had placed on Lafayette and other family members.

Another was to locate the remains of her mother, grandmother, and sister. When Adrienne found the site of the mass grave, in which more than thirteen hundred victims of the Terror had been dumped, she bought it, gave it to the Ladies of the Sacred Heart and of the Perpetual Adoration, and allowed them to watch over the burial ground.

Lafayette was unwelcome in Paris and confined to La Grange. The man of action chafed, and his wife's frequent absences became "unbearably long." He had regained his health after prison, although not his hair. But he'd discovered a love for his wife that the busy crusader of bygone days never had time to cultivate. He was reduced to begging for her return, "even if" it was for just "one day."[310]

His wife seemed touched, and also bemused, by his neediness. The thing that hadn't changed was his impetuous nature: he still wanted the world, and he wanted it now. As Adrienne trudged from place to place in Paris, shrewdly negotiating to recapture what had been lost, she knew how much work it would take to rehabilitate the family fortune, and the family name. She was quite successful, but the process dragged on far more slowly than her impatient husband could understand.

"I would like at least to have something consoling to say to you," she wrote. "But what should I say, my dear Gilbert?"[311]

---

[310] Lane, *General and Madame de Lafayette*, 251.
[311] Lane, *General and Madame de Lafayette*, 251.

There would still be much for both of them to say to one another. The occasion for those conversations would be Adrienne's battered body finally giving out.

11

She never fully recovered after the two years she spent in Olmütz. No doubt, the punishing—albeit productive—schedule she kept after her release did her no favors. But when she became sick again in August 1807, doctors couldn't arrest her decline. Even moving her to Paris from La Grange, for treatment from the personal physician of Napoleon, now emperor of France, had little effect.

Lafayette spent hours and hours by his wife's bedside. Many of the heart-to-heart discussions they had in her final months were captured in his letters. They chronicle the sadness of a man who has recently learned about a precious gift he's actually owned for most of his life. That regret is dispelled, though, by the steady beacon of his wife's faith.

In her illness, Adrienne suffered through some delirious moments. But, according to her husband, she remained clearheaded about the man she married—and still hopeful for his soul.

> I never knew her to be wrong about me save once, when for a few moments she was convinced that I had become a fervent Christian. But the mistake was fleeting and accompanied by doubts and questions which proved that what she had said was as much the expression of a wish as an illusion.
>
> "You are not a Christian, are you?" she said one day. Then, since I made no answer: "Ah! I know what you are: you are a Fayettist!'"

Gently, Lafayette attempted to return his wife's joke about his ego.

> "You must think me very bumptious," I replied, "but are you not something of one yourself?"
>
> "Indeed, yes!" she exclaimed. "With all my heart! I would give my life for that sect."

This she said with a very discerning look, and added: "But you admire Jesus Christ, do you not?" I told her, as I had often done before, that I did. "Well then, since you admire him so much, you will end by recognizing his divinity."[312]

She had seen her own country, and the whole world, change—some of it thanks to her husband, and some of it thanks to her. But that final wish was one that, as far as we know, Adrienne Lafayette would not live to see fulfilled.

On Christmas Eve, her body exhausted from its labors, she died at age forty-eight. Her last words were to her husband. *"Je suis toute á vous,"* she whispered—"I am yours entirely."[313]

There were few people left who would understand. One of them was Thomas Jefferson, who had lost his own wife, Martha, while he was serving in Paris in 1782. Jefferson was now in his second term as president, and Lafayette reached across the ocean to seek and offer solace.

"I have long ago, from my heart, pitied you, my dear Jefferson," Lafayette wrote his old friend, "and yet, before this blow, I confess I did not know what it is to be unhappy."[314]

The "Hero of Two Worlds," who had faced death a hundred times, who had been humiliated and despised by the people he tried to save, had been brought to his lowest point. "I feel," he confessed to Jefferson, "irresistibly overpowered."[315]

12

That assessment, made in grief, was premature. Old and bashed about as he was, Lafayette's life concluded with a final, glorious third act. He reentered French politics one final time, at age seventy-three, once again calming the passions of the country during the revolution of 1830. For a single day, he once again had the powers of a dictator.

[312] Maurois, *Adrienne*, 464.
[313] Unger, *Lafayette*, 338.
[314] Unger, *Lafayette*, 338.
[315] Gaines, *For Liberty and Glory*, 438.

He faced a choice, however. He could try to establish a constitutional monarchy, with Louis Philippe, the duc d'Orléans, on the throne. Or he could make another effort at turning France into a republic, like his beloved America. But his advisers made it clear: the only way a republic could work would be if Lafayette did the thing he'd avoided forty years earlier. He would have to become president.

The blood-spattered memories of 1789 were still as fresh and graphic as ever for Lafayette. Yet the dream of at last bringing the American Revolution to Paris remained seductive enough that he wavered.

"What will our friends say if they learn we have proclaimed the republic?" Lafayette asked American ambassador William C. Rives. The ambassador answered bluntly: "They will say that forty years of experience are lost on the French."[316]

With that barb, Lafayette stepped aside. "There is the most republican solution we were able to find," he said of Louis Philippe.[317] He was probably wrong: Lafayette quickly lost faith in the new king, who declared martial law to maintain order. Lafayette's efforts in the Chamber of Deputies to press for reforms ended in failure. The dream of a French republic was as elusive as ever.

It was different in America, which Lafayette had visited on a grand farewell tour in 1824 and 1825. Everywhere he went in the thriving new nation, adoring crowds lined up elbow to elbow — in public plazas, in theaters, by the roadside between towns — to see the man they still credited with their independence. There were fireworks, there were songs and speeches, there were military drills, and there were even reunions with the soldiers he'd served with in the Continental Army. More than once, the aged general, hobbling on a broken leg that had never healed properly, broke down and wept.

But nothing could stir his emotions like the memory of Adrienne. The boy who grew up haunted by the ghost of his heroic father was now in thrall to an even more persistent spirit.

---

[316] Unger, *Lafayette*, 367.
[317] Unger, *Lafayette*, 369.

He preserved her bedroom at La Grange like a shrine, "a spot too sacred to be defiled by the feet of the profane," as biographer André Maurois described it.[318] "On certain anniversary days Lafayette entered it alone through a secret door. He never mentioned his wife's name without visible emotion, and each morning on waking spent a few silent moments thinking of her."

Christmas Eve, the anniversary of Adrienne's death, was the saddest moment of each year. On one gloomy holiday, Lafayette went there, candles flickering, to write at her old desk. The letter went to Marie-Josephe Beauchet, Adrienne's personal maid. Lafayette wanted to write to someone else who knew and remembered Adrienne on "this cruel anniversary.... For a friend such as you are, dear Madame, not twenty years could efface so many tender and painful impressions. I am sure that on this melancholy anniversary evening your heart is with me."

For anyone who claimed Adrienne had "preached" at Lafayette, he disagreed. "That was not her way," he said after her death.

> In her delirium she had often expressed the thought that she would go to heaven, though, may I add, this thought was not enough to console her for leaving me. She several times said: "This life is short and troubled. Let us be reunited in God and pass together into eternity." She prayed that the peace of God should be given to me and to all of us. That is how this sweet angel spoke in her last illness, just as she had done in the Will she had drawn up some years previously. It is a model of delicacy, elevated thought and eloquent feeling.[319]

Elevated thought and eloquent feeling weren't enough to convince the skeptical Lafayette. Yet the promises he made to her weighed heavily on him, especially those she had insisted on as she lay dying. A letter he wrote to his business agent, and Marie-Josephe's husband, Philippe Beauchet, captured his struggles:

[318] Maurois, *Adrienne*, 479.
[319] Maurois, *Adrienne*, 471.

My dear friend, you will realize how eager I am to observe the wishes of my poor, angelic wife. I have found in a letter of 1785 a request that I should read certain books which she thought likely to bring me round to her religious opinions. You know with what delicacy of feeling she always feared to importune me in this matter, and with what tenderness she prayed for me. The request to which I have referred has the adorable character which marked everything that came from her, and I should be stricken with qualms of conscience should I fail to read with the closest attention of which I am capable the following books:

(1) Pascal's Pensdes [*sic*],
(2) Verité de la religion chrétienne by [*sic*] Abadie,
(3) Bossuet's Discours sur Histoire Unwerselle [*sic*],
(4) the works of Father de la Berthonie in defence of religion.

"You will realize," he added, "that among those there are many not new to me."[320]

He asked Beauchet to purchase the best editions possible of all four books and to have them bound with Adrienne's monogram on each cover. In life, Lafayette had never been patronizing of his wife's Christianity. His honesty would not permit him to lie about a subject so serious, even if such a lie might have brought his wife happiness.

Did he read the books she recommended, there in her bedroom, as the seasons changed at La Grange, as life outside died and was reborn? Again, his integrity makes it likely he kept his promise. But did those volumes help him regain the faith he'd lost, somewhere long ago? That is a question we are unlikely to have answered in this lifetime.

Even in his old age, there were still people who wanted a glimpse of the old Lafayette: the war hero on two continents, who had been the most loved and hated man in France. And right up until the end, he obliged them.

---

[320] Maurois, *Adrienne*, 479.

That was not, however, the only Lafayette. There was also the man who had outlasted all the French revolutionaries, years of prison, and Napoleon. And there was the man who had never outgrown his own revolutionary fervor, who was still "too easily inclined to believe any casual patriot he met who spoke to him of liberty and the rights of man."

"All these he was, and last of all, the more secret Lafayette, and the best, who at La Grange went through the concealed door into Adrienne's room, there to sit beside the empty bed and read in Pascal or in Bossuet as she had asked him to," Maurois wrote, "now and again saying to himself: 'What if it were true?....'"[321]

Following her death, Lafayette wore around his neck a pendant with Adrienne's picture, and a lock of her hair. When he breathed his last, close to thirty years later, in May 1834, he would do so clutching that portrait.

After Adrienne made her last confession, she told her husband, "If I am going to another world, you know how busy I shall be there for you."[322] Is she busy there still?

That may be what it takes to get the Hero of Two Worlds into a third. And if so, it seems unwise to bet against the astounding and heroic faith of the Marquise de Lafayette.

[321] Maurois, *Adrienne*, 485.
[322] Lane, *General and Madame de Lafayette*, 263.

Chapter 9

The Code Word Was Rochambeau

1

From an early age, it was clear the boy was meant to be a priest.

Now Pentecost was not far away. He was ready to have his head shaved in the traditional tonsure and take his vows as a Jesuit. Because he was small, here at the school in Blois people had not-so-teasingly called him the little grand vicar.

The current grand vicar, the Abbé de Beaumont, who would one day become the archbishop of Paris, smiled when he heard this. He didn't doubt, however, that one day it would come true. The boy had been a sickly youth, but he was now fifteen, devout, and an excellent student.

So when the local bishop, François de Crussol d'Uzès, came to fetch the boy one spring afternoon in 1740, the young man assumed it had something to do with his lessons, or perhaps a last-minute detail before he took the minor orders. Instead, the bishop was about to change the entire course of his life, and of history.

Gently but simply, Bishop Crussol broke the news: the boy's brother, Césaire, had just died unexpectedly. This was a deep shock: Césaire had been only a year older, and they had been close as children. But it was followed immediately by an even more earthshaking pronouncement.

The boy who had been training faithfully for the priesthood since he was six was now his family's oldest son. He would have to forget everything the bishop had told him about his future career as a Jesuit. Instead, he was to immediately leave the school at Blois and begin the military career expected of the family heir.

"You must now prepare to serve the King as loyally in the army and with the same zeal and devotion you would have served God on the altar," the bishop told him.

"I was deeply grieved," the boy remembered in his memoirs. But there was no time to mourn, and nothing to dispute. The bishop "took me into his carriage and carried me at once to my parents."[323]

Just that abruptly, one of the most brilliant military careers in history began. It made an international hero of the Marshal Jean-Baptiste Donatien de Vimeur, better known as the Comte de Rochambeau. And that tragedy, and the response to it, would one day save the American Revolution.

2

Even though he never appears onstage in the Broadway musical *Hamilton*, one of the most memorable moments occurs when Rochambeau's name is shouted in the chorus of "Yorktown (The World Turned Upside Down)":

> The code word is "Rochambeau," dig me?
> Rochambeau!
> You have your orders now, go, man, go![324]

That's not just poetic license. At the critical Battle of Yorktown, Rochambeau's name was in fact used as a password by Alexander Hamilton's troops, who were attacking a key British redoubt. Afraid gunfire would give away their position during the moonless night assault, the patriots successfully stormed the fortification with bayonets, shouting "Rochambeau!"

Rochambeau did far more than just lend his name to the battle, however. If not for his calm, experienced presence, Yorktown might have been

---

[323] Jean Edmond Weelen, *Rochambeau, Father and Son: A Life of the Maréchal de Rochambeau*, trans. Lawrence Lee (New York: H. Holt, 1936), 11.

[324] Lin-Manuel Miranda, "Yorktown (The World Turned Upside Down)," Genius, September 25, 2015, https://genius.com/Original-broadway-cast-of-hamilton-yorktown-the-world-turned-upside-down-lyrics.

the site of a completely different military outcome in the fall of 1781: the rescue of the British army. New York City, meanwhile, would likely have hosted an epic battle instead. Carnage would have been assured for both sides, but success for the patriots would have been unlikely.

After turning his sights from the priesthood to the battlefield, Rochambeau assembled a distinguished thirty-year military career. It was in his blood. His home, the Château de Rochambeau, three miles west of Paris, was filled with reminders of his heroic ancestors. That line stretched back to the Crusades.

Rochambeau's contribution to that lineage included service in the War of Austrian Succession and the Seven Years' War. He might then have eased into a well-deserved retirement at the family château, recovering from rheumatism and watching the swans glide past on the nearby river Loire. But in 1780 he was summoned by King Louis XVI to play his greatest role.

Rochambeau is one of several Catholic heroes of the Revolution from France. We've already met Beaumarchais in chapter 5 and the Lafayettes in chapter 8. Adm. François Joseph Paul de Grasse was critical to the victory at Yorktown. So was Armand-Louis Gontaut, the duc de Lauzun, whose Legion helped defend the Gloucester Peninsula and prevent Cornwallis from a last-minute escape.

Meanwhile, Adm. Charles de Ternay, the commanding officer of the French fleet, didn't live to see Yorktown. He died of typhus in December 1780. But he played an important part in the final stages of the Revolution and was given a hero's funeral in Newport, Rhode Island.

However, what makes Rochambeau of particular interest is how unlike some other well-known Frenchmen of his day he was.

During that time, the extramarital affairs of noblemen — and women — were common knowledge, and even encouraged. Yet Rochambeau and his wife, Jeanne-Thérèse Telles d'Acosta, had by all accounts a faithful and loving relationship that lasted for decades. He would write: "My star gave me a wife who was all I could wish for ... but especially a personality and an education which was most highly praised among all my friends. She brought me happiness all my life. I hope for my part, to have made her happy by the tenderest affection, which has never wavered for a single moment for nearly sixty years."

Meanwhile, while many upper-class Frenchmen, like Lafayette, paid only lip service to Catholicism, Rochambeau apparently took his faith far more seriously. His father, crippled from birth but beloved by his neighbors, had been a devoted practitioner of "a very simple Christianity" and "was constantly giving thanks to God for 'the benefits bestowed on himself and his family.'"[325]

Although Rochambeau ended up a soldier instead of a priest, those lessons of his early days stuck with him. "Above all other," he wrote, "a soldier must be inspired by his respect for God and his religion." Like George Washington, he made it a point to insist on regular church services for his men. Both men believed this was important not only for instilling discipline but also as a way of ensuring God's favor. "We can have little hope of the blessing of Heaven on our army," Washington thought, "if we insult it by our impiety and folly."[326]

A third quality that differentiated Rochambeau from some other prominent French soldiers was his ego—or rather, the lack of it.

From the very beginning of the partnership between France and the colonies, French assistance had been for the country's leaders a means to an end: a way to strike back at Great Britain. As we saw in chapter 5, the original plan was not just to fund the colonial uprising but also to have a French military dictator lead it.

That attitude trickled down to some of the officers who joined the colonial cause. A good example is the brilliant engineer Louis Duportail, a recent graduate of France's military academy when he was sent to the colonies by King Louis XVI in February 1777. Duportail quickly became one of Washington's most trusted advisers, and later outlined a plan to create the army's Corps of Engineers.

---

[325] Jini Jones Vail, *Rochambeau, Washington's Ideal Lieutenant: A French General's Role in the American Revolution* (Tarentum, PA: Word Association Publishers, 2011), 7.

[326] Vail, *Rochambeau*, 27.

Yet "Duportail thought very highly of himself"[327] — so much so that his long list of demands included promotions for himself and his fellow engineers, pay raises all around, servants, and multiple horses. All "before the French king's engineers lifted a gun or stuck a shovel in the ground."

Rochambeau, aged fifty-five when he was promoted to lieutenant general and chosen to lead the Expédition Particulière, was different. He had been a soldier for forty years when he came to America in 1780. He probably had more experience than any colonial soldier — including George Washington.

Yet, unlike French officers such as the duc de Broglie, and English immigrants like Charles Lee and Horatio Gates, Rochambeau never intrigued for Washington's job. In fact, he became known as "Washington's ideal lieutenant" — the title of Jini Jones Vail's comprehensive biography — precisely because he resolved not to let rank get in the way of his job.

One of his first acts on landing at Newport, Rhode Island, in July 1780, was to write Washington and define his position: "Being ordered by the King, my master, to come and [place] myself under your command, I arrive with the deepest feelings of submission, of zeal, and of veneration for your person, and for the distinguished talents which you display in supporting an ever memorable war. We are now, Sir, under your command."[328]

In Newport, Rochambeau and his troops spent much of their time in a state of expectation. They were waiting for France to act: to send the second division of soldiers that had been requested; to send money; and to send naval reinforcements.

When the two generals finally met face-to-face in Hartford that September, they agreed the last point was critical. And since America's navy was still a tiny collection of retrofitted ships, no serious action could be taken without the help of a French fleet to secure the coastline.

---

[327] Storozynski, *The Peasant Prince*, 41.

[328] Count de Rochambeau, "Count de Rochambeau to General Washington, On the Arrival of the French Army at Newport," July 12, 1780, in *The Writings of George Washington*, vol. 7, *Correspondence and Miscellaneous Papers Relating to the American Revolution*, ed. Jared Sparks (New York: Harper and Brothers, 1847), 511.

The waiting game stretched through the winter and into the next spring. Yet Rochambeau's discipline and attention to detail made the long layover remarkably incident-free. "Not a man has left his camp, not a cabbage has been stolen, not a complaint has been heard," Rochambeau wrote.[329]

Contemporaneous accounts back up his assertion. The *Connecticut Courant* had nothing but praise for Rochambeau's men: "The exact discipline of the troops, and the attention of the officers to prevent any injury to individuals, have made the march of this army through the country very agreeable to the inhabitants."[330]

The good behavior wasn't an accident. As France's inspector of infantry, Rochambeau had spent years disciplining troops. He played a major role in turning the French army into the professional, formidable force it now was. His simple but effective principles—troops needed to be both well-trained and well-supplied—won him the loyalty of his men, who affectionately called him "Papa."

The troops' conduct, though, was more than a matter of etiquette. It was also strategically necessary. The British army had pillaged its way through many of the cities and towns where it stayed. Yet memories of the Seven Years' War, in which the British had been allies and the French had been the enemy, were still fresh in the minds of many colonists.

And there was suspicion about the motives of the French. Some of it was reasonable. (Were the French using the war to help themselves? Absolutely.) And some was the product of anti-Catholicism encouraged by the British. Louis Duportail had observed, three years earlier, that "the people here, although at war with England, hate the French even more than they do the English."[331]

The Comte de Clermont-Crèvecoeur, an officer who served under Rochambeau, added that the British had fed colonial prejudices at every turn. "They had made the French seem so odious to the Americans,"

---

[329] Vail, *Rochambeau, Washington's Ideal Lieutenant*, 73.

[330] Vail, *Rochambeau, Washington's Ideal Lieutenant*, 126.

[331] Storozynski, *The Peasant Prince*, 62.

he wrote, "saying that we were dwarfs, pale, ugly specimens who lived exclusively on frogs and snails."[332]

That made Rochambeau's disciplined leadership all the more important, added Clermont-Crèvecoeur. The avoidance of unpleasant incidents during his command helped win the friendship of Americans, "who were not naturally drawn toward our nation."

Rochambeau also possessed the gifts of a diplomat. When an eager Lafayette encouraged an assault on New York City, the older man gently put the young lieutenant general in his place.

"My dear marquis," his reply began. "Allow an old father to reply to you as a dear son whom he loves and infinitely esteems.

"It is always good to think the French invincible, but I am going to tell you a secret learned from forty years' experience," he continued. "There are no easier men to defeat than those who have lost confidence in their leaders, and they lose it at once when they have been endangered through personal and selfish ambition."[333] An abashed Lafayette apologized, but Rochambeau admired his zeal and took care not to diminish it.

When Rochambeau felt he'd waited long enough for Washington to visit Newport and survey his troops, he wrote a letter in February 1781. It was not a complaint, however, but a gentle reminder in the form of a birthday wish. He told Washington that his troops planned to celebrate the commander in chief's birthday, "with the sole regret that Your Excellency is not a witness to the gladness of our hearts."

"The response was immediate,"writes Jini Jones Vail.[334] Washington was under extreme pressure at the time, dealing with a troop mutiny in Pennsylvania and the frustrating wait for French support. But he "was so moved by the unexpected warmth of Rochambeau's note that he wrote back saying he would come visit soon."

The respect between the two men was obvious. They were physical opposites: Washington towered over the five-foot six-inch Rochambeau,

---

[332] Vail, *Rochambeau, Washington's Ideal Lieutenant*, 58.

[333] Ferreiro, *Brothers at Arms*, 224.

[334] Vail, *Rochambeau, Washington's Ideal Lieutenant*, 89.

"a small, keen-looking man but with the dignity and simplicity of the French country gentleman."[335] But Washington, who complained early in the war about the foreign-born officers he'd been sent, must have been grateful Rochambeau was after neither glory nor his job.

"In the most crucial situations, when Washington and Rochambeau disagreed profoundly on essential matters relating to the conduct of battle," wrote the Rev. Jacques Bossière, "the French general always showed his willingness to submit to his superior's opinion."[336]

Rochambeau seems to have had only one serious argument with Washington during their time together. It just so happened to be the most important argument of the entire Revolutionary War.

And it just so happened that Rochambeau was right.

3

For almost the entire war, George Washington had been obsessed with New York.

It was a reasonable obsession, strategically. New York City was even then a hub of commerce, and its waterways provided a natural division of the colonies. But the focus was also personal. The British army under Gen. William Howe had chased Washington out of the city in 1776, and had held it ever since.

It was a sharp slap of reality after the patriots' early successes, and it called into question Washington's fitness to lead. In a letter that autumn to his cousin Lund, Washington wrote despairingly, "Such is my situation that if I were to wish the bitterest curse to an enemy on this side of the grave, I should put him in my stead with my feelings."[337]

So, in the spring of 1781, when he was faced with two options—heading south to take on Lord Cornwallis or going toe-to-toe with Gen. Henry

---

[335] Vail, *Rochambeau, Washington's Ideal Lieutenant*, 91.

[336] Vail, *Rochambeau, Washington's Ideal Lieutenant*, xvi.

[337] "From George Washington to Lund Washington, 30 September 1776," Founders Online, National Archives, https://founders.archives.gov/documents/Washington/03-06-02-0341.

Clinton in a battle for New York—Washington badly wanted to choose the second option and redeem himself.

He had supporters. Alexander Hamilton, for one, was skeptical of the southern strategy. Lafayette's troops were keeping Cornwallis boxed in, but Hamilton believed the British could easily evade the Continental Army if threatened.

The French disagreed. In a letter written to Rochambeau in August 1780, the French ambassador, Anne-César de La Luzerne, raised the possibility of a march south as an alternative to an invasion of New York. Rochambeau immediately saw the wisdom of trying to surprise Cornwallis, but the man described as "strong as an oak with the bending qualities of a willow"[338] had to use both attributes to win over Washington.

In their frequent conversations, "the confident Rochambeau watered the seeds of concentrating the campaign in the South," Jones Vail writes, "and gently nourished them through the fall, winter, and spring following the original planting."[339]

It still took a "rare, unpleasant"[340] discussion between the two men to settle matters. Rochambeau was forced to point out to Washington that the key piece of either strategy—a French fleet led by Admiral de Grasse that was sailing north from the Caribbean—was technically not under Washington's command.

Jones Vail highlights three events that added weight to Rochambeau's argument. The first was a reconnaissance of New York that July. It showed the British presence in the city was far more formidable than suspected. This was backed up by a discouraging report from engineer Louis Duportail about how difficult it would be to breach the British defenses there.

The third, and most important, factor was that Rochambeau had learned Admiral de Grasse's fleet was on its way. At Rochambeau's urging, it was headed to Chesapeake Bay, instead of New York. This was the naval support Washington and Rochambeau had agreed was critical.

---

[338] Vail, *Rochambeau, Washington's Ideal Lieutenant*, 163.
[339] Vail, *Rochambeau, Washington's Ideal Lieutenant*, 164.
[340] Vail, *Rochambeau, Washington's Ideal Lieutenant*, 150.

Ironically, the same reason that made Cornwallis choose Yorktown to defend—its deepwater harbor, which could have allowed him and his army to be rescued by sea—was also a key argument for having de Grasse head there as well. His fleet would be unable to get over the sandbar leading to New York Harbor, so the Virginia coast was his natural option.

In addition, de Grasse was on a strict timetable. He and his fleet were assisting the Spanish navy in the Caribbean, and they could only be spared for a limited duration. Therefore, the closer destination was also the better one. "When combined with the eight ships already at Newport," author Larrie D. Ferreiro points out, "the French would have an overwhelming naval advantage over the British, but only for a brief window of time."[341]

So Rochambeau and Washington headed south, leaving enough troops and fortifications behind to make Clinton believe an attack on New York was still imminent. For Rochambeau's army, it was a particularly grueling march. In the stifling late-summer heat, they trekked more than six hundred miles from Rhode Island to Virginia.

The patriots were helped by the indecision of Clinton. He missed several chances to stop the Continental Army on its way to Virginia. Then he dallied before sending a British fleet to rescue Cornwallis—two weeks too late. Cornwallis, meanwhile, was stubbornly dug in on the bluffs of Yorktown, with his back to the sea. His single-minded strategy made a bailout by the British navy his only option.

That became less likely after the Battle off the Capes in early September, when de Grasse's fleet chased off British vessels that had come to help Cornwallis. It was a "tactical stalemate" but "would turn out to be the crucial strategic victory that allowed the French and American forces to envelop and dominate Cornwallis in just a few weeks."[342]

At six feet four inches, with a booming voice and an infectious confidence, de Grasse was a formidable figure. Since the age of eleven, he'd

---

[341] Ferreiro, *Brothers at Arms*, 236.
[342] Ferreiro, *Brothers at Arms*, 263.

been a member of the Knights of Malta, one of the Catholic Church's oldest military orders. He seemed every bit the answer to the patriots' prayers.

But flushed with this success, de Grasse had to be talked into sticking around rather than heading back to the Caribbean to fulfill his commitments to the Spanish. Then, later that month, when rumors of a British fleet headed toward Virginia reached de Grasse, the impetuous admiral wanted to abandon the cordon around Yorktown and engage his foes.

In both cases, it was Rochambeau who served as the voice of reason.

"My dear admiral, you are the most amiable admiral that I know," Rochambeau wrote soothingly. "You meet all of our wishes and I believe that we are going to turn this into a good business."[343] But he also made clear how bad a decision it would be for de Grasse to leave his position. Mollified, de Grasse agreed to stay through October. His presence ensured Cornwallis would remain trapped on the coastline.

The siege of Yorktown itself, during the first two weeks of October, was decisive, as most people know. Although the war would not officially end for almost two years, popular support in Great Britain plummeted after Yorktown, and a new government would make peace its goal.

Yet Rochambeau's decision to go south didn't just effectively end the war: it did so with surprisingly little loss of life. By the time the humiliated British signed the Articles of Capitulation on October 19, less than a thousand soldiers had been killed on all sides at Yorktown. A battle for New York would likely have been far more deadly.

When Rochambeau returned to France, Louis XVI appointed him a *Maréchal de France*, an honorary rank. Yet perhaps the most telling sign of the esteem people had for Rochambeau is this: in 1787, on a trip to London, he was the guest of his old adversary Cornwallis. In fact, "all of the officers of Cornwallis' army who were in the metropolis wished to pay tribute to the loyalty and the generosity of their opponent who had

---

[343] Charles Lee Lewis, *Admiral de Grasse and American Independence* (Annapolis: Naval Institute Press, 1945), 180.

known how to reconcile the demands of the human conscience with his duties as a Frenchman."[344]

That all meant nothing when the revolution came to France in 1789. As Rochambeau had once written to Washington, the difference between the Americans and the French could be observed by how they ate soup. The former let the soup cool before eating it; the latter simply shoveled it in and burned their mouths.[345] So it was with the two revolutions.

Nearly seventy and suffering from his old war wounds, Rochambeau was thrown into prison at the height of the Terror in 1794. He was slated for execution, and saved only by the death of Robespierre, which ended the bloodshed.

After a life of adventuring, the rest of his time was peaceful. The gentle River Loire still unwound lazily outside the window of his bedchamber at the Château de Rochambeau. "At last I am to enjoy philosophical quiet," he wrote gratefully to his old friend Washington, "in the shade of my own laurel tree."[346] He died at age 82 in the room where he was born, in May 1807.

He'd already been saved from the guillotine when he wrote it, but a line from one of Rochambeau's letters seeking release from prison could serve nicely as an epitaph for this general of rare humility and tact.

"I have never been a schemer nor ambitious for power," he wrote. "I have never looked for enterprises, they have sought me out."[347]

None were greater than the battle for American freedom. And the modest character Rochambeau accurately described is one of the primary reasons it was successful.

[344] Weelen, *Rochambeau, Father and Son*, 126.

[345] Vail, *Rochambeau, Washington's Ideal Lieutenant*, 91–92.

[346] Count de Rochambeau, "What France Did for America: Memoirs of Rochambeau," trans. M. W. E. Wright, *North American Review* 205, no. 738 (May 1917): 787.

[347] Weelen, *Rochambeau, Father and Son*, 169.

Chapter 9 Supplement

Yo Solo ... Pero No Solamente
(I Alone ... But Not Only I)

1

Many of the sailors were angry. Some were close to mutiny. Even the commander of the fleet flatly told the general he was a coward and had his "cannon ass-backwards."[348] What was being proposed seemed like a suicide mission to them all.

Bernardo de Gálvez wasn't listening to any of it.

He was prepared to run his brig, the *Galveztown*, through the shallow inlet that led to Pensacola Bay. The ship would immediately come under heavy fire from artillery on the Red Cliffs above. And the narrow inlet would not allow a ship to turn around.

Trying to assault the cliffs by land had already been a failure: they were fiercely defended by British troops, as well as Choctaw and Creek warriors.

So it seemed impossible to gain access to the bay. But Gálvez threw down a defiant challenge to his troops in a note.

"He who has honor and valor, follow me," wrote Gálvez, the Spanish governor of Louisiana. "I am going ahead on the *Galveztown* to take away your fear."[349]

The fleet commander, José Calvo de Irazábal, snorted in disbelief when he read these words. But he and the sailors of the Spanish fleet bobbing

---

[348] Ferreiro, *Brothers at Arms*, 236.
[349] Ferreiro, *Brothers at Arms*, 250.

at the mouth of the bay couldn't help watching. They were horrified, yet fascinated, as Gálvez and his crew prepared to run the gauntlet.

It was a Sunday afternoon in March 1781, and the emerald green waters glistened in the sun. The scene was a deceptively serene setting for a man with a death wish—whose luck appeared ready to run out.

For the past two years, since Spain had formally declared war on Great Britain, Bernardo de Gálvez had led a charmed life. As the governor of Louisiana, he had pursued a pro-patriot policy throughout the Revolution. Beginning in 1779, he'd led a military campaign that weakened the British hold on the south. At battles in Fort Bute, Baton Rouge, Natchez, and Mobile, Gálvez's forces had bested the redcoats.

The last of those battles involved a two-week siege of Fort Charlotte, at present-day Mobile, Alabama, in February 1780. It was a defensive maneuver, since Fort Charlotte was close enough to be a threat to Gálvez's home city, New Orleans. But its success had also reduced the British hold on West Florida to a single post: the capital of Pensacola, defended by Fort George.

There was little reason to believe that was going to change this afternoon, as Gálvez directed his brig into the inlet. Everyone collectively tensed as the ship neared the cliffs and cannonballs rippled the waters.

Only Gálvez himself, fingers laced over his girth, appeared calm. He'd studied the British redoubt and concluded that the artillery mounted on the Red Cliffs would not be able to reach his ships. Trying to stay out of range, the *Galveztown* carefully hugged the contours of Santa Rosa Island, the long finger of land opposite the cliffs.

And though shrapnel from the cannonballs ripped holes in the brig's rigging and sails, Gálvez was proven correct. There were no direct hits to the ship itself, and soon he and his crew were floating safely inside the bay. Everyone exhaled.

Gálvez wasted no time issuing his "I-told-you-so." Addressing his exultant crew, he announced, "I alone went to sacrifice myself so as not to expose any soldier or member of my army."[350] As author Larrie D.

---

[350] Ferreiro, *Brothers at Arms*, 250.

Ferreiro points out, that conveniently ignored the fact that the crew of the *Galveztown* had also been part of that sacrifice.

But "I alone"—*Yo solo*—was an important part of Gálvez's mystique. It was important enough that after the war, Spain's King Carlos III allowed Gálvez to place the phrase on his coat of arms.

Of course, Gálvez was far from alone in the two-month battle for Pensacola, which essentially ended on May 8 with a lucky shot. A Spanish grenade lobbed into a redoubt blew up a store of gunpowder and munitions. More than a hundred British troops were killed, and surrender became inevitable.

But Gálvez, who was wounded during the siege, had been the longest, loudest voice in favor of the assault on Pensacola. And now that he'd been proven right, the Revolution would be all but ended within six months.

It couldn't have happened without Gálvez. Nor without Spain. Nor without the Catholic patriots who captured the American West, so that the Revolution could be won in the East.

One of those patriots, Oliver Pollock, described well the situation of his fellow travelers.

"I dwelt in an obscure corner of the universe," Pollock wrote in a letter to Congress, after the war, "alone and unsupported."[351] But to paraphrase his friend and colleague, Bernardo de Gálvez, Pollock was "alone ... but not only I."

2

As chapter 5 argued, Americans have long been unaware of how important France was to the patriot cause. So it might be surprising to some that Spain played any role at all.

Historian Ferreiro sums up the relationship in the final chapter of his 2016 book *Brothers at Arms*: "America could have never won the

---

[351] Ward Bond, "Oliver Pollock: Forgotten Patriot," Doggesbreakfast.com, September 13, 2010, http://www.doggesbreakfast.com/history/oliver-pollock-forgotten.html.

war without France, and France could have never succeeded without Spain."[352]

It's true that Spain didn't officially enter the war until 1779. There were several reasons for this, but a major factor was that Spain had to ensure the safety of two important fleets. One of them was transporting a load of Mexican silver—worth about $50 billion today. The other was bringing home troops from Buenos Aires. A British attack at sea would have caused "irreparable damage to Spain's economy and military."[353]

Meanwhile, most of the Spanish assistance happened in the western and southern theaters of the Revolution—out of view of most colonial leaders.

Spain had been helping the patriots covertly since before the war even began. As early as 1775, Spanish businessman Diego de Gardoqui was shipping muskets to Jeremiah Lee in Massachusetts.

It was a big risk for a man who did lucrative business with the British. But Gardoqui was not only willing to take it, he would eventually become "Spain's Beaumarchais"[354]—in other words, a crucial middleman funded by the Spanish government, who traded arms and supplies to the patriots in exchange for tobacco.

Yet, even after Spain officially became an ally, the American response to its assistance was tepid.

George Washington himself, when informed of Gálvez's victory at Pensacola, wrote only a "cursory reply." It was a brief note of congratulations "in the success of His Catholic Majesty's Arms at Pensacola." Washington added that he had "no doubt but a recital of the particulars will reflect much honor upon General Don Gálvez and the troops under his command."[355]

But Gálvez's capture of Penascola set into motion the events that would ultimately end the war. By helping neutralize Britain's naval

---

[352] Ferreiro, *Brothers at Arms*, 336.
[353] Ferreiro, *Brothers at Arms*, 95.
[354] Ferreiro, *Brothers at Arms*, 67.
[355] Ferreiro, *Brothers at Arms*, 255.

advantage in the Gulf of Mexico and the West Indies, Gálvez freed the French fleet, commanded by Admiral de Grasse, to head north.

That fleet, as we saw in chapter 9, played a decisive role in the patriots' victory at Yorktown. It trapped Cornwallis's troops and made their rescue by sea impossible. And it allowed Washington and Rochambeau to lead their forces south, where they linked up with Lafayette's troops and ultimately forced the British surrender.

It was Lafayette's friend Alexander Hamilton who wrote despairingly, after the British seized Charleston in 1780, "If we are saved France and Spain must save us."[356] It was a startling admission from a man who was once afraid of Catholic immigrants overrunning his nation, but he was right. And it would take both countries to save America.

3

Throughout most of this book, we've talked about Catholics in colonial America as a distinct minority. But that doesn't include the territory of Spanish Louisiana, a massive area twice the size of the thirteen colonies. It stretched from the Mississippi River to the Rockies, and followed the Mississippi north from the territory's capital, New Orleans, to Canada.

The territory had passed from French to Spanish hands after the Seven Years' War: it was a gift from one Bourbon monarch (France's Louis XV) to another (his cousin, Spain's Charles III). France preferred to keep Louisiana away from the British, and gave it secretly to Spain in 1762's Treaty of Fontainebleau.

Not all of its residents were Catholic, but as the property of two consecutive Catholic monarchies, Spanish Louisiana was far more hospitable than most colonial locales. While sparsely populated, some five thousand Acadians—Catholic refugees from the Canadian province of Acadia who had been forced from their homes by the British—wound up in Louisiana. Today we call their descendants "Cajuns."

Several Catholics in the territory would play crucial roles in the War of Independence. One of them was Oliver Pollock, who became known

---

[356] Ferreiro, *Brothers at Arms*, 218.

at the "Financier of the American Revolution in the West." Like some of the men we met in chapter 4, he was an Irishman by birth, emigrated to Philadelphia, and spent time in the West Indies pursuing business interests.

But unlike Thomas Fitzsimons or George Meade, he headed west when he returned to America. Pollock ended up in New Orleans in 1768, when he was about thirty years old. There he owned several plantations and befriended the Spanish governor, Luis de Unzaga.

Having spent time in Havana, Pollock could speak and write Spanish and quickly became Unzaga's confidant. There was an even more practical reason for the friendship: Spain needed wealthy and well-connected British[357] merchants like Pollock "if the colony's economy were to continue functioning."[358]

Pollock was a man of many connections. That included a close relationship with Philadelphia's Robert Morris, the Revolution's primary financier. It's because of Pollock's invoices to Morris, in fact, that we now use what we've come to call the "dollar sign." The symbol was created when Pollock was using shorthand for "pesos"—and began mashing up the letters "p" and "s."

The Mississippi River was naturally the focus of trade in Spanish Louisiana, including trade with the British colonies to the east. In the fall of 1776, it became a vital military supply line as well. Pollock oversaw a shipment of ten thousand pounds of Cuban gunpowder that was sent north to Fort Pitt. Soon, the river would carry clothes, arms, and medicine—especially Peruvian quinine, which helped fight off malaria—to the patriots. "These supplies proved to be the lifeline," Ferreiro writes, "that kept American troops fighting the British in the western theater of operations."[359]

---

[357] Ireland was under British rule. So Pollock was Irish by ethnicity and British by political rule.

[358] Light T. Cummins, "Oliver Pollock's Plantations: An Early Anglo Landowner on the Lower Mississippi, 1769–1824," *Louisiana History* 29, no. 1 (Winter 1988): 38, http://www.jstor.org/stable/4232633.

[359] Ferreiro, *Brothers at Arms*, 63.

Pollock was soon named the official American agent in Spanish Louisiana—by his own request, so he would become a prisoner of war if he were captured.

He never was, and his service continued through the Revolution. With his own money, he bought and refitted a captured British warship successfully used in skirmishes on Lakes Pontchartrain and Maurepas, and on the lower Mississippi. His funding helped George Rogers Clark seize a string of forts in the west, as we'll read in chapter 11.

In all, Pollock would contribute three hundred thousand pesos—well over half a billion dollars in today's funds—to the patriot cause. Yet, even after he found himself in dire financial straits by 1779, with his credit gone and his property mortgaged to the hilt, he still volunteered as an aide-de-camp in the battles of Fort Bute and Baton Rouge.

Why did he do it? For reasons his fellow Irish Catholics Thomas Fitzsimons, Stephen Moylan, John Barry, and many others would have immediately understood.

He explained himself, in part, when he requested that Congress approve him as its official agent in Louisiana, so that he could "merit the confidence and approbation of the country to which I owe everything but my birth."[360]

Pollock was modest enough, in fact, that he turned down a commission in the Spanish army because he said his "feeble services"[361] weren't worth it. That was in marked contrast to the man who offered him the commission: Unzaga's successor as governor, Bernardo de Gálvez.

4

Thirty-one when he became governor of Louisiana, Gálvez came from Spanish aristocracy. His father Matías would become the viceroy of New Spain; his uncle José was Spain's highest-ranking colonial official, the minister of the West Indies. Yet Gálvez "had gained his position less

---

[360] Bond, "Oliver Pollock."
[361] Bond, "Oliver Pollock."

through nepotism and more through competence, physical courage, and sheer force of will."[362]

He served in the Seven Years' War when Spain invaded Portugal. When he came to America, he led a series of expeditions to defend Spanish settlements in Mexico against Apache attacks. In one of those excursions, Gálvez rallied his reluctant troops with the line he'd later use at Pensacola: "I alone will go if no one will accompany me."[363] As was the case in Florida a dozen years later, it worked.

Gálvez endeared himself to his new subjects in Louisiana by marrying Félicité de St. Maxent d'Estrehan, the daughter of a wealthy Creole fur trader. And he endeared himself to Americans by making New Orleans a trading hub for the colonies while cracking down on British smuggling.

For the first three years of the Revolution, Gálvez had to do this while maintaining public neutrality. This got trickier in 1778 when he chose to protect an American raiding party, financed by Oliver Pollock, that had been looting British outposts along the Mississippi. Despite threats from the British to cannonade the city if the rebels and their stolen goods weren't handed over, Gálvez didn't blink.

It was the same resolve he showed at Pensacola, in perhaps the most important battle of the Revolution that no one knows about. Gálvez tried to inform the public: he later commemorated his accomplishment by writing an epic poem. In two parts and more than two hundred lines long, it was translated into English for the first time in 2018.

Reading "The Triumphant Victory at Pensacola," though, it's easy to see that Gálvez was motivated by more than just his pride. The poem opens with the declaration, "The Trumpet sounds of the fame / from the ethereal Regions / of the Catholic Armies / proclaiming laurels, feats, / praises, and victories."

And it goes on to suggest that England's inevitable fall isn't simply a matter of military might:

---

[362] Ferreiro, *Brothers at Arms*, 133.
[363] Ferreiro, *Brothers at Arms*, 133.

A severe God
desires that she return to his Church,
desires that she embrace the Faith,
desires that she do penance.

5

"Of all the nations that fought in the War of American Independence," Ferreiro writes, Spain "came closest to achieving the goals it originally had set out."[364] Those goals included regaining Florida, getting Britain out of Central America and the Gulf of Mexico, and recovering the Balearic island Minorca, lost to England in the Seven Years' War.

Bernardo de Gálvez did not get to enjoy those triumphs for long. He died, most likely of typhus, in Mexico City in 1786.

But he would probably have seen the success of Spain's aims in the War of Independence to have been divinely ordained. As he wrote about his home country, at the close of his ode to his own success at Pensacola,

Long live the Faith that adorns her,
long live the zeal, the care,
long live her beloved Patron
the Immaculate Star
of the Pure Conception,
and the Apostle Saint James.
Long live, long live the Gospel,
long live our King Charles
that his Reign be
defended, protected, and true.

---

[364] Ferreiro, *Brothers at Arms*, 301.

Chapter 10

God's Johnny Appleseed

1

The disbanding of the Jesuit order, as we've already seen in chapter 3, had dramatic consequences for the revolutionary effort. But while Fr. John Carroll became a critical figure in the fight for independence, he wasn't the only Jesuit who played a major role in that struggle.

In particular, two missionary priests — one in the east, one in the west — might have been even more important. And while Fr. Carroll could occasionally escape wartime tensions at his family estate in Maryland, the two men featured in the next two chapters spent most of the Revolution in more dangerous territory. They didn't just face Native American attacks, treacherous weather, and the hardships of the road: both men came under repeated scrutiny for their loyalties — to both Catholicism and America. That scrutiny could easily have led to their deaths; it cost one of these men dearly, regardless.

Whether it's the dog days of summer or the depths of winter as you read this, put yourself in the saddle with these priests. Imagine the stifling humidity and the crackling blue cold; the weight of clothes soaked by a rainstorm and an autumn gust forcing its prying fingers under your collar. Imagine it all for years and years and years of cycling seasons, of Masses and baptisms, weddings and funerals. Imagine how deeply these men must have loved their faith, and their idea of a new country.

Imagine. Put on your warmest clothes, but be sure to travel light. Keep your breviary and the Eucharist well hidden. And you might want to pack a pistol. Or two.

2

The rider shivered. His horse stomped and shook the moisture off its flanks. A jagged wind rustled the grasses of the riverbank, and the rider shrank in the saddle. The March sun was far too weak to dry his black woolen greatcoat. It was just luck, or providence, that the icy water hadn't reached the valuables stored in his saddle roll.

Crossing the creek had saved him precious time. The melting snow and spring rains, however, had swollen the stream to greater depths than he'd guessed. Now it was already midafternoon, and he found himself, chilly and wet, at the edge of a field. Someone had cleared it: that might mean a house nearby. A house where he could sit by the fire, steam the dampness out of his clothes, and perhaps even spend the night.

A man suddenly appeared at the end of a nearby lane. He squinted up at the horseman, chin thrust forward. The rider considered, as he always did, other possibilities. Instead of conversation, there might be suspicion. Instead of a warm hearth, there might be smoldering anger. Instead of a night indoors, there might be hours in freezing darkness, searching for shelter in a rotted tree stump or on a bed of sticky pine needles.

There would be many evenings like this on his journey. It would take the rider nearly 150 miles, from Salem, New Jersey—just across the river from Philadelphia—to the state's northern border. There, he hoped to visit a community near an ironworks called Long Pond.

First, though, he had to appease the man who was studying him carefully. What the cautious farmer saw was a horseman who appeared to be middle-aged. He was slim, wiry, and dressed as plainly as a Quaker, in sober browns and grays. When the rider spoke, his German accent was unmistakable.

Beneath his broad-brimmed beaver hat, the rider's face was weather-marked and travel-worn. He'd been on these roads for more than a decade now. But his eyes were gray and mild, and his smile was genuine. One day, years from this, someone would describe that expression as "almost seraphic."

The man at the edge of his field agreed, that windy March afternoon. He invited the rider into his nearby farmhouse, to share a meal and dry his waterlogged coat. After spending the night on a bed of hay in the nearby stable, the rider continued his journey. He would be grateful for this night of grace, and hopeful there would be others on the road ahead.

The rider would give thanks as well for the questions that had not been asked. Who was he, and why was he traveling these lonely paths? If he'd had to answer truthfully, there was no guarantee of the friendly reception he'd gotten. More than once, he'd had to hurry onto the road again, folded arms and frowns at his back. There was no guarantee that the frowns wouldn't be accompanied by muskets, either.

Gently, he slapped his horse's reins and rode into the brisk morning, deep in thought. Fr. Ferdinand Farmer mused about a day when there would be no need to hide his name, or his purpose, here in his adopted country. He didn't live to see that happen everywhere. But few people did more in colonial America to bring it about.

3

The forgotten hero among colonial Catholics must be Fr. Ferdinand Farmer. He might not have been the most significant of the many Jesuits who served in the colonies—that honor belongs to Archbishop John Carroll—but it's almost certain he racked up the most miles in service of his faith.

Writing about him in 1946, Fr. John M. Daley, S.J., tried to explain his low profile: "That Fr. Ferdinand Farmer is not better known is not entirely the fault of a lack of interest but is partially due to the obscurity which surrounds his personal life. He slips in and out of the pages of American Catholic histories much as it must have been necessary for him to slip in and out of farmhouses in the days when his ministry was not regarded favorably by the authorities."[365]

[365] John M. Daley, S.J., "Pioneer Missionary: Ferdinand Farmer, S.J., 1720–1786," *Woodstock Letters* 75, no. 2 (June 1946): 103, Jesuit Online Library.

Fr. Daley's sketch of Ferdinand Farmer is, with one exception, the best biography of the man popularly known as the "priest on horseback." That nickname became the title of a children's book published in 1958 by Eva K. Betz. It's a partly fictionalized account of Fr. Farmer's life during the spring of 1768. But while some scenes from *Priest on Horseback* are imagined, and though its scope is limited, this little volume also offers the clearest glimpse of the man who spent more than two decades in the saddle, ministering to a geographic triangle that stretched nearly two hundred miles from point to farthest point.

From his home parish of St. Joseph's in Philadelphia, Fr. Farmer made regular trips across the Delaware River into New Jersey. He traveled that state's length and breadth each spring and autumn. Later, he would go even farther north, into even more dangerous territory: New York, where Catholic priests were forbidden on penalty of death.

Through storms and snows, through hardships and hostility, over thousands and thousands of miles, he kept a protective hand cupped gently around the flame of frontier Catholicism. Some of the babies he baptized grew up to fight for freedom: their own freedom to worship as they chose, and their country's freedom as well.

Later, Fr. Farmer served as a pastor of the nation's first, and most important, Catholic church: Philadelphia's Old St. Joseph's. He would not only travel freely to New York but would also bring Catholicism to its largest city. He would remain loyal to the patriot cause, turning down a plea to serve the British army. He would gain renown not just as a man of the cloth but as a man of scientific letters as well. And when he died, no less an authority than John Carroll, America's first bishop, would say simply, "he died the model of pastors and all priests."[366]

Maybe even more significant was the tribute from the many non-Catholics who knew and loved the priest on horseback. "Men of every religious persuasion followed his remains to the tomb," historian J. D.

---

[366] "Rev. Ferdinand Farmer S.J.: A Priest of Pennsylvania, 1752–1786," *American Catholic Historical Researches* 7, no. 3 (July 1890): 120, https://www.jstor.org/stable/44373669.

Rupp wrote more than fifty years after Farmer's death, "the last and un-sought tribute of their respect for his many virtues."[367]

4

Who was this tireless priest, then, who won the respect of just about everyone who knew him? There are still gaps in our knowledge nearly as broad as the territory he covered.

The common complaint among Fr. Farmer's biographers is the lack of details about his life before he came to America. Even his name contains confusion, just like the names of many immigrants in those days of suspect record-keeping. He was apparently born Andreas (or Andrew) Steinmeyer (or "Steenmeyer"). But his first name is usually listed as "Ferdinand." And when he came to America, he took the last name "Farmer"—sometimes explained as a simpler translation of Steinmeyer, which means, in German, the manager of a large estate.

Much of what we know about Fr. Farmer was apparently not disclosed until after his death. In the sermon at his funeral in 1786, his superior, Fr. Robert Molyneux, S.J., told mourners Farmer was born to "reputable parents" in Germany on October 13, 1720. He came from a province then known as Swabia, located between Bavaria and Switzerland. His home-town is usually listed as Weissenstein, in what is now Baden-Württemberg, about two hundred miles south of Berlin.

Fr. Farmer, according to Molyneux, was, from an early age, "initiated in the duties of piety and the elements of liberal learning."[368] What Farmer learned, exactly, is the subject of debate. Fr. Molyneux mentions "a course in philosophy" and then three years in "a special study of physics." Other commentators claim he was a medical student; some say he was a professor for a time at the University of Freiburg in Breisgau. What's clear is that his interests were wide, significant, and not limited to one area of the sciences. As a pioneer priest, he would demonstrate abilities as a doctor, a botanist, and an astronomer, among other skills.

[367] "Rev. Ferdinand Farmer," 121.
[368] Daley, "Pioneer Missionary," 104.

Sometimes his interests might even have given him cover in areas that did not welcome Catholics. *Priest on Horseback* imagined one such story: Fr. Farmer accidentally drops his prayerbook, but is mistaken for a doctor—because the prayers are in Latin, which no one else can read. He sits up all night treating a sick boy with a poultice made from violets, and the boy recovers. The story is fictional, but plausible.

In September 1743, Farmer joined the Jesuits. He entered the novitiate at Landsperge (Landsberg), a town located in southwest Bavaria. In his funeral homily, Fr. Molyneux offered a "good conjecture"[369] that Farmer was ordained a priest around 1750. At that point, he would have been a candidate to join one of the Jesuit missions around the world. According to Molyneux and other sources, the new priest was assigned to China.

What would he have done there? It's difficult to say today. We do know that Jesuits in China at that time had just lost a decades-long battle called "The Rites Controversy," which pitted them against members of other orders, especially the Franciscans and the Dominicans.

The issue was whether the ancient Chinese rituals of Confucianism and ancestor worship were secular—and therefore safe for Christians to practice—or religious, and therefore blasphemy.

The great seventeenth-century Jesuit priest, Fr. Matteo Ricci, S.J., well known for his sympathy to Chinese culture, argued the rituals were compatible with Christianity. But the Spanish Franciscans, in particular, felt otherwise. In 1742, Pope Benedict XIV came down on their side: he forbade ancestor worship and ended further discussion of the issue.

So Fr. Farmer would have been entering a particularly challenging situation. He wouldn't just have been struggling to evangelize the Chinese but would have found himself battling fellow Catholics as well.

We're told by Fr. Molyneux that Farmer was disappointed he didn't get to go to China. If so, we don't have any official record of it. *Priest on Horseback* gives us a small window into Fr. Farmer's feelings on the subject.

---

[369] Daley, "Pioneer Missionary," 105.

"I was afraid life would be too easy in the Colonies," he thinks—but again, this comes from a fictional recounting of his life.[370]

If Fr. Farmer ever did entertain such thoughts, he must have found out quickly how wrong they were.

5

It was "the finger of Providence," Fr. Molyneux told the mourners at Ferdinand Farmer's funeral, that brought him to America.[371]

It was also simple, old-fashioned need.

In the early 1740s, German immigrants in Pennsylvania and Maryland were desperate for a priest who would not only visit every now and then but also speak their language. There weren't a lot of these immigrants yet: a 1756 census showed only 1,365 adult Catholics in the entire state of Pennsylvania.

But "three out of five were German, and the bulk of them lived along the rural frontier," according to author Jay Dolan.[372]

To serve these settlers, the Society of Jesus sent two missionaries: Fr. Theodore Schneider, S.J., and Fr. William Wappeler, S.J.

A letter from Jesuit Fr. Henry Neale. S.J., in April 1741 to his superior shows how anxious the locals were for German priests. "Their presence is very much wanted," Neale wrote. "My heart has yearned when I've met with some poor Germans desirous of performing their duties, but whom I have not been able to assist for want of language."[373]

When they finally arrived, their impact was significant. Fr. Wappeler built a chapel at Conewago and rode a circuit as far west as Harrisburg, although his health forced him to return to Europe before the end of the 1740s.

[370] Eva K. Betz, *Priest on Horseback: Father Farmer, 1720–1786* (1958; Long Prairie, MN: Neumann Press, 2019), 1.

[371] Daley, "Pioneer Missionary," 105.

[372] Dolan, *The American Catholic Experience*, 87.

[373] Paul G. Gleis, "German Jesuit Missionaries in 18th Century Maryland," *Woodstock Letters* 75, no. 3 (October 1946): 200, Jesuit Online Library, https://jesuitonlinelibrary.bc.edu/?a=d&d=wlet19461001-01.2.3.

Fr. Schneider, meanwhile, became a legendary figure. Tall, with a high forehead and freckles, he became a favorite of Catholics throughout Pennsylvania. He had stepped down as rector at the University of Heidelberg to come to America, and his educational background—he had taught philosophy—led him to start several schools in his territory.

Just south of Allentown, he also built a log chapel to serve as the headquarters of the Mission of St. Paul, popularly called the "Goshenhoppen Mission" because of its location. And he rode a circuit that stretched from Lancaster in the west to well past Philadelphia in the east. Bishop John Carroll called him a "a person of great dexterity in business, consummate prudence, and undaunted magnanimity."[374]

But by the turn of the decade, Wappeler had returned to Europe, and Schneider was left alone on the Pennsylvania frontier. He had a growing audience far too large for one man to serve. There were also nearly five hundred acres of property at Goshenhoppen that he needed to develop into a Jesuit plantation, which might supply needed revenue. Enter Fr. Ferdinand Farmer, in June 1752.

During his first six years as an American missionary, Fr. Farmer took charge of the Lancaster mission. As is the case with his background in Germany, details about Farmer's time in Lancaster are scarce. Some of this is because the area's earliest set of registers—logbooks in which a priest recorded baptisms, marriages, and sometimes celebrations of Mass—were misplaced in the late 1800s. These registers, which would have covered the years from 1732 to 1758, could have given valuable details about Farmer's Lancaster years.

We know that within his first year as a priest in Pennsylvania, he founded a new church: the Donegal mission of St. Mary of the Assumption in Elizabethtown, nearly twenty miles from Lancaster. Built of logs on the farm of parishioner Henry Eckenroth, the church would serve the

[374] John Gilmary Shea, *The Hierarchy of the Catholic Church in the United States: Embracing Sketches of All the Archbishops and Bishops from the Establishment of the See of Baltimore to the Present Time; Also an Account of the Plenary Councils of Baltimore, and a Brief History of the Church in the United States* (New York: Office of Catholic Publications, 1886), 387.

local community for nearly fifty years. In 1799, it was replaced by the stone chapel of St. Peter's, which still stands.

We also know that in 1757, near the end of Fr. Farmer's time in Lancaster, a survey of Catholics was requested by Pennsylvania's governor. This survey showed that through his circuit rides, Farmer was serving a group of nearly four hundred Catholics in Lancaster, Berks, Chester, and Cumberland counties. Most were German, though there were also quite a few Irish Catholics as well. (If four hundred Catholics sounds unimpressive, it was still more Catholics than lived in the town of Philadelphia.)

Philadelphia, however, was to be Fr. Farmer's new home. Once again, the need for a priest who could help minister to the city's growing population of German Catholics was too great to ignore. That man had been Fr. Theodore Schneider, who traveled to Philadelphia as part of his circuit. But he now had his hands full at Goshenhoppen.

So Ferdinand Farmer was once more the natural choice to replace him. Over the next three decades, he became a Philadelphia institution. In New Jersey and New York, he became more important still—for renewing and cultivating further the Faith in these hostile territories. We know this because we still have the records of his travels, written in his own hand.

6

His registers begin on August 29, 1758, with a baptism. In neat, careful script is the notation *"Baptizati a me Ferdinando Farmer, Soc. Jesu Missionary, nisi aliter notetur."*

The last three words of the Latin translate as "unless otherwise indicated." For the next fifteen years, seldom would anyone else be indicated. Fr. Farmer performed many more baptisms—more than five hundred on his mission trips alone. He would officiate at more than five hundred weddings, some at St. Joseph's and others on his travels. And he would record all these ministerial services in his register, which was small enough to fit into the pocket of his greatcoat.

It was important that he traveled light. Not just because he traveled often, but because he also had to travel—like Fr. Greaton and Fr. Schneider before him—in what amounted to a disguise. The simple clothing he wore made some mistake him for a Quaker. And the knowledge he'd gained while studying with the Jesuits in Germany made it plausible to imagine him as a doctor.

His impressive bearing must have helped sustain that belief, too. An acquaintance wrote: "He was tall and upright, of ruddy, pleasing countenance, graceful in manners and fluent in conversation; full of bonhomie and anecdotes. In his deportment he was gentle like his Model, but showing by the bright flash of his light grey eyes that he could feel for his Master's honor and defend His cause."[375]

That cause would have led him to carry a breviary, with the daily offices written in Latin. He would have guarded especially the precious items he carried in his saddle roll: his vestments and stole, a Roman Missal, a small altar stone, containers of wine and oil, and a special case for the Eucharist.

His new territory was widespread. It covered all of southeastern Pennsylvania and southern New York, as well as the entire state of New Jersey. As the Jesuit periodical *The Woodstock Letters* noted in a 1915 sketch of Fr. Farmer, "Well-known towns of to-day, such as Kensington, Goshen, and Bristol in Pennsylvania; Ringwood, Long Pond, Gloucester, Deerfield, and Salem in New Jersey; and Fishkill in New York, benefited by his ministrations, and that for a term of long years."[376]

He was relatively familiar with the landscape in and around Philadelphia, and no doubt benefited from the state's comparatively tolerant atmosphere. He also found friendship with the two Englishmen who served as his superiors: Fr. Robert Harding, who was the pastor at St. Joseph's until his death in 1771; and then his replacement, Fr. Robert Molyneux, who arrived the next year.

It's easy to imagine Fr. Farmer and Fr. Molyneux, on a winter's evening in Philadelphia, sharing spirited discussions about science and philosophy

---

[375] John F. Quirk, S.J., "Father Ferdinand Farmer: An Apostolic Missionary in Three States," *Woodstock Letters* 44, no. 1 (February 1915): 65, Jesuit Online Library, https://jesuitonlinelibrary.bc.edu/?a=d&d=wlet 19150201-01.2.8.

[376] Quirk, "Father Ferdinand Farmer," 65.

by the fireside. Both men would become members of the American Philosophical Society, as well as trustees of the University of Pennsylvania.

While he can't have had much time to pursue them, we know from Fr. Molyneux's eulogy that Fr. Farmer also maintained the interests in math and astronomy he must have developed in Germany. The eulogy mentioned "his correspondence with Fr. Myers, late astronomer to the elector Palatine, now Duke of Bavaria."[377] That "late astronomer" was actually the Moravian astronomer Fr. Christian Mayer, S.J., a Jesuit who pioneered the study of binary stars.

Busy as he stayed, Philadelphia became a real home for Fr. Farmer. There he enjoyed good friends, intriguing conversations, and diverting hobbies — as well as the respect of both Catholics and members of other faiths. The other two states where he worked were quite another story.

Even before it became a royal colony in 1702, New Jersey restricted office-holding to Protestants. The sparsely populated province was still home to a variety of religious groups. Puritans, Baptists, Lutherans, and Quakers, as well as Anglicans, Presbyterians, and Methodists could all be found among the state's fourteen thousand residents. When New Jersey was officially accepted as a colony, Queen Anne allowed local officials to grant liberty of conscience to believers in all these faiths.

Only one Christian denomination — Catholicism — was excluded. Fr. Farmer kept a similar prohibition, issued by New Jersey governor Francis Bernard, pasted in the flyleaf of his register — as if he could ever forget it.

To get to New Jersey, Fr. Farmer had to take a ferry across the Delaware River. The crossing was short — maybe three hundred yards — but still dangerous for an unaccompanied priest. Here was one bit of good luck: the ferryman, Patrick Colvin, was rumored to be the only Catholic living in Trenton.

He shared not only a faith with Fr. Farmer, but also a patriotic spirit. On a bitterly cold and stormy Christmas night in 1776, it was Colvin

---

[377] Robert Molyneux, "Funeral Sermon on the Death of the Rev. Ferdinand Farmer ...," *American Catholic Historical Researches* 7, no. 3 (July 1890): 125, https://www.jstor.org/stable/44373670.

who lent his boat to Gen. George Washington and his troops for their famous crossing of the Delaware, to surprise the Hessians at the Battle of Trenton. Years later, he would personally ferry Washington across the river for an equally momentous occasion: his inauguration as America's first president.

There was nothing so momentous in the many trips Colvin made across the river with Fr. Farmer. Nor was there anything dramatic in the modest shelter he offered the priest, in his own home, before Farmer began his long trek into the swamps and pine barrens of New Jersey. But that night before the fire might have been the only warm bed and hot meal Farmer would get for weeks. It's probably not exaggerating to say that his trips would have been nearly impossible without Colvin's friendship and aid.

Yet New Jersey was positively welcoming compared to New York. In her book, *Priest on Horseback*, Eva Betz noted, "Each time Fr. Farmer went across the river from Bergen County or by boat, from Elizabeth, in New Jersey, to New York, he risked his life."[378]

Things hadn't always been that way. A century earlier, New York had been governed by Thomas Dongan, an Irish Catholic committed to the cause of religious liberty. Dongan was able to get a Charter of Liberties passed that extended liberty of conscience to all Christians. When Jewish merchants requested the freedom to trade and practice their faith, Dongan acquiesced.

The fallout from England's Glorious Revolution of 1688 changed things dramatically. By 1700, the Act Against Jewish and Popish Priests made it a crime to be a Catholic priest or Jewish rabbi[379] or to harbor one. Life imprisonment was the sentence in either case, unless you escaped and were retaken. Then, the penalty was death. That applied even if, like the unfortunate Anglican priest, the Rev. John Ury, who was hanged in 1741, you were only mistaken for a Catholic.

---

[378] Betz, *Priest on Horseback*, 138.

[379] Despite the New York law, Jews haven't had priests since the Temple was destroyed in AD 70. They have rabbis who lead their congregations.

Not surprisingly, New York Catholics kept so low a profile as to be invisible. Writing in 1748, an Episcopal clergyman could state confidently, "There is not in New York the least face of Popery."

He was wrong, but Fr. Ferdinand Farmer's visits to New York were kept decidedly undercover. He must have used all his tricks—his Quaker's outfit; his scientific knowledge; his ready smile—to stay incognito. He celebrated Mass clandestinely at the homes of two Spanish officials in Lower Manhattan, and perhaps at other locations: at the home of a fellow German near Wall Street and in the loft of a carpenter's house on nearby Water Street.

His visits to the city are rumored throughout the 1760s, although the earliest recorded visit to New York in his registers comes on October 6 and 7, 1781, when he baptized fourteen children in Fishkill.

From these humble and hidden beginnings would arise a revitalized Catholicism in the heart of New York City. That includes a historic church building that stills stand today, more than two centuries later. There might not be a better example of how Fr. Farmer's patience and nurturing spirit paid off in the long run.

7

At this point, the reader might well ask a question.

No doubt Ferdinand Farmer was an important Catholic during the Revolutionary Era. He was an important *American* Catholic, too. The work he did to build the Church in the colonies is well established. So is his long-standing friendship with Fr. John Carroll. In addition to their correspondence, Farmer and Carroll apparently visited one another regularly. The man who would become the country's first bishop counted the priest on horseback as one of his most trusted confidants.

But was Fr. Farmer actually a *patriot*? Did he, like Fr. John Carroll, truly advance the American cause? Especially given the fact that, as a missionary who necessarily traveled in disguise, he had personally experienced the anti-Catholicism common in his adopted country?

The answer might rest on a single but revealing incident—and some context for it.

Near the end of September 1777, the British captured Philadelphia, the de facto capital of the colonies. It was a devastating development for the rebels, and an ominous one for Fr. Farmer and Fr. Molyneux. Now that redcoats controlled the city, would the pair be able to continue serving their growing parish and their widening missionary territory?

So Fr. Farmer went to visit Gen. William Howe in his headquarters on Second Street. No doubt he hoped to get some sense of how things stood for Catholics in Philadelphia under British control.

The meeting must have been a cordial one, because Howe asked the priest to join the British army as the chaplain of Roman Catholic volunteers to the loyalist cause.

What happened next has been the subject of some confusion. General Howe's plan was to form a regiment of Catholic soldiers, to be led by Lt. Col. Alfred Clifton. A regiment is usually made up of a thousand soldiers. Some histories claim Howe began with five hundred deserters from the Continental Army, many of them Irishmen. And a list of the regiment published in 1778 cites "Frederick Farmer" as the regiment's chaplain.

But the numbers, and the participation of Fr. Farmer, both appear to be mistaken. The provincial "regiment" only attracted 172 men to wear its green coats when it first mustered that November. Nearly fifty members reportedly deserted not long afterward.

Meanwhile, Fr. Farmer wrote, in March 1778, to Fr. John Austin, S.J., in Dublin, "Perhaps it will please you to hear that your British General on arriving here upon my waiting on him, proposed the raising of a Regiment of Roman Catholick Volunteers. Mr. Clifton, an English gentleman of an Irish mother, is the Lt. Col. and commanding of it. They desire me to be their Chaplain which embarrasseth me on account of my age and several other reasons."[380]

It wasn't unheard of for a priest as old as Fr. Farmer — then fifty-seven — to serve in this role. Just the year before, at age sixty, the Rev.

---

[380] John M. Daley, S.J., "Pioneer Missionary: Ferdinand Farmer, S.J., 1720–1786 (continued)," *Woodstock Letters* 75, no. 3 (October 1946): 221, Jesuit Online Library, https://jesuitonlinelibrary.bc.edu/?a=d&d=wlet 19460601-01.2.4.

Michael Schlatter, a Reformed German minister, had served as a British chaplain—although he would quickly be imprisoned for his sympathy to the rebels.

That leads us to Fr. Farmer's "several other reasons," which we never learn from any other source.

The evidence supports the simplest explanation: the most important "other reason" was that Fr. Farmer supported the patriot cause. Jesuit historian Fr. John Daley makes a compelling case for this view.

One significant point is Farmer's friendship with Fr. John Carroll, including the letter of introduction he gave him in 1776 on his Canadian mission. That letter caused both Carroll and the recipient, the priest Fr. Pierre René Floquet, plenty of trouble, as we saw in chapter 3.

Fr. Farmer knew well why the Americans were headed to Montreal —and what the reaction there was likely to be. He did himself no favors by getting involved. As Fr. Daley noted, "One could hardly judge from his participation in this incident, indirect though it was, that he was an enemy of the Revolution."[381]

In June of 1778, the British evacuated Philadelphia. The French had officially become America's ally, and the redcoats were needed in New York to counter this shift. By that fall, the much-touted Catholic regiment had shrunk to about eighty men. There wasn't much of a force left for Fr. Farmer to serve, and there is no evidence he ever did.

What he *had* done while the British occupied Philadelphia was perform weddings for British soldiers and their Hessian allies. That, Fr. Daley observed, was not surprising. "Naturally, Fr. Farmer would offer the ministrations of the Church to friend or foe, for his Captain recognized no such distinctions."

But the last such marriage was recorded at the beginning of May 1778. It's entirely possible the marriages stopped because Fr. Farmer took an oath of allegiance to the government of Pennsylvania. It's almost certain he'd done this by the following year, when he was named a trustee of the College of Pennsylvania, representing one of "the six principal religious

---

[381] Daley, "Pioneer Missionary (continued)," 220.

denominations."[382] He was the first Catholic priest to hold such an office in the state.

Fr. Daley again: "It is not likely that the government of Pennsylvania would have approved of the choice of and respected the oath of a man who had been in the British army the year previous."[383] There are records of priests in the city who refused the oath, and were jailed as a result — something that would certainly have been noted if it had happened to Fr. Farmer.

There is one other point relevant to loyalties. At least twice, St. Mary's in Philadelphia offered Masses at the request of the French: on July 4, 1779, and in November 1781, following the stunning British surrender at Yorktown. While it isn't certain Fr. Farmer and Fr. Molyneux were the celebrants, it seems likely. And, as Fr. Daley adds, "It is hardly possible that the use of the church would have been permitted for the celebrations if the Pastor and his associate were foes of the cause which sponsored them."[384]

Implied in this argument is that Fr. Farmer's time as a pioneer inevitably made him a patriot. All those years spent building a faith in the wilds and lonely places of the colonies simultaneously built a new nation, as surely as the soldiers who fought for its independence.

As Fr. Daley concludes, "Ferdinand Farmer did not fight the country's wars, nor did he make its laws. He was, nevertheless, an heroic figure in American history. The early days of this country were days that called for pioneers to mold that indescribable something which is now called, 'the American Way.' In that 'American Way,' religion and the religion professed by Fr. Farmer, played and must still play an important part."[385]

[382] Griffin, *Thomas FitzSimons*, 11–12.
[383] Daley, "Pioneer Missionary (continued)," 223.
[384] Daley, "Pioneer Missionary (continued)," 224.
[385] John M. Daley, S.J., "Pioneer Missionary: Ferdinand Farmer, S.J., 1720–1786 (continued [2])," *Woodstock Letters* 75, no. 4 (December 1946), 321, Jesuit Online Library, https://jesuitonlinelibrary.bc.edu/?a=d&d=wlet 19460601-01.2.4.

8

Fr. Farmer spent more than thirty-five years—more than half his life—in the saddle. Fittingly, he stayed there until almost the very end.

In the spring of 1786, the Revolution was over. His work was not. The new nation was, if not entirely welcoming of Catholics, far less hostile, at least. There was no better example than in New York.

"Suddenly and beyond all expectation, most of the legal barriers against Catholics and other religious minorities crumbled," Msgr. Florence Cohalan wrote about postwar New York. "No single reason or event explains the change."[386]

One reason was undoubtedly the work Fr. Farmer had done covertly in the city. By the spring of 1785, things had changed dramatically enough that a group of twenty-two Catholic laymen began looking for a site for a church. They had the help of the French consul and the mayor, and Trinity Episcopal Church agreed to sell the group some land in Lower Manhattan. It was a situation unthinkable just a few years earlier, when Fr. Farmer had slipped into town to say secret Masses.

That April 1785, Fr. Farmer set off once again from Philadelphia on his usual tour. He returned to the ironworks at Long Pond in northern New Jersey, before returning home in early May. But his friends could see all was not well.

"He was very weak when he left here; if he lives to return, I wish some means would be devised to prevent him going any more," fretted Fr. Molyneux, in a letter to Fr. John Carroll. "He is no more fit to take that journey than I am to fast forty days and nights like St. Stylites without eating and drinking."[387]

He returned at last, but confessed—in a letter of his own to Fr. Carroll—that the years had taken their toll. Apologizing for not writing sooner, he admitted, "Such is my weakness of late that the

---

[386] Florence D. Cohalan, *A Popular History of the Archdiocese of New York*, 2nd ed. (1983; Yonkers, NY: United States Catholic Historical Society, 1999), 12.

[387] Daley, "Pioneer Missionary (continued [2])," 319.

exercise and application, both of body and mind, must be short and interrupted."[388]

Weary but resolute, he saddled up once more in April 1786. The registers once again tell an eloquent story: "He crossed over into New York and baptized seven near Warwick in Orange County. On May 4 he was at Greenwich, New Jersey, on May 9 near Mt. Hope. From May 12 to May 16, he was at Ringwood, New Jersey, where he baptized seven."[389]

The last baptism is recorded in Philadelphia on July 30. The final marriage took place on August 2. Just two weeks later, at age sixty-five, the weary priest on horseback breathed his last.

Sadly, Fr. Farmer did not live to see so many of the seeds he planted come to fruition. The first was Old St. Peter's Church, which opened in New York City in November 1786.

But many other sites he'd cultivated would bloom into full, vibrant parishes. Writing in 1946, Fr. John Daley noted some of them: "in Pennsylvania, St. John the Baptist, Haycock, founded in 1798, St. Peter's, Elizabethtown, founded in 1799, St. Malachy's, Chester County, begun in 1808 and in New Jersey, St. John the Baptist, in Trenton, founded in 1814.

"Due to his efforts the Church in New York, New Jersey, and especially in Pennsylvania was furthered in its infant days and the ground work was laid for the present beautiful and massive structure."[390]

At Fr. Farmer's funeral Mass on August 17, the numerous guests included many non-Catholics. There were Protestant clergymen, members of the Philosophical Society, and professors and fellow trustees from the University of Pennsylvania.

Because so many people attended, in fact, Fr. Farmer's body had to be carried from St. Joseph's to the larger St. Mary's, before it was brought back to St. Joseph's for burial. His friend Fr. Robert Molyneux delivered the homily, reminding those gathered about the many other mourners not present. "His fatiguing and extensive excursions through a neighboring

---

[388] Daley, "Pioneer Missionary (continued [2])," 319.
[389] Daley, "Pioneer Missionary (continued [2])," 319.
[390] Daley, "Pioneer Missionary (continued [2])," 321.

State and various parts of this, in search of little flocks scattered in the wilderness, will be long retained in their minds and preserved in their breasts as grateful monuments of his unwearied zeal and unbounded charity, and as perennial proofs of the faithful performance of the duties of his ministry."[391]

As the crowd fanned itself in the August heat, a poem was read. It had been composed by John Stanwick, a state assemblyman from Philadelphia who later served in Congress. Besides his interest in politics, Stanwick had a habit of turning out verse for special occasions like this. In eleven quatrains dedicated to Fr. Molyneux, Stanwick commiserated with the priest on the loss of his friend.

But one couplet stands out. It spoke directly to the people who were perhaps most affected by Fr. Farmer's death: those he visited on horse-back, recorded in his registers, and shepherded through uncertain and dangerous times to a new era.

> His distant flocks shall now expect in vain
> The annual season of his wish'd return.

Tomorrow, the members of those flocks would undoubtedly focus on a horizon promising better days. Today, however, they would listen once more for the sound of hooves and look longingly for the sight of a slender, gray-eyed rider with a gentle smile. After all those faithful years, who could blame them?

---

[391] Molyneux, "Funeral Sermon," 126.

Chapter 11

The Priest Who Won the West

1

Now we travel across the not-quite nation, from east to west. These territories are wilder, less familiar to Europeans, and probably more dangerous. Especially if you happen to be a priest living in the middle of a camp of British soldiers, answering to a bishop who wholeheartedly supports the redcoats.

If that were you, and the rebels suddenly turned your world upside down, you'd have to believe pretty strongly in your God—and their promise of liberty—to follow them.

2

Fr. Pierre Gibault, S.J., rapped softly at the door of the cabin. A harsh voice commanded him to enter.

Around a table that had become a makeshift desk, several men were gathered. Their buckskins were crusted with dried mud, and every inch of their clothing was patched and stained. They scowled at the visitor, squinting through red-rimmed eyes. One of them, a strapping man in his midtwenties, stood imposingly when the priest entered. He was six feet tall, and his hair was fiery red. The Indians in this territory called him "Long Knife," and for good reason.

As he bowed his tonsured head in deference, Fr. Gibault prepared himself to die.

Like most Jesuit missionaries who had served on the Western frontier for the past century and a half, he was *always* ready to die. The dangers in this territory were too numerous, and too well-known.

Martyrdom at the hands of hostile Native Americans was always a possibility. Some souls nearly experienced it twice. In the seventeenth century, Fr. Isaac Jogues, S.J., had been held captive and tortured by the Iroquois for more than a year. They mutilated his hands, cutting off several fingers. Yet after he was ransomed and escaped, he insisted on coming back to America. His return was brief: he was beheaded by Mohawks who thought he was practicing witchcraft.

A priest might also perish at the hands of the elements. Winters were severe here in the Illinois Country; floods and famine were common. The constant travel was punishing, especially for a priest past forty.

Now, on the morning of July 5, 1778, the country was two years into the War of Independence. And the fort at Kaskaskia, on the eastern side of the Mississippi River, had just been captured by American rebels.

The commander, Philippe de Rocheblave, had been surprised as he slept the night before, by a small force of 175 men. Rocheblave was a Frenchman who'd agreed to work for the British after they emerged victorious in the Seven Years' War. He'd spent the previous evening across the Mississippi, enjoying several bottles of wine at a dinner with Spanish officials. Rocheblave might have been drinking to forget the rebellion brewing in his backyard: not long before, he'd been amazed to hear his own young daughter happily singing a rebel song.

Now he'd readily surrendered to the Americans, led by Long Knife — otherwise known as George Rogers Clark — who now studied his priestly guest, hands folded in his black cassock. To Fr. Gibault, the tall, intense, Clark presented a formidable figure.

He struck most others the same way. Clark had begged for the chance to pull off this invasion, taking his case straight to Patrick Henry, the governor of his home state, Virginia. The previous summer, a letter had reached Clark. It was from Francis Vigo, a Catholic merchant who traded in the western territories along the Mississippi and Ohio Rivers. The letter claimed that many of the forts now controlled by the British were poorly supplied and lightly defended.

In addition, the residents were mostly French. They had stayed after the Seven Years' War, and might even have taken a loyalty oath to King George III. But deep down, they owed no allegiance to the British. The case of Rocheblave's daughter was no isolated incident.

Clark, the head of the Virginia militia, saw a rare opportunity. With just a small, handpicked force, he argued, he could capture this string of forts. At the very least, he could cut off the supply chain that led northward to Detroit, and make things much more difficult for the Crown. His dream was to use these outposts as a base to invade Fort Detroit, the jewel of British holdings in the West.

Success there would unlock a huge advantage. "If the British posts south of the Lake line could be destroyed, a single army, and that not large, would be able to hold the whole of Canada at bay with the fort at Detroit," author Pauline Lancaster Peyton wrote.[392] It was a tantalizing prospect: an answer to the Canada problem that had plagued the colonies and a solution perfect for the manpower-poor rebels.

Patrick Henry was convinced, and the first invasion as Kaskaskia had now been a success. Now Fr. Gibault was convinced, as well—certain he was negotiating for the last wishes of himself and his people.

He asked Clark for permission to offer Mass that morning, and Clark gruffly agreed. "I have nothing to do with churches more than to defend them from insult," he muttered.

The priest led his frightened parishioners into the church, where Clark later noted that they stayed "a considerable time."[393] Fr. Gibault tried to console them by offering the Eucharist.

---

[392] Pauline Lancaster Peyton, "Pierre Gibault, Priest and Patriot of the Northwest in the Eighteenth Century," *Records of the American Catholic Historical Society of Philadelphia* 12, no. 4 (December 1901): 481, https://www.jstor.org/stable/44207808.

[393] J. P. Dunn, "Father Gibault: The Patriot Priest of the Northwest," *Transactions of the Illinois State Historical Society* (1905), http://www.museum.state.il.us/RiverWeb/landings/Ambot/Archives/transactions/1905/Gibault.html.

It was difficult. The French citizens were convinced they would lose their property, their families—maybe even their lives. So when Fr. Gibault returned to the cabin Clark and his men had commandeered, he had another request.

Earnestly, the priest begged the invaders not to separate the French families. He also requested that women and children be allowed to keep some of their clothes and a few of their possessions.

Clark looked at his guest in amazement.

"Do you think we're savages?" he asked incredulously. "Are we here to make war on women and children, or upon the church?"

Surprised, Fr. Gibault didn't answer this rhetorical question, so Clark continued.

"We are here to prevent innocent bloodshed. Now that the King of France has joined us, we hope to soon see the end of this war," Clark insisted, tapping a map spread across the table for emphasis. It was true: the Treaty of Alliance had been signed between France and the colonies in February. The news, when it reached French citizens on the western frontier, could hardly help but make them sympathetic to the Americans.

"So you and your congregation can decide to take whatever side you please," Clark concluded. "But I can tell you that the United States makes no war on any man's religion."

This was, of course, wonderful news for Fr. Gibault and his flock, who took to the streets to celebrate. The church bell, donated by Louis XV, was rung, and people would later call it "The Liberty Bell of the West." Bonfires were lit. The chapel was crowded again with grateful French settlers.

It was wonderful news for the Americans as well. George Rogers Clark didn't realize it at the time, but he had just made an ally who would help him win a good chunk of the western frontier. The French men and women at Kaskaskia, happily taking loyalty oaths to the United States of America, offered a scene that would be repeated elsewhere.

And it was thanks to a pioneer priest who was just as strong, just as formidable, and just as convincing as George Rogers Clark. Neither man would end up getting his due during his lifetime. But the Revolutionary War would have been quite different without their unlikely friendship.

3

The long Canadian winter was nearing an end when Pierre Gibault entered the world on April 7, 1737. The streets of Montreal, a growing town which then had about six thousand residents, were probably still icy on that day in early spring when the boy was born.

His father, also Pierre, was a bank clerk and teacher, but his mother Marie helped his education by reading to him. His favorite stories, we're told, were of the missionary saint, Francis Xavier, who once evangelized throughout Asia.[394] It would be a telling choice.

When he was seven, he entered the local Jesuit school; at thirteen, he left home to enroll at the Jesuit College in Quebec, about 150 miles northeast up the St. Lawrence River. Built in 1634, the school had recently expanded and was now housed in a stone building on the site of the current Quebec City Hall.

His father, who died in 1761, would not live to see it, but Pierre Gibault followed his wishes and entered the priesthood. He was ordained on March 19, 1768, and there was an immediate job waiting for the thirty-year-old priest, with an impressive title. Not long after his ordination, Fr. Gibault became the vicar general of the Illinois territory.

It was a huge swath of land with a complicated history and an even murkier present. In theory, the area stretched from the Appalachian Mountains to the Mississippi River, and from the Great Lakes to New Orleans. During the eighteenth century, the territory had shrunk somewhat, both diplomatically and practically. At the end of the Seven Years' War, the land west of the Mississippi River had been ceded to Spain. The British claimed the land to the east, which became part of Quebec.

But the European population was concentrated mostly in a string of forts and settlements along the Mississippi River. And while those

---

[394] Joseph Dispenza, *Forgotten Patriot: A Story of Father Pierre Gibault* (Notre Dame, IN: Dujarie Press, 1968), 9–10.

outposts were nominally under British control, they were still mostly populated by French Catholics, who decided to stay even after France gave up the territory.

Further muddling matters in the west was France's suppression of the Jesuits in 1763. Priests from the order were expelled from the Louisiana territory then held by the French. Most were ordered back to France, their property seized and sold.

But one was allowed to make his way north to the Illinois Country, where he had once served. His name was Fr. Sébastien Louis Meurin, S.J. And while he had pledged himself to serve the Capuchin bishop of New Orleans, the territory he served was under the control of Quebec's Bishop Jean-Olivier Briand, a loyalist whom we met in chapter 3.

In 1766, Fr. Meurin wrote to Bishop Briand, for the first time in three years, to report on conditions in Illinois. He had both good and bad news. The good was that, thanks to improved water travel, he had been able to visit settlements such as Vincennes, Sainte Genevieve, and Cahokia at least once, and sometimes twice, a year to offer the sacraments. Fr. Meurin had even been able to visit a new settlement to the north. Some called it Paincourt, but others had dubbed it St. Louis, after the French king.

The bad news was that the life of a frontier missionary had simply worn Fr. Meurin out. The next year, he made his position even clearer in a second letter to the bishop. He wrote,

> I am only sixty-one years old; but I am exhausted, broken down by twenty-five years mission work in this country, and of these nearly twenty years of malady and disease show me the gates of death. I am incapable of long application or of bodily fatigue. I cannot therefore supply the spiritual necessities of this country, where the stoutest man could not long suffice, especially as the country is intersected by a very rapid and dangerous river. It would need four priests. If you can give only one, he should be appointed for [Cahokia].[395]

---

[395] Dunn, "Father Gibault."

Bishop Briand took him seriously. In the spring of 1768, he dispatched the newly ordained Fr. Gibault to the Illinois territory at once. Gibault made the trip of more than fifteen hundred miles south, reaching Kaskaskia at the beginning of September. He was accompanied on this difficult journey by his mother and sister. These uninvited guests annoyed the bishop when he found out about them — the first rupture between the two men. It would grow into a chasm.

Nevertheless, Fr. Gibault performed his first baptism almost immediately on arrival. And he quickly agreed to serve as the priest for Kaskaskia, which was protected by an earthen fort constructed atop a bluff overlooking the village. He gave control of the parish at Cahokia, just across the Mississippi from St. Louis, to the older, wearier Fr. Meurin.

But Fr. Gibault would not stay in one place for long. His territory was vast, and in some places it had been years since a priest had visited.

One example occurred at Vincennes, located on the Wabash River two hundred miles from Kaskaskia. Fr. Gibault finally was able to reach this territory late in 1769, with winter conditions complicating travel and another Indian attack on the settlement likely.

He was dressed "in the rudest of home-spun," head covered "with the skin of some wild animal, captured in the wilder forests." As he mounted his horse, he had to "take care that the flint lock gun and pair of pistols, which are an essential part of his equipment, be in good order."[396]

They were, and he later reported that the trip was a success: "On my arrival, all crowded down to the banks of the river Wabash to receive me, some fell on their knees, unable to speak; others could speak only in sobs.... Some cried out: 'Father, save us, we are almost in hell;' others said: 'God has not then yet abandoned us, for He has sent you to us to make us do penance for our sins. Oh sir, why did you not come sooner,

---

[396] Joseph J. Thompson, "Penalties of Patriotism: An Appreciation of the Life, Patriotism and Services of Francis Vigo, Pierre Gibault, George Rogers Clark and Arthur St. Clair, 'The Founders of the Northwest,'" *Journal of the Illinois State Historical Society* 9, no. 4 (January 1917): 414, https://www.jstor.org/stable/40194522.

my poor wife, my dear father, my dear mother, my poor child, would not have died without the sacraments.'"[397]

Wherever he found Catholics, Pierre Gibault ministered to them. The young priest's energy astounded and delighted the aging Fr. Meurin, who wrote, "The English soldiers in the garrison from the Eighteenth Royal Irish Regiment were chiefly Catholics, and with the consent of the British authorities, Fr. Gibault ministered to them as chaplain. He gathered up the scattered remnants of religion and knitted the people into a homogeneous community. He not only established good relations between the people of the Illinois country, French, Americans and even Indians, but exchanged courtesies with the Spaniards across the Mississippi."[398]

But the years in the wild wore on him. In 1774, his mother took ill and died while he was traveling. His sister had married not long after coming to Illinois, and settled elsewhere in the territory. The flock at Kaskaskia that had welcomed him eagerly was now grumbling. That was partly because he was gone for long stretches doing mission work—and also because of money. Under British control, a priest had to be paid by tithes from the congregation. The settlers began to whisper that Fr. Gibault enjoyed alcohol a bit too much and too often.

In addition, the Jesuits had now been formally suppressed by Pope Clement XIV. The members of the order serving in America were left with an uncertain future. Fr. Gibault loyally kept reporting to Bishop Briand, but he was now tired, lonely, and unhappy. In October 1775, he implored the bishop to recall him to Canada. Afraid that winter would trap him in Illinois, he set out for Detroit in early November before receiving a reply.

It was a miserable journey, through freezing weather and in the most primitive conditions. No boats were left when he reached Lake Huron, but Fr. Gibault was so determined to escape Illinois that he crossed the ice-choked lake in a bark canoe. He traveled with another

[397] Dunn, "Father Gibault."
[398] Thompson, "Penalties of Patriotism," 414.

man and a child who were on their first voyage, so he was in charge of the tiny craft.

"Having had no experience with a boat for sixteen years, asleep during the nights and often during the day, and consequently knowing nothing of the dangerous places, which are not uncommon — in this miserable conveyance, resolved to overcome every obstacle, myself through ice, in snow, of which there were eight inches in the level country, amidst high winds and tempests, at a season when no one in the memory of man has ever ventured forth, in twenty-two days I reached Detroit."[399]

Exhausted, he became ill from his travels. Then received the bishop's answer. It was no.

Crushed, Fr. Gibault returned to Kaskaskia that May. Awaiting him was Fr. Meurin, who knew his friend was "full of indignation against his parish which he wishes absolutely to leave as soon as he has set his affairs in order."[400] But less than a year later, the older priest would be dead.

Now Fr. Gibault felt even more friendless and abandoned. Years later, he would describe how difficult those years had been in another letter to his bishop.

He remembered "all the pains and hardships I have undergone in my different journeys to most distant points, winter and summer, attending so many villages in Illinois distant from each other, in all weathers, night and day, snow or rain, wind, storm or fog on the Mississippi, so that I never slept four nights in a year in my own bed, never hesitating to start at a moment's notice." Still, he'd had "no other view than God's glory, and the salvation of his neighbor, with no pecuniary reward, almost always ill-fed, unable to attend to both spiritual and temporal needs."[401]

He must have doubted those sacrifices were worth it. American history suggests otherwise.

[399] Pierre Gibault, "Letter to the Bishop of Quebec, May 22, 1788," *Kaskaskia Records, 1778–1790*, ed. and trans. Clarence Walworth Alvord (1909; Springfield: Illinois Historical Library, Classic Reprint, 2016), 208.

[400] Peyton, "Pierre Gibault," 478.

[401] Dunn, "Father Gibault."

4

After the joyous celebration at Fort Kaskaskia, Fr. Gibault surprised his new friend George Rogers Clark.

He suggested they advance to the next target, Cahokia, that very day. It was about sixty miles away, and Clarke objected: his men were worn out and needed rest after capturing Kaskaskia in the wee hours.

"You won't need many men," Fr. Gibault assured Clark.[402] He was right. A detachment of just thirty militiamen and a few residents of Kaskaskia was sent north that afternoon. With the priest's calming word as assurance, the fort at Cahokia was taken without a shot. The French settlers who knew Gibault and the late Fr. Meurin readily pledged their support.

The same thing happened at the settlements of Prairie du Rocher and St. Philippe, and by week's end, more than three hundred people had taken loyalty oaths to the Americans. Considering that represented close to a third of the European population in the whole Illinois territory, it was a stunning turn of events.

A bigger prize loomed. Clark and Fr. Gibault now turned their attention to Fort Sackville at Vincennes. This was a town of about five hundred residents on the Lower Wabash River, located between present-day Evansville and Terre Haute, Indiana.

Scouts reported that the fort's commander, Lt. Gov. Henry Hamilton, had traveled to Detroit. Another golden opportunity was at hand, but Clark again hesitated. He called in Fr. Gibault and proposed waiting until the spring to take the fort, when he could summon reinforcements.

The priest was resolute. He explained to Clark that he could once again convince the settlers to defect to the American side. And once again, he was correct.

"He had great influence over the people," Clark later wrote, "and Post Vincennes was under his jurisdiction.... He informed me ... he would take this business on himself, and had no doubt of his being able

---

[402] Dispenza, *Forgotten Patriot*, 43.

to bring that place over to the American interest without my ... marching against it."[403]

Fr. Gibault arrived in Vincennes at the beginning of August, accompanied only by a doctor named Jean Laffont and an American militiaman, Capt. Leonard Helm. One of Gibault's loyal parishioners, a fur trader and store owner named François Bosseron, met the party and vouched for his priest. After a few days of discussions and the celebration of Mass, the citizens of Vincennes pledged themselves to the Americans, and to the government of Virginia.

"Before Almighty God, I swear to renounce all fidelity to King George III of Britain, and to his successors," the oath went in part, "and to be a faithful and true subject of the Republic of Virginia as a free and independent state."

Afterward, Fr. Gibault helped take down the Union Jack and raised the Stars and Stripes over Fort Sackville for the first time.

Two people were furious when they heard the news. The first, of course, was British Lt. Gov. Henry Hamilton. When word reached him in Detroit, he made immediate plans to take back Fort Sackville. And when he learned of Fr. Gibault's role in the takeover, he indignantly declared the Jesuit traitor should be hanged.

The second was Bishop Briand, who felt his loyalty to Great Britain had been compromised by his renegade priest. The situation between the two men, difficult before, was now impossible.

Hamilton's response came first. "It appeared to me expedient," he explained later, "to attack them as soon as possible, & before they should

---

[403] George Rogers Clark, "George Rogers Clark Memoir, Part 4," in William Hayden English, *Conquest of the Country Northwest of the River Ohio 1778–1783 and Life of Gen. George Rogers Clark* (Indianapolis and Kansas City: Bowen-Merrill, 1897), Indiana Historical Bureau, https://www.in.gov/history/for-educators/download-issues-of-the-indiana-historian/the-fall-of-fort-sackville/the-fall-of-fort-sackville-focus/memoir-of-campaigns-against-the-british-posts-northwest-of-the-river-ohio/george-rogers-clark-memoir-part-four/.

be reinforced, or have time to engage the Indians in their interest."[404] That October, he assembled a force of about three hundred British troops and Native Americans.

On the morning of December 6, 1778, they descended on Fort Sackville. Most of Clark's men had returned home to Kentucky County in Virginia for the winter, and the British retook the fort without a struggle. It was only the first step for Hamilton, who planned to retake soon the other lost properties in Illinois.

The people at Fort Sackville were unhappy, and became unhappier when Hamilton and his men announced they'd be hunkering down at the fort before restarting the campaign in the spring. But the settlers retook the loyalty oath to King George and stayed quiet.

In the meantime, Clark faced a quandary. He'd heard about Hamilton's recapturing Vincennes, but he was short of both troops and money. He was able to get the latter from Francis Vigo, the Catholic trader who was a friend of Fr. Gibault—and from Gibault himself.

By February 1779, Clark had scraped together a coalition of about 130 men, including French settlers from Kaskaskia and the nearby forts. He was determined not to wait for spring to attack Fort Sackville. The element of surprise, he decided, would make up for his inferior forces.

Fr. Gibault saw them off with a prayer and an admonition: "If you have God on your side, you have already won the war."[405]

The company must have doubted anyone at all was on their side, because conditions were so awful. The little band of rebels trudged 250 miles through rain, snow, sleet, and muck. They were forced to cross the Wabash River in a sleet storm, slogging through icy water that was chest high. Thoroughly soaked, frozen, hungry, and disillusioned, it says something for Clark's abilities as a motivator that they ever reached Vincennes.

---

[404] John D. Barnhart, "Lieutenant Governor Henry Hamilton's Apologia," *Indiana Magazine of History* 52, no. 4 (December 1956): 389, https://www.jstor.org/stable/27788392.

[405] Dispenza, *Forgotten Patriot*, 54.

What happened next also says something about his skills as a strategist. The entire assault on Fort Sackville was one elaborate bluff. First, Clark had a friendly French trapper deliver a message to the town's inhabitants. Those who wanted liberty should stay safely in their homes. Anyone loyal to King George, meanwhile, should head for the fort and prepare to help defend it.

"Every person found under arms on my arrival," the message read, "will be treated as an enemy." To put a cherry atop the daring hoax he'd whipped up, Clark promised no mercy for those enemies.

Clark's troops found mostly allies instead. Some citizens even dug up powder and arms they had secretly buried when Hamilton took over the fort. They gave the supplies to the Americans—which was lucky indeed, since the march across the Wabash River had ruined most of their powder.

Next, Clark spread out his men in a zigzag formation, giving every seventh man a flag to hold. As they approached the fort, the staggered ranks gave the illusion of a much larger force. The British panicked, and some Indian allies quickly deserted.

In truth, the fort was in poor condition and difficult to defend. Hamilton called it a "miserable picketed work" that was "so ill set up that a man might pass his closed fist" between the logs. This, he noted, "gave a great advantage to people armed with rifles."[406]

Clark's men began their assault on the fort at dusk, and kept changing positions to cover up just how few men they had. French citizens of Vincennes, meanwhile, brought food to the rebel troops through the night.

By the next morning, February 24, the British were perilously low on food and ammunition. They also believed they were surrounded by a force of as many as a thousand men. A chastened Lt. Gov. Hamilton was forced to surrender the fort, and the town. Clark's audacious gamble had worked: the Americans had lost only a single soldier.

Clark was later named a brigadier general by Thomas Jefferson as a reward for his efforts. He never reached Detroit—he finally got to march

---

[406] Howard H. Peck, *Indiana: A History* (Urbana: University of Illinois Press, 2003), 26.

on the fort in 1781, but his reinforcements were ambushed, and the attack was called off. But it turned out that taking Fort Detroit wasn't necessary. Thanks to Clark's efforts, the Americans now controlled the entire Ohio River valley. The British hold on the frontier had been weakened, and the western campaign of the Revolutionary War was nearly finished.

It was the best kind of military victory: the kind that involved little loss of life. And it would never have been possible without the patriot priest, Fr. Pierre Gibault.

5

If this story had a happy ending, it would no doubt conclude with Pierre Fr. Gibault and George Rogers Clark both rewarded handsomely for winning the West.

The truth is that both men had apparently used up their good fortune on the frontier. Life for both became much unhappier after this patriotic high point.

Clark's story was a mixture of missed opportunities and the fate of so many old soldiers: the amnesia of his government and the public. His longtime lament about not capturing Detroit—"It would have been mine"[407]—could apply to the rest of his life as well.

In 1783, the governor of Virginia, Thomas Jefferson, proposed Clark to lead the adventure of a lifetime. The mission: to travel and map out the untamed wilds of the Northwest Territory. But Clark reportedly turned down the appointment to return to Kentucky County and put his affairs in order.

Twenty years later, Jefferson had become president and made the Louisiana Purchase with France that would transform the new nation. Now the territory to be explored was far vaster. But it demanded a younger man: not one, like Clark, on the wrong side of fifty.

The "Clark" of Lewis and Clark fame was instead the general's younger brother, William. George Rogers Clark helped William win a spot on the

---

[407] George Rogers Clark, *George Rogers Clark Papers, 1771–1784*, ed. James Alton James (Springfield, IL: Trustees of the Illinois State Historical Library, 1912), 382.

historic exploration and mentored him for the challenges ahead. The missed opportunity, though, must have been hard to accept.

His military successes were now just a memory. The adventure in his life was mostly provided by dodging creditors. He'd dipped into his own savings to provide for his soldiers during the war, and came home nearly penniless. His request for reimbursement from the Virginia government was denied: the record-keeping was called fraudulent. Clark was forced to deed the compensation he did receive—thousands of acres of property—to his brother and other relatives, so that his debtors couldn't seize the land.

Health problems multiplied. One of his legs was amputated, after he was badly burned by falling into a fireplace. And when he was issued a ceremonial sword by the state of Virginia in 1812 for his wartime service, a stroke left him unable to hold it. Another stroke the following year finished him off—not long after the Virginia General Assembly finally approved for Clark a $400-a-year pension.

"My country has proved notoriously ungrateful for my services," he once complained.[408] His biographer James Alton James noted simply that, in Clark's later years, "life was at best lonely for him."[409]

The same could be said for Fr. Pierre Gibault. The help he'd given the Americans had not gone unnoticed. Unfortunately, the people who noticed didn't approve. His bishop, in particular, had watched with growing displeasure. And loyalists aware of Fr. Gibault's role in foiling the Crown's plans were only too happy to pass on rumors and accusations to Quebec.

Henry Hamilton, still bitter about the role Fr. Gibault played in the loss of Fort Sackville, wrote, "To enumerate the vices of the inhabitants would be to give a long catalogue, but to assert that they are not in possession of a single virtue is no more than truth and justice require; still

---

[408] F. R. Hall, "Genet's Western Intrigue, 1793–1794," *Journal of the Illinois State Historical Society* 21, no. 3 (October 1928): 371.

[409] James Alton James, *George Rogers Clark—Civilian* (Springfield, IL: Phillips Bros., 1928), 94.

the most eminently vicious and scandalous was the Reverend Monsieur Gibault."[410]

Gibault moved to Vincennes after the war. In a 1786 letter to his bishop, he reported that he hoped soon to banish the "gross ignorance"[411] from the settlers there. The grateful parishioners built him a church of wood and stone. It was called St. Francis Xavier on the Wabash, after his childhood hero.

He wrote again to Bishop Briand, then to Briand's replacement, Bishop Louis Philippe d'Esglis, who was also a loyalist. The response was always the same: silence. This treatment was apparently judged the best punishment for Fr. Gibault's support of the Americans.

In May 1788, Fr. Gibault begged the bishop once again to allow him to return to Quebec. It was the groveling letter of a desperate man.

Even though he'd never had "more than a swallow" of brandy, he said it had been more than a year since he'd had liquor in his home: "I think no longer about it." Believing it would help his cause, he even disavowed his part in the Revolution. His health was failing; there was "no reason," he added, "that I should expect this neglect."[412] But there was still no reply.

However, the new bishop, Jean-François Hubert, did write to John Carroll, who would soon become America's first bishop. In the letter, Hubert disowned Fr. Gibault. He cited "complaints of various kinds," including a charge of treason. Bishop Hubert added, "After the disadvantageous opinion that the government has formed of him, I can not prudently consent to his return."[413]

---

[410] Dunn, "Father Gibault."

[411] Peyton, "Pierre Gibault, Priest and Patriot," 476.

[412] Pierre Gibault, "Letter to the Bishop of Quebec, May 22, 1788, *Kaskaskia Records, 1778–1790*, ed. and trans. Clarence Walworth Alvord (Springfield, IL: Illinois Historical Library. Classic Reprint, [1909] 2016), 583–584.

[413] "The Bishop of Quebec [Jean-François Hubert] to Right Reverend John Carroll," October 6, 1788, in *Collections of the Illinois State Historical Library*, vol. 5, 586–590 (Springfield: Illinois State Historical Library), 589.

Instead, Bishop Hubert suggested the Americans take the problematic priest off his hands. Fr. Carroll agreed, but his letter to Fr. Gibault contained a further indignity: he would have to give up his title of vicar general, since there was already one appointed for that territory.

Like Clark, Fr. Gibault had invested substantial amounts of his own resources in the American cause. He estimated that he contributed nearly eight thousand French livres worth of money and goods — which in today's funds would equal about fifty thousand dollars. As in Clark's case, Fr. Gibault's repayment never occurred.

Fr. Gibault accepted these humiliations stoically, although his frustrations sometimes showed themselves in his letters. How, he asked in one unanswered missive to Quebec, "can you know such a priest zealous to fulfill the duties of his holy ministry, careful to watch over his flock. instruct them in the most important tenets of religion, instruct the young unceasingly and untiringly not only in Christian doctrine but teaching the boys to read and write, as one who gives scandal, and is addicted to intoxication?"[414]

Although he had become settled in Vincennes, he moved to Cahokia when the priest there was lured across the Mississippi into Spanish-controlled territory. It was there that he received one final reminder of how little was thought of his wartime sacrifices.

In Cahokia, Fr. Gibault lived on five acres of land that had always belonged to missionaries. Congress had authorized the transfer of land to militia members, and Fr. Gibault decided to request that the title to the land be transferred to his name. It was small enough payment, he felt, for the money he had given supporting independence. Now fifty-three and worn out from a missionary's life, he dreamed only of settling down and planting an orchard on the little patch of ground.

"The love of his country and of liberty has also led your memorialist to reject all of the advantages offered him by the Spanish government," he wrote to Arthur St. Clair, the governor of the Northwest Territory, in

---

[414] Dunn, "Father Gibault."

the spring of 1790. Now he hoped to "at last receive acknowledgment" of this sacrifice.[415]

St. Clair passed the request on to Washington, saying, "I believe no injury would be done to anyone by his request being granted, but it was not for me to give away the lands of the United States."[416]

Some claim Bishop Carroll objected to this request, saying Church property should not be transferred to priests. Others say the matter reached the office of George Washington himself, but was turned down by a secretary for a similar reason.

Regardless, this must have been the final straw for the broken priest. In 1793, he finally gave in to "the advantages offered him by the Spanish government" and crossed the Mississippi River. He became the priest at New Madrid, a town in southern Missouri. There, he undoubtedly was reunited with some of his former parishioners.

While details of Fr. Gibault's final years in exile are scarce, it was undoubtedly a difficult, demanding life. More than a century later, French-American solider and historian Edmond Mallet speculated that Gibault spent his last days "in unmerited poverty and obscurity among his compatriots of the Mississippi Valley."

It's believed he died in New Madrid in 1804, but parish records were destroyed during the Civil War, so the date is uncertain. Then, as if to cement his obscurity, a series of earthquakes struck New Madrid in 1811 and 1812, swallowing the parish cemetery where Fr. Gibault was most likely buried.

There were a few who recognized what had been lost. In 1896, author William Hayden came to Fr. Gibault's defense in the history *Conquest of the Northwest*:

> There was no reason, however, why his great services should not have been properly recognized, but they never were. As far as the author is advised, no county, town or post office bears his name;

---

[415] Dunn, "Father Gibault."
[416] Peyton, "Pierre Gibault," 496.

no monument has been erected to his memory, and no headstone marks his grave, as its location is entirely unknown. It is well for him that he could turn to the religion of which he had been so faithful, and find consolation in the trust that there was a heaven where meritorious deeds, such as his, find reward since they were so poorly appreciated and requited on earth.[417]

Belatedly, things have changed. Americans have honored Fr. Pierre Gibault by giving his name to a hospital, a high school, and even a warship—an irony that might have puzzled the patriot priest, who helped win the West without firing a shot.

There's also a statue, appropriately enough, at George Rogers Clark State Park in Vincennes, Indiana. It stands directly in front of the Basilica of St. Francis Xavier, the saint who inspired young Pierre Gibault to accept the life of a missionary.

Even more appropriately, the park is located on the approximate site of Fort Sackville. It's the place where Clark and Fr. Gibault reached a collective career high point in the cause of liberty. Eyes raised beseechingly to heaven, the sculpture is a bronze-cast reminder that those sacrifices are often not rewarded until long after we all pass on.

[417] William Hayden English, *Conquest of the Country Northwest of the River Ohio, 1778–1783, and Life of Gen. George Rogers Clark* (1896; n.p.: British Library, Historic Print Editions, 2011), 189–190.

Chapter 12

The Greatest Catholic That Never Was:
George Washington's Enlightened Tolerance

1

An estimated one thousand books have been written about the life of George Washington. Add books about the Revolutionary War, and you're looking at a number perhaps ten times that.

There's a story about Washington, however, that has made it into few, if any, of those books. Yet it's fascinating for what it suggests — and not just about Washington himself.

The tale goes something like this:

During the bitter winter of 1777, as the rebel troops struggled against the elements at Valley Forge, George Washington was visited in his office one afternoon by a mysterious woman, "a singularly beautiful female." The figure didn't speak at first, and an unnerved Washington began to feel as if he were dying.

Then the woman broke her silence, saying, "Son of the Republic, look and learn." Washington saw an angel, who revealed to him a series of mysterious visions.

From beneath a mist of heavy white vapor, all the countries of the world appeared. The angel dipped his hands into the ocean and sprinkled water on both America and Europe. A cloud was created, which drifted westward and covered America. From beneath it, Washington could hear "smothered groans and cries." The cloud lifted, and Washington then saw cities springing up across the American continent.

Next, he watched as an "ill-omened specter" drifted from Africa to America, apparently causing the inhabitants to battle one another. He saw a "bright angel, on whose brow rested a crown of light, on which was traced the word 'Union,' bearing the American flag which he placed between the divided nation, and said, 'Remember ye are brethren.'" The fighting ceased.

The worst vision, however, was still to come. Once again, the mysterious woman commanded, "Son of the Republic, look and learn." And Washington saw "the dark, shadowy angel" give three blasts on a trumpet, and sprinkle ocean water on Europe, Asia, and Africa. "Then my eyes beheld a fearful scene: From each of these countries arose thick, black clouds that were soon joined into one."

Moving with these clouds were "hordes of armed men" who came by land and sea to invade America. "I saw these vast armies devastate the whole county," Washington remembered, "and burn the villages, towns and cities that I beheld springing up."

Yet, when all seemed lost, the dark angel once again blew his trumpet, and the light of "a thousand suns" flooded across the nation. "The angel upon whose head still shone the word Union, and who bore our national flag in one hand and a sword in the other, descended from the heavens attended by legions of white spirits. These immediately joined the inhabitants of America, who I perceived were well nigh overcome, but who immediately taking courage again, closed up their broken ranks and renewed the battle."

The bright angel then cried out, "'While the stars remain, and the heavens send down dew upon the earth, so long shall the Union last.' And taking from his brow the crown on which blazoned the word 'Union,' he placed it upon the Standard while the people, kneeling down, said, 'Amen.'"

Shaken, Washington turned to his visitor for an explanation. "Son of the Republic, what you have seen is thus interpreted," the woman said. "Three great perils will come upon the Republic. The most fearful is the third, but in this greatest conflict the whole world united shall not prevail against her. Let every child of the Republic learn to live for his God, his land and the Union."

At that, the vision disappeared. In his frigid office, with evening drawing in, Washington was left to ponder what he had seen and heard. He concluded "that I had seen a vision wherein had been shown to me the birth, progress, and destiny of the United States."

2

Only George Washington knows what really happened that afternoon at Valley Forge. But it seems probable that, like the more familiar tales of young George chopping down the cherry tree and tossing a silver dollar across the Potomac River, this story is also a fake.

The tale was allegedly told on July 4, 1859, by a Revolutionary War veteran named Anthony Sherman, who would have been a teenager during the war. Sherman was ninety-nine when he supposedly recounted this story to a writer who went by the name Wesley Bradshaw, Esq., in Philadelphia's Independence Square. Bradshaw then published the account in 1861 as a broadside titled *Washington's Vision*.

The author's real name was Charles Wesley Alexander, a Philadelphia journalist who had founded a publication titled *The Soldier's Casket*, aimed at Union veterans of the Civil War. He also wrote novels and several other "sketches" recounting visions that had appeared to historical figures.

One was called *General McClellan's Dream*, where the Union general is visited by the ghost of George Washington. Washington reveals Confederate plans to McClellan and warns him that there is "a traitor in his midst." Another tract billed itself as *Jeff Davis' Confession*. It was supposedly discovered "on the dead body of a rebel!" and urged the United States to "get rid of the incubus" of slavery.

Doubt has been cast on the identity of "Anthony Sherman," Washington's former soldier. A solider by that name reportedly served under Benedict Arnold at Saratoga at the end of 1777, around the time Washington's vision was supposed to have taken place. But while nearly a dozen soldiers with that last name of Sherman were at Valley Forge, the official muster roll doesn't show that a soldier named Anthony Sherman served there. (Sherman himself, meanwhile, apparently only *overheard* Washington's story, which the general was relating to a "confidential officer.")

There's a good explanation for why Alexander would choose to fabricate such a tale. Writing for the website Snopes.com, David Mikkelson observes that *Washington's Vision* "was an obvious allegory for Unionists whose America was facing its greatest crisis since the revolution: a civil war pitting one half the country against the other in a struggle that threatened the existence of the Republic."[418]

It's now commonly known that many of the things people long believed about George Washington are embellished, or just plain false. One of the most cherished tales, of course, is a young Washington confessing to his father that he "cannot tell a lie" about using his hatchet to chop down a prized cherry tree.

The cherry tree myth appeared in the very first biography of Washington, published the year after his death (although the story wasn't included until the book's fifth edition). The author of *The Life of Washington* was Mason Locke Weems, otherwise known as "Parson Weems." As Jay Richardson of George Mason University points out, "Weems had several motives when he wrote *The Life of Washington* and the cherry tree myth."

"Profit was certainly one of them; he rightly assumed that if he wrote a popular history book about Washington it would sell," Richardson says. "Weems was also able to counter the early tradition of deifying Washington by focusing on his private virtues, rather than his public accomplishments."[419] Weems also wanted to provide moral instruction —something that was emphasized when the cherry tree story wound up in the popular *McGuffey Reader* for students.

"Washington's Vision," like those other stories, is generally thought to be a fabrication. Yet is there some deeper truth about this tale that has allowed it to endure?

---

[418] David Mikkelson, "George Washington's Vision," Snopes, May 12, 2002, https://www.snopes.com/fact-check/george-washingtons-vision/.

[419] Jay Richardson, "Cherry Tree Myth," in *The Digital Encyclopedia of George Washington*, ed. James P. Ambuske (n.d.), George Washington's Mount Vernon, https://www.mountvernon.org/library/digitalhistory/digital-encyclopedia/article/cherry-tree-myth/.

3

The story of Washington's mysterious visitor at Valley Forge inevitably speaks to Catholics in a way it most likely wouldn't to a Protestant. For one thing, the revelations have echoes of the apparitions of Fatima. On a hillside in Portugal in 1916, three children—Lucia dos Santos and her cousins Francisco and Jacinta Marto—said they were visited by an angel three times while watching over their sheep.

The next year, just outside Fatima, the children reported they were visited again by a "Lady of dazzling light." That October, thousands witnessed an event called "the Miracle of the Sun," in which the sun seemed to change colors and move rapidly across the sky.

The apocalyptic tone, the presence of similar imagery, and, of course, the messenger—who seems, in the Washington story, very similar to the Virgin Mary—make some comparisons inevitable.

The fascination with Washington among Catholics goes further than this story. Rumors of Washington's deathbed conversion to Catholicism have surfaced periodically. A piece that appeared in the *Denver Catholic Register*, a Catholic newspaper, in February 1957, gives a good summation.

> It was a long tradition among both the Maryland Province Jesuit Fathers and the Negro slaves of the Washington plantation and those of the surrounding area that the first President died a Catholic. These and other facts about George Washington are reported in the Paulist *Information* magazine by Doran Hurley.

The *Register* then quoted Hurley, who explained the story of Washington's death this way:

> The story is that Fr. Leonard Neale, S.J., was called to Mount Vernon from St. Mary's Mission across the Piscatawney River four hours before Washington's death. Tradition also holds that shortly after Washington's death Fr. Neale sent a heavily sealed packet to Rome. If this be true, it may yet turn up in the Vatican archives, or it may have been lost during the Jesuits' hidden years.

Hurley added the claim that "the General made the Sign of the Cross at meals," something he said had been reported by Washington's slave Juba Carter. "He may have learned this," Hurley speculated, "from his Catholic lieutenants, Stephen Moylan or John Fitzgerald."[420]

Washington might also have learned it from his Catholic friends in Maryland, the Carrolls. But, as many people have pointed out, there is no record of all this from those present at Washington's death. In fact, skeptics about Washington's Christian beliefs are quick to point out that there's no mention of any religious observance in his final hours.

A tale also told numerous times, and which is somewhat more plausible, is credited to the Fr. Ambrose Marechal, a French immigrant who would later become the archbishop of Baltimore. Marechal was passing through Philadelphia in the spring of 1792, on his way to Maryland, where he would be a professor at St. Mary's Seminary.

Washington, then living at the President's House on Market Street, invited Fr. Marechal to breakfast. After the meal, Marechal wanted to visit Washington's library. To get there, he had to pass through the president's bedroom.

There he was surprised to find a portrait of the Virgin Mary at the foot of the bed. Fr. Marechal asked Washington about it, and he allegedly replied, "I cannot love the Son without honoring the Mother."[421]

Perhaps this is the portrait of the Blessed Virgin, holding a prayer book, that hung on the wall of the dining room at Mount Vernon. In recent years, it was restored to its place there, along with a painting of St. John the Evangelist.

We don't know a lot about either painting, besides the fact that both are pastels. Jessie MacLeod, an associate curator at Mount Vernon, says the identity of the artist or artists is unknown. "The donor of the Virgin Mary noted a family tradition that the pastel was a 'gift from a Frenchman,'"

---

[420] Slaves of the Immaculate Heart of Mary, "Slaves Held Washington Became a Catholic on His Deathbed," Catholicism.org, October 14, 2008, https://catholicism.org/washington-slaves.html.

[421] A. A. Lambing, "Washington's Devotion to Mary Immaculate," *Donahoe's Magazine* 11, no. 2 (February 1884): 110–112.

MacLeod writes in an email. "However, we have no further evidence to support this story."

The fact the Washingtons hung these paintings in such prominent places also invites comment. The portrait of Mary is the first thing a visitor to the dining room sees. It seems clear these pictures were important to the Washingtons in some way.

Meanwhile, a century after Washington led the Continental Army to triumph, Pope Leo XIII wrote admiringly of his contributions not just to liberty but also to further explaining the founding principles of the Catholic Church.

"Without morality the State cannot endure," said the pope, "a truth which that illustrious citizen of yours, whom We have just mentioned, with a keenness of insight worthy of his genius and statesmanship, perceived and proclaimed."[422]

The point of all this is not to argue, as some have done, that Washington was secretly a Catholic. But it's worth exploring why the figure of Washington has been so appealing to Catholics over the last three centuries. We should also ask why the idea of a secular Father of Our Country is equally appealing to many people—and why that idea might be even more fanciful than a Catholic Washington.

4

If you want to start a long disagreement almost guaranteed to end unsatisfactorily, bring up the subject of the Founding Fathers' religious views.

Were they devout Christians? Or skeptical deists? Were they committed to biblical principles? Or were they determined to build an imaginary wall between church and state? It's an argument that has for centuries gotten people passionate.

In *The Faiths of the Founding Fathers*, his 2006 study of a half-dozen founders and their beliefs, historian David L. Holmes summarized the

---

[422] Pope Leo XIII, Encyclical Letter *Longinqua* (January 6, 1895), no. 4, http://www.vatican.va/content/leo-xiii/en/encyclicals/documents/hf_l-xiii_enc_06011895_longinqua.html.

division. Writers, he said, "have tended to place the founders' religion into one of three categories—non-Christian Deism, Christian Deism, and orthodox Christianity. Those best remembered by history—Franklin, Washington, and Jefferson, for example—were Deists of varying degrees."

But Holmes also pointed out, "In recent decades evangelical writers, decrying a secular bias among academic historians, have argued that all but a few of the founders genuinely adhered to Christian belief."[423]

This is actually an old argument. Three decades after Washington's death, his former pastor, Bishop White, wrote to another Episcopal priest, who was curious about Washington's beliefs. People had begun to speculate that Washington was an orthodox Christian, but White disagreed. "I do not believe that any degree of recollection will bring to my mind any fact," he wrote, "which would prove General Washington to have been a believer in the Christian revelation."[424]

That was hardly the end of the matter. As Holmes put it, "The fervor and devoutness of Washington's religion has long been the subject of conflicting assertions."[425]

Some thought Washington simply didn't reflect much upon his faith. In 1830, his fellow founder James Madison was interviewed by a biographer, who wrote, "Mr. Madison does not suppose that Washington had ever attended to the arguments for Christianity, and for the different systems of religion, or in fact that he had formed definite opinions on the subject. But he took these things as he found them existing."[426]

Holmes comes down—mostly—on the side of Washington as a deist, "the dominant interpretation of religion"[427] among men in Virginia. He gives the evidence of the Rev. Bird Wilson, the son of Founding Father James Wilson. The younger Wilson, an Episcopal priest whose father knew Washington well, called him and the other founders deists in an 1831

[423] David L. Holmes, *The Faiths of the Founding Fathers* (Oxford: Oxford University Press, 2006), 68.
[424] Holmes, *The Faiths of the Founding Fathers*, 162–163.
[425] Holmes, *The Faiths of the Founding Fathers*, 61.
[426] Holmes, *The Faiths of the Founding Fathers*, 71.
[427] Holmes, *The Faiths of the Founding Fathers*, 164.

sermon. "If anyone in 1831 knew the difference between appearance and reality in the religious beliefs of the founding fathers," Holmes stated, "it would have been Bird Wilson."[428]

Holmes also mentioned that Washington rarely referred to Jesus Christ, and used more general, deistic terms such as "Providence" to represent God. This providence, Holmes claimed, was "partially distant and impersonal."[429]

Like Madison, Holmes described Washington as unbothered by life's deepest questions. "He seemed to have no interest in theology. Unlike Jefferson and Adams, he did not seem particularly interested in why the world was so."[430]

Yet the smoking gun that would prove Washington's unbelief remains elusive. For example, the fact that he frequently skipped out before communion when he attended church is sometimes cited as evidence — but it's also true that most Episcopalians did the same during this time.

The question became persistent enough that author Michael Novak was approached by administrators at Mount Vernon to write a book examining Washington's elusive faith. With his daughter Jana's help, in 2006 Novak wrote *Washington's God*, a convincing case for the first president as a private but devout Christian.

First is what we might call the physical evidence — what is verifiable. Washington was raised an Anglican, and not only attended Anglican church services regularly as an adult but also served as a member of the vestry at two different churches. He did this while living some distance from both places, meaning that a day of worship or vestry business was a significant commitment.

He was the godfather to eight children of family and close friends. This, the Novaks point out, would have been a hypocritical commitment for a Christian unbeliever: Thomas Jefferson turned down the chance to serve as a godfather multiple times for just that reason.

---

[428] Holmes, *The Faiths of the Founding Fathers*, 162.
[429] Holmes, *The Faiths of the Founding Fathers*, 66.
[430] Holmes, *The Faiths of the Founding Fathers*, 66.

Washington also took special pains to ensure that his troops were served by a chaplain, and spoke on many occasions of the necessity of prayer and religious observance among his soldiers. "He often warned that they could not expect the favor of God's help in their cause," the Novaks write, "unless they lived in a way worthy of it."[431]

On at least one occasion, when addressing the chiefs of the Delaware tribe in 1779, he even used a term no deist would countenance: "You do well to wish to learn our arts and ways of life," Washington told the tribal officials, "and, above all, the religion of Jesus Christ."[432]

Turning to the interpretive evidence, Washington's common term for God, "Providence," may sound impersonal, the Novaks admit—but that reflects Washington's acknowledgment of religious differences, both in the men he commanded and in the country he led. A neutral term was simply good politics—then, and now.

More significant is the form Providence takes in Washington's writings and speeches. It is not the distant, "cosmic watchmaker" of deist belief, who takes no interest in human affairs. Instead, over and over again, the Novaks show Washington's Providence to be a force that moves among men—a force which can, and should, be appealed to, and which works its own designs in mysterious ways.

Washington made such appeals himself and encouraged his troops and his countrymen to do the same. One of his noteworthy General Orders to the Continental Army even put it in writing: "The Commander in Chief is confident, the Army under his immediate direction, will shew their Gratitude to providence, for thus favoring the Cause of Freedom and America; and by their thankfulness to God, their zeal and perseverance in this righteous Cause, continue to deserve his future blessings."[433]

It's hard to get less impersonal than that.

---

[431] Michael and Jana Novak, *Washington's God: Religion, Liberty, and the Father of Our Country* (New York: Basic Books, 2006), 218.

[432] Novak and Novak, *Washington's God*, 137.

[433] Novak and Novak, *Washington's God*, 65.

From the time he was a young soldier, Washington kept Providence close to his heart. He carried with him a privately printed prayer book. He read from it when he led the burial service for Gen. Edward Braddock, slain in a surprise attack at Fort Duquesne in July 1755. The prayer book was a copy of the 1662 Anglican Book of Common Prayer. Washington had copies printed for family members as well, and he specified that the books should be pocket-size so he could always have his with him.[434]

It's true that Washington was undemonstrative, and turned down even direct appeals to declare his faith. Yet this was hardly rare in Washington's time. Among moderate Anglicans, latitudinarianism—defined by the *Oxford Dictionary* as "showing no preference among varying creeds and forms of worship"—was common. The more outward, evangelical form of Christianity, where declarations of belief were expected, and public, was still new to the American landscape.

But in George Washington's reluctance to reveal himself also lies a large part of his particular genius. It is a genius for which he is rarely given credit. To become the true father of a country, none of your children must believe you have disowned them.

5

Catholics provide the best example of this Washingtonian strength. Go back to the Quebec Act in 1774, and the colonial response to it.

In offering the residents of Quebec the freedom to practice their Catholic faith, Great Britain set a trap for the colonists. Clearly, the gesture—coming from a nation with centuries of repression against Catholics—could be interpreted as insincere. But, as mentioned in chapter 3, it was also sound policy to let native peoples retain their culture. And it threw the ball back into the colonists' court. They promptly fumbled it, with a vehemently anti-Catholic response guaranteed to alienate Canadian and American Catholics alike.

One founder, however, understood what was at stake—which was why, in 1775, he put a halt to his troops' participation in "Pope's Night"

---

[434] Vail, *Rochambeau, Washington's Ideal Lieutenant*, 171

activities. Washington's stinging reprimand showed the sort of wisdom that would serve him well beyond his military career:

> As the Commander in Chief has been apprized of a design form'd for the observance of that ridiculous and childish custom of burning the Effigy of the pope — He cannot help expressing his surprise that there should be Officers and Soldiers in this army so void of common sense, as not to see the impropriety of such a step at this Juncture; at a Time when we are solliciting, and have really obtain'd, the friendship and alliance of the people of Canada, whom we ought to consider as Brethren embarked in the same Cause. The defence of the general Liberty of America: At such a juncture, and in such Circumstances, to be insulting their Religion, is so monstrous, as not to be suffered or excused; indeed instead of offering the most remote insult, it is our duty to address public thanks to these our Brethren, as to them we are so much indebted for every late happy Success over the common Enemy in Canada.[435]

Catholics would remember well Washington's leadership, so different from what they'd come to expect. They remembered his example during the war, when he welcomed troops of all races and faiths — including the men profiled in this book. They remembered a man who, in short, walked the walk, instead of merely talking the talk.

Even in just talking the talk, however, we can observe an important difference in Washington.

When he was elected president in 1789, a group of Catholics — including Fr. John Carroll, soon to become America's first bishop, as well as his brother Daniel and his cousin Charles Carroll of Carrollton — wrote him a congratulatory letter.

After praising his military and political acumen, they offered special thanks for the service he had provided to American Catholics, and showed they understood his idea of Providence:

---

[435] Novak and Novak, *Washington's God*, 230.

It is your peculiar talent, in war and in peace, to afford security to those, who commit their protection into your hands. In war, you shield them from the ravages of armed hostility: in peace you establish public tranquillity by the justice and moderation, not less than by the vigour of your government. By example as well as by vigilance, you extend the influence of laws on the manners of our fellow citizens to encourage respect for religion, and inculcate, by words and actions, that principle, on which the welfare of nations so much depends, that a superintending Providence governs the events of the world, and watches over the conduct of men.[436]

Washington replied on March 15, 1790. He was gracious, but more important, his words show that he assumed the Revolution had settled an important question about Catholics. That question was a cloud that had hung unpleasantly in the air of America for the past 150 years. If Washington's words didn't entirely dispel its stench, they certainly let every Catholic patriot know that their leader could see through the smoke, and that their sacrifices had been justified:

As mankind become more liberal they will be more apt to allow, that all those who conduct themselves as worthy members of the Community are equally entitled to the protection of civil Government. I hope ever to see America among the foremost nations in examples of justice and liberality. And I presume that your fellow-citizens will not forget the patriotic part which you took in the accomplishment of their Revolution, and the establishment of their Government: or the important assistance which they received from a nation in which the Roman Catholic faith is professed.[437]

---

[436] "From George Washington to Roman Catholics in America, c. 15 March 1790," Founders Online, National Archives, https://founders.archives .gov/documents/Washington/05-05-02-0193.

[437] 'From George Washington to Roman Catholics."

Washington made similar declarations to Jewish Americans, as well as to Baptists, Quakers, and Presbyterians. He thanked each group for its service to America. Using his beloved metaphor from Micah 4:4, he also sketched out a vision of religious tolerance as eloquent as any of its better-known expressions.

"Every one shall sit in safety under his own vine and fig tree," he reassured the Hebrew congregation of Newport, Rhode Island, "and there shall be none to make him afraid."[438]

But those are just words, some might argue, and words are cheap in politics. Perhaps. Yet if so, why didn't any other Protestant founder use them so directly?

6

If there were a Hall of Fame of Clichés, the plaque that reads "You can't be all things to all people" would undoubtedly have a prominent place.

It was St. Paul, though, who inverted the phrase in his first letter to the Corinthians. "I have become all things to all, to save at least some," he wrote. "All this I do for the sake of the gospel, so that I too may have a share in it" (1 Cor. 9:22–23, NABRE).

George Washington was not a saint, and his primary concerns were undoubtedly secular. Yet he probably doesn't get enough credit for the way he followed this advice of Paul — whether by design or instinct. As the Novaks write:

> If it was George Washington's intention to maintain a studied ambiguity (and personal privacy) regarding his own deepest religious convictions, so that all Americans, both in his own time and for all time to come, might feel free to approach him on their own terms — and might also feel like full members of the new republic, equal with every other — that is an intention, if such it was, he abundantly fulfilled.

[438] "From George Washington to the Hebrew Congregation in Newport, Rhode Island, 18 August 1790," Founders Online, National Archives, https://founders.archives.gov/documents/Washington/05-06-02-0135.

Nowadays, the most atheist professor, the rebel from any church, the Mason, and with them the devout Baptist, the serious Catholic, and the active Presbyterian, along with the academic or the lawyer committed to Stoic philosophy who wears even less overlay of religion than Washington, and perhaps even such other American immigrants as Buddhists, Hindus, and Muslims (secular and religious) — all find it possible to repair to Washington as to a figure with whom to identify in spirit.[439]

Forests have been felled to praise the intellectuals of the Revolution: Jefferson, Franklin, even John Adams. All were to great extent Enlightenment deists, heirs to the humanistic (and sometimes anti-Catholic) philosophy of John Locke.

None of them, however, could have done what Washington did, and they knew it. Historian Joseph J. Ellis alludes to this in *His Excellency: George Washington*:

> It seemed to me that Benjamin Franklin was wiser than Washington; Alexander Hamilton was more brilliant; John Adams was better read; Thomas Jefferson was more intellectually sophisticated; James Madison was more politically astute. Yet each and all of these prominent figures acknowledged that Washington was their unquestioned superior.[440]

Part of that superiority involved striking the delicate balance — his "studied ambiguity" in faith — that Washington managed not just during his lifetime, but over two centuries afterward. To successfully lead the army, and the nation, he led, at the time he led them, it could have been no other way. The latitudinarian practice of his beliefs allowed room for the religious pluralism necessary to win a revolution, and build a country.

In fact, we could argue that Washington's view of religious plurality is the one that has traditionally been recognized by Americans. Vincent

[439] Novak and Novak, *Washington's God*, 222.
[440] Joseph J. Ellis, *His Excellency: George Washington* (New York: Alfred A. Knopf, 2011), 15.

Phillip Muñoz, the Tocqueville associate professor of Religion and Public Life at the University of Notre Dame, has written one of the most thorough examinations of what the founders thought about religion, and the modern implications of those beliefs. His 2009 book *God and the Founders* explores the views of Washington, Jefferson, and Madison.

Muñoz shows, using a variety of examples, that Washington believed government could, and sometimes should, support religion—if there was a legitimate civic reason to do so. For Washington, that reason was often the need for encouraging moral behavior.

"Washington recognizes that for most men most of the time, virtue and morality are not choice-worthy in and of themselves," Muñoz writes. "Republican government needs religion because virtue and morality depend on religious faith."[441]

Washington's view, therefore, was more realistic than Madison's stricter separation of church and state or Jefferson's belief in a civic religion based on reason alone. Part of its realism stemmed from Washington's view of human nature. Unlike Jefferson and even Madison, Washington believed government could not take for granted the moral character, nor the reason, of the people it governed.

The idea that government could be involved in shaping the morals of its people was "an unhallowed perversion of the means of salvation,"[442] Madison wrote. Some may see it as ironic, given the private nature of his own personal faith, that Washington believed the opposite. But he had seen enough of human nature not to trust it solely on its own merits.

Part of the realism of Washington's position was also its pluralism. It assumed government could support any faith, as long as the faith supported the goals of government.

"Washington venerates virtue and morality because they prompt citizens to act in a decent, truthful, and law-abiding manner," Muñoz adds. "Virtuous citizens govern themselves voluntarily and respect the

[441] Vincent Philip Muñoz, *God and the Founders: Madison, Washington, and Jefferson* (New York: Cambridge University Press), 55.
[442] Muñoz, *God and the Founders*, 56.

rights of others, thereby reducing the need for government to secure rights through the coercive force of law. Virtue and morality are indispensable because they make self-government possible."[443]

This is the understanding most Americans have held for nearly 250 years. When people speak of the secularization of America, it's easy to infer that they're speaking of a move away from this commonsense view of how government and religion interact.

It may be, then, that Washington thought quite a bit more about Christianity than James Madison, or any of the other founders, realized. It may also be that the reason we live, even still, in the America he imagined is because of the way he thought about Christianity, and religion generally.

There's little evidence that Washington was a Catholic. There's abundant evidence all around us in America, however, that he might have been the greatest Catholic that never was.

---

[443] Muñoz, *God and the Founders,* 55.

Epilogue

Revolutions and Revelations

1

The pain from the boiling tar was almost indescribable. Underneath it, his naked skin had puckered and blistered. He could barely feel the sharp October wind off the ocean, as he lay there gasping on the rough wood of the wharf.

He had blacked out, but was slowly regaining consciousness. He could barely remember balancing on the rail they had forced him to straddle as they rode him out of town, jeering and guffawing. Turning his head slowly, he saw a trail of chicken feathers, their shafts coated a sticky black, that marked his path down the jetty.

It was easier to recall what had happened earlier, though no more pleasant. From inside the house where he'd planned to stay the night, he could hear the mob assembling on the street outside. When they smashed in the cellar door, he had surrendered himself willingly: his hosts were terrified, and it was wrong to put them in danger, too.

They'd stripped him—"You'll be getting a new suit of clothes soon, mackerel snapper!" one of them spat through his beard—and lashed him to a tree in the forest. A few of them punched him in the face, and one of his eyes began to swell, but he could tell they were impatient for the main event.

Would it be a hanging? That's what some of the mob seemed to want. "Say, maybe the Pope can resurrect you!" a short man exclaimed, giggling as he fiddled with a length of cord.

He wouldn't die tonight, though. He would just wish that he had. The burns from the hempen rope felt like caresses when the tar cascaded over his body.

As he shifted now on the wharf in the wee hours of the morning, hours after the attack, he could only moan. He closed his eyes and replayed scenes of the saints he could recall. Then he said a prayer for their souls, before he passed out again.

2

Unbelievably, Fr. John Bapst, S.J., would celebrate Mass later that morning, after being beaten, tarred, and feathered by a mob in Ellsworth, Maine. His hair and eyebrows had to be shaved off, and he was badly blistered from the burning tar. But he showed up to worship.

This was not an attack that occurred during the American Revolution. Instead, it happened three-quarters of a century later. No one was ever charged in the assault against Fr. Bapst, a Swiss priest who had run afoul of the locals for suggesting a Catholic Bible be used in the local schools.

Although he later became the first president of Boston College, he never came back to Ellsworth, and he never forgot the events of October 14, 1854. Years later, confined to an asylum, he often awoke screaming, sure his assailants were climbing through his window.[444]

John Adams claimed the real American Revolution was "in the minds and hearts of the American people." And as Catholic historian Jay P. Dolan observed, when it officially ended in 1783 with the Treaty of Paris, for "the small colony of Catholics, the change was especially dramatic."[445] After fighting alongside Protestant patriots for a shared liberty, Catholics were beginning to reap its benefits.

The roughly thirty years that followed the American Revolution were mostly peaceful ones in Catholic-Protestant relations. Historian Maura Jane Farrelly notes that it was an era when Protestants made an effort to focus on religious similarities instead of differences. During this period,

---

[444] Hennesey, *American Catholics*, 125.
[445] Dolan, *The American Catholic Experience*, 101.

"Catholics didn't have to struggle against laws that restricted their rights, and they didn't have to prove their loyalties—or even their legitimacy as Christians—to their countrymen."[446]

Protestants attended Masses, contributed to the building of Catholic churches, and sometimes even sent their children to Catholic schools. "Catholics and Protestants were partners in politics," Jay Dolan pointed out, especially since restrictions against Catholic office-holding were being lifted, "and mixed marriages were commonplace."[447]

The real disputes were within the developing Catholic Church itself. But this period of outward calm was critical. It allowed Church leaders time to develop a philosophy that would see American Catholics through the crisis that followed.

As we read in chapter 3, the key figure in American Catholicism during this time was Fr. John Carroll. In 1784, he became the first superior of the Church in the United States. In 1789, he was elected its first bishop. And in 1808, he became the first archbishop of America's first archdiocese, overseeing Baltimore, Philadelphia, New York, Boston, and Bardstown, Kentucky.

But his importance reflected far more than just a title. As chapter 3 suggested, Carroll also developed a distinctly American identity for the Church, one that went hand in hand with his support of the Revolution. Included among the Church in America's principles were religious freedom; a respect for and reliance on laypeople and trustees in supporting priests in running parishes; and a clear, reason-based presentation of the Gospel, which could be understood by all, in celebrating the liturgy.

The overlap between republic and "republican Church" wasn't just intentional, but also natural. For example, Catholics who had been repressed found ways to celebrate Mass privately, often in their homes. Necessity had made them used to having control over their worship, and they were reluctant to turn that control back over to priests.

---

[446] Farrelly, *Anti-Catholicism in America*, 97.
[447] Dolan, *The American Catholic Experience*, 102.

Meanwhile, as we've seen, American Catholics became revolutionaries in part because they were resisting state control of religion. It was expected that they would resist it after they won their freedom as well.

This developing Church in America also took steps toward having Masses in English, rather than the traditional Latin. Influential Catholic publisher Mathew Carey, who is buried in Old St. Mary's churchyard, which we visited in chapter 4, produced an English Catholic version of the Bible—sometimes called the "Carey Bible"—in 1790. "One of his most energetic salesmen," observed Jay P. Dolan, "was Bishop John Carroll."[448]

This vision of the Church is one many Catholics today may recognize. If it sounds a lot like the Church that emerged after Pope St. John XXIII's Second Vatican Council in the 1960s, that's because Vatican II marked a return to many of these ideas.

However, they didn't last long after the American Revolution. A chapter in Fr. James Hennesey, S.J.'s *American Catholics* is titled "The Failure of Carroll's Plans."[449] That reflects a not-uncommon view of the thirty years that Archbishop John Carroll led the renewed Church in America.

Some would argue Archbishop Carroll didn't *fail* as much as he *adapted*. Events well beyond his control had much to do with his changing views.

In 1785, Fr. Carroll estimated there were about sixteen thousand Catholics in Maryland, and another seven thousand in Pennsylvania—still by far the two most heavily Catholic states. A mere twenty-one priests served those twenty-three thousand parishioners—nineteen in Maryland, and just two in Pennsylvania.[450]

Carroll began a network of schools to train homegrown priests—most notably, Georgetown University, which opened in 1791—as well as female religious. But the growth of these institutions could not keep up with demand.

[448] Dolan, *The American Catholic Experience*, 110.
[449] Hennesey, *American Catholics*, 89–100.
[450] Hennesey, *American Catholics*, 73.

So Archbishop Carroll frequently had to import clergy from Ireland, Germany, and France. These Europeans were used to a different model of how parish life should operate, which was a change from what a good number of Catholics in America envisioned. For priest immigrants, the clergy ran the Church without significant lay collaboration. And state involvement with religion was expected, if not always welcomed.

In addition, some of the French priests Carroll brought to the United States had just escaped their own revolution—one that, as we saw in chapter 8, was nothing like the one in America. These priests had good reason to fear a "republican church," and they fought against it.

Conflict was thus inevitable, wrote Dolan, who noted that "the older he got," the more committed Archbishop Carroll became to a more "traditional understanding of Roman Catholicism."[451] In his younger days as a priest, according to Dolan, Father Carroll favored a more collaborative role for laypeople in parish life. However, after he became a bishop and then archbishop, and increasingly had to rely on immigrant priests who were used to a more traditional model, the archbishop moderated his views.

By the time of Carroll's death in 1815, Dolan added, the Church faced a choice: a parish life informed more by new experiences in America or the traditional European one. Immigration, Dolan argued, would decide in favor of the latter.

Even before the potato famine of the 1840s, more than a quarter-million Irish came to America between 1820 and 1840. Over the five years of the famine, a million more emigrated to the United States, and that growth continued into the new century.

Add to that more than five million Germans who came to America between 1820 and 1920, and a million more Italians between 1880 and 1900—with three million more in the twenty years that followed.

Put another way, by 1790 there were about thirty-five thousand Catholics in the United States—less than 1 percent of the total population. By the end of the nineteenth century, that number had jumped to more than seventy-six million Catholics, or 16 percent of all Americans. That

[451] Dolan, *The American Catholic Experience,* 123–124.

number would continue to climb. This tidal wave of immigration had dramatic effects on the Church in America.

One of them was an increase in anti-Catholicism. Anti-Catholic literature, like the lurid novel *Six Months in a Convent*, began to proliferate. It may have inspired the attack on an Ursuline convent near Boston, which was burned down by an angry mob in 1834. Ten years later, anti-Catholic riots in Philadelphia leveled two churches and thirty homes, and led to a gun battle outside St. Philip Neri Church that left dozens dead or wounded.

The nativist movement gave birth to the Know-Nothing Party, which favored restrictions on immigration and the rights of immigrants. In practice, supporters backed up those sentiments with the kind of mob violence that opened this chapter. A key part of these anti-Catholic beliefs was a very old fear: that Catholic Americans were more Catholic than American, and were beholden to Rome instead of Washington.

Conspiracy theories abounded. The pope was directing masses of unwashed, uneducated immigrants to America. They would vote as he told them—or perhaps, in more apocalyptic scenarios, they were just the foot soldiers for his inevitable invasion.

The Civil War put an end to Know-Nothings, but not to Know-Nothing attitudes about Catholicism. Maura Jane Farrelly points out that the Blaine amendments that exist in thirty-seven state constitutions today, named for Maine senator James G. Blaine, are the legacy of this bigotry. They're also the source of the "separation of church and state" that many Americans erroneously believe the founders intended for schools.

The success of Catholic education after the Civil War stirred fears that public schools couldn't compete.

The Blaine amendments adopted by states soon afterward were an effort to minimize the growth and impact of Catholic schools in America. They ensured that no religious institutions—first and always foremost, Catholic schools—could receive taxpayer funds. Yet, in the summer of 2020, the landmark U.S. Supreme Court decision in *Espinoza v. Montana Department of Revenue* threatened to make the Blaine amendments irrelevant at last.

The case was heard on behalf of three Montana families whose children were excluded from a state scholarship program because they attended religious schools. In the 5–4 ruling, Chief Justice John Roberts wrote that the Constitution "condemns discrimination against religious schools and the families whose children attend them. They are 'member[s] of the community too.'"[452]

Since that bleak March day in 1634, when the new Marylanders onboard the *Ark* and the *Dove* reached the north shore of the Potomac and celebrated Mass, the dream of American Catholics has been, in Chief Justice Roberts's words, to be "members of the community too."

The men and women in this book all played some role in securing that membership—not least because they also helped create that community.

We'll give the last words to Charles Carroll of Carrollton, who did as much as any American to build it. Writing to his friend James McHenry in 1800, well after the American Revolution had concluded, Carroll reflected on the importance of Catholicism to the colonial struggle for independence. It was a timely observation: the terror of the French Revolution was now widely known. The fact that the French had spurned religion in their own quest for liberty, equality, and fraternity surely played a role in those horrors, Carroll thought:

> Divine revelation has been scoffed at by the Philosophers of the present day, the immortality of the soul treated as the dreams of fools, or the invention of knaves, & death has been declared by public authority an eternal sleep.... Remove the hope & dread of future reward & punishment, the most powerful restraint on wicked action, & ye strongest inducement to virtuous ones is done away. Now, what motive can be stronger than ye belief, founded on revelation, that a virtuous life will be rewarded by a happy immortality?

[452] Espinoza v. Montana Department of Revenue, 591 U.S. __ (2019), slip opinion at 22, https://www.supremecourt.gov/opinions/19pdf/18-1195_g314.pdf.

Without morals a republic cannot subsist any length of time; they therefore, who are decrying the Christian religion, whose morality is so sublime & pure, which denounces against the wicked eternal misery, & insures to the good eternal happiness are undermining the solid foundation of morals, the best security for the duration of free government.[453]

A quarter-century later, in 1826, just a few years before his death—he would be the last of the signers of the Declaration of Independence to expire—an elderly Carroll wrote to a woman who had drafted a poem in his honor.

He explained in just a couple of sentences the principles that joined his faith and his service to his country. It's an epitaph worthy of all the Catholic men and women mentioned in this book, who followed this advice in helping create the United States of America.

"Who are deserving of immortality?" Carroll asked his admirer. "They who serve God in truth, and they who have rendered great, essential, and disinterested services and benefits to their country."[454]

---

[453] Birzer, *American Cicero*, 186.
[454] Rowland, *The Life of Charles Carroll of Carrollton*, 346.

Acknowledgments

After the Mass at Old St. Mary's, I approached the priest on the sidewalk outside. When I told him I was writing a book about Catholics in the American Revolution, he looked at me tiredly and frowned.

"There are already a lot of those," he observed.

What could I say? He was right. So that's the best place to begin these acknowledgments.

Anyone who sets out to write a popular history (or what they hope will be a popular history) does it on the backs of those who have come before. In the field of Catholic history, that includes people like Martin Griffin, who did an astounding amount of research and writing in his lifetime. It includes historians who created sweeping narratives of the Faith in America that are still required reading today, people like Jay Dolan and James Hennesey. And it includes a group of more recent writers whose work shaped this book, like Bradley Birzer, Fr. Charles Connor, Robert Emmett Curran, Maura Jane Farrelly, and Scott McDermott. To all of them, and many others, I owe my gratitude. To paraphrase the old saying: my debts to them are considerable; the mistakes are mine alone.

Thanks to the team at Sophia Institute Press, including Carley Casella, who first worked with me on this proposal; John Barger; and Anna Maria Dube, who did a wonderful job shepherding it to completion. I'm proud to have this book come out through such a great and supportive publisher.

The careful and sensitive edits that Dr. Kevin Schmiesing and Tom Nash did on this manuscript have been a blessing. As at least one high-profile examination of the Revolutionary War has recently shown us, the first goal of a work like this has to be historical accuracy. Dr. Schmiesing and Mr. Nash have contributed immeasurably to achieving that objective: their work has prevented me from making both factual and doctrinal errors. In addition, their suggestions have substantially improved the book. The mistakes, as stated, are all mine, but Dr. Schmiesing and Mr. Nash's keen eyes have certainly saved me—and the readers—from some of them.

This book began in the Perpetual Adoration Chapel at St. Monica Parish one blustery Sunday evening in March 2019. I was reading Prof. Anthony Esolen's column in *Magnificat*, "How the Church Changed the World." The subject that month was the Polish cavalryman Casimir Pulaski, "A Hero of Two Nations." Professor Esolen is a compelling writer, and a line from this piece nearly shouted out at me in the quiet of the chapel. Speaking of Pulaski, he said, "if the contribution of such men, many of them Catholic (Pulaski, Kościuszko, Lafayette, Rochambeau), escaped the notice of some, it did not escape that of the tolerant and great-hearted Washington." In that single sentence, the idea for this book—and many of its major characters—resided. Thank you to Professor Esolen for that inspiration.

My journey back to the Catholic Faith I was born into is a story for another time, but the person who most helped to get me there is my best friend, Stephen Catanzarite. This book would not exist without his years of patient, faithful witness. I have always tried to emulate him, and he'll probably never know how much I have relied on his example. To him and his wife, Rachel, his sons, Thomas and Henry, and the rest of their family, I will remain forever grateful.

Every week, I say a prayer of thanks that I can participate in Mass in a parish where the priests are faithful to the Gospels in every way, and aren't afraid to tell hard truths from the pulpit. Fr. Kim Shreck, Fr. John Naugle, Fr. Ladis Cizik, Fr. Bill Schwartz, and Deacon Harry DeNome are a major reason this book exists.

Acknowledgments

I'm grateful to all the administration, faculty, staff, and students at Lincoln Park Performing Arts Charter School and Lincoln Park Performing Arts Center, who have supported my "other" career for the past fifteen years. With love and particular gratitude, I recognize the other two members of the Writing and Publishing department: Deanna Baringer and Cindy West. Working with someone who is writing a book usually involves picking up some of the writer's slack. Their grace in doing so has been considerable and uncomplaining. I could not ask for better colleagues and friends.

The same sentiment applies to all my wonderful Writing and Publishing students, who had to share me with this book for eighteen months. My pride in them, which is considerable and deep, extends to their willingness to make that sacrifice.

Writing a book like this during a worldwide pandemic made research a bit more challenging than it might have been otherwise. Special thanks to Lesley Carey at St. Joseph's University, Pierre Lafontaine of the Archdiocese of Quebec, and Jessie MacLeod at Mount Vernon for going above and beyond to help answer my questions.

I am blessed to have the support of as stalwart and loving a group of family members and friends as anyone could wish. They include my brother, Drew LeRoy, and my nephews Alex, Matt, and Connor; my brother-in-law Devin Nutter, his wife, Melissa, and my niece Charlotte; Carolyn Tallman, Jamie Tallman, Heather, Chad, and Lily Sigmon; and Nancy, Steve, and Rachel Kovac.

Professionally, I owe Michael Lipton everything: he started my writing career and made everything that has happened to me possible. For years, D. X. Ferris and Peter Relic have been the sort of right-hand friends that no writer can survive without.

Finally, my parents, Louie D. and Polly G. LeRoy. I grew up in a home with more than one Christian heritage, but it was at all times — and in fact, still is — a home where God was honored, where parents put their children's needs first, and where dreams were supported. That is a debt I will never be able to repay. I can only say, publicly and with the greatest love, how humbled I am to have the chance to try, in my own household.

In such a home, spouses and children are charged the heaviest price when a book is written. In the same way every writer wants to make their parents proud, we hope the same is true—if we're honest—in the case of our wives and children. Not to be cool (far too late for that!), nor to be great. We want it only to try to make up for all those lonely hours we were absent, and the many more when we were only halfway there. To Carys, Greer, and Grant—I love you all, and thank you for always giving me the time, and the understanding.

I can only add, in the case of my long-suffering and beloved wife, Kiena Nutter, that what Alexander Hamilton wrote to Eliza goes double here. Best of wives, best of women—I am more grateful than I can say that you have always been both.

Endnotes

Prologue: Song of the South

There are three major sources for the story of Stono. One is Peter Charles Hoffer's book *Cry Liberty: The Great Stono River Slave Rebellion of 1739*, which retraces the steps of the South Carolina slaves who rose up against their owners. As mentioned in the prologue, Hoffer's view is that the riot was a tragic accident: a simple incident of rule-breaking that rapidly spun out of control.

University of South Carolina history professor Mark M. Smith's anthology *Stono: Documenting and Interpreting a Southern Slave Revolt* is an invaluable collection of just about everything significant written about Stono up to 2005. That includes John K. Thornton's essay "African Dimensions," cited in the prologue, as well as "Account of the Negroe Insurrection in South Carolina," which was written the month after the rebellion by an author whose identity is contested. (James Oglethorpe, the founder of the colony of Georgia, is credited. But as Smith points out, "other historians are less certain.")

The book also includes Smith's essay "Time, Religion, Rebellion." This is an updated version of his 2001 essay "Remembering Mary, Shaping Revolt: Reconsidering the Stono Rebellion," first published in the *Journal of Southern History*.

I also went back to read Peter H. Wood's entire pioneering study *Black Majority: Negroes in Colonial South Carolina from 1670 through the Stono*

Rebellion, which is excerpted in Smith's book. I gained additional insight into the way the rebellion affected colonial thought from University of Mississippi professor Jack Shuler's 2011 book *Calling Out Liberty: The Stono Slave Rebellion and the Universal Struggle for Human Rights.*

We still struggle to interpret this event. We don't know for certain what caused it, nor who led it, nor what their motivations might have been — beyond an obvious desire for "liberty," as the slaves apparently called out on their march.

Hoffer's thesis has the advantage of extensive on-the-ground research. To cite just one example, he locates a plausible spot for Hutchenson's general store, where the rebellion is believed to have started. His account, filled with the sights and sounds of the Low Country, also has Occam's Razor on its side. That is, the simplest explanation is usually the best.

Yet the question of why the slaves simply stopped in a field by the Savannah River continues to nag. They were undoubtedly tired. They might have been waiting in hopes of attracting a larger group, which seems to have happened. But they all would have known the local authorities would soon be on their heels — and that a violent death was the inevitable result of being caught. It's hard to shake the idea that the slaves might have believed larger forces were on their side.

I think Mark M. Smith's focus on the unusual timing of the rebellion, while controversial in some quarters, offers the best explanation of the unanswered question above: Why did the slaves stop when and where they did? If nothing else, the Stono River slave rebellion offers us an uncomfortable, yet necessary, window seat on the sometimes violent, always complicated relationship between Catholicism and slavery.

Chaper 1: Bless Those That Curse You

There are still lots of people who will remember reading *Johnny Tremain* in grade school or middle school. That fictional account of a young apprentice silversmith on the eve of the American Revolution won a Newbery Medal. But the author, Esther Forbes, also received a Pulitzer Prize for her account of Paul Revere's life, published just a couple of years later. A lot of the qualities that have made *Johnny Tremain* one of the most famous works of historical fiction carry over into Forbes's biography of Revere. It's a rich and detailed account, and it is one of the primary sources for the reconstruction of Pope's Night in Boston, 1764.

Did Paul Revere himself participate in Pope's Night? In 1764, he would have been nearly thirty, and he had a young daughter at home. So perhaps he sat out this celebration. Yet ten years later, following the passage of the Quebec Act, he did a popular engraving called "The Mitred Minuet." It depicts four Anglican bishops, hand in hand, dancing gleefully around a copy of the "Quebec Bill." British officials Lord Bute—shown playing the bagpipes—and Lord North, observe the scene, while Satan himself looks on approvingly. You can see the engraving at https://www.nga.gov/collection/art-object-page.182398.html.

The point is that Anglicans are now in league with the forces of the devil, i.e., Catholicism. So it's pretty clear Revere would have been at Pope's Night in spirit, at least.

There are several other sources, from those who were eyewitnesses to Pope's Nights, that add color to this account. One of them is printer Isaiah Thomas's 1810 book *The History of Printing in America: With a Biography of Printers, and an Account of Newspapers*. Another is the notebooks of Boston resident Samuel Breck, preserved by the Library of Congress.

Sect. 6. The estimate that 70 percent of the Allied forces in the Revolution were Catholic comes from Lewis Leonard's biography of Charles Carroll of Carrollton. Part of that number includes Irish-Americans, who are represented in this book in chapter 4. But how many? Historian Martin Griffin states numerous times in his work that the majority of Irish patriots were Presbyterians, not Catholics. But as later Carroll biographer Scott McDermott says, "The question of how many Irish-American soldiers were actually Catholic has received little scholarly attention and awaits further research."

Chapter 2: First Citizen

There are fewer biographies than you might imagine for a Founding Father of Charles Carroll of Carrollton's stature. Luckily, the four that exist all have strengths I've tried to use in assembling this portrait of the most important Catholic founder.

The oldest, Kate Mason Rowland's two-volume *The Life of Charles Carroll of Carrollton, 1737–1832*, draws heavily on his voluminous correspondence. Rowland's reputation for careful scholarship gives it added weight. Ellen Hart Smith's *Charles Carroll of Carrollton* is a more literary work that gives us a readable, humane depiction of Charles Carroll the man.

The third book, Scott McDermott's 2001 biography *Charles Carroll of Carrollton: Faithful Revolutionary*, offers the most complete picture of Carroll's life. It takes a hard look at the relationship between Charles Carroll and his father. It was unquestionably loving, yet also had negative effects on the eager-to-please son. If these effects inflamed Charles Carroll's patriotic fervor — if they made him determined to prove himself to his father in a way that helped lead to American independence — then it's yet another reminder of the high cost that liberty can exact.

McDermott also does a great job of placing Carroll's political career into a wider context. From the way William of Occam and John Duns Scotus's rejection of universals paved the way for the Catholic Church's decline, to the way Charles Carroll helped reinstill an appreciation for natural law that still survives in America, this book gives a clear-eyed portrait of Carroll's life and work. (McDermott also offers the most detail about Carroll's slave holdings, sometimes inflated by abolitionists.)

Finally, Brad Birzer's 2010 book *American Cicero* goes even deeper into the origins of Carroll's political ideas, which were so influential to America's founding. He examines not just Cicero's influence but also Montesquieu's theory of mixed government, which we can still observe in our system of checks and balances.

Perhaps as much as any biography, the poignant collection of letters *Dear Papa, Dear Charley: The Peregrinations of a Revolutionary Aristocrat* illustrates the depth of the unusual relationship between Charles Carroll of Annapolis and his son.

I drew as well on a couple of other histories of colonial Catholicism for this chapter. Robert Emmett Curran's *Papist Devils* and Father Charles Connor's *Pioneer Priests and Makeshift Altars* helped flesh out the picture of Charles Carroll's Maryland and the way it changed—thanks in large part to his own efforts.

Sect. 1. George Washington's quote about no "thinking man in all North America" comes from an October 9, 1774, letter to his old friend from the Seven Years' War, Robert MacKenzie (Washington 1889, 444).

Sect. 3. Details about the increase in Maryland chapels can be found in Curran 2014, 177.

Sect. 4. Some of the material on Bohemia Academy comes from Annabelle Melville's 1955 biography of Charles Carroll's cousin, *John Carroll of Baltimore*.

Sect. 5. Additional material for this chapter—especially about Maryland colonial history and the development of political thought in the colony—came from Maura Jane Farrelly's two books, *Papist Patriots* and *Anti-Catholicism in America, 1620–1860*. I think the single most important insight about Carroll comes from Farrelly's work. That is, the roots of American independence can be found in the struggles of American Catholics in Maryland, who tried to show that their history and destiny were separate from England's. That revelation, when applied to the other colonies, helped lead to revolution. As a Catholic, Charles Carroll realized this earlier than perhaps any other founder. I'm indebted to Farrelly for explaining it so clearly.

Sect. 6. Carroll's "First Citizen" letters can, and should, be read in their entirety. Professor Peter Onuf's 1974 book *Maryland and the Empire, 1773: The Antilion-First Citizen Letters* is still the best edition available.

Sect. 7. Some of the material about the 1776 mission to Canada comes from Annabelle Melville's *John Carroll of Baltimore*. H. W. Brands's biography of Benjamin Franklin, *The First American*, gives additional background about the Canadian mission.

Sect. 8. "Heaven has been determined to save your Country . . ." (Washington 1778a). Conway, it should be pointed out, was one of the foreign soldiers sent to America by Beaumarchais, as described in chapter 5.

The detail about spontoons (or, as they were also known, "epontoons") at Valley Forge comes from the Smithsonian's website. ("Spontoon" n.d.)

Washington's Christmas dinner at Valley Forge is mentioned in "Winter at Valley Forge: George Washington's Most Dismal Christmas Ever" (Clavin and Drury 2020).

While it's a children's book, Milton Lomask's *Charles Carroll and the American Revolution* provides some additional color for Carroll's activities at Valley Forge (and is consistent with Ellen Hart Smith's account).

Leonard Lewis's *Life of Charles Carroll of Carrollton* provides the unsourced but tantalizing quote about Carroll possibly helping negotiate with the French during the American Revolution. Unfortunately, I can't find any supporting evidence for it anywhere (Leonard 1918, 175).

Sect. 11. Carroll's troubled relationships with his children are examined in some detail in Scott McDermott's biography. Charles Carroll of Homewood alienated his father with his alcoholism, but McDermott also raises the possibility that the boy's mother, Molly, might have taken laudanum while she was pregnant with him; "if so, Homewood's addictive personality is no mystery." Homewood also infuriated his father with his extravagance in building Homewood House in Baltimore. Today it's considered one of the finest Georgian homes in the country, but at the time, it went over budget by four times its projected amount, costing today's equivalent of half a million dollars.

For all Charles Carroll of Carrollton's struggles with his children, however, McDermott does note that Carroll's daughter Kitty "remained Catholic throughout her life, and Carroll also guided his granddaughters toward the Faith." Those three Caton granddaughters, Mary Ann, Elizabeth, and Louisa—"the Three Graces"—charmed European society, and all became members of the British aristocracy by marriage.

∞

To return to the question of slavery, online records available through the Maryland State Archives (at http://slavery2.msa.maryland.gov/) show that between 1808 and 1856, Carroll (or his estate, since some of the manumissions were delayed and occurred after his death) manumitted nearly fifty slaves. Thirty of them served on Carroll's Poplar Island plantation, which had failed to generate profits. The database shows that seven more were members of the same family, the Mahoneys — "six children and their mother" — who were freed in 1808. There may be further manumissions, of course, that are not part of this database.

The idea that Carroll should have manumitted all his slaves is one of those "it's easy for you to say" propositions that deserves a bit more explanation. As Scott McDermott points out, much of Carroll's wealth was tied up in landholdings and slaves, which made him more, not less, dependent on slave labor as the years went on. He still earned money by lending, but was a conservative investor. He sank considerable amounts of money into the support of his three children and his grandchildren. Yet he was also tightfisted enough to once turn down George Washington's request for a loan!

This is back-of-the-envelope math at its worst — especially when we're talking about the value of human beings — but we could consider these figures. Let's use 185 million pounds sterling in today's money — a little less than $300 million — to represent Carroll's net worth. (Scott McDermott quotes this figure by using Officer and Worth's "economic status" multiplier.)

The average value of a slave is difficult to calculate because there are so many factors to consider: age, skills, location, ownership terms, etc. If we err on the high side and use a figure of $300 per slave, and err on the high side again in assuming Carroll owned about three hundred slaves he did not manumit, we get a figure of roughly $3 million in current prices. (That's using the chart in the footnotes for chapter 5, and multiplying the $300 per slave by about $30, using the Real Price Comparator.)

Carroll would presumably have to have replaced the labor the slaves provided (except on Poplar Island), which means the total cost of total manumission would have been considerably higher. Yet the thorny question posed in the chapter about whether Carroll could have, and should have, done more, stands. (For a valuable and detailed look at slaveholding in Maryland at this time, it's worth consulting T. Stephen

Whitman's *The Price of Freedom: Slavery and Manumission in Baltimore and Early National Maryland.*)

∞

The statistic about Maryland's history of manumission can be found in Fields 1985, 1.

Chapter 2 Supplement: Of Dangerous Consequence. The information used in this section, and in these charts, comes from the following sources:
   Bradley J. Birzer's *American Cicero: The Life of Charles Carroll*
   Patrick W. Carey's *Catholics in America: A History*
   Fr. Charles P. Connor's *Pioneer Priests and Makeshift Altars: A History of Catholicism in the Thirteen Colonies*
   Robert Emmett Curran's *Papist Devils: Catholics in British America*
   Jay P. Dolan's *The American Catholic Experience: A History from Colonial Times to the Present*
   Maura Jane Farrelly's *Papist Patriots* and *Anti-Catholicism in America, 1620–1860*
   Fr. James Hennesey, S.J.'s *American Catholics: A History of the Roman Catholic Community in the United States*
   Scott McDermott's *Charles Carroll of Carrollton: Faithful Revolutionary*
   Kate Mason Rowland's *Life of Charles Carroll of Carrollton, 1737–1832: With His Correspondence and Public Papers*
   Ellen Hart Smith's *Charles Carroll of Carrollton*

Chapter 3: The Pope Who Helped the Patriots

The two major biographies of John Carroll mentioned in this chapter — by Msgr. Peter Guilday and Annabelle Melville — were the main sources here. I also consulted Jay P. Dolan's *The American Catholic Experience* and Fr. James Hennesey's *American Catholics*. Both books have substantial sections about Father Carroll; the latter is refreshingly critical of some of his clerical shortcomings. The first biography of Archbishop Carroll, published in 1843 by his great-nephew, John Carroll Brent, was also a useful source of information. Another account worth noting also predates both of the major biographies of Archbishop Carroll: John Gilmary Shea's 1888 account of Carroll's life.

Eva Betz's charming children's book *Priest, Patriot and Leader: The Story of Archbishop Carroll* added color to this chapter. So did Ellen Hart Smith's 1942 biography of Archbishop Carroll's cousin, *Charles Carroll of Carrollton*. Meanwhile, H. W. Brands's biography of Benjamin Franklin, *First American*, gives additional insight into Franklin's friendship with Carroll, which played such a significant role in American Catholicism.

Sect. 1. What exactly is a "prefect of the sodality"? A sodality is just a small group within a church or order, dedicated to a specific purpose. In some cases, the sodality exists to venerate a figure such as the Blessed Virgin Mary.

Sect. 3. You can see Jack Manley Rosé's 1943 mural *The Burning of the Peggy Stewart*, and learn more about it in "Rebellious Anniversary: Burning the Peggy Stewart Ended Annapolis' Golden Era," https://www.capital-gazette.com/maryland/annapolis/ph-ac-cn-peggy-stuart-1014-20161014-story.html.

There is another, earlier, well-known painting of the same name, done in 1896 by Francis Blackwell Mayer. It is part of the Maryland State Archives: https://msa.maryland.gov/msa/speccol/sc1500/sc1545/001100/001111/text/label.html, and you can learn more about it on the Maryland Historical Society's website: https://www.mdhs.org/underbelly/2014/10/16/the-burning-of-the-peggy-stewart/.

Dates have been a constant issue for Carroll's biographers—especially his birthdate and the date of his ordination to the priesthood. Thomas W. Spalding's 1985 article "John Carroll: Corrigenda and Addenda" in the *Catholic Historical Review* seems to settle these nagging questions, and I'm using the dates he has fixed: January 19, 1736, as Carroll's birth date, and Valentine's Day 1761, as his ordination date.

Sect. 4. Father Ferdinand Farmer's unpublished letter, translated from Latin, about Bishop Briand's proposed visit to America, can be found in the Jesuits' online archive at https://jesuitonlinelibrary.bc.edu/?a=d&d =wlet18991001-01.2.2&e=--------en-20--1--txt-txIN------- (Spillane 1899).

Sect. 5. You can read more about the ferryman Patrick Colvin—who also played a major role in the story of Father Ferdinand Farmer, the subject of chapter 10— in McCormack 1887.

The full text of Congress's "Instructions to the Commissioners to Canada, 20 March 1776" can be found online at https://founders.archives .gov/documents/Adams/06-04-02-0001-0004 (Adams 1776).

To read Benjamin Franklin's witty "Dialogue Between Franklin and the Gout," visit https://www.bartleby.com/109/3.html.

Sect. 6. As far I know, the fact that Bishop Carroll was not excommunicated by Bishop Briand has never been publicly refuted—which seems like kind of a big deal. I can find no record of it before Cardinal Foley mentioned it in August 2008. It has, however, been repeated several times since then in biographies of John Carroll.

Pierre Lafontaine, the archivist for the Archdiocese of Quebec, was generous enough to do a complete search of the archives, and found no record of Father Carroll's excommunication. His quotes all come from an email conversation we conducted in June 2020. As Lafontaine points out, the most likely explanation is confusion over the bishop's interdict of Father Floquet. It seems clear Bishop Briand was angry with both priests!

For those who are curious about the difference between an interdict and an excommunication, here's a definition from the *Catholic Encyclopedia*, via the website New Advent:

> Whereas excommunication is exclusively a censure, intended to lead a guilty person back to repentance, an interdict, like suspension, may be imposed either as a censure or as a vindictive punishment. In both cases there must have been a grave crime; if the penalty has been inflicted for an indefinite period and with a view to making the guilty one amend his evil ways it is imposed as a censure; if, however, it is imposed for a definite time, and no

reparation is demanded of the individuals at fault, it is inflicted as a punishment. (Boudinhon [1910] 2020)

Sect. 7. The quotes from John Thorpe are from Annabelle Melville's *John Carroll of Baltimore*, 69.

Chapter 3 Supplement: A Man of Few Words. Important sources for this chapter were the two major biographies of Daniel Carroll's younger brother, Archbishop John Carroll, by Peter Guilday and Annabelle Melville. Also useful were the four major biographies of Charles Carroll of Carrollton (by Kate Mason Rowland, Ellen Hart Smith, Scott McDermott, and Bradley Birzer).

In addition, Sr. Mary Virginia Geiger's 1943 biography *Daniel Carroll: A Framer of the Constitution* provides some useful financial context about Carroll's life. And Richard J. Purcell's 1941 biographical sketch "Daniel Carroll, Framer of the Constitution" from *Records of the American Catholic Historical Society of Philadelphia* is the source of Georgia delegate William Pierce's recollection of Carroll.

There are many excellent books about the events of Philadelphia during the summer of 1787, when the Constitution was drafted. For this chapter, I consulted J. Moss Ives's 1936 history *Ark and the Dove: The Beginning of Civil and Religious Liberties in America* and the more recent *Plain, Honest Men: The Making of the American Constitution* by Richard R. Beeman. (However, the dates Beeman gives for Carroll's attendance are apparently mistaken. He says Carroll did not arrive until August 6 and then stayed only eleven days. But numerous other records show that Carroll arrived—late—on July 9, and apparently stayed until the end. He signed the Constitution with thirty-eight other delegates on September 17, when the convention adjourned.

∞

"Nervous complaints" (D. Carroll 1787). This is from Daniel Carroll's letter to Michael Morgan O'Brien, dated May 25, 1787. In it, Carroll confides to O'Brien that because of his delicate health, "I dare not think of residing in Philada. during the Summer months." This was not just a hypochondriac's lament. Poor sanitation, crowded conditions, and ever-present mosquitoes meant outbreaks of disease were always a possibility. In 1793, mosquitoes spread yellow fever among Philadelphia residents, and an estimated five thousand of them died.

Therefore, in the letter, Carroll instructs O'Brien "to look out for a convenient and economical situation where I can board in a small family somewhere near my former temporary residence near German Town. I would prefer the Situation from it being High, healthy, and at a suitable distance."

Carroll did apparently stay in Germantown during the Constitutional Convention. He also adds a note at the end of the letter that is in line with the Carroll family's parsimonious nature: "It is necessary to attend to economy in this business." Read the letter at https://www.consource.org/document/daniel-carroll-to-michael-morgan-obrien-1787-5-25/.

Here's something that has vexed historians (and many Catholics). Daniel Carroll, like his friend George Washington, was a Freemason. The Masons had been censured, as Annabelle Melville notes, by Pope Clement XII. She adds that this association upset Daniel's brother, Archbishop John Carroll. Even today, Catholics "who enroll in Masonic associations are in a state of grave sin and may not receive Holy Communion," according to the 1983 *Declaration on Masonic Associations*. And yet at least some Catholic patriots — including Lafayette and Casimir Pulaski — attended Masonic events or became Masons themselves.

The question of why is beyond the scope of this book to answer, but a letter by John Carroll is suggestive. Regarding the ban on freemasonry for Catholics, he wrote in 1794, "I do not pretend that these decrees are received generally by the Church, or have full authority in this diocese. But they ought to be a very serious warning to all good Christians not to expose themselves to dangers that the head of the church has judged to be so contagious" (Melville, Annabelle McConnell 1955, 156).

In short, the benefits of freemasonry — the connections and political clout — clearly outweighed the ban for some Catholics, who were an often-persecuted minority group. This was especially true, no doubt, because there were so few priests and churches at the time to enforce the prohibition.

∞

You can read the 1790 letter written on behalf of American Catholics that is quoted here, as well as new president George Washington's response to it, at https://founders.archives.gov/documents/Washington/05-05-02-0193.

Chapter 4: The Philadelphia Story

My own visits to Old St. Joseph's and Old St. Mary's, as well as to St. Mary's churchyard, are the source for some of the material in this chapter. I have also drawn on a trip to the archives of the Francis Drexel Library in Philadelphia, where I had access to a number of documents about church history. (More about the archives, and the remarkable material they house, can be found in the notes for chapter 10.)

Eleanor C. Donnelly's 1886 biography *A Memoir of Father Felix Joseph Barbelin, S.J.*, provided some color for the section about the early days of Old St. Joseph's. Martin Griffin's histories of St. Joseph's and St. Mary's served the same function, as well as providing numerous historical details. Griffin also wrote short biographies of Thomas Fitzsimons, Stephen Moylan, and John Barry, which were useful here. Meanwhile, Tim McGrath's comprehensive biography, *John Barry: An American Hero in the Age of Sail*, is a naval historian's dream. And the collection of Catholic histories cited elsewhere — books by Connor, Curran, Dolan, Farrelly, and Hennesey — helped complete the picture of Catholic life in colonial Pennsylvania.

Sect. 1. Agnes Repplier's quote comes from her book *Philadelphia: The Place, and the People*.

You can read the complete text of William Penn's Charter of Privileges online at https://avalon.law.yale.edu/18th_century/pa07.asp.

According to an untitled, typewritten document from the records of Old St. Joseph's Church at the Francis Drexel Library, the Rev. Thomas

Mansell, S.J.—who was also the founder of Bohemia Manor in Maryland, and went under the alias Thomas Harding—said the first public Mass in Philadelphia on September 8, 1707. Presumably this Mass was held at his residence, on Third Street and Strawberry Alley. The document states he had purchased this property earlier that year.

A Seasonable Caveat Against Popery, Or, a Warning to Protestants is an essay written by Penn in 1700. Joseph J. Casino notes in his essay "Anti-Popery in Colonial Pennsylvania" that as far back as 1678, Penn felt it necessary to deny before Parliament that he was a "Papist." Nor, he added, was he "a seminarist, a Jesuit, an emissary of Rome, and in the pay of the Pope." By 1708, however, things were going badly for Penn. That year, he spent time in prison for debt. Therefore, Penn's demand for more information about "publick Mass" came at a time when he was under a great deal of pressure in England.

Thomas Penn's quotes: Delaurentis and Hershey 1991, 26.

Sect. 2. Author Martin Griffin was skeptical about the claim that Greaton was disguised as a Quaker, pointing out that a Quaker "disguise" most likely just meant dressing modestly, in dark colors. Griffin also tracked down the deed to the property that Greaton bought from John Dixon, a barber, and his wife, Mary, in 1733—and not a "Mrs. Doyle," who may have been the "wealthy matron" in this story. As a side note, most sources seem to agree that Father Greaton lived on the land before he purchased it. However, based on the testimony of other sources cited in this chapter, the idea that Greaton might have kept his identity concealed does not seem far-fetched.

Richard Henry Lee's June 7, 1776, resolution to create a declaration of independence can be read online at https://avalon.law.yale.edu/18th_century/lee.asp.

"Legend has it Benjamin Franklin himself...." Based on research, this claim appears to be mostly legend. It seems significant that it does not appear in the numerous writings on the subject of Old St. Joseph's by Martin Griffin and Eleanor Donnelly. It appears, uncited, in the *Frommer's* blurb about the church, but I have been unable to track down its original source.

Frommer's describes Old St. Joseph's as "Greek Revival merging into Victorian," https://www.frommers.com/destinations/philadelphia/attractions/old-st-josephs-church.

Sect. 3. John Adams's famous quote about Mass at Old St. Mary's can be found in many places. You can read his complete letter to his wife, Abigail, at https://founders.archives.gov/documents/Adams/04-01-02-0111. We should cut the second president some slack, however: he was the leading non-Catholic contributor to the building fund for Boston's Holy Cross Church (Lally n.d.).

There is a very handy online calendar of George Washington's church attendance, as recorded in his diaries, http://candst.tripod.com/GeoW-churchchart.html.

"A Spanish gentleman of distinction ..." (Griffin 1893b, 56). We're told that De Miralles, who was not an official representative of the Spanish government but was treated as a visiting diplomat anyway, got sick during an April 1780 visit to Washington's camp at Morristown, New Jersey, and was buried there.

"The Church, which was filled to its utmost capacity ..." (Donnelly 1886, 115). In some accounts of this Mass, the church is mistakenly listed as St. Joseph's — which wouldn't have been nearly big enough for such a service.

Sect. 4. "The vast majority of Catholic patriots ..." (Curran 2014, 264). Martin Griffin's research suggested about three hundred Irish Catholics from Pennsylvania served in the Continental Army.

Sect. 5. A note about the variant spellings of "Fitzsimons": I have decided to use the simplest spelling here, except in direct quotes from other sources.

∞

The most complete information I found about the missing faces in Howard Chandler Christy's *Scene at the Signing of the Constitution of the United States* comes from https://teachingamericanhistory.org/resources/convention/christy-about/. Here is the full explanation:

There was no verified official portrait in the 1930s of Pierce Butler of South Carolina and Thomas Fitzsimmons of Pennsylvania, so Christy has their faces hidden by the raised arms of the South Carolina delegation. There is also a blur of faces in the corner to the right of Washington. Christy has been very creative: he has placed John Dickinson, whom Christy has listed as the thirty-eighth signer—who actually wasn't there at the signing because of health reasons, but who had George Read sign on his behalf—disguising the face of Jacob Broom, whom Christy lists as the thirty-ninth and last of the signers. There was no official portrait of Broom available in the 1930s.

∞

The story about the rediscovery of Thomas Fitzsimons's portrait appeared, appropriately enough, on St. Patrick's Day: ("Thomas Fitzsimons Portrait by Stuart Believed Found" 1965)

Information about the City Tavern comes from its website, https://www.citytavern.com/city-tavern-timeline/.

Fitzsimons's firm, Meade and Company, donated about £5,000 to the Continental Army (at least $750,000 in today's funds). Morris made a personal donation of twice that amount, and also financed $1.4 million of "Morris Notes," using his own credit, to keep the government running. Today that would equal about $40 million. ("Robert Morris" n.d.)

Fitzsimons's and Morris's financial losses are explained in Purcell 1938, 288. An even more detailed explanation is in the Addendum in Griffin 1887, 112–114.

Sect. 6. The story of the long search for the originator of "The United States of America" can be read at the New York Historical Society's blog (Touba 2014). Byron DeLear's *Christian Science Monitor* story is also worth consulting (DeLear 2013).

Two more Moylan brothers served the revolutionary cause: James, who helped the colonies as a commercial agent in France; and John, who became the clothier-general of the Continental Army. The Moylans also had a half-brother, Jasper, who joined the Pennsylvania militia late in the war. James and Jasper both lived in Philadelphia and were members of the Friendly Sons of St. Patrick.

Washington apparently insisted that all captured red coats be dyed immediately (Washington 1777).

Background on the rift between Moylan and Casimir Pulaski comes from Frank Monaghan's "Stephen Moylan in the American Revolution," in *Studies: An Irish Quarterly Review*, 484. For further details, see Joseph Wroblewski's "The Winter of His Discontent: Casimir Pulaski's Resignation as Commander of Horse" (Wroblewski 2016).

"Merry appearance ..." (Griffin 1909b, 175). Colorful as it sounds, this was apparently the standard outfit for Moylan's regiment.

Sect. 7. The story about Barry and his men helping to get Pennsylvania to ratify the Constitution is expertly, entertainingly told by Tim McGrath in *John Barry: An American Hero in the Age of Sail.*

Sect. 8. "The Continental Navy was first proposed by John Adams ..." In fact, in the summer of 1775, George Washington had commissioned privateers from Massachusetts and Rhode Island to make raids on British vessels—so he has a claim on the title "Father of the American Navy" as well (Ferreiro 2016, 168).

Martin Griffin's wonderfully titled "Was John Commodore Barry Any Kind of a Catholic?" tries to answer that question in detail. He gives Barry a "demerit mark" for his Protestant second wife, but points out that he "repaired the dereliction" by converting her. (Griffin also notes that Barry might have converted both his wives to Catholicism.) Regarding Barry's habit of Bible reading onboard his ships, Griffin says, "A record made by one of his petty officers says that Barry 'although Roman Catholic, always was present at worship on board performed by a Presbyterian minister, and enforced a strict attention and orderly conduct.' Moral theologists will determine the extent of his offense." Griffin adds, "Barry was known as a Catholic, so much so that a Church of Englander who applied for chaplaincy of his frigate in 1800 thought it necessary in his letter to Barry to tell him that he admired the devotion of Roman Catholics as he saw it on frequent visits to church. Barry must have been publicly known as a staunch enough Catholic to have had that said to conciliate him."

"Savage as they were …" (McGrath 2011, 242). McGrath's description of the mutiny and how Barry handled it is in the chapter "Mutiny" and is one of the most vivid recountings you could ever wish to read.

Sect. 10. Chesterton's full quote, from *The Everlasting Man*, is, "Christendom has had a series of revolutions and in each one of them Christianity has died. Christianity has died many times and risen again; for it had a God who knew the way out of the grave."

Chapter 5: The Most Important Receipt in American History

Key sources for this chapter include Elizabeth Kite's *Beaumarchais and the War of American Independence* and Harlow Unger's more recent biography, *Improbable Patriot: The Secret History of Monsieur de Beaumarchais, the French Playwright Who Saved the American Revolution*.

Thomas Schaeper's book *Edward Bancroft: Scientist, Author, Spy* was used to provide some background material on the tragic fate of Silas Deane, while Jini Jones Vail's *Rochambeau: Washington's Ideal Lieutenant* gives more information about the covert career of Jeremiah Lee.

In addition, I've drawn on Larrie D. Ferreiro's 2016 book *Brothers at Arms: American Independence and the Men of France and Spain Who Saved It*, which gives a painstakingly complete picture of the contributions of France and Spain to the American Revolution. (One of the many fascinating details is that one of the first French spies in America was actually a Scottish Catholic, Charles Murray, who represented a London wine merchant and sold Madeira to George Washington, among others. In 1765, he also began sending reports on conditions in the colonies to France.)

I've also borrowed from Ferreiro what I think is the most sensible way of translating currencies, and use it throughout the book. Ferreiro sets a base year of 1775 for evaluating currencies, since it was the last stable year before the American Revolution. He uses an exchange rate of 1 pound (Britain) = 5 dollars (America) = 23.5 livres (France) = 6.3 pesos (Spain).

He then employs two measures, the Real Price Comparator and the Economy Cost Comparator, to evaluate prices. Individual goods and salaries are compared using the first measure; "large national outlays," like the arms deal discussed in this chapter, are compared using the second measure.

Nation	Currency	Real Price Comparator	Economy Cost Comparator
Great Britain	Pound (£)	$149	$13,127
America	Dollar ($)	$29.40	$77,500
France	Livre	$6.30	$560
Spain	Peso	$24	$2,083

So, using this table, the roughly five million livres funneled from France to the colonies in 1777, multiplied by the Economy Cost Comparator, equals about $2.8 billion in today's dollars. The 480 livres Beaumarchais provided as the passage for Casimir Pulaski, by contrast, works out to a little more than $3,000 today, using the Real Price Comparator.

Sect. 1. The French aid was no secret in the colonies. Nor was its importance. "I firmly believe that unless these arms had thus been timely furnished to the Americans, Burgoyne would have made an easy march to Albany," said Caleb Stark of the First New Hampshire Militia Regiment, the son of American general John Stark, after Saratoga. Stark called the weapons "Beaumarchais arms," showing people knew exactly who was responsible (Ferreiro 2016, 73).

Sect. 2. As Larrie Ferreiro relates, one of Beaumarchais's spying successes was retrieving the plans for a French invasion of Britain from the Chevalier d'Éon, who was living in London and using the plans as leverage against the French government. The Chevalier was one of the more colorful characters of a colorful age: he liked to dress in women's clothing, and there was even a betting pool on the London Stock Exchange as to whether he was actually a man or woman. (An autopsy showed it was the former.)

Voltaire's quote about Beaumarchais can be found in the introduction to the 1964 edition of *The Barber of Seville* and *The Marriage of Figaro*.

The CIA "profile" of Beaumarchais, "Beaumarchais and the American Revolution," can be found online at https://www.cia.gov/library/center-for-the-study-of-intelligence/kent-csi/vol14no1/html/v14i1a01p_0001.htm.

Sect. 3. "How can you allow your vessels …" and "How can you suffer …" (Storozynski 2010, 17). Did Beaumarchais mean "vassals" or "vessels" here? In context, the former makes a bit more sense, but you could make a case for either interpretation.

"We must aid the Americans …" (Ferreiro 2016, 53). Ferreiro also points out that Vergennes had an ulterior motive: he was less convinced by the "silver tongue" of Beaumarchais and more by the desire to "prevent Portugal from expanding its war with Spain onto the European continent." If France armed the rebels, it would keep the British occupied. Therefore, Britain would be less likely to aid Portugal in a conflict against Spain. Therefore, those two nations' conflict in South America would be less likely to turn into a full-scale European war—one that would inevitably have invoked France.

Sect. 4. "After nearly a decade and a half of boring peace …" (Brands 2002, 535). Washington's complaint appears on the same page. Franklin's all-purpose recommendation letter is on page 536 of the same source.

Sect. 5. Elizabeth Kite's biography includes letters from Beaumarchais claiming he was never repaid for the loans he made von Steuben and Casimir "Pulasky." The sad state of Beaumarchais's final reckoning with Congress is well summarized in the CIA "profile" of Beaumarchais.

Chapter 6: Polish Patriots …

The best recent biography of Casimir Pulaski available is Francis Casimir Kajencki's *Casimir Pulaski: Cavalry Commander of the American Revolution*. It is focused primarily on Pulaski's wartime service, but provides a wealth of military detail, rendered authoritatively by a West Point graduate. Kajencki also wrote a second book about Pulaski, *The Pulaski Legion in the American Revolution*, which takes a deep dive into the contributions of Pulaski's ill-fated group.

This chapter also draws from Clarence Manning's 1944 biography, *Casimir Pulaski: A Soldier of Liberty*, which gives the most complete account of Pulaski's life as a young man in Poland, as well as the indefatigable Martin Griffin's substantial profile of Pulaski, "General Count Casimir Pulaski: The Father of the American Cavalry," from the American Catholic Historical Researches.

Alex Storozynski's biography *The Peasant Prince: Thaddeus Kościuszko and the Age of Revolution* provides additional scope to this chapter. Meanwhile, *Cavalry Hero: Casimir Pulaski*, by Dorothy Adams and Irena Lorentowicz, is for children. However, it does contain a colorful—if romanticized—portrait of Pulaski that is worth considering.

One additional name that deserves citation is Edward Pinkowski, who tracked down Pulaski's bones. Pinkowski passed away in January 2020 at the age of 103. He was a tireless historian who probably did more to raise awareness of Polish patriots like Pulaski and Thaddeus Kościuszko than any other American. (He also bought the Philadelphia rooming house where Kościuszko stayed in 1797–1798. Jefferson was one of his visitors. Today, the house is a museum, with Kosciuzsko's living quarters restored.) Pinkowski won numerous awards for his work, including the Ellis Island Medal of Honor. His research was a great help to this chapter and the next; you can read more of it at poles.org.

Sect. 1. Information about Jasna Góra and its Black Madonna can be found in Dr. Anna Hamling's "The Power of an Image: The Black Madonna of Częstochowa," https://think.iafor.org/the-power-of-an-image-the-black-madonna-of-czestochowa/. Additional information comes from Drusilla Menaker's article "Poland's Black Madonna" (Menaker 1990).

It's also possible to take a virtual tour of the monastery and chapel at the Jasna Góra website: http://www.zdjecialotnicze.pl/wirutalnyspacer/JasnaGoraPL.html.

The family shrine to Mary at the Pulaski family estate is mentioned in Pienkos 1976, 13.

Sect. 2. "Count Pulaski of Poland ..." (Griffin 1910a, 6–7). Pulaski didn't deliver just this letter to Washington: he also delivered a letter from Lafayette's wife to her husband — instantly endearing Pulaski to a grateful Lafayette.

Sect. 3. If you have a chance to visit Brandywine Creek, you will see that Andrew Wyeth was right: it is one of the loveliest sites in America.

The descriptions of Pulaski's uniform are partly drawn from the historical reconstruction mentioned in the Smithsonian Channel's *America's Hidden Stories* episode about Pulaski.

Sect. 4. While it's possible Pulaski and some of his troops may have attended Masses while in Maryland, the only record of him attending a church service there is mentioned in Clarence Manning's *Casimir Pulaski: A Soldier of Liberty*:

> In Poland, he had been a devout Roman Catholic and in the United States there were very few Roman Catholic priests. We have no record of his attending any church services but on Maundy Thursday, April 16 (1778), he and Colonel Kowacz suddenly appeared at the evening service of the Moravian sisters at Bethlehem near Easton. It is said that Pulaski had been obliged to protect the sisters against the outrages of some soldiers. Be this as it may, it is interesting to note that there is this definite record of his attendance at a Protestant service, when we consider his former devotion as a Knight of the Holy Cross.

∞

The quote "the best cavalry the rebels ever had" comes from the diary of British Major Francis John Skelly, who wrote, "Polaskey (a great partizan) had advanced his legion consisting of about a hundred foot and eighty Horse. The foot was posted behind a kind of Breastwork thro which was a large entrance. Polaskey with his horse (the best Cavalry the rebels ever had) advanced towards our dragoons."

This quote is sometimes taken as a tribute to Hungarian Colonel Michael Kováts, who died during this battle. Kováts, by all accounts a brilliant horseman, certainly deserves credit for his work with the cavalry, but it's clear Skelly was speaking about Pulaski instead.

∞

The most convincing defense of Pulaski's importance at Charleston is made by Francis Kajencki in *The Pulaski Legion in the American Revolution*. Kajencki makes the case that Pulaski's cavalry, while it took heavy losses, succeeded in its main goal: to keep the British army occupied until reinforcements could arrive.

Sect. 5. Pulaski's last words were probably spoken on the battlefield, not on the *Wasp*, where he may never have regained consciousness. They were reported by Maj. Maciej Rogowski, who was apparently one of the first soldiers of the Legion to assist his fallen commander. This is recorded in Griffin 1910a, 108.

Sect. 6. The information about Pulaski's possible intersex condition comes from the 2019 episode "The General Was Female?," in the Smithsonian Channel's *America's Hidden Stories* series.

"I likewise took on board the Americans that were sent down ..." is quoted by Edward Pinkowski (who discovered the letter) at http://www.poles.org/p_body.html.

The Smithsonian Channel documentary on Pulaski did not answer the questions about Pulaski to everyone's satisfaction. For a response to some of the issues that the research raised, The Affair at Egg Harbor Historical Society released a statement that can be read here: https://poland.us/strona,13,33452,0,a-statement-on-the-smithsonian-documentary-about-pulaskis-skeleton-as-female-or-intersex-hermaphrodite.html.

Chapter 7: ... and Postponed Promises

Alex Storozynski's excellent biography, *The Peasant Prince: Thaddeus Kościuszko and the Age of Revolution*, is the chief source for this chapter.

Liberty's Lions

I have also drawn on Martin Griffin's *General Thaddeus Kościuszko: The Father of the American Artillery Service of the United States*, and Monica Mary Gardner's *Kościuszko: A Biography*.

Dr. Nicholas Michael Sambaluk's article "Making the Point — West Point's Defenses and Digital Age Implications, 1778–1781" in the *Cyber Defense Review* gives useful insight into the magnitude of Kościuzsko's accomplishment at West Point.

Sect. 2. Kościuszko was a talented visual artist and craftsman. At West Point, he also reportedly composed a piece of music that became known as "The Kościuszko Polonaise." It played "an important role in Polish history, featuring prominently in the nineteenth-century patriotic Polish soundtrack and becoming an inspiration for many other musical pieces." There is some question about whether Kościuszko actually composed the piece, but music was apparently one of his many gifts (Gliński 2019).

"But what they really needed …" As Larrie D. Ferreiro points out, the patriots needed both engineers and artillerists. Engineers handled fortification and "laying sieges"; artillerists specialized in "the movement and emplacement of heavy weaponry." The two jobs often overlapped, as was true in Kościuszko's case. This is why he's sometimes called "The Father of American Artillery" (Ferreiro 2016, 120).

Sect. 6. In a sort of after-the-fact foreshadowing, Kościuszko would not sustain the head wound shown in the painting for three more years. By the time he did, in 1794, the constitution — and Poland — effectively no longer existed.

Sect. 8. "Accept nothing from traitors" (Gardner [1919] 2010, 184). The czar's money, we're told, "lay untouched in an English bank till Kościuszko's death."

Louise Sosnowska, who became Princess Louise Lubomirska, did remain in contact with Kościuszko. After she was widowed, she "even offered to give him her hand for their twilight years" (Storozynski 2010, 274).

∞

Kościuzko's will is reproduced on pages 181–182 of *Kościuszko: A Biography*. It reads:

> I, Thaddeus Kościuszko ... being just in my departure from America, do hereby declare and direct that should I make no other testamentary disposition of my property in the United States thereby authorize my friend Thomas Jefferson to employ the whole thereof in purchasing negroes from among his own as any others and giving them liberty in my name, in giving them an education in trades or otherwise, and in haying them instructed for their new condition in the duties of morality which may make them good neighbours, good fathers or mothers, husbands or wives, and in their duties as citizens, teaching them to be defenders of their liberty and country and of the good order of society and in whatsoever may make them happy and useful, and I make the said Thomas Jefferson my executor of this.
>
> *T. Kościuszko. 5th day of May, 1798*

Chapter 8: She Stooped to Conquer

In writing this chapter, I thought sometimes about a quote from the introduction of Linda K. Kerber's *Women of the Republic*: "The war raised once again the old question of whether a woman could be a patriot—that is, an essentially political person—and it also raised the question of what form female patriotism might take" (Kerber 1980, 9).

There can be little doubt that Adrienne de Lafayette was a patriot —and a "political person." Yet what made her so remarkable is that her patriotism and politics weren't a performance to prove a theory about gender or nationality or political ideology. Her actions were motivated by love of God and of her family. For all her husband's singular qualities, it is this question of motivation that makes his wife, in my view, the more remarkable half of the pair.

Liberty's Lions

This chapter draws on several biographies of the Lafayettes for its portrait. One of the most useful was Jason Lane's *General and Madame de Lafayette*, which gives Adrienne deserved equal time. Also consulted frequently were Harlow Unger's *Lafayette*; André Marois's *Adrienne: The Life of the Marquise de La Fayette*; Constance Wright's *Madame de Lafayette*; and James R. Gaines's *For Liberty and Glory: Washington, Lafayette, and Their Revolutions*.

Besides those works, two illuminating sources of material about the French Revolution were Simon Schama's classic *Citizens: A Chronicle of the French Revolution* and David Andress's *The Terror: The Merciless War for Freedom in Revolutionary France*.

Some may find my own view of the French Revolution too harsh. For that, I make no apology. One can acknowledge the serious failings of the clergy and the monarchy in France and still find the revolution they unleashed unworthy of celebration. Yet all too often, the way it's taught in schools (when it's taught at all) is as an amped-up version of the American Revolution, where people finally threw off the shackles of kings and priests—and then there was that unfortunate bit at the end where people got a *little* crazy. But hey, they meant well! Events during the summer of 2020, and the way the French Revolution was referenced admiringly by young radicals, are proof this view resonates with more than a few Americans.

One of the few contemporary retellings that gets it exactly right is Lin-Manuel Miranda's musical *Hamilton*; you could learn more truth about the French Revolution from "Cabinet Battle #2" than you ever would in the average American public school.

Sect. 4. Some of these musketeers (from before Lafayette's time, of course) became the basis for Alexandre Dumas's 1844 novel *The Three Musketeers*.

Author Geri Walton details the affair between Lafayette and Comtesse Diane-Adélaïde de Simiane on her blog. Included is the allegation that Adélaïde's husband, Charles, the Marquis of Miremont, is believed to have killed himself—even though he was also gay. He was still jealous of his beautiful wife, and his death in March 1787, which occurred while he was hunting, was thought to be no accident (Walton 2017).

Sect. 5. De Broglie (pronounced *de Broy*) had also been "Louis XV's most trusted member of the *Secret*," the covert organization of spies that Louis XVI disbanded upon becoming king (Ferreiro 2016, 17).

The French had already sent Kalb to America, as early as 1768, to report on colonial attitudes. He believed the colonists would eventually revolt against Britain, but that it wouldn't happen until their "population exceeds that of Great Britain" (Ferreiro 2016, 25–26).

Sect. 6. Invasions of Great Britain's vulnerable coasts had been discussed internally by the French for years. As early as 1767, France and Spain developed a plan to assault the shores near Portsmouth and Sussex with a combined fleet of 140 ships, stopping just "short of a full-out assault on London, which could frighten other Continental powers ..." (Ferreiro 2016, 20).

Sect. 12. "This cruel anniversary ..." (Maurois 1961, 481). In what must have been a doubly bittersweet coincidence, Christmas Eve also happened to be the birthday of George Washington Lafayette, born in 1779.

∞

The books Lafayette requested are all worth a brief mention. It seems clear why his wife chose them, as they all have some connection with religious conversions.

1. The seventeenth-century mathematician Blaise Pascal's *Pensées* (which means "thoughts") is a compilation of his insights into theology and philosophy. Pascal is most famous for his "wager," which states that humans who don't believe in God are making a "bad bet," since they're gambling a few temporary pleasures for eternity.

2. Hugo Grotius's *Verité de la religion chrétienne* (The truth of the Christian religion) was published in 1627 with the aim of showing unbelievers (as well as Jews, Muslims, and members of other faiths) the truth of Christianity.

3. French Catholic bishop Jacques-Bénigne Bossuet's 1681 book *Discours sur L'histoire Universelle* is regarded as something of a sequel to St. Augustine's *City of God*.

4. This is apparently the most recent of the authors recommended. It seems likely the Marquise had in mind one book in particular. Published in 1784 and written by Pierre-Thomas La Berthonie, *Relation of the Conversion and Death of M. Bouguer, Member of the Royal Academy of Sciences*, is a work whose title speaks for itself.

Chapter 9: The Code Word Was Rochambeau

The main sources for this chapter include Jean Edmond Weelan's 1936 *Rochambeau, Father and Son: A Life of the* Maréchal de Rochambeau, and Jini Vail Jones's fine recent biography, *Rochambeau, Washington's Ideal Lieutenant: A French General's Role in the American Revolution.*

Sect. 1. "You must now prepare to serve the King ..." (Downing 1919, 99). Downing relates a further encounter between the bishop of Blois and Rochambeau, on the eve of the French Revolution. Rochambeau confessed to his former mentor that he could no longer see the three estates of French society, but only two: "the privileged and the unprivileged, and his vote and his sword are for the oppressed."

Sect. 2. "My star gave me a wife ..." (Vail 2011, 15). We have to assume here that "star" is a reference to "God."

Sect. 3. "Since the age of eleven ..." (Ferreiro 2016, 256). The Admiral de Ternay was also a member of this order, long associated with the French Navy.

De Grasse broke everyone up when he first met Washington—who apparently was an inch or so shorter, at six foot two—and hugged him, exclaiming, "My dear little general!"

Chapter 9 Supplement: Yo Solo ... Pero No Solamente. The chief source here is Larrie D. Ferreiro's *Brothers at Arms*, the definitive history of America's allies during the Revolution. "Oliver Pollock: Financier of the

American Revolution in the West," by George Rogers Clark's biographer James Alton James, also provided some key details.

Sect. 1. "Spain's King Carlos III allowed Gálvez ..." In 1784, "the king also acknowledged that the victory was not only Gálvez's (pero no solamente 'yo') but also belonged to the men who fought with him." One of them was Captain-General José Solano y Bote—given "the title Marques de Socorro for the aid (socorro) he provided to Gálvez at the crucial moment" (Ferreiro 2016, 254).

Sect. 4. "The Trumpet sounds of the fame ..." It's amazing to learn that Gálvez's poem was only translated into English—by Jonathan Tharin, "from a rare copy graciously provided by the Library of Congress"—so recently (Gálvez 2018).

Sect. 5. "Long live the Faith ..." (Gálvez 2018). Gálvez's name lives on in Galveston, Texas, among other places. In 2014, he became just the eighth honorary American citizen. He's the third Revolutionary hero to get that recognition, after Lafayette and Casimir Pulaski.

Chapter 10: God's Johnny Appleseed

Sect. 2. If there's a character in this book who deserves his own biography, it's Fr. Farmer. I've taken the liberty of reconstructing the opening sequence from a passage in Eva K. Betz's *Priest on Horseback*. While it's fictionalized, it is in line with what we know of Fr. Farmer's life and the territory he served.

"Almost seraphic" ("Rev. Ferdinand Farmer S.J.: A Priest of Pennsylvania, 1752–1786" 1890, 120). The uncredited writer—quite possibly Martin Griffin—adds, "My childish imagination even personified him as one of the Apostles."

Sect. 4. "He sits up all night treating a sick boy ..." (Betz [1958] 2019, 45–55). Fr. Farmer's skills as a botanist are mentioned in conjunction with the Geiger/Kiger House. This home in Salem, New Jersey, is still standing today, and was a regular stop on the circuit of Fr. Farmer (and Fr. Schneider before him) for private Masses. "The hemlock tree before its door and the pond lilies in the Sharptown Millpond nearby are said to have been planted by Father Farmer" (Francis 1941).

Sect. 5. Like Ferdinand Farmer, Fr. Schneider must also have been a natural adventurer. Stories abound of Schneider passing himself off as a doctor to enter hostile territory, and making narrow escapes from Indian arrows and settlers' muskets when his Catholic message was unwelcome. As early as 1744, he made a trip into New Jersey to visit Catholic families — most likely Germans who had taken jobs at the glassworks in Wistarburg. He was also known for carrying his own, handwritten copy of the Roman Missal. That was either the result of his vow of poverty or, more likely, the risk such "Popish" literature might pose if he were stopped and questioned.

One interesting family detail that I've never run across elsewhere is that Fr. Farmer had a brother back in Swabia who was also a priest. In the archives at St. Joseph's University there is an extract from a letter dated November 24, 1757, which Fr. Farmer wrote to his brother in the Upper Rhine Province. He mentions the tensions that had been raised for Catholics by the Seven Years' War. "The opponents of our faith attribute all the evil which they experience or fear — I don't know for what reason — to us priests," he writes. Pennsylvania's leaders, he adds, treat Catholic priests as French spies. "Ridiculous!" he exclaims. This might be the strongest language Fr. Farmer ever used.

Sect. 6. The first thing you think, upon being handed Fr. Farmer's two ledgers of baptisms and marriages, is, "I shouldn't be allowed to touch these."

But if you visit the Francis Drexel Library, on the campus of St. Joseph's University in Philadelphia, you can. There certainly isn't enough space here to give them justice. (I do hope to write more about these registers elsewhere.)

Both volumes have been rebound in bright red cloth. However, the pages inside are the same ones Fr. Farmer spent almost thirty years writing upon, in freehand columns, in Latin. The very first page of the second register, which spans the years 1769 to the end of Fr. Farmer's life in

1786, has been damaged by water (and remounted onto another page). When Fr. Farmer started this new ledger, was he crossing a river swollen by spring rains, as described in the beginning of this chapter? Did his saddlebag get submerged, and the register soaked?

Even more than being able to touch a document like the Declaration of Independence, flipping through these registers is humbling. They are not just the record of a historical moment, but the chronicle of a life — one spent, by all accounts, well indeed.

∞

"That 'mathematician' was the Moravian astronomer." In the archives of St. Joseph's, there is an extract from a handwritten letter (in Latin!) dated May 4, 1774, from Mayer to Farmer. It came from the collection of the American Philosophical Society. Mayer was also, apparently, the "mathematician" Fr. Molyneux mentioned in the eulogy when he claimed that the American Philosophical Society "is indebted for some curious pieces of that celebrated mathematician on the transit of Venus, dedicated to the empress of Russia."

"There is not in New York ..." (Daley 1946a, 105). The priest was evidently a "Rev. Mr. Backhouse, an Episcopal clergyman, speaking of the colony in a letter from Chester."

He said Mass clandestinely at the homes ... (Cohalan [1983] 1999,12–14). There are conflicting reports about when, exactly, Fr. Farmer began saying Mass in New York City. The earliest date given, by the *Encyclopedia of New York*, is 1756, which seems a bit premature (Shelley 2010).

∞

The first recorded date of Fr. Farmer being in New York is in his registers: he visited Fishkill, New York, in October 1781. "Whether or not Father Farmer was in New York prior to the date of that entry, 1781, we can not say for certain. Some have surmised that he was there prior to the Revolution but no evidence for the fact is extant" (Daley 1946b, 221). Daley also adds:

Liberty's Lions

Tradition has it that he was there earlier in 1781–1782 and said Mass in a loft over a carpenter's shop near Barclay street, which was then in the outlying district of the city. Mass was later celebrated in the home of Don Thomas Stoughton, the Spanish consul and in 1785 in the home of Don Diego de Gardoqui, the Spanish Ambassador. Greenleaf states that in 1784, Father Farmer said Mass in a house on Water Street and that the first place of worship used by the Catholics after they became organized, was a building erected for public purposes in Vauxhall Garden.

Sect. 7. "And a list of the regiment published in 1778 ..." The regiment is reproduced here in Clifton 1907.

"The provincial 'regiment' only attracted 172 men." A fair amount has been written regarding this loyalist Catholic regiment. Some historians have denied the presence of Catholic Tories altogether, while others have overplayed their numbers — especially in this regiment. I think the most convincing explanation comes from John Daley, who examines the evidence and points out several flaws with earlier interpretations of the numbers of this regiment, as well as Fr. Farmer's alleged participation (Daley 1946a, 221–225).

"Naturally, Fr. Farmer would offer the ministrations ..." (Daley 1946b, 222). It's worth nothing that in Fr. Farmer's registers, there are no mission trips recorded during the fall and spring of 1777–1778, when the British were occupying the city. It probably made sense to stay close to home during that time and not attempt anything that might be viewed as a provocation. One other note: Martin Griffin points out that it's unlikely the British used Old St. Mary's during their occupation of Philadelphia. "A map of the time induces the belief that the old chapel in the Alley across the street, sufficed for the services required" (Griffin 1893b, 55).

Sect. 8. "Besides his interest in politics, Stanwick had a habit ..." ("Rev. Ferdinand Farmer S.J.: A Priest of Pennsylvania, 1752–1786" 1890, 122–23). You can find the full text of Stanwick's poem in this document. As mentioned in chapter 4, Stanwick was not a Catholic, but he did subscribe to a pew at Old St. Mary's and was a friend of Fr. Farmer. He also defeated Thomas Fitzsimons in the congressional election of 1794. One of the issues working against Fitzsimons and his fellow Federalists that year was the suppression of the Whiskey Rebellion.

Chapter 11: The Priest Who Won the West

As is the case with his colleague Ferdinand Farmer, there is no true biography of Fr. Gibault. However, there are several fairly detailed sketches of his life available, including Pauline Lancaster Peyton's "Pierre Gibault, Priest and Patriot of the Northwest in the Eighteenth Century"; J. P. Dunn's "Father Gibault: The Patriot Priest of the Northwest"; and Joseph J. Thompson's appropriately titled "Penalties of Patriotism: An Appreciation of the Life, Patriotism and Services of Francis Vigo, Pierre Gibault, George Rogers Clark and Arthur St. Clair, 'The Founders of the Northwest.'" George Rogers Clark's memoirs were also a good source of information about the events on the western frontier.

While some of the figures in this book deserve new full-length biographies, many of them are the subject of books for young readers. Fr. Gibault is one of them; Joseph Dispenza's 1968 volume, *Forgotten Patriot: A Story of Father Pierre Gibault*, was helpful as well.

Sect. 2. "I have nothing to do with churches...." This is a paraphrase of Clark's recounting of the meeting in his memoirs. These memoirs are available online at the website of the State of Indiana's Historical Bureau. Part 2 contains the section "July 4, 1778 — taking Kaskaskia."

"Do you think that we're savages?," "We are here to prevent ...," and "So you and your congregation ..." Further paraphrases of Clark's recounting of the meeting in his memoirs.

Sect. 4. "Before Almighty God, I swear to renounce ..." The oath of allegiance Fr. Gibault led might have been similar to this one, which was approved by Congress for use in the Continental Army: (Hamilton 1778).

"Every person found under arms on my arrival ..." Clark reproduces the "placard" he wrote for the residents of Vincennes in his memoirs (Clark 1897b).

Sect. 5. "Fr. Gibault begged the bishop once again …" According to Fr. Peter Guilday, S.J., the archives in Quebec contain a letter from Bishop Briand dated June 29, 1780, recalling Fr. Gibault to Quebec. Fr. Guilday adds, "There is nothing to show he obeyed" (Guilday 1922). It's certainly possible the letter simply got lost, a tragic little metaphor for the misunderstandings between bishop and priest.

∞

"Fr. Gibault had invested substantial amounts of his own resources." There is a reasonable question to be asked here: where did this money come from? We do not have a conclusive answer, although Fr. Gibault did claim, in his appeal to Congress, that he "parted with his tithes and his beasts only to set an example to his parishoners." This suggests that he contributed both contributions and livestock to the war effort, which probably didn't help his already-fraught relationship with his bishop.

The subject is further addressed by author Joseph J. Thompson in his 1917 essay "Penalties of Patriotism." After pointing out that the Catholic merchant Francis Vigo was left so poor by Congress's failure to repay his contributions to the war effort that his funeral expenses went unpaid for forty years, Thompson writes:

> It should be noted, too, that Father Gibault played a most important part in the financial world of that day. If Vigo was the financial rock upon which the structure of the new country was reared, Father Gibault is at least entitled to be regarded as the mortar in which the rock was laid, for he not only ably seconded Vigo in his efforts of persuading the inhabitants to accept the continental scrip, but himself took it at par and eventually sold every earthly possession, beggared himself to sustain the worthless currency that the officers of the commonwealth were obliged to foist upon the community.
>
> After speaking of his patriotism, as before indicated, [J. P.] Dunn further remarks: "Perhaps even more important were his services in a financial way, for he 'publicly sold his own property

to the Americans, accepting for it Virginia scrip, at face value, and by his example he induced the French settlers and merchants to do the same.' It has been established that out of his meager resources he raised in some manner and sacrificed 7,800 livres in money and goods to aid Clark and the Virginia government" (Thompson 1917, 408, 417–418).

"Some claim Bishop Carroll objected to Gibault's request . . ." J. P. Dunn finds no evidence that Carroll rejected Gibault. "No one else had any authority to make the donation except Congress," Dunn writes, "and there is nothing to indicate any movement in that direction by Congress. It was a case of seeking relief from a wrong source." The sure thing is that Fr. Gibault did not get the land, nor any other compensation. "It is not surprising that after years of weary waiting Father Gibault at length abandoned the country of his choice," Dunn writes, "and went to the Spanish settlements beyond the Mississippi, where he might at least hope to avoid starvation."

Chapter 12: The Greatest Catholic That Never Was

Much has been written about the faith of the founders, and of Washington in particular. I have drawn on several of those sources here, including David Holmes's *The Faiths of the Founding Fathers*. The Novaks' account of Washington's beliefs seems to me particularly convincing. I think it does the best job of putting Washington's religious circumspection into context. It should be considered in light of common behavior for Anglicans at the time, and—even more important—of his awareness of his need to be "all things to all people."

On a related note, Washington's understanding of the importance of religious pluralism explains his appeal to minority groups—especially Catholics. Vincent Muñoz's *God and the Founders* shows convincingly how this understanding never meant that church and state were to be artificially separated. If you read his book, you will recognize the commonsense ways religion did, and still does, inform public policy. You may marvel at how far we have drifted from what was a widespread consensus regarding this belief. And some people, at least, will probably realize George Washington was a lot smarter than they thought.

Sect. 1. You can read the full text of "George Washington's Vision," as well as the Snopes rebuttal in Mikkelson 2002.

Sect. 2. You can read "General McClellan's Dream" (Alexander 1862) and "Jeff Davis' Confession!" (Alexander 1861) online.

The muster roll for Valley Forge is available online ("Valley Forge Muster Roll") and, as advertised, does not show an "Anthony Sherman." However, I also do not find any record of an "Anthony Sherman" serving at Saratoga—at least not in muster rolls from 1777, around the time of the Battle of Saratoga.

Sect. 3. Author Carlos Caso-Rosendi makes a good argument for the similarities between Washington's "vision" and the events of Fatima on his blog: https://casorosendi.wordpress.com/2015/08/08/a-vision-attributed -to-george-washington/.

∞

The paintings of the Virgin Mary and Saint John that you see at Mount Vernon are copies. The reason is that pastels are highly light-sensitive and unstable and should be displayed for no more than three months at a time, says assistant curator Jessie MacLeod. Also, the painting of Saint John is privately owned, and has been returned from its loan to Mount Vernon. Meanwhile, MacLeod adds, "The Virgin Mary is now safely in our collections storage."

Regarding the paintings' placement, MacLeod writes:

> The placement of almost all the artworks in the New Room is conjectural—while the inventory of the room lists the titles of the pieces, it does not indicate their placement (instead, it groups them by type). We determined the locations by noting that nearly every piece of artwork was part of a pair, and the style of the 18th century prized symmetrical arrangements and often had items

arranged vertically in descending order of size (i.e., the biggest paintings at the top), called a "salon-style" hang. From there, it was like solving a puzzle to determine how we could arrange 21 pieces of artwork and have everything fit. While we don't know exactly where George Washington placed the pastels in the room, the fact that he displayed them in the New Room — the grandest and most up-to-date room in the house — does suggest that he (or perhaps Martha) saw them as significant (MacLeod, pers. comm.).

Sect. 6. Maybe the best example of Washington's belief that religion and government weren't automatically meant to be separated is this: his reaction to a controversial 1784 bill, proposed by Patrick Henry in the Virginia Assembly, that would have provided tax support for religious instruction.

"I must confess, that I am not amongst the number of those who are so much alarmed at the thoughts of making people pay towards the support of that which they profess," Washington wrote to George Mason, "if of the denominations of Christians; or declare themselves Jews, Mahomitans or otherwise, & thereby obtain proper relief."

In the end, Washington opposed Henry's bill — but not because it would have allowed government support for religion. That was acceptable, Washington thought, as long as the education in question promoted the general welfare. He simply felt the bill had become too controversial. But his belief that government could support religion, yet should not arbitrarily favor or punish any particular religion, remained consistent (Muñoz 2009, 50–51).

Epilogue: Revolutions and Revelations

Sect. 1. The attack on Father Bapst has been recreated from several different accounts. These include a recent one in the *Bangor Daily News* (Burnham 2018), one from the New England Historical Society ("Fr. John Bapst Survives Tar & Feathers, Becomes 1st Boston College President" 2014), and one from the newspaper at Boston College (Consodine 1925).

Sect. 2. Figures on immigration come from the chapter "Immigrant Catholics: A Social Profile" in The American Catholic Experience (Dolan 1992, 127–157).

Beecher's proposal has become an accepted part of educational philosophy, though it's deeply ironic. Back in 1784, just after the Revolution, Catholics in the Maryland Assembly strongly opposed a bill that would have given taxpayer support to churches of all denominations. The principle was clear: no state entanglement with religion, to *preserve* religion. The Protestants who followed Beecher's suggestion also opposed state involvement with religion—and the negative effect on religion since then would be difficult to calculate.

The discussion of Catholic schools and Blaine amendments is drawn partially from *Anti-Catholicism in America, 1620–1860* (Farrelly 2018, 123–125). The actual "Blaine Amendment" was a federal constitutional amendment introduced by Maine senator James G. Blaine in 1875. This amendment failed, but some states had already adopted similar measures designed to keep Catholic schools (and other parochial schools) from receiving public funding. Ultimately, thirty-seven states passed some form of this legislation. "Blaine Amendment" became a blanket term to describe these laws.

Bibliography

Adams, Dorothy. *Cavalry Hero: Casimir Pulaski*. Rev. ed. Illustrated by Irena Lorentowicz. Bathgate. ND: Bethlehem Books, 2018.

Adams, Geoffrey. *The Huguenots and French Opinion, 1685–1787: The Enlightenment Debate on Toleration*. Waterloo, ON: Wilfrid Laurier University Press, 1991.

Adams, John. 1771. "Adams's Diary Notes on the Right of Juries," February 12. 1771. Founders Online, National Archives. https://founders.archives.gov/documents/Adams/05-01-02-0005-0005-0004.

———. "Adams to Abigail Adams, 9 October 1774." Founders Online, National Archives. https://founders.archives.gov/documents/Adams/04-01-02-0111.

———. "Adams to Jedidiah Morse, 2 December 1815." Founders Online, National Archives. https://founders.archives.gov/documents/Adams/99-02-02-6548.

———. "Instructions to the Commissioners to Canada, 20 March 1776." Founders Online, National Archive. https://founders.archives.gov/documents/Adams/06-04-02-0001-0004.

———. *Papers of John Adams*. Vol. 2, *September 1755–April 1775*. Edited by Robert J Taylor, Mary-Jo Kline, and Gregg L Lint. Cambridge, MA: Belknap Press of Harvard University Press, 2003.

An Old Soldier. "Address to the Soldiers." 1775. Printed Ephemera Collection. Library of Congress. https://www.loc.gov/resource/rbpe.0380300a/?st=text.

Alexander, Charles Wesley. "Jeff Davis' Confession! A Singular Document Found on the Dead Body of a Rebel!" Philadelphia: as printed by the author, c. 1861. Printed Ephemera Collection, Library of Congress. https://www.loc.gov/resource/rbpe.15702300/?st=text.

———. "General McClellan's Dream." March 8, 1862. Digital Library, Theodore Roosevelt Center. https://www.theodorerooseveltcenter.org/Research/Digital-Library/Record?libID=o51499.

Andress, David. *The Terror: The Merciless War for Freedom in Revolutionary France*. New York: Farrar, Straus, and Giroux, 2005.

Auricchio, Laura. *The Marquis: Lafayette Reconsidered*. Novato, CA: Presidio, 2015.

Bancroft, George. *History of the United States of America, from the Discovery of the Continent*. Vol. 5. Buffalo, WY: Creative Media Partners, 2017.

Barnhart, John D. "Lieutenant Governor Henry Hamilton's Apologia." *Indiana Magazine of History* 52, no. 4 (December 1956): 383–396. https://www.jstor.org/stable/27788392.

Bass, Streeter. "Beaumarchais and the American Revolution." Studies Archive Index 14, no. 1, September 22, 1993. Central Intelligence Agency.

Beaumarchais, Pierre Augustin. *The Barber of Seville* and *The Marriage of Figaro*. Translated by John Wood. Harmondsworth, UK: Penguin Books, 1964.

Beeman, Richard R. *Plain, Honest Men: The Making of the American Constitution*. New York: Random House, 2010.

Betz, Eva K. *Priest on Horseback: Father Farmer, 1720–1786*. Long Prairie, MN: Neumann Press, 2019.

———. *Priest, Patriot and Leader: The Story of Archbishop Carroll*. Bathgate, ND: Bethlehem Books, 2017.

Birzer, Bradley J. *American Cicero: The Life of Charles Carroll*. Wilmington, DE: ISI Books, 2010.

Blakemore, Erin. "The Revolutionary War Hero Who Was Openly Gay." History. Updated February 6, 2020. https://www.history.com/news/openly-gay-revolutionary-war-hero-friedrich-von-steuben.

Bond, Ward. "Oliver Pollock: Forgotten Patriot." Doggesbreakfast.com, September 13, 2010. http://www.doggesbreakfast.com/history/oliver-pollock-forgotten.html.

Boudinhon, A. "Interdict." In *The Catholic Encyclopedia*. Vol. 8. New York: Robert Appleton, 1913. https://www.newadvent.org/cathen/08073a.htm.

Bradshaw, Wesley, and Anthony Sherman. *Washington's Vision: Strange Forecast of the Destiny of the American Nation*. Benton Harbor, MI: House of David, n.d.

Brands, H. W. *The First American: The Life and Times of Benjamin Franklin*. Norwalk, CT: Easton Press, 2002.

Breck, Samuel. *Recollections of Samuel Breck, with Passages from His Notebooks (1771–1862)*. Edited by Horace Elisha Scudder. London: Porter & Coates, 1877.

Brent, John Carroll, ed. *Biographical Sketch of the Most Rev. John Carroll, First Archbishop of Baltimore: With Select Portions of His Writings*. Baltimore: John Murphy, 1843.

Burnham, Emily. "164 Years Ago, This Bangor Priest Was Tarred, Feathered and Ridden on a Rail." *Bangor Daily News* (Bangor, ME), June 19, 2018. https://bangordailynews.com/2018/06/19/news/bangor/164-years-ago-this-bangor-priest-was-tarred-feathered-and-ridden-on-a-rail/.

Campbell, B. U. "Memoirs of the Life and Times of the Most Rev. John Carroll." *U.S. Catholic Magazine and Monthly Review* 3 (1844): 40.

"Cardinal Foley Entertains Knights' Dinner, Asks for Lifting of Excommunication." Catholic News Agency. August 5, 2008. https://www.catholicnewsagency.com/news/cardinal_foley_entertains_knights_dinner_asks_for_lifting_of_excommunication.

Carey, Patrick W. *Catholics in America: A History*. Lanham, MD: Rowman and Littlefield, 2008.

Carroll, Charles. *Dear Papa, Dear Charley: The Peregrinations of a Revolutionary Aristocrat, as Told by Charles Carroll of Carrollton and His Father, Charles Carroll of Annapolis, with Sundry Observations on Bastardy, Child-Rearing, Romance, Matrimony, Commerce, Tobacco, Slavery, and the Politics of Revolutionary America*. Edited by Ronald Hoffman, Sally D. Mason, and Eleanor S. Darcy. Chapel Hill: University of North Carolina Press, 2001.

Carroll, Daniel. Carroll to Michael Morgan O'Brien, May 25, 1787. Constitutional Sources Project. https://www.consource.org/document/daniel-carroll-to-michael-morgan-obrien-1787-5-25/.

Carroll, John. "John Carroll to Benjamin Franklin, 11 May 1776." Founders Online, National Archives. https://founders.archives.gov/documents/Franklin/01-22-02-0257.

Casino, Joseph J. "Anti-Popery in Colonial Pennsylvania." *Pennsylvania Magazine of History and Biography* 105, no. 3 (July 1981): 279–309. https://www.jstor.org/stable/20091589.

Caso-Rosendi, Carlos. "A Vision Attributed to George Washington." *Carlos Caso-Rosendi* (blog). August 9, 2015. https://casorosendi.wordpress.com/2015/08/08/a-vision-attributed-to-george-washington/.

"Charter of Privileges Granted by William Penn, esq. to the Inhabitants of Pennsylvania and Territories, October 28, 1701." In *The Federal and State Constitutions, Colonial Charters, and Other Organic Laws of the States, Territories, and Colonies Now or Heretofore Forming the United States of America.* Compiled and edited by Francis Newton Thorpe. Washington, DC: Government Printing Office, 1909. Online at Avalon Project, Yale Law School, Lillian Goldman Law Library. https://avalon.law.yale.edu/18th_century/pa07.asp.

Chaussé, Gilles. "Bishop Briand and the Civil Authorities." In *A Concise History of Christianity in Canada*, edited by Terrence Murphy, 70–75. Toronto: Oxford University Press, 1996. Online at The Quebec History Encyclopedia. http://faculty.marianopolis.edu/c.belanger/quebechistory/encyclopedia/BishopBriandandtheCivilAuthorities.html.

Checkley, Samuel. "Diary of the Rev. Samuel Checkley, 1735." In *Publications of the Colonial Society of Massachusetts.* Vol. 12, *Transactions, 1908–1909*, 270–306. Boston: Massachusetts Colonization Society, 2012.

"City Tavern Timeline." City Tavern, n.d. Accessed August 17, 2020. https://www.citytavern.com/city-tavern-timeline/.

Clark, George Rogers. "George Rogers Clark Memoir, Part 2." In William Hayden English, *Conquest of the Country Northwest of the River Ohio 1778–1783 and Life of Gen. George Rogers Clark.* Indianapolis and Kansas City: Bowen-Merrill, 1897. Indiana Historical Bureau. https://www.in.gov/history/for-educators/download-issues-of-the-indiana-historian/the-fall-of-fort-sackville/the-fall-of-fort-sackville-focus/memoir-of-campaigns-against-the-british-posts-northwest-of-the-river-ohio/george-rogers-clark-memoir-part-2/.

———. "George Rogers Clark Memoir, Part 4." In William Hayden English, *Conquest of the Country Northwest of the River Ohio 1778–1783 and Life of Gen. George Rogers Clark.* Indianapolis and Kansas City: Bowen-Merrill, 1897. Indiana Historical Bureau. https://www.in.gov/history/for-educators/download-issues-of-the-indiana-historian/the-fall-of-fort-sackville/the-fall-of-fort-sackville-focus/memoir-of-campaigns-against-the-british-posts-northwest-of-the-river-ohio/george-rogers-clark-memoir-part-four/.

———. "George Rogers Clark Memoir, Part 7." In William Hayden English, *Conquest of the Country Northwest of the River Ohio 1778–1783 and Life of Gen. George*

Rogers Clark. Indianapolis and Kansas City: Bowen-Merrill, 1897. Indiana Historical Bureau. https://www.in.gov/history/for-educators/download-issues-of-the-indiana-historian/the-fall-of-fort-sackville/the-fall-of-fort-sackville-focus/memoir-of-campaigns-against-the-british-posts-northwest-of-the-river-ohio/george-rogers-clark-memoir-part-seven/.

———.*George Rogers Clark Papers, 1771–1784*. Edited by James Alton James. Springfield, IL: Trustees of the Illinois State Historical Library, 1912.

Clary, David A.. *Adopted Son: Washington, Lafayette, and the Friendship That Saved the Revolution*. New York: Bantam Books, 2008.

Clavin, Tom, and Bob Drury. "Winter at Valley Forge: George Washington's Most Dismal Christmas Ever." History. February 4, 2020. https://www.history.com/news/valley-forge-george-washington-worst-christmas.

Clifton, Alfred. "The Roman Catholic Regiment." *American Catholic Historical Researches* 3, no. 4 (October 1907): 324–338. https://www.jstor.org/stable/44374703.

Cohalan, Florence D. *A Popular History of the Archdiocese of New York*. 2nd ed. Yonkers, NY: U.S. Catholic Historical Society, 1999.

"Colonel Stephen Moylan: 2nd Quartermaster School Commandant, June 1776–September 1776." Updated February 21, 2019. U.S. Army Quartermaster Corps. https://quartermaster.army.mil/bios/previous-qm-generals/quartermaster_general_bio-moylan.html.

"Committee at Camp to Henry Laurens." *Letters of Delegates to Congress*. Vol. 9, *February 1, 1778–May 31, 1778*. February 24, 1778. American Memory, Library of Congress. http://www.memory.loc.gov/cgi-bin/query/r?ammem/hlaw:@field(DOCID+@lit(dg009125)).

Connor, Charles P. *Pioneer Priests and Makeshift Altars: A History of Catholicism in the Thirteen Colonies*. Irondale, AL: EWTN, 2017.

Consodine, William A. "The Tarring of Father John Bapst." *The Heights*, March 31, 1925. Online at Boston College Libraries. https://newspapers.bc.edu/?a=d&d=bcheights19250331.2.16.

"The Constitution of the United States: A Transcription." America's Founding Documents, National Archives. September 24, 2018. https://www.archives.gov/founding-docs/constitution-transcript.

"Continental Congress to the People of Great Britain, October 22, 1774." *Journals of the American Congress: From 1774–1788*. Vol. 1, *September 5, 1774 to December 31, 1776*. Washington, DC: Way and Gideon, 1823.

Cresson, W. P. *Francis Dana: A Puritan Diplomat at the Court of Catherine the Great.* New York: L. MacVeagh, Dial Press, 1930.

Crowl, Philip A. "Charles Carroll's Plan of Government." *American Historical Review* 46, no. 3 (April 1941): 588–595.

Cummins, Light T. "Oliver Pollock's Plantations: An Early Anglo Landowner on the Lower Mississippi, 1769–1824." *Louisiana History* 29, no. 1 (Winter 1988): 35–48. http://www.jstor.org/stable/4232633.

Curran, Robert Emmett. *Intestine Enemies: Catholics in Protestant America, 1605–1791.* Washington, DC: Catholic University of America Press, 2017.

———. *Papist Devils: Catholics in British America, 1574–1783.* Washington, DC: Catholic University of America Press, 2014.

Daley, John M., S.J. "Pioneer Missionary: Ferdinand Farmer, S.J., 1720–1786." *Woodstock Letters* 75, no. 2 (June 1946): 103–115. Jesuit Online Library. https://jesuitonlinelibrary.bc.edu/?a=d&d=wlet19460601-01.2.2.

———. "Pioneer Missionary: Ferdinand Farmer, S.J., 1720–1786 (continued)." *Woodstock Letters* 75, no. 3 (October 1946): 207–231. Jesuit Online Library. https://jesuitonlinelibrary.bc.edu/?a=d&d=wlet19461001-01.2.4.

———. "Pioneer Missionary: Ferdinand Farmer, S.J., 1720–1786 (continued [2])." *Woodstock Letters* 75, no. 4 (December 1946): 311–321. Jesuit Online Library. https://jesuitonlinelibrary.bc.edu/?a=d&d=wlet19461201-01.2.4.

Delaplaine, Edward S. "Chief Justice Roger B. Taney — His Career at the Frederick Bar." *Maryland Historical Magazine* 13, no. 2 (June 1918): 109–142.

DeLaurentis, Ann, and Bernadine Hershey. *Church of the Assumption of the Blessed Virgin Mary, Lancaster, PA: "Old St. Mary's," 1741–1991.* Lancaster, PA: St. Mary's of Lancaster, 1991.

DeLear, Byron. "Who Coined 'United States of America'? Mystery Might Have Intriguing Answer." *Christian Science Monitor*, July 4, 2013. https://www.csmonitor.com/USA/Politics/2013/0704/Who-coined-United-States-of-America-Mystery-might-have-intriguing-answer.

Devitt, Edward I., S.J. "Centenary of the Restoration of the Jesuits in the United States." *Messenger* 44, no. 2 (August 1905): 106–119.

———. "Letter of Father Joseph Mosley, S.J., and Some Extracts from His Diary (1757–1786) (continued)." *Records of the American Catholic Historical Society of Philadelphia* 17, no. 3 (September 1906): 289–311. https://www.jstor.org/stable/44207979.

Dispenza, Joseph. *Forgotten Patriot: A Story of Father Pierre Gibault.* Notre Dame, IN: Dujarie Press, 1968.

Dolan, Jay Patrick. *The American Catholic Experience: A History from Colonial Times to the Present.* Notre Dame, IN: University of Notre Dame Press, 1992.

Donnelly, Eleanor C. *A Memoir of Father Felix Joseph Barbelin, S.J.* New York: Christian Press Association, 1886.

Downing, Margaret. "Washington's Associate at Yorktown." *Catholic World* 110, no. 1 (October 1919): 95–103.

Dunn, J. P. "Father Gibault: The Patriot Priest of the Northwest." Transactions of the Illinois State Historical Society. http://www.museum.state.il.us/RiverWeb/landings/Ambot/Archives/transactions/1905/Gibault.html.

Duras, Duchesse de. *Prison Journals during the French Revolution.* Translated by Mrs. M. Carey. New York: Dodd, Mead, 1891.

Ellis, Joseph J. *American Sphinx: The Character of Thomas Jefferson.* New York: Vintage, 1998.

———. *His Excellency: George Washington.* New York: Alfred A. Knopf, 2011.

English, William Hayden. *Conquest of the Country Northwest of the River Ohio, 1778–1783, and Life of Gen. George Rogers Clark.* N.p.: British Library, Historic Print Editions, 2011.

Esolen, Anthony. "How the Church Has Changed the World: A Hero of Two Nations." *Magnificat* 20, no. 13 (March 2019): 208–212.

Espinoza v. Montana Department of Revenue. 591 U.S. 1 (2019). https://www.supremecourt.gov/opinions/19pdf/18-1195_g314.pdf.

Farrelly, Maura Jane. *Anti-Catholicism in America, 1620–1860.* Cambridge: Cambridge University Press, 2018.

———. *Papist Patriots: The Making of an American Catholic Identity.* Oxford: Oxford University Press, 2012.

Fea, John. "Religion and Early Politics: Benjamin Franklin and His Religious Beliefs." *Pennsylvania Heritage* 37, no. 4 (Fall 2011). Accessed online at http://www.phmc.state.pa.us/portal/communities/pa-heritage/religion-early-politics-benjamin-franklin.html.

Ferling, John. "Myths of the American Revolution." *Smithsonian Magazine,* January 2010. https://www.smithsonianmag.com/history/myths-of-the-american-revolution-10941835/.

Ferreiro, Larrie D. *Brothers at Arms: American Independence and the Men of France & Spain Who Saved It.* New York: Alfred A. Knopf, 2016.

Fields, Barbara Jeanne. *Slavery and Freedom on the Middle Ground: Maryland during the Nineteenth Century*. New Haven, CT: Yale University Press, 1985.

Fogarty, Gerald P. "Property and Religious Liberty in Colonial Maryland Catholic Thought." *Catholic Historical Review* 72, no. 4 (October 1986): 573–600. www.jstor.org/stable/25022406.

Forbes, Esther. *Paul Revere and the World He Lived In*. Birmingham, AL: Palladium Press, 2005.

"Fr. John Bapst Survives Tar & Feathers, Becomes 1st Boston College President." New England Historical Society. November 2, 2014. https://www. newenglandhistoricalsociety.com/fr-john-bapst-survives-tar-fathers-becomes -1st-boston-college-president/.

Francis, Carroll Hampton. "First Mass in West Jersey." *Camden* (Camden, N.J.) *Courier-Post*, January 20, 1941.

Franklin, Benjamin. "Dialogue between Franklin and the Gout." In *The Oxford Book of American Essays*, edited by Brander Matthews. New York: Oxford University Press, 1914. Online at Bartleby. https://www.bartleby.com/109/3. html.

Gaines, James R. *For Liberty and Glory: Washington, Lafayette, and Their Revolutions*. New York: W. W. Norton, 2009.

Gallagher, Eugene B. "Two Hundred and Fifty Years Ago: The Beginnings of St. Joseph's Church." *Records of the American Catholic Historical Society of Philadelphia* 93, no. 1/4 (March–December 1982): 3–8. https://www.jstor .org/stable/44216420.

Gálvez, Bernardo de. "Triumphant Victory at Pensacola." Edited by Nicole Darbois. Translated by Jonathan Tharin. Early Visions of Florida, 2018. https:// earlyfloridalit.net/bernardo-de-galvez-triumphant-victory-at-pensacola/.

Gardner, Monica Mary. *Kościuszko: A Biography*. Charleston, SC: Nabu Press, 2010.

Geiger, Mary Virginia. *Daniel Carroll: A Framer of the Constitution*. Washington, DC: Catholic University of America, 1943.

"George Washington's Church Attendance as Recorded in His Diaries." The Constitutional Principle: Separation of Church and State. http://candst. tripod.com/GeoWchurchchart.html.

Gibault, Pierre. Gibault to the Bishop of Quebec, May 22, 1788. In *Kaskaskia Records, 1778–1790*. Edited and translated by Clarence Walworth Alvord. Springfield: Illinois Historical Library, 2016.

Gleis, Paul G. "German Jesuit Missionaries in 18th Century Maryland." *Woodstock Letters* 75, no. 3 (October 1946): 199–206. Jesuit Online Library. https://jesuitonlinelibrary.bc.edu/?a=d&d=wlet19461001-01.2.3.

Gliński, Mikołaj. "Was Kościuszko an Artist?" Culture.Pl. May 26, 2019. https://culture.pl/en/article/was-kosciuszko-an-artist.

Gordon, William W. "Count Casimir Pulaski." *Georgia Historical Quarterly* 13, no. 3 (September): 167–227. http://www.jstor.org/stable/40576081.

Griffin, Martin I. J. "The Apostate Lord Baltimore and Acts of Hostility against the Catholics of Maryland." *American Catholic Historical Researches* 1, no. 2 (April 1905): 156–157.

———. *Catholics and the American Revolution.* Vol. 1. Ridley Park, PA: printed by the author, 1907.

———. "General Count Casimir Pulaski." *American Catholic Historical Researches* 6, no. 1 (January 1910): 1–128. https://www.jstor.org/stable/44374799.

———. "General Thaddeus Kosciuszko." *American Catholic Historical Researches* 6, no. 2 (April 1910): 129–216. https://www.jstor.org/stable/44377883.

———. "George Meade." *American Catholic Historical Researches* 6, no. 3 (July 1889.): 98–118.

———. *The History of Commodore John Barry.* Reprinted from the *Records of the American Catholic Historical Society.* Edited by F. T. Furey. Philadelphia: American Catholic Historical Society, 1897.

———. *History of Old St. Joseph's, Philadelphia.* London: Forgotten Books, 2016.

———. "Old St. Joseph's Philadelphia, Birthplace of Religious Freedom." *American Catholic Historical Researches* 4, no. 3 (July 1908): 284–288. https://www.jstor.org/stable/44374760.

———. "Rev. Joseph Greaton, S.J.: Planter of the Faith in Philadelphia and Founder of Old St. Joseph's Chapel." *American Catholic Historical Researches* 16, no. 2 (April 1899): 59–106.

———. "Revolutionary Catholic Notes." *American Catholic Historical Researches* 5, no. 4 (October 1909): 332–347. https://www.jstor.org/stable/44374787.

———. "Stephen Moylan, Muster-Master General, Secretary and Aide-de-Camp to Washington, Quartermaster-General, Colonel of 4th Pennsylvania Light Dragoons and Brigadier-General of the War for American Independence—the First and the Last President of the Friendly Sons of St. Patrick of Philadelphia." *American Catholic Historical Researches* 5, no. 2 (April 1909): 97–235. https://www.jstor.org/stable/44374763.

———. "The Story of St. Mary's." *American Catholic Historical Researches* 10, no. 1 (January 1893): 2–16, and no. 2 (April 1893): 50–72.

———. "The *Te Deum* at St. Mary's, Philadelphia, July 4th, 1779." *American Catholic Historical Researches*, no. 4 (October 1907): 315–18. https://www.jstor.org/stable/44374700.

———. "The *Te Deum* at St. Mary's, Philadelphia for the Victory at Yorktown." *American Catholic Historical Researches* 3, no. 4 (October 1907): 311–314. https://www.jstor.org/stable/44374699.

———. *Thomas FitzSimons: Pennsylvania's Catholic Signer of the Constitution of the United States*. Philadelphia: Press of the American Catholic Historical Researches. 1887.

———. "Was John Commodore Barry Any Kind of a Catholic?" *American Catholic Historical Researches* 20, no. 3 (July 1903): 100–106. https://www.jstor.org/stable/44374370.

Guay, Tom. "Rebellious Anniversary: Burning the Peggy Stewart Ended Annapolis' Golden Era." *Capital Gazette*, October 14, 2016. https://www.capitalgazette.com/maryland/annapolis/ph-ac-cn-peggy-stuart-1014-20161014-story.html.

Guilday, Peter. *The Life and Times of John Carroll*. Vol. 1. New York: Encyclopedia Press, 1922.

Hall, F. R. "Genet's Western Intrigue, 1793–1794." *Journal of the Illinois State Historical Society* 21, no. 3 (October 1928): 359–381.

Hamilton, Alexander. "Alexander Hamilton to Elizabeth Hamilton, [4 July 1804]." Founders Online, National Archives. https://founders.archives.gov/documents/Hamilton/01-26-02-0001-0248.

———. "Oath of Allegiance, [12 May 1778]." Founders Online, National Archives. https://founders.archives.gov/documents/Hamilton/01-01-02-0453.

———. "Remarks on the Quebec Bill: Part Two, [22 June 1775]." Founders Online, National Archives. https://founders.archives.gov/documents/Hamilton/01-01-02-0059.

Hamling, Anna. "The Power of an Image: The Black Madonna of Częstochowa." *THINK*. March 30, 2017. https://think.iafor.org/the-power-of-an-image-the-black-madonna-of-czestochowa/.

Hennesey, James, S.J. *American Catholics: A History of the Roman Catholic Community in the United States*. New York: Oxford University Press, 1983.

———. "An Eighteenth Century Bishop: John Carroll of Baltimore." *Archivum Historiae Pontificiae* 16 (1978): 171–204. www.jstor.org/stable/23563998.

Hoffer, Peter Charles. *Cry Liberty: The Great Stono River Slave Rebellion of 1739.* New York: Oxford University Press, 2012.

Hoffman, Ronald. "The Carroll Family of Maryland." *Proceedings of the American Antiquarian Society* 117, no. 2 (October 2007): 331–350. https://www.americanantiquarian.org/proceedings/44539656.pdf.

Holmes, David L. *The Faiths of the Founding Fathers.* Oxford: Oxford University Press, 2006.

Gibault, Pierre. Gibault to Bishop Briand, December 4, 1775. In Joseph J. Thomson, "Illinois' First Citizen—Pierre Gibault (continued)." *Illinois Catholic Historical Review* 4, no. 1 (July 1921): 197–213.

Hubert, Jean-François. Bishop of Quebec [Jean-François Hubert] to Right Reverend John Carroll, October 6, 1788. In *Collections of the Illinois State Historical Library,* vol. 5, 586–590. Illinois State Historical Library. https://babel.hathitrust.org/cgi/pt?id=uc1.$b687580&view=1up&seq=684.

Ives, J. Moss. *The Ark and the Dove: The Beginning of Civil and Religious Liberties in America.* New York: Cooper Square, 1969.

James, James Alton. *George Rogers Clark—Civilian.* Springfield, IL: Phillips Bros., 1928.

———. "Oliver Pollock: Financier of the American Revolution in the West." *Studies* 18, no. 72 (December 1929): 633–647. http://www.jstor.org/stable/30095212.

Jefferson, Thomas. "Declaration of Independence: A Transcription." America's Founding Documents, National Archives. Reviewed July 24, 2020. https://www.archives.gov/founding-docs/declaration-transcript.

———. "From Thomas Jefferson to Horatio Gates, 21 February 1798." Founders Online, National Archives. https://founders.archives.gov/documents/Jefferson/01-30-02-0083.

———. *The Writings of Thomas Jefferson.* Vol. 1, *1760–1775.* Collected and edited by Paul Leicester Ford. New York: G. P. Putnam's Sons, 1892.

Juliani, Richard N. *Building Little Italy: Philadelphia's Italians before Mass Migration.* University Park: Pennsylvania State University Press, 1999.

Kajencki, Francis C. *The Pulaski Legion in the American Revolution.* El Paso: Southwest Polonia Press, 2004.

Kajencki, Francis Casimir. *Casimir Pulaski: Cavalry Commander of the American Revolution.* El Paso: Southwest Polonia Press, 2002.

Katz, Brigit. "Was the Revolutionary War Hero Casimir Pulaski Intersex?" *Smithsonian Magazine*, April 29, 2019. https://www.smithsonianmag.com/smart-news/was-revolutionary-war-hero-casimir-pulaski-intersex-180971907/.

Kelly, John Barry. "Named in Honor of Commodore John Barry [USS Barry]." 1995. https://www.public.navy.mil/surfor/ddg52/Pages/Namesake.aspx.

Kerber, Linda K. *Women of the Republic: Intellect and Ideology in Revolutionary America*. Chapel Hill: Omohundro Institute of Early American History and Culture and the University of North Carolina Press, 1997.

Kite, Elizabeth Sarah. *Beaumarchais and the War of American Independence*. Whitefish, MT: Kessinger, 2010.

Klugewicz, Stephen M. "An Extraordinary Revolution: The Creation of the Catholic Church in America." The Imaginative Conservative. May 17, 2011. https://theimaginativeconservative.org/2011/05/john-carroll-and-creation-catholic.html.

Kruk, Jonathan. *Legends and Lore of the Hudson Highlands*. Charleston, SC: History Press, 2018.

Lafayette, Virginie du Motier Lasteyrie du Saillant, Marquise de. *Life of Madame de Lafayette*. Paris: L. Techener, 1872.

Lally, Robert Johnson. "Building the Church in Boston." Archdiocese of Boston. https://www.bostoncatholic.org/historical-sketch-archdiocese-boston/building-church-boston.

Lambing, A. A. "Washington's Devotion to Mary Immaculate." *Donahoe's Magazine* 11, no. 2 (February 1884): 110–112.

Lane, Jason. General and Madame de Lafayette: Partners in Liberty's Cause in the American and French Revolutions. Lanham, MD: Taylor Trade, 2003.

Lee, Richard Henry. "Lee's Resolutions, June 7, 1776." Avalon Project, Yale Law School, Lillian Goldman Law Library. https://avalon.law.yale.edu/18th_century/lee.asp.

Leonard, Lewis A. *Life of Charles Carroll of Carrollton*. New York: Moffat, Yard, 1918.

Leepson, Marc. "George Washington and the Marquis de Lafayette." In *The Digital Encyclopedia of George Washington*. Edited by James P. Ambuske. George Washington's Mount Vernon. https://www.mountvernon.org/library/digitalhistory/digital-encyclopedia/article/george-washington-and-the-marquis-de-lafayette/.

Leo XIII, Pope. Encyclical letter *Longinqua* (January 6, 1895). http://www.vatican.va/content/leo-xiii/en/encyclicals/documents/hf_l-xiii_enc_06011895_longinqua.html.

Léonard, Louis. *Beaumarchais and His Times: Sketches of French Society in the Eighteenth Century from Unpublished Documents*. Translated by Henry S. Edwards. New York: Harper, 1857.

Lewis, Charles Lee. *Admiral de Grasse and American Independence*. Annapolis: Naval Institute Press, 1945.

Lomask, Milton. *Charles Carroll and the American Revolution*. Rev. ed. Bathgate, ND: Bethlehem Books, 2017.

Lori, William. "Offered for the Eternal Salvation of Charles Carroll of Carrollton, of the Deceased Members of the Carroll Family, and of All the Faithful Departed." November 22, 2013. Archdiocese of Baltimore. https://www.archbalt.org/offered-for-the-eternal-salvation-of-charles-carroll-of-carrollton-of-the-deceased-members-of-the-carroll-family-and-of-all-the-faithful-departed/.

Manning, Clarence Augustus. *Casimir Pulaski: A Soldier of Liberty*. New York: Philosophical Library, 1944.

Mapp, Alf J., Jr. *The Faiths of Our Fathers: What America's Founders Really Believed*. Lanham, MD: Rowman and Littlefield, 2005.

Marie, Sister Blanche. "The Catholic Church in Colonial Pennsylvania." *Pennsylvania History: A Journal of Mid-Atlantic Studies* 3, no. 4 (October 1936): 240–258. https://www.jstor.org/stable/27766216.

"Marquis de Lafayette." American Battlefield Trust. February 2, 2017. https://www.battlefields.org/learn/articles/marquis-de-lafayette.

Maurois, André. *Adrienne: The Life of the Marquise de La Fayette*. Translated by Gerard Hopkins. London: Jonathan Cape, 1961.

Maynard, W. Barksdale. *The Brandywine: An Intimate Portrait*. Philadelphia: University of Pennsylvania Press, 2015.

McCarthy, Charles Hallan. "The Importance of Stresses and Omissions in the Writing of American History." *Catholic Historical Review* 10, no. 1 (April 1924): 27–46. www.jstor.org/stable/25012042.

McCarthy, Joseph F. X. "Stephen Moylan: An American Military Career," Peter & Lynne's Place. http://www.pmoylan.org/pages/family/KenMoylan/Stephen_Moylan.html.

McClarey, Donald R. "Catholics in the American Revolution." The American Catholic, September 23, 2011. https://www.the-american-catholic.com/2011/09/23/catholics-in-the-american-revolution/.

McCormack, John D. "Patrick Colvin, the Ferryman of '76, and Friend of Washington — Trenton's First Catholic." *American Catholic Historical Researches* 3, no. 3 (January 1887): 19–26. https://www.jstor.org/stable/44373518.

McDermott, Scott. *Charles Carroll of Carrollton: Faithful Revolutionary*. New York: Scepter, 2018.

McDougall, Alexander. "To George Washington from Major General Alexander McDougall, 13 April 1778." Founders Online, National Archives. https://founders.archives.gov/documents/Washington/03-14-02-0461.

McGrath, Tim. *John Barry: An American Hero in the Age of Sail*. Yardley, PA: Westholme, 2011.

Meany, William Barry. *Commodore John Barry: The Father of the American Navy*. New York: Harper and Brothers Publishers, 1911.

Melville, Annabelle McConnell. *John Carroll of Baltimore: Founder of the American Catholic Hierarchy*. New York: Charles Scribner's Sons, 1955.

Menaker, Drusilla. "Poland's Black Madonna." *New York Times*, July 22, 1990. https://www.nytimes.com/1990/07/22/travel/poland-s-black-madonna.html.

Metzger, Charles H. *Catholics and the American Revolution: A Study in Religious Climate*. Chicago: Loyola University Press, 1962.

———. "Some Catholic Tories in the American Revolution," Part I. *Catholic Historical Review* 35, no. 3 (October 1949): 276–300. www.jstor.org/stable/25015030.

Mikkelson, David. "George Washington's Vision." Snopes, May 12, 2002. https://www.snopes.com/fact-check/george-washingtons-vision/.

Miranda, Lin-Manuel. "Yorktown (The World Turned Upside Down)." Genius, September 25, 2015. https://genius.com/Original-broadway-cast-of-hamilton-yorktown-the-world-turned-upside-down-lyrics.

Molyneux, Robert. "Funeral Sermon on the Death of the Rev. Ferdinand Farmer, Who Departed This Life the 17th of August, 1786, in the 66th Year of His Age." *American Catholic Historical Researches* 7, no. 3 (July 1890): 124–128. https://www.jstor.org/stable/44373670.

Monaghan, Frank. "Stephen Moylan in the American Revolution." *Studies* 19, no. 75 (September 1930): 481–486. https://www.jstor.org/stable/30094651.

Morton, Brian N., and Donald C. Spinelli. *Beaumarchais and the American Revolution*. Lanham, MD: Lexington Books, 2003.

Mosley, Joseph. "Letters of Father Joseph Mosley, S.J., and Some Extracts from His Diary (1757–1786) [continued]." Compiled by Edward I. McDevitt, S.J. *Records of the American Catholic Historical Society of Philadelphia* 17, no. 3 (September 1906): 289–311. https://www.jstor.org/stable/44207979.

Muñoz, Vincent Philip. *God and the Founders: Madison, Washington, and Jefferson.* Cambridge: Cambridge University Press, 2009.

Novak, Michael, and Jana Novak. *Washington's God: Religion, Liberty, and the Father of Our Country.* New York: Basic Books, 2006.

Oglethorpe, James. *The Publications of James Edward Oglethorpe.* Edited by Rodney M. Baine. Athens: University of Georgia Press, 1994.

"Old St. Joseph's Church." Frommer's. https://www.frommers.com/destinations/philadelphia/attractions/old-st-josephs-church.

Onuf, Peter S., ed. *Maryland and the Empire, 1773: The Antilon-First Citizen Letters.* Baltimore: Johns Hopkins University Press, 1974.

Peckham, Howard H. *Indiana: A History.* Urbana: University of Illinois Press, 2003.

Penn, William. *A Seasonable Caveat against Popery, or, a Warning to Protestants* (1700). Cambridge, UK: EEBO Editions, ProQuest, 2011.

Peyton, Pauline Lancaster. "Pierre Gibault, Priest and Patriot of the Northwest in the Eighteenth Century." *Records of the American Catholic Historical Society of Philadelphia* 12, no. 4 (December 1901): 452–498. https://www.jstor.org/stable/44207808.

Philbrick, Nathaniel. *In the Hurricane's Eye: The Genius of George Washington and the Victory at Yorktown.* New York: Penguin, 2019.

Pienkos, Angela. "A Bicentennial Look at Casimir Pulaski: Polish, American and Ethnic Folk Hero." *Polish American Studies* 33, no. 1 (Spring 1976): 5–17. https://www.jstor.org/stable/20147942.

Pinkowski, Edward. "General Pulaski's Body." Poles in America Foundation, October 1997. http://www.poles.org/p_body.html.

"Prospect Hill. Bunker's Hill" (ca. 1775). Collections Online, Massachusetts Historical Society. https://www.masshist.org/database/viewer.php?item_id=534&pid=3.

"Pulaski Monument Vandalized with Spray Paint in Baltimore's Patterson Park." WJZ-13–CBS Baltimore, May 23, 2019. https://baltimore.cbslocal.com/2019/05/23/pulaski-monument-vandalized-patterson-park/.

Purcell, Richard J. "Daniel Carroll, Framer of the Constitution." *Records of the American Catholic Historical Society of Philadelphia* 52, no. 2 (June 1941): 65–87. https://www.jstor.org/stable/44209385.

———. "Daniel Carroll, Framer of the Constitution (continued)." *Records of the American Catholic Historical Society of Philadelphia* 52, no. 3 (September 1941): 137–160. https://www.jstor.org/stable/44209394.

———. "Thomas Fitzsimons: Framer of the American Constitution." *Studies* 27, no. 106 (June 1938): 273–290. http://www.jstor.org/stable/30097546.

Putnam, Israel. "To George Washington from Major General Israel Putnam, 13 January 1778." Founders Online, National Archives. https://founders.archives.gov/documents/Washington/03-13-02-0190.

Quirk, John F., S.J. "Father Ferdinand Farmer: An Apostolic Missionary in Three States." *Woodstock Letters* 44, no. 1 (February 1915): 55–67. Jesuit Online Library. https://jesuitonlinelibrary.bc.edu/?a=d&d=wlet19150201-01.2.8.

Repplier, Agnes. *Philadelphia: The Place, and the People*. Illustrated by E. C. Peixotto. New York: Macmillan, 1898.

"Rev. Ferdinand Farmer S. J.: A Priest of Pennsylvania, 1752–1786." *American Catholic Historical Researches* 7, no. 3 (July 1890): 120–123. https://www.jstor.org/stable/44373669.

Richardson, Jay. "Cherry Tree Myth." In *The Digital Encyclopedia of George Washington*, edited by James P. Ambuske. George Washington's Mount Vernon. https://www.mountvernon.org/library/digitalhistory/digital-encyclopedia/article/cherry-tree-myth/.

"Robert Morris (1734–1806)." Encyclopedia.com. https://www.encyclopedia.com/people/history/us-history-biographies/robert-morris.

Rochambeau, Count de. Rochambeau to General Washington, on the Arrival of the French Army at Newport"(July 12, 1780). In *The Writings of George Washington*, vol. 7, *Correspondence and Miscellaneous Papers Relating to the American Revolution*, 511. Edited by Jared Sparks. New York: Harper and Brothers, 1847.

———. "What France Did for America: Memoirs of Rochambeau." Translated by M. W. E. Wright. *North American Review* 205, no. 738 (May 1917): 788–802.

Rousseau, Jean-Jacques. *The Major Political Writings of Jean-Jacques Rousseau: The Two Discourses and Social Contract.* Translated and edited by John T Scott. Chicago: University of Chicago Press, 2014.

Rowland, Kate Mason. *Life of Charles Carroll of Carrollton, 1737–1832: With His Correspondence and Public Papers.* N.p.: Sagwan Press, 2018.

Sambaluk, Nicholas Michael. "Making the Point: West Point's Defenses and Digital Age Implications, 1778–1781." *Cyber Defense Review* 2, no. 2 (Summer 2017): 141–154. https://www.jstor.org/stable/26267348.

"Scene at the Signing of the Constitution of the United States by Howard Chandler Christy." Teaching American History. https://teachingamericanhistory.org/resources/convention/christy-about/.

Schaeper, Thomas J. *Edward Bancroft: Scientist, Author, Spy.* New Haven: Yale University Press, 2012.

Schama, Simon. *Citizens: A Chronicle of the French Revolution.* London: Folio Society, 2004.

Schroth, Raymond A., S.J. "American Jesuits, Buried and Brought Back, Part II: The Maryland Plantation Jesuits." *America,* November 18, 2014. https://www.americamagazine.org/issue/american-jesuits-buried-and-brought-back-part-ii.

Shea, John Gilmary. *The Hierarchy of the Catholic Church in the United States: Embracing Sketches of All the Archbishops and Bishops from the Establishment of the See of Baltimore to the Present Time; Also an Account of the Plenary Councils of Baltimore, and a Brief History of the Church in the United States.* New York: Office of Catholic Publications, 1886.

Shelley, Thomas J. "Catholics." In *The Encyclopedia of New York City,* 2nd ed., edited by Kenneth T. Jackson, Lisa Keller, and Nancy Flood, 215–218. New Haven: Yale University Press. Online at Virtual New York City. https://virtualny.ashp.cuny.edu/EncyNYC/catholics.html.

Shuler, Jack. *Calling Out Liberty: The Stono Slave Rebellion and the Universal Struggle for Human Rights.* Jackson: University Press of Mississippi, 2011.

Slaves of the Immaculate Heart of Mary. "Slaves Held Washington Became a Catholic on His Deathbed." Catholicism.org. October 14, 2008. https://catholicism.org/washington-slaves.html.

Smith, Ellen Hart. *Charles Carroll of Carrollton*. Cambridge, MA: Harvard University Press. 2014.

Smith, Mark M. "Remembering Mary, Shaping Revolt: Reconsidering the Stono Rebellion." *Journal of Southern History* 67, no. 3 (August 2001): 513–534. https://www.jstor.org/stable/3070016.

———. *Stono: Documenting and Interpreting a Southern Slave Revolt*. Columbia: University of South Carolina Press, 2005.

Smith, Paul Hubert, ed. *Letters of Delegates to Congress, 1774–1789*, vol. 9, *February 1–May 31*. Washington, DC: Library of Congress, 1982.

Smith, Sydney Fenn. *The Suppression of the Society of Jesus*. Edited by Joseph A. Munitiz. Leominster, UK: Gracewing, 2004.

"South End Forever' [cut] North End Forever. *Extraordinary Verses on Pope-Night. or, A Commemoration the Fifth of November, Giving a History of the Attempt, Made by the Papishes, to Blow Up King and Parliament, A. D.*" Boston, 1768. In "Printed Ephemera Collection." Library of Congress.https://www.loc.gov/item/rbpe.03602800/.

Spalding, Thomas W. "John Carroll: Corrigenda and Addenda." *Catholic Historical Review* 17, no. 4 (October 1985): 505–518. https://www.jstor.org/stable/25022122.

Spillane, Fr. Edward. "Why There Were No Bishops in Colonial Times: An Unpublished Letter of Father Ferdinand Farmer." *Woodstock Letters* 28, no. 2 (October 1899): 173–177. https://jesuitonlinelibrary.bc.edu/?a=d&d=wlet18991001-01.2.2.

"Spontoon." The Price of Freedom: Americans at War. Smithsonian National Museum of History. https://amhistory.si.edu/militaryhistory/collection/object.asp?ID=703.

Storozynski, Alex. *The Peasant Prince: Thaddeus Kościuszko and the Age of Revolution*. New York: Thomas Dunn Books, 2010.

Szymański, Leszek. *Casimir Pulaski: A Hero of the American Revolution*. New York: Hippocrene Books, 1994.

"A Statement on the Smithsonian Documentary about Pulaski's Skeleton as Female or 'Intersex.'" *Polish Daily News*, April 17, 2019. https://poland.us/strona,13,33452,0,a-statement-on-the-smithsonian-documentary-about-pulaskis-skeleton-as-female-or-intersex-hermaphrodite.html.

"Thomas Fitzsimons Portrait by Stuart Believed Found." *New York Times*, March 17, 1965. https://www.nytimes.com/1965/03/17/archives/thomas-fitzsimons-portrait-by-stuart-believed-found.html.

Thomas, Isaiah. *The History of Printing in America: With a Biography of Printers, and an Account of Newspapers*. Worcester, MA: Isaiah Thomas Jr., 1810.

Thompson, Joseph J. "Penalties of Patriotism: An Appreciation of the Life, Patriotism and Services of Francis Vigo, Pierre Gibault, George Rogers Clark and Arthur St. Clair, 'The Founders of the Northwest.'" *Journal of the Illinois State Historical Society* 9, no. 4 (January): 401–449. https://www.jstor.org/stable/40194522.

Thompson, Marshall P. "Rochambeau, (Part I)." *The Magazine of History, with Notes and Queries* 22 (June 1916): 220–229.

Thornton, John K. "African Dimensions of the Stono Rebellion." *American Historical Review* 96, no. 4 (October 1991): 1101–1113. https://www.jstor.org/stable/2164997.

Touba, Mariam. "Who Coined the Phrase 'United States of America'? You May Never Guess." New York Historical Society. November 5, 2014. http://blog.nyhistory.org/coined-phrase-united-states-america-may-never-guess/.

"Two Milestones in Jesuit History." *Woodstock Letters* 62, no. 2 (June 1933): 288–304. Jesuit Online Library. https://jesuitonlinelibrary.bc.edu/?a=d&d=wlet19330601-01.2.9.

Unger, Harlow G. *Improbable Patriot: The Secret History of Monsieur de Beaumarchais, the French Playwright Who Saved the American Revolution*. Hanover NH: University Press of New England, 2011.

———. *Lafayette*. New York: Wiley, 2003.

Vail, Jini Jones. *Rochambeau, Washington's Ideal Lieutenant: A French General's Role in the American Revolution*. Tarentum, PA: Word Association, 2011.

"The Muster Roll Project." Valley Forge Park Alliance. Updated February 4, 2020. http://valleyforgemusterroll.org/index.asp.

Walton, Geri. "Lafayette and Diane of Simiane: Their Love Affair." April 7, 2017. https://www.geriwalton.com/love-affair-lafayette-and-diane-of-simiane/.

Warren, Joseph. "The Suffolk Resolves." September 9, 1774. https://www.nps.gov/mima/learn/education/upload/The%20Suffolk%20Resolves.pdf.

"Washington and Catholicism." George Washington's Mount Vernon. https://www.mountvernon.org/george-washington/religion/george-washington-and-catholicism/.

Washington, George. "From George Washington to the Hebrew Congregation in Newport, Rhode Island, 18 August 1790." Founders Online, National Archives. https://founders.archives.gov/documents/Washington/05-06-02-0135.

———. "From George Washington to Henry Laurens, 31 January 1778." Founders Online, National Archives. https://founders.archives.gov/documents/Washington/03-14-02-0537.

———. "From George Washington to James Mease, 12 May 1777." Founders Online, National Archives. https://founders.archives.gov/documents/Washington/03-09-02-0394.

———. "From George Washington to John Hancock, 25 September 1776." Founders Online, National Archives. https://founders.archives.gov/documents/Washington/03-06-02-0305.

———. "From George Washington to Lafayette, 8 December 1784." Founders Online, National Archives. https://founders.archives.gov/documents/Washington/04-02-02-0140.

———. "From George Washington to Lund Washington, 30 September 1776." Founders Online, National Archives. https://founders.archives.gov/documents/Washington/03-06-02-0341.

———. "From George Washington to Major General Horatio Gates, 4 January 1778." Founders Online, National Archives. https://founders.archives.gov/documents/Washington/03-13-02-0113.

———. "From George Washington to Roman Catholics in America, c. 15 March 1790." Founders Online, National Archives. https://founders.archives.gov/documents/Washington/05-05-02-0193.

———. *Writings of George Washington: 1758–1775*. New York: G.P. Putnam's Sons, 1889.

Weelen, Jean Edmond. *Rochambeau, Father and Son: A Life of the Maréchal de Rochambeau*. Translated by Lawrence Lee. New York: H. Holt, 1936.

Whitehead, Maurice. *English Jesuit Education: Expulsion, Suppression, Survival and Restoration, 1762–1803*. Burlington, VT: Ashgate, 2013.

———. "From Expulsion to Restoration: The Jesuits in Crisis, 1759–1814." *Studies* 103, no. 412 (Winter 2014): 447–461. https://www.jstor.org/stable/24347842.

Whitman, T. Stephen. *The Price of Freedom: Slavery and Manumission in Baltimore and Early National Maryland*. Lexington: University Press of Kentucky, 1997.

Wickham, Jonathan. "The General Was Female?" *America's Hidden Stories*, April 8, 2019. Smithsonian Channel. https://www.smithsonianchannel.com/video/series/americas-hidden-stories/66986.

Wright, Constance. *Madame de Lafayette*. New York: Holt, Rinehart and Winston, 1962.

Wright, Robert K., and Morris J. MacGregor. *Soldier-Statesmen of the Constitution*. Washington, DC: Center of Military History, U.S. Army, 2007.

Wroblewski, Joseph E. "The Winter of His Discontent: Casimir Pulaski's Resignation as Commander of Horse." *Journal of the American Revolution*, November 14, 2016. https://allthingsliberty.com/2016/11/winter-discontent-casimir-pulaskis-resignation-commander-horse/.

About the Author

Dan LeRoy is an author, journalist, and teacher. His work has appeared in the *New York Times*, *Rolling Stone*, *Newsweek*, the *Village Voice*, *Alternative Press*, Esquire.com, and *National Review*. He is certainly the only person in history to have contributed to publications founded by William F. Buckley Jr. and by Gene Simmons of KISS.

Since 2006, he has been the director of writing and publishing at Lincoln Park Performing Arts Charter School, near Pittsburgh, Pennsylvania.

He has written three books, including one about the Beastie Boys' classic *Paul's Boutique*, for Bloomsbury's 33 1/3 series. His next book, *Different Drummer: The Secret History of the Drum Machine*, will be published by Bloomsbury in 2022.

Sophia Institute

Sophia Institute is a nonprofit institution that seeks to nurture the spiritual, moral, and cultural life of souls and to spread the Gospel of Christ in conformity with the authentic teachings of the Roman Catholic Church.

Sophia Institute Press fulfills this mission by offering translations, reprints, and new publications that afford readers a rich source of the enduring wisdom of mankind.

Sophia Institute also operates the popular online resource CatholicExchange.com. *Catholic Exchange* provides world news from a Catholic perspective as well as daily devotionals and articles that will help readers to grow in holiness and live a life consistent with the teachings of the Church.

In 2013, Sophia Institute launched Sophia Institute for Teachers to renew and rebuild Catholic culture through service to Catholic education. With the goal of nurturing the spiritual, moral, and cultural life of souls, and an abiding respect for the role and work of teachers, we strive to provide materials and programs that are at once enlightening to the mind and ennobling to the heart; faithful and complete, as well as useful and practical.

Sophia Institute gratefully recognizes the Solidarity Association for preserving and encouraging the growth of our apostolate over the course of many years. Without their generous and timely support, this book would not be in your hands.

www.SophiaInstitute.com
www.CatholicExchange.com
www.SophiaInstituteforTeachers.org